COMPUTER AND JOB-SHOP
SCHEDULING THEORY

COMPUTER AND JOB-SHOP SCHEDULING THEORY

EDITED BY
E. G. COFFMAN, JR.
PENNSYLVANIA STATE UNIVERSITY

COAUTHORS:
**J. L. BRUNO, E. G. COFFMAN, JR.,
R. L. GRAHAM, W. H. KOHLER, R. SETHI,
K. STEIGLITZ, AND J. D. ULLMAN**

A WILEY-INTERSCIENCE PUBLICATION
JOHN WILEY & SONS
NEW YORK / LONDON / SYDNEY / TORONTO

Library of Congress Cataloging in Publication Data
Main entry under title:

Computer and job-shop scheduling theory.

    "A Wiley–Interscience publication."
    Bibliography: p.
    Includes index.
    1. Scheduling (Management)—Mathematical models.
2. Scheduling (Management)—Data processing.
I. Coffman, Edward Grady.

TS157.5.C65   658.5′1   75-19255
ISBN 0-471-16319-8

Printed in the United States of America

10 9 8 7 6 5 4 3 2 1

PREFACE

In the past several years interest and new results in the theory of deterministic scheduling have mounted at an increasing rate. This book is an attempt to represent the current position of the field in terms of research and the types of problems currently being investigated. As a result, most of the material covered is relatively recent and cannot be found elsewhere in textual form. Although the book consists of six coordinated contributions, it is not to be considered an edited collection of papers, but rather a multiple-author text written specifically for its purpose. Simply because of the number of coauthors, it was necessary to have an editor to coordinate the overall effort of seven people.

The book provides a theoretical treatment of sequencing problems arising in computer and job-shop environments. However, the models are simple in structure and are consequently meaningful in a very large variety of applications. Briefly, the general model studied assumes a set of tasks or jobs and a set of resources to be used in executing or servicing the tasks. In almost all cases the models are deterministic in the sense that the information describing tasks is assumed to be known in advance. This information includes task execution times, operational precedence constraints, deferral costs, and resource requirements. The principal sequencing problems examined are the minimization of schedule lengths, minimization of the mean time in system (weighted by deferral costs), and scheduling to meet due dates or deadlines. A number of closely related problems are also studied. The results presented include efficient optimal algorithms, heuristics and their performance bounds, efficient enumerative and iterative methods, and mathematical descriptions of the complexity of a wide variety of sequencing problems.

Computers arise in the subject matter in at least three ways. First, they represent an almost universal job shop for our purposes. The appearance of virtually all the problems we analyze can be observed or envisioned in the design or operation of general-purpose computer systems, although the prime importance of specific problems may exist in other applications. Second, computers must be considered in the implementation of the enumerative and iterative approaches to sequencing problems. Finally, the field of computer science is the origin of the complexity theory that we introduce and then apply to problems of sequence.

As in other areas of applied mathematics, scheduling theory spans many academic disciplines; in our case these include Industrial Engineering, Management Science, Business Administration, Operations Research, Computer Science, and Electrical Engineering. The book is directed primarily to these departments of research institutes and of the academic world in which graduate students and faculty are performing research in deterministic scheduling theory. Because of the nature of the material, substantial mathematical maturity must be assumed on the part of the reader. Thus as a text or supplementary material one must assume a course with graduate students towards the end, at least, of the first year of study.

I acknowledge the *Institut de Recherche d'Informatique et d'Automatique* (Rocquencourt, France) for the primary support in the production of this book. The initial phases and much of the work reported in Chapters 2 and 3 were supported in part by the National Science Foundation under grant NSF-28290 at the Pennsylvania State University. The work in Chapter 6 was supported by the National Science Foundation under grants NSF-GK-37400 and NSF-GK-42048, and the U.S. Army Research Office under contract DAHCO4-69-C-0012. Thanks are due to Mrs. Teddi Potter and Mrs. Hannah Kresse for typing portions of the manuscript.

Finally, special thanks are due to Drs. M. R. Garey and D. S. Johnson for their valuable efforts in examining and correcting the manuscript. They have been of particular help to me, as editor, except insofar as they have, through a constant stream of new results, attempted to antiquate the book before its appearance.

E. G. COFFMAN, JR.

University Park, Pennsylvania
May 1975

CONTENTS

COMPUTER AND JOB-SHOP
SCHEDULING THEORY

CHAPTER ONE

INTRODUCTION TO DETERMINISTIC SCHEDULING THEORY

E. G. COFFMAN, JR.
INSTITUT DE RECHERCHE D'INFORMATIQUE ET D'AUTOMATIQUE,
ROCQUENCOURT, FRANCE*

In this chapter we introduce and put into a common context the contents of the remainder of the book. In so doing, we present common notation for models analyzed in subsequent chapters, as well as some additional results serving as background or complementary material extending and unifying the coverage of the book. As a result, it is recommended that the reader examine the present chapter before attempting to read Chapters 2 through 6. Although each of Chapters 2 through 6 may be read without any essential recourse to material in the others, the reader will note that there are reasons for the sequence chosen for the chapters.

The mutual independence of Chapters 2 through 6 is of course a convenience and to some extent a result of a multiple-author book in which appear several different styles of writing and approaches to notation. However, the subject matter has been partitioned in such a way that this mutual independence is not unnatural. Consequently, any discontinuities in style and presentation experienced in passing from one chapter to another should be tolerable, especially if one first makes reference to relevant material in this chapter.

In Section 1.1 the objectives and motivations of the book are discussed; the general model to be studied is presented in Section 1.2. Section 1.3 discusses background results drawn primarily from Conway, Maxwell, and Miller [CMM]. Section 1.4 reviews the results of Chapters 2 through 6, making use of tabular presentations where possible. A number of related topics, covered in Section 1.5, complement the material in Chapters 2 through 6. Finally, in Section 1.6 some comments are made on the notation used in subsequent chapters.

---

* On leave from The Pennsylvania State University.

1.1 OBJECTIVES AND MOTIVATIONS

In very general terms, the scheduling problems studied in this book assume a set of resources or servers and a fixed system of tasks which is to be serviced by these resources. Based on prespecified properties of and constraints on the tasks and resources, the problem is to find an efficient algorithm for sequencing the tasks to optimize or tend to optimize some desired performance measure. The primary measures studied are schedule length and the mean time spent in the system by the tasks. The models of these problems we analyze are deterministic in the sense that all information governing the scheduling decision is assumed to be known in advance. In particular, the tasks and all information describing them are assumed to be available at the outset, which we normally take as time $t = 0$.

Since one can not organize an effective work day, plan examination periods at universities, or even prepare a nontrivial meal without frequently encountering such problems, it does not seem necessary to dwell on motivations for the study of these problems. On the other hand, our interest must focus on problem formulations that reflect applications in which poor sequencing decisions incur intolerably large costs. Thus the assumptions by which the problem is formalized ought, for example, to reflect general industrial job shops. In fact, because of primary associations and interests of the authors, the original context of the models analyzed is often computer systems.

Readers who are well-informed about general-purpose computer architectures and the problems of economical computer operation will realize at once that we are sacrificing very little in generality. One seldom finds basic sequencing problems that do not have interesting and important counterparts in existing or proposed computer systems. But it is worth noting here, also as a justification for the book's title, that specific questions of application will not be discussed. For, as we shall see later, the book reflects the fact that significant theoretical results (apart from general complexity issues) are largely confined to rather simplistic models that apply over a broad spectrum of real-life scheduling problems.

Many similar terms are used abstractly in this book without being formally defined. For example, unless otherwise noted, jobs, tasks, programs (in a computer), and customers can all be regarded as equivalent for our purposes. Also, resources may be referred to as machines, storage devices, and most commonly, processors. With respect to appropriate resources jobs may be performed, run, executed, stored, or serviced. We may use rule, procedure, or an appropriate function or mapping instead of algorithm; and the terms scheduling, sequencing, allocation, and assignment are used synonymously or analogously, depending on context. As customary in current literature, nontrivial algorithms are specified using an informal Algol-like notation; no special devices appear that will not be transparent to the reader.

Broadly speaking, the goal of this book is a presentation and analysis of deterministic sequencing problems which is sufficiently comprehensive to ensure that

(1) the status of recent and ongoing research in this field is adequately covered, and

(2) the significant principles that can be abstracted from current and past analyses and formal approaches to these problems are well represented.

In these days, any attempt at a book that is an unqualified success in both respects is bound to fail; it would be in a constant state of writing. Of course, the primary reason for this is the usual difficulty in remaining *au courant* in a field that has accumulated as much momentum as scheduling theory. But the problem is aggravated enormously because scheduling theory spans several disciplines, each of which is large and vigorous in its own right. We are referring to the many industrial research as well as academic departments of Operations Research, Management Science, Computer Science, Industrial Engineering, Electrical Engineering, and Applied Mathematics, in which one finds the (increasingly) many researchers currently engaged in the advancement of scheduling theory. It would be impossible to cover the great variety of specific systems that form the principal motivations in these disciplines. Thus the more modest goal is to focus on tractable, generic models of simple structure whose combinatorial complexity and analysis resembles or specializes that of the various structures encountered in the above-mentioned disciplines.

After a more formal discussion of the results of subsequent chapters we return to the question of objectives vis-à-vis the types of problems and approaches not treated in detail. We conclude this section with some remarks on the literature as it bears on our point of departure. The emphasis of subsequent chapters is on results which have appeared within the last 7 or 8 years; in fact, most of these have appeared within the last 4 or 5 years. Thus in terms of textual material, the initial chapters of the book by Conway, Maxwell, and Miller [CMM], which was published in 1967, form a natural basis for the present work. We especially recommend this book to the reader desiring engineering motivation beyond that provided here. For again, we emphasize that our treatment is almost wholly mathematical, with very little recourse to discussions of pragmatics. The applicability (and, of course, inapplicability) of our work will be quite evident in virtually all cases, owing primarily to the simplicity of the models. But in [CMM] one obtains good insight into the general problems in practice and the many features of such problems that extend the models analyzed here but for which comparable results are not known (see also [Bak]).

This book presents virtually all the theoretical results in [CMM] that fall within the boundaries of deterministic scheduling theory. They form the background for the new results. Indeed, this background material occupies only a couple of brief sections in Chapters 1 and 2. Additional background material concerned with computer sequencing problems and relevant to parts of Chapters 2 and 5 can be found in a more recent text [CD] on operating-systems theory. In fact, the third chapter of the latter book forms a small subset whose limitations motivated the conception of the present work. Thus the present book is largely new material not appearing elsewhere in textual form. For recent survey papers dealing with many of the subjects of this book, the reader is referred to [G3], [Co], [B1], and [BLR].

1.2 A GENERAL MODEL

The scheduling model, from which subsequent problems are drawn, is described by considering in sequence the resources, task systems, sequencing constraints, and performance measures. (At the end of the chapter we describe briefly the notational questions relevant to this and subsequent chapters).

1.2.1 Resources

In the majority of the models studied, the resources consist simply of a set $P = \{P_1, \ldots, P_m\}$ of processors. Depending on the specific problem, they are either identical, identical in functional capability but different in speed, or different in both function and speed.

In the most general model there is also a set of additional resource types $\mathcal{R} = \{R_1, \ldots, R_s\}$, some (possibly empty) subset of which is required during the entire execution of a task on some processor. The total amount of resource of type R_j is given by the positive number m_j. In the computer application, for example, such resources may represent primary or secondary storage, input/output devices, or subroutine libraries.* Although it is possible to include the processors in $\mathcal{R}$, it is more convenient to treat them separately because

---

* In this chapter, unless noted otherwise, and in Chapter 4 a resource type R_i is to be regarded as a set of m_i identical resources. In the somewhat more general model of Chapter 5, m_i is the *amount* of resource R_i usually normalized to 1, any fraction of which may be required for executing a given task.

(1)   they will constitute a resource type necessarily in common with all tasks (although two different tasks need not require the same processors), and
(2)   they are discretized with the restriction that a task can execute on at most one processor at a time.
These constraints need not apply to the resource types R_i, $1 \le i \le s$.

1.2.2   Task Systems

A general task system for a given set of resources can be defined as the system $(\mathcal{T}, <, [\tau_{ij}], \{\mathcal{R}_j\}, \{w_i\})$ as follows:

1. $\mathcal{T} = \{T_1, \ldots, T_n\}$ is a set of tasks to be executed.

2. $<$ is an (irreflexive) partial order defined on $\mathcal{T}$ which specifies operational precedence constraints. That is, $T_i < T_j$ signifies that T_i must be completed before T_j can begin.

3. $[\tau_{ij}]$ is an $m \times n$ matrix of execution times, where $\tau_{ij} > 0$ is the time required to execute T_j, $1 \le j \le n$, on processor P_i, $1 \le i \le m$. We suppose that $\tau_{ij} = \infty$ signifies that T_j cannot be executed on P_i and that for each j there exists at least one i such that $\tau_{ij} < \infty$. When all processors are identical we let τ_j denote the execution time of T_j common to each processor.

4. $\mathcal{R}_j = [R_1(T_j), \ldots, R_s(T_j)]$, $1 \le j \le n$, specifies in the ith component, the amount of resource type R_i required throughout the execution of T_j. We always assume $R_i(T_j) \le m_i$ for all i and j.

5.   The weights w_i, $1 \le i \le n$, are interpreted as deferral costs (or more exactly cost rates), which in general may be arbitrary functions of schedule properties influencing T_i. However, the w_i are taken as constants in the models we analyze. Thus the "cost" of finishing T_i at time t is simply $w_i t$.

This formulation contains far more generality than we intend to embrace in subsequent chapters, but each problem studied can be represented as a special case of the model. One particular restriction worth noting is the limitation on operational precedence. We cannot, for example, represent loops in computer programs modeled as task systems. Note that the partial order $<$ is conveniently represented as a directed, acyclic graph (or *dag*) with no (redundant) transitive arcs. Unless stated otherwise, we assume $<$ is given as a list of arcs in such a graph. In general, however, the way in which a partial order is specified in a given problem may influence the complexity of its solution. (We return to this point later.)
In Fig. 1.1 for example, the notation T_i/τ_i is introduced for labeling

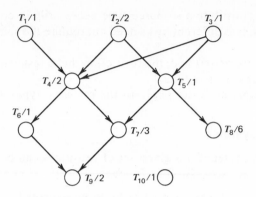

Task/execution time, identical processors

Figure 1.1   A dag representation of $(\mathcal{T}, <, \{\tau_i\})$.

Notation and properties:
1. Acyclic.
2. No transitive edges: (T_1, T_6) would be such an edge.
3. T_1, T_2, T_3, T_{10} are initial vertices; T_8, T_9, T_{10} are terminal vertices.
4. For example, T_7 is a successor of T_1, T_2, T_3, T_4, T_5 but an immediate successor of only T_4, T_5; T_5 is a predecessor of T_7, T_8, T_9 but an immediate predecessor of only T_7, T_8.
5. Levels: 8   9   8   7   7   3   5   6   2   1
                T_1 T_2 T_3 T_4 T_5 T_6 T_7 T_8 T_9 T_{10}
6. Critical paths: T_2, T_5, T_8 and T_2, T_4, T_7, T_9.

vertices. Tasks are occasionally referred to simply by their indices (e.g., "task 1" may be used rather than T_1, especially when graph vertices are more conveniently labeled with integers).

As the reader might expect, we make heavy use of graphical methods for defining task systems, rather than defining them as appropriate five-tuples. In so doing we choose a number of more or less commonly used terms concerning dags. In particular, a *path* of length k from T to T' in a given graph G is a sequence of vertices* (tasks) $T_{i_1}, \ldots, T_{i_k}$ such that $T = T_{i_1}$, $T' = T_{i_k}$ $(k \geq 1)$ and $(T_{i_j}, T_{i_{j+1}})$ is an arc in G for all $1 \leq j \leq k - 1$. Moreover, if such a path exists, T will be called a *predecessor* of T' and T' a *successor* of T. If $k = 2$ the terms *immediate predecessor* and *immediate successor* will be used. *Initial* vertices are those with no predecessors, and *terminal* vertices are those with no successors. The graph forms a *forest* if either each vertex has at most one predecessor, or each vertex has at most one successor. If a forest has in the first case exactly one vertex with no predecessors, or in the second case, exactly

*The term *node* is used synonymously with vertex.

one vertex with no successors, it is also called a *tree*. In either case, the terms *root* and *leaf* have the usual meaning. The *level* of a vertex T is the sum of the execution times associated with the vertices in a path from T to a terminal vertex such that this sum is maximal. Such a path is called a *critical path* if the vertex T is at the highest level in the graph.

1.2.3   Sequencing Constraints

By "constraint" we mean here a restriction of scheduling algorithms to specific (though broad) classes. Two main restrictions are considered.

1. *Nonpreemptive* scheduling: with this restriction a task cannot be interrupted once it has begun execution; that is, it must be allowed to run to completion. In general, *preemptive* scheduling permits a task to be interrupted and removed from the processor under the assumption that it will eventually receive all its required execution time, and there is no loss of execution time due to preemptions (i.e., preempted tasks resume execution from the point at which they were last preempted).

2. *List* scheduling: in this type of scheduling an ordered list of the tasks in $\mathcal{T}$ is assumed or constructed beforehand. This list is often called the *priority list*. The sequence by which tasks are assigned to processors is then decided by a repeated scan of the list. Specifically, when a processor becomes free for assignment, the list is scanned until the first unexecuted task T is found which is ready to be executed; that is, the task can be executed on the given processor, all predecessors of T have been completed, and sufficient resources exist to satisfy $R_i(T)$ for each $1 \le i \le s$. This task is then assigned to execute on the available processor. We assume the scan takes place instantaneously. Also, if more than one processor is ready for assignment at the same time, we assume they are assigned available tasks in the order P_1 before P_2 before P_3, etc. As a matter of notation we assume that the list is ordered (and scanned) from left to right and written in the form $L = (T_{i_1}, \ldots, T_{i_n})$. Preemptions are not considered; thus list schedules form a subset of nonpreemptive schedules.

Before discussing performance measures, let us illustrate the means by which schedules are to be represented graphically, assuming $s = 0$. We use the type of timing diagram illustrated in Fig. 1.2 for the task system shown in Fig. 1.1. In the obvious way the number of processors determines the number of horizontal lines which denote time axes. The hatching shown in the figure represents periods during which processors are idle. When the need arises to refer to idle periods, the symbol $\emptyset$, appropriately subscripted when necessary, is used. Also, the symbol D denotes these diagrams, when such notation is desired. The symbols s_i

and f_i denote, respectively, the start and finishing times of T_i. When necessary for indicating the dependence on a particular schedule S, the notation $s_i(S)$ and $f_i(S)$ is used.

For problems assuming additional resources, we will have occasion to draw timing diagrams only for $s = 1$. In this case the vertical axis denotes the amount of additional resource required, the number of vertical segments being bounded by the given number of processors. An example is given shortly (Fig. 1.4b).

The timing diagram of Fig. 1.2 gives an informal and intuitive notion of schedule. Somewhat more formally, a schedule can be defined as a suitable mapping that in general assigns a sequence of one or more disjoint execution intervals in $[0, \infty)$ to each task such that

1. Exactly one processor is assigned to each interval.
2. The sum of the intervals is precisely the execution time of the task, taking into account, if necessary, different processing rates on different processors.
3. No two execution intervals of different tasks assigned to the same processor overlap.
4. Precedence and additional-resource usage constraints are observed.
5. There is no interval in $[0, \max\{f_i\}]$ during which no processor is assigned to some task (i.e., a schedule is never allowed to have all processors idle when uncompleted tasks exist).

For nonpreemptive schedules there is exactly one execution interval for each task, and for list schedules we further require that no processor can be idle if there is a task ready and able to execute on it. We do not attempt to further formalize the notion of schedules—a wholly mathematically definition is unnecessary and very elaborate for the general model.

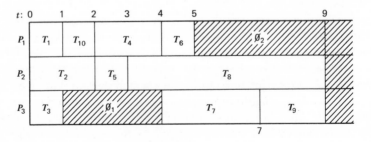

Figure 1.2   Example timing diagram for Fig. 1.1 ($m = 3$).

1.2.4 Performance Measures

Two principal measures of schedule performance that we consider are the *schedule-length* or *maximum finishing* (or *flow*) *time*

$$\omega(S) = \max_{1 \leq i \leq n} \{f_i(S)\} \tag{1}$$

and the *mean weighted finishing* (or *flow*) *time*

$$\bar{\omega}(S) = \frac{1}{n} \sum_{i=1}^{n} w_i f_i(S) \tag{2}$$

The basic problems, therefore, are to find efficient algorithms for the minimization of these quantities over all schedules S, drawn perhaps from a specific class of schedules as defined earlier.

At this point it is convenient to illustrate that preemptive, nonpreemptive, and list scheduling disciplines can be distinct in terms of minimum schedule length and mean weighted flow time and that the "power" of these disciplines decreases in the order given. A graph of a task system, a minimum-length preemptive (i.e., unrestricted) schedule, a minimum-length nonpreemptive schedule, and a minimum-length list schedule appear in Fig. 1.3a, b, c, and d, respectively. (The exercise of verifying the optimality of the schedules is left to the reader). Note that for $w_i = 1$ $(1 \leq i \leq n)$ the mean weighted flow-time performance is optimal in each case and concurs with the ordering in terms of minimum schedule lengths just given.

Even for $<$ empty, preemptive schedules can be shorter than non-preemptive schedules (e.g., consider $m = 2$ and three unit length tasks). However, for nonpreemptive scheduling on identical processors, a minimum-length list schedule is a minimum-length nonpreemptive schedule when $<$ is empty. For mean weighted flow time (non-negative weights) on identical processors, the optimal list schedule is an optimal preemptive schedule when $<$ is empty, thus removing any distinction between the disciplines in these circumstances.

A good many of the results, especially those related to problem complexity and efficient enumerative or approximate algorithms, can be readily extended to a number of other performance measures of interest in job-shop or computer sequencing. For example, suppose we have identical processors and we define $W_i(S) = f_i(S) - \tau_i$ as the *waiting time* of T_i in S. Then it is easily seen that a schedule minimizing $\bar{\omega}$ also minimizes the mean, weighted waiting time.

Now suppose the general model is extended to permit a positive number d_i $(1 \leq i \leq n)$ called the *due date* to be given for each task T_i. The

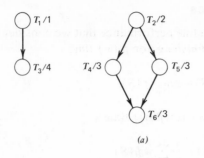

(a)

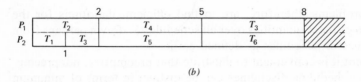

(b)

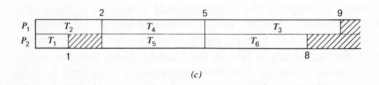

(c)

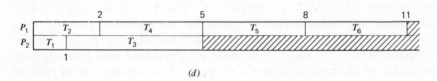

(d)

Figure 1.3 Discipline hierarchy. (a) $m = 2$ identical processors, $s = 0$, $\omega_i = 1$ ($1 \leq i \leq n = 6$). (b) Optimal preemptive schedule, $\omega = 8$, $\bar{\omega} = 29/6$. (c) Optimal nonpreemptive schedule, $\omega = 9$, $\bar{\omega} = 30/6$. (d) Optimal list schedule, $\omega = 11$, $\bar{\omega} = 32/6$.

due date expresses the time at which it is desired to have a task finished. Then the *lateness* of T_i in S is defined as $f_i(S) - d_i$, and the *tardiness* is defined as $\max\{0, f_i(S) - d_i\}$. The maxima and weighted means of lateness and tardiness are also interesting performance measures. As with waiting times, it is easily seen that sequences minimizing mean weighted flow time also minimize mean weighted lateness; however, this is not true for the mean weighted tardiness.

When we consider problems in which due dates *must* be respected (i.e., $f_i(S) \leq d_i$, $1 \leq i \leq n$), the due dates are also called *deadlines*. One such problem to which we devote considerable attention assumes $d_i = d$, $1 \leq i \leq n$, $<$ is empty, $s = 0$, identical processors, and seeks to minimize the number of processors required to meet the common deadline d. This problem is referred to as the bin-packing problem in Chapter 5. Interestingly, we find that this problem is equivalent to the schedule-length minimization problem for identical processors, $<$ empty, $\tau_i = 1$ ($1 \leq i \leq n$), $m \geq n$, and $s = 1$. Figures 1.4a and b illustrate this equivalence. Note that if we remove the restriction $m \geq n$ in the parameter list, we have an equivalence to the problem of scheduling to meet a common deadline with the constraint of at most m tasks per processor and the objective of minimizing the number of processors. Although there was no need, for Chapters 2 through 6, to introduce deadlines as another component in the general model, the augmented system with an arbitrary set $\{d_i\}$ is discussed briefly in the next section on single-machine results and in section 1.4.1.

As a final performance measure of broad interest we consider the mean number of tasks, $\bar{N}(S)$, in the system calculated over the interval $[0, \omega(S)]$. In general, such a measure is useful in expressing expected inventory or storage requirements for tasks in the job-shop or computer. We can write

$$\bar{N}(S) = \frac{1}{\omega(S)} \int_0^{\omega(S)} N(t)\, dt$$

where $N(t)$ is the number of uncompleted tasks in the system at time t. Clearly $N(t)$ takes the form of a decreasing staircase function with changes in value occurring at task completion times (subsets of which may, of course, be coincident). Indeed, one can express the integral as the sum

$$\bar{N}(S) = \frac{1}{\omega(S)} \{f_1(S) \times n + [f_2(S) - f_1(S)](n - 1)$$
$$+ \cdots + [f_n(S) - f_{n-1}(S)] \times 1\}$$

where the task indexing is assumed to be such that $f_i(S) \leq f_j(S)$ for $1 \leq i < j \leq n$. Assuming unit weights in (2), this reduces directly to

$$\bar{N}(S) = n \frac{\bar{\omega}(S)}{\omega(S)} \tag{3}$$

which we note has been obtained independently of scheduling disciplines,

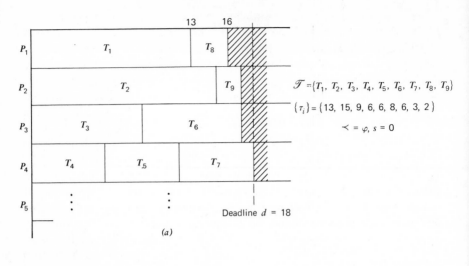

$$\mathcal{T} = \{T_1, T_2, T_3, T_4, T_5, T_6, T_7, T_8, T_9\}$$
$$\{\tau_i\} = \{13, 15, 9, 6, 6, 8, 6, 3, 2\}$$
$$\prec = \varphi, s = 0$$

Deadline $d = 18$

(a)

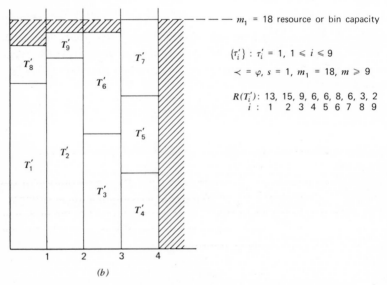

m_1 = 18 resource or bin capacity

$\{\tau'_i\} : \tau'_i = 1, 1 \leqslant i \leqslant 9$
$\prec = \varphi, s = 1, m_1 = 18, m \geqslant 9$

$R(T'_i)$: 13, 15, 9, 6, 6, 8, 6, 3, 2
i :   1   2 3 4 5 6 7 8 9

(b)

Figure 1.4 An equivalence of two sequencing problems. (a) Scheduling $\{T_1, \ldots, T_9\}$ to meet deadline $d = 18$ on minimum number (4) of processors. (b) Scheduling unit-length tasks with single-resource requirements to minimize schedule length.

number of processors, or any property other than finishing times. From this expression we note immediately that for $m = 1$ processors $\bar{N}(S)$ is minimized when $\bar{\omega}(S)$ is minimized, since $\omega(S)$ is in fact not a function of S for $m = 1$. Later we consider the case for $m \geq 2$.

1.3 BACKGROUND IN SINGLE-PROCESSOR RESULTS

In this section we cover classical results for the special case of one processor ($m = 1$), $<$ empty, and $s = 0$. For $m = 1$ the problem of minimizing max $\{f_i\}$ vanishes; hence we are concerned only with the other measures mentioned in the previous section. The important results are summarized in the following theorems.

Theorem 1.1 [Sm] The mean weighted flow time, lateness, and waiting time are minimized by sequencing the tasks in an order of nondecreasing ratio τ_i/w_i. Since max $\{f_i\}$ is fixed, it is clear from (3) that $\bar{N}$ must also be minimized by this sequence.

Now suppose our system includes a set of due dates for the tasks, and our problem is to optimize performance with respect to the lateness and tardiness measures. We have the following result.

Theorem 1.2 [Ja2] The maximum lateness and maximum tardiness are minimized by sequencing the tasks in an order of nondecreasing due dates.

Finally, for the due-date problem, let us define the *slack time* of T_i at time t in a schedule as $d_i - \tau_i - t$. The result of sequencing by the intuitively appealing rule of nondecreasing slack time is given by the following somewhat unexpected result.

Theorem 1.3 [CMM] Sequencing in an order of nondecreasing slack time maximizes the minimum lateness and minimum tardiness.

All these theorems are subject to the same type of proof, which proceeds as follows. Suppose there is a sequence S having the desired optimal performance but violating the ordering. (Since resolution of ties is arbitrary, on selection of a tie-breaking rule we obtain a linear order in the case of each theorem.) Then there must exist adjacent tasks in S whose properties are such that they violate the ordering. Reversing the two tasks shows that the performance improves, which contradicts the original assumption. Let us illustrate this procedure by proving the first part of Theorem 1.1 concerned with mean weighted flow time.

Let the above-mentioned hypothetical sequence S be such that $f(i)$, $\tau(i)$, and $w(i)$ denote, respectively, the finishing time, execution time, and deferral cost of the ith task sequenced in S, and suppose

$$\frac{\tau(k)}{w(k)} > \frac{\tau(k+1)}{w(k+1)} \qquad \text{or} \qquad w(k)\tau(k+1) < w(k+1)\tau(k) \qquad (4)$$

Now consider the effect on the mean weighted flow time $\bar{\omega}$ of interchanging the kth and $(k + 1)$st tasks in the sequence. Interchanging delays the finishing time of the kth task by $\tau(k + 1)$ units contributing an additional $(1/n)w(k)\tau(k + 1)$ to $\bar{\omega}$; at the same time the $(k + 1)$st task now finishes $\tau(k)$ units earlier, decreasing $\bar{\omega}$ by $(1/n)w(k + 1)\tau(k)$. As a consequence, we have

$$\bar{\omega}' = \bar{\omega} + [w(k)\tau(k + 1) - w(k + 1)\tau(k)]/n$$

Hence by (4) we have $\bar{\omega}' < \bar{\omega}$ and the desired contradiction.

Single machine results for problems involving due-dates and the tardiness performance measure have received considerable attention. See [La1], [HK1], and [RLL] (which contains a recent survey) for results related to the approaches described in Chapter 6. In section 1.4 we discuss the complexity of these problems.

A well-known related result in [Mo] concerns the problem of finding a sequence that minimizes the number of late tasks. An optimal algorithm can be described as follows. First, the tasks are sequenced in the order of Theorem 1.2. The algorithm then finds the first late task T in this sequence and eliminates that task T' in the initial subsequence terminated by T, which has the largest execution time. The process is then iterated on the resulting sequence (with T' removed) until a sequence is obtained with no late tasks. Any sequence beginning with the initial subsequence determined by the above process minimizes the number of late tasks. Extensions have been examined in [Si2].*

Another problem using as a performance measure the maximum of the weighted finishing times has been studied in [La2]. A simple algorithm is produced for $<$ arbitrary which minimizes max $\{w_i f_i\}$ on one processor.

It is clearly interesting to assess the importance of sequencing algorithms by comparing their performance with that achieved under a random selection procedure. Moreover, it is also of considerable interest to analyze an algorithm that is optimal under the assumptions of known execution times, under weaker conditions in which only partial information (specifically, a probability distribution) is available. Examination of the difficulties presented by such an analysis of the models in subsequent chapters reveals the general intractability of this approach in virtually all cases of interest. However, we present below some results for single-processor problems to illustrate the value of probability models.

We examine the random and shortest-processing-time (SPT) sequencing rules under the assumptions of $m = 1$, $w_i = 1$ $(1 \leq i \leq n)$, and a distribution function $F(\tau)$ governing execution times $\{\tau_i\}$ regarded as independent random variables. We let $E(\tau)$ denote the first moment of $F(\tau)$.

---

* For further discussion and references see [Bak].

First, if $\tau(i)$ is the execution time (random variable) of the ith task scheduled, we observe

$$\sum_{i=1}^{n} f(i) = \sum_{i=1}^{n} \sum_{j=1}^{i} \tau(j) = \sum_{j=1}^{n} (n - j + 1)\tau(j)$$

Thus if we sequence at random we obtain

$$E(\bar{\omega}_R) = \frac{n+1}{2} E(\tau) \tag{5}$$

Now suppose we sample the execution times and then sequence them in SPT order. To calculate the expected value $E(\bar{\omega}_S)$ of the mean flow time of the resulting schedule, we calculate first the corresponding value $E(\bar{\omega}_L)$ for the reverse, largest-processing-time (LPT) schedule, and then transform this result in a simple way to $E(\bar{\omega}_S)$. Thus if the samples of execution times are indexed in the order of increasing magnitude ($\tau_1 \leq \tau_2 \leq \cdots \leq \tau_n$) we have

$$E(\bar{\omega}_L) = E\left[\frac{1}{n} \sum_{i=1}^{n} (n - i + 1)\tau(n - i + 1)\right] = E\left[\frac{1}{n} \sum_{i=1}^{n} i\tau(i)\right] = \frac{1}{n} \sum_{i=1}^{n} iE[\tau(i)]$$

Computing the distribution $F_i(\tau)$ of the ith ordered execution time (or consulting standard texts in statistics), one obtains

$$dF_i(\tau) = \frac{n!}{(i - 1)!(n - i)!} F^{i-1}(\tau)[1 - F(\tau)]^{n-i} dF(\tau)$$

from which one can obtain $E[\tau(i)] = \int_0^{\infty} \tau \, dF_i(\tau)$. Specifically, one finds

$$E(\bar{\omega}_L) = E(\tau) + (n - 1) \int_0^{\infty} \tau F(\tau) \, dF(\tau)$$

Now we have the relation

$$E(\bar{\omega}_S) = \frac{1}{n} \sum_{i=1}^{n} (n - i + 1)E[\tau(i)] = (n + 1)E(\tau) - E(\bar{\omega}_L)$$

and hence

$$E(\bar{\omega}_S) = nE(\tau) - (n - 1) \int_0^{\infty} \tau F(\tau) \, dF(\tau) \tag{6}$$

This provides us with a means of comparing SPT sequencing with the result in (5) of random sequencing. Notice that $E(\bar{\omega}_S)$ is maximum when the variance of $F(\tau)$ is zero and it takes on the value of $E(\bar{\omega}_R)$.

Next, we describe an analysis of a problem in which incomplete information is available under the same assumptions used previously. Suppose we have a family $\{G_i(\tau)\}$ of distributions describing the respective independent random variables $\tau_1, \tau_2, \ldots, \tau_n$. If we know at the outset only the expected values $E(\tau_i)$ and we sequence in nondecreasing order of $E(\tau_i)$, we obtain immediately

$$E_1(\bar{\omega}) = \frac{1}{n} \sum_{i=1}^{n} (n - i + 1) E(\tau_i) \tag{7}$$

as the corresponding expected mean flow time. Now we want to measure the average cost incurred by this procedure, which results from knowing only expected values.

Thus suppose the execution times are sampled according to the $G_i(\tau)$ and then sequenced in nondecreasing order. The following result can be proved for the expected mean flow time in such an experiment [CMM]:

$$E_2(\bar{\omega}) = \sum_{j=1}^{n} \left[E(\tau_j) - \frac{1}{n} \int_0^{\infty} \tau \left(\sum_{i \neq j}^{n} G_i(\tau) \right) dG_j(\tau) \right] \tag{8}$$

The idea of the proof is as follows. Consider the (outer) summand, to be denoted $E_2[\bar{\omega}(j)]$, which represents the contribution to $E_2(\bar{\omega})$ of task T_j. For a given value τ of the execution time of T_j let $p_{in}(\tau)$ denote the probability that T_j occupies the ith position in sequence when there are n tasks. A straightforward argument leads to the recurrence relation

$$p_{i,n+1}(\tau) = p_{i,n}(\tau)[1 - G_{n+1}(\tau)] + p_{i-1,n}(\tau) G_{n+1}(\tau), \qquad i = 2, 3, \ldots, n$$

$$p_{1,n+1}(\tau) = p_{1,n}(\tau)[1 - G_{n+1}(\tau)]$$

$$p_{n+1,n+1}(\tau) = p_{n,n}(\tau) G_{n+1}(\tau)$$

from which we may fashion an induction argument for $E_2[\bar{\omega}(j)]$, whose basis $(n = 1)$ is trivially true from (8). In particular, letting $E_2[\bar{\omega}_n(j)]$ denote the result for n tasks, we can write

$$E_2[\bar{\omega}_{n+1}(j)] = \frac{1}{n+1} \int_0^{\infty} \tau \sum_{i=1}^{n+1} [(n+1) - i + 1] p_{i,n+1}(\tau) \, dG_j(\tau)$$

or

$$E_2[\omega_{n+1}(j)] = \frac{n}{n+1} E_2[\omega_n(j)] + \frac{E(\tau_j)}{n+1} - \frac{1}{n+1} \int_0^{\infty} \tau G_{n+1}(\tau) \, dG_j(\tau)$$

from which we complete the induction step by substituting for $E_2[\bar{\omega}_n(j)]$ from (8)

$$E_2[\bar{\omega}_{n+1}(j)] = E(\tau_j) - \frac{1}{n+1} \int_0^{\infty} \tau \left(\sum_{i \neq j}^{n+1} G_i(\tau) \right) dG_j(\tau)$$

Thus comparison of (7) and (8) affords us a means for assessing the performance of sequencing with only the expected values available for the sequencing decisions.

1.4   RESULTS IN SCHEDULE-LENGTH AND MEAN FLOW-TIME MINIMIZATION AND APPROXIMATION PROBLEMS

It is convenient to discuss the results of Chapters 2 and 3 in conjunction with those of Chapter 4 because the results on problem complexity in Chapter 4 help describe the significance and limitations on extensions of the results in Chapters 2 and 3. However, this necessitates preliminary remarks on measures of complexity. These comments are rather brief, but should be sufficient to permit appreciation of the results described in this section. A careful presentation of these notions appears in Chapter 4.

In general, the "complexity" of an algorithm solving a given problem refers only to its execution time, expressed as a function of the input-length; i.e. the number of bits needed to describe an instance of the problem. For our purposes we will usually specify complexity as a function of basic problem parameters, primarily the number n of tasks. In some cases, this is a considerable simplification, but not an inappropriate one for our purposes. (In effect, we are assuming that numbers can be read and operated on in constant time, which is reasonable in practice.)

The detailed specification of the functions representing complexity depend on the details of algorithm and data structure design in which we take no special interest. Thus we use the order-of-magnitude notation $O(.)$, which concentrates on the terms of a function that dominate its behavior. Thus if we say that an algorithm has complexity $O(n^2)$, we simply mean that there exists a constant c such that the function cn^2 bounds the execution time as a function of n. As a specific example, if a sequencing rule depends essentially on the ordering of an arbitrary permutation of n execution times, we know that algorithms exist, using binary comparison operations only, whose complexity is $O(n \log_2 n)$. But the specific functions of execution time, for different algorithms, usually consist also of terms $O(n)$, $O(\log_2 n)$, or $O(1)$ and may differ in the coefficient of the $n \log_2 n$ term.

Any sequencing algorithm whose complexity is bounded by a polynomial in n is called a polynomial-time algorithm or an algorithm that runs in polynomial time. The corresponding problem is said to have a polynomial-time solution (algorithm). Henceforth we consider an algorithm to be *efficient* if it runs in polynomial time. The practical motivations of this terminology are strong, especially for large n. In this respect we should note that the sequencing problems we study are or can be reduced to finite problems, in the sense that the solution space is finite. Thus our notion of efficient algorithm can be associated with nonenumerative algorithms; "inefficient" algorithms are those which effectively require a search (enumeration) of the solution space and have a complexity that is at least some exponential in n. (However, Chapter 6 on approximate and enumerative algorithms concentrates on the notion of efficiency as it is normally thought of; i.e., without the special meaning just given.)

There exists a set of problems, each of which is called *NP-complete* (sometimes called polynomial complete, or simply complete), which includes many classical, hard problems. Such problems include the traveling salesman problem, finding the chromatic number of a graph, and the knapsack problem, just to mention a few. It is known that in terms of complexity, all the NP-complete problems are equivalent in the following intuitive sense. If one can find a polynomial-time algorithm to solve one of these problems, one can find a polynomial-time algorithm for every other problem in the class, according to a procedure that normally varies from one problem to another. Thus either there exist polynomial-time algorithms for all the NP-complete problems, or none of them has a polynomial-time algorithm; we do not know which of these two assertions is the correct one. However, despite the lack of an answer to this "ultimate" question, there is strong evidence to suggest that all NP-complete problems are inherently intractable. As we shall see, almost all sequencing problems stated in complete generality are NP-complete.

The above intuitive discussion of course is very informal. More formally, one must proceed by defining a common mathematical basis for representing algorithms and instances of problems, defining problem complexity in terms of the model, and defining the transformation (or reduction) of one problem to another. With such a formalism one can address for specific problems such questions as deciding their complexity in terms of desirable problem parameters, the tradeoff between storage and execution-time complexity, the essential aspect of a problem that contributes to its complexity, and so on. These mathematical aspects are left to Chapter 4. Later, however, we illustrate, again informally, the techniques for taking a new combinatorial problem and showing that it admits of a polynomial-time solution only if some known NP-complete problem has such a solution.

1.4.1 Schedule-Length Minimization Problems

Chapter 2 concerns schedule-length minimization problems, obviously for $m \geq 2$. Table 1.1 summarizes the results presently known for these problems. To help interpret the table, the following remarks are in order.

1. The columns correspond to the possible parameters of an algorithm that solves a problem defined by the assumptions given in a row of the table. Those entries in which a value is specified eliminate a "free"

parameter. For example, in problem (row) 2 we find that m is not a parameter but is fixed at $m = 2$. Similarly, $\{\tau_i\}$ is not a parameter, for the specific common value of the τ_i does not influence the algorithm. The partial order is a free parameter, but no preemptions are allowed and there is no additional resource requirement that can be specified. Here and throughout the book, n is always a free parameter.

2. The entries in the column on complexity given as "open" simply mean that the question of the complexity of the corresponding problem has not been resolved.

3. For each of the nonpreemptive problems for which polynomial-time optimal algorithms are known, there in fact exists an optimal list-scheduling algorithm.

4. An important point concerning the NP-complete problems indicated in Table 1.1 is that they represent the simplest cases for which NP-completeness is known. Thus the reader can and should make appropriate inferences regarding more general problems. Generalizing any one of the parameter restrictions in a given problem (e.g., assuming as appropriate, non-identical processors, nonempty partial orders, additional resources, etc.) obviously produces a problem at least as hard as the original one.

One important observation in this respect concerns a comparison of rows such as 6 and 4. Since problem 6 is NP-complete, it is easy to see that so also is the problem for m a free parameter. However, the converse is not necessarily true. Problem 4 is NP-complete, but it is not known whether for any fixed $m \geq 3$ the corresponding problem (problem 3) is NP-complete (and in fact a considerable effort has been invested in resolving this problem for $m = 3$).

5. Regarding polynomial-time algorithms, we do not in all cases claim that the complexity shown is minimal. As the analysis of subsequent chapters indicates, however, there is virtually conclusive evidence to this fact in a number of cases. For example, algorithms necessarily depending on an ordering of execution times must surely be of at least $O(n \log_2 n)$ complexity, assuming an unordered list to begin with. Algorithms depending on precedence constraint structure must surely have a complexity at least $O(n^2)$, since there are $O(n^2)$ edges in a general precedence graph (see problem 2, e.g.). However, complexity must also depend on data structures, as demonstrated in Chapter 2. For example, if a graph is specified by an edge list containing redundant transitive edges, the complexity may well increase. Problem 2 is a relevant example, for the complexity shown depends on the absence of transitive edges; the problem of removing such edges from a dag edge list has $O(n^{2.8})$ complexity according to the best algorithm currently known [AGU]. Thus

TABLE 1.1 RESULTS FOR MINIMIZING $\omega = \max \{f_i\}$

Problem complexity	m	$\{\tau_i\}^*$	$\prec$	Rule†	Resources		References
					s	$\{m_i\}$	
1. $O(n)$	—	Equal	Forest	Nonpr	0		[H]
2. $O(n^2)$	2	Equal	—	Nonpr	0		[CG]
3. Open	Fixed $m \geq 3$	Equal	—	Nonpr	0		
4. NP-complete	—	Equal	—	Nonpr	0		[U1]
5. NP-complete	Fixed $m \geq 2$	$\tau_i = 1$ or 2 for all i	—	Nonpr	0		[U1]
6. NP-complete	Fixed $m \geq 2$	—	φ	Nonpr	0		
7. $O(n \log_2 n)$	—	—	Forest	Pr	0		[MC]
8. $O(n^2)$	2	—	—	Pr	0		[MC]
9. Open	Fixed $m \geq 3$	—	—	Pr	0		
10. NP-complete	—	—	φ	Pr	0		(See Chapter 4)
11. $O(n^3)$	2	Equal	φ	Nonpr	—	—	[GJ1]
12. NP-complete	Fixed $m \geq 2$	Equal	Forest	Nonpr	1	—	[GJ1]
13. NP-complete	Fixed $m \geq 2$	Equal	—	Nonpr	1	$m_1 = 1$	(See Chapter 4)
14. NP-complete	Fixed $m \geq 3$	Equal	φ	Nonpr	1	—	[GJ1]
15. $O(n \log_2 n)$	2	Flow shop	—	Nonpr	0		[Jo]

16. NP-complete	Fixed $m \geq 3$	Flow shop		Nonpr	0	[GJS]
17. NP-complete	Fixed $m \geq 2$	Job shop		Nonpr	0	[GJS]
18. NP-complete	Fixed $m \geq 2$	—	φ	Σf_i is minimum	0	[CS]

* Identical processors assumed throughout, except for problems 15–17.
† Nonpr and pr are abbreviations for nonpreemptive and preemptive, respectively.

without the assumption of the absence of transitive edges, problem 2 would have a complexity dominated by this latter algorithm.

The optimization algorithms for problems 1, 2, 7, and 8 are essentially critical path algorithms (called *level-by-level* algorithms in Chapter 2), since the scheduling priority at any point is given sequentially to the remaining tasks at the highest level. (Actually, in problem 2 this criterion must be augmented by another property of tasks which, in the sense of the precedence graph, is locally computable.) Clearly, the complexity of these algorithms is dominated by the complexity of the graph operations needed to find critical paths. Note that "first-order" generalizations of these problems are NP-complete as shown in problems 4, 5, and 10.

Problem 15 is solved essentially by an appropriate ordering of the tasks; hence the complexity is determined by the complexity of sorting. This is the earliest result (1954) in schedule-length minimization. Apart from problem 1 (1961) and special cases of problem 16 (covered in Chapter 2), the remaining results date from 1968.

The *flow-shop* problem referred to in problems 15 and 16 is defined as follows. Each task system consists of a set of n/m chains of length m, usually called jobs in the literature, with the restriction that the ith task in a chain must be executed on processor P_i (n is a multiple of m). In terms of $[\tau_{ij}]$ in our original model, columns $km + i$, $k = 0, 1, \ldots, n/m - 1$, correspond to tasks that must execute on P_i, so that $\tau_{j,km+i} = \infty$ for all $j \neq i$. The T_{km+i}, $i = 1, 2, \ldots, m$, will correspond to the sequence of tasks in the job k.

Problem 17 concerns the complexity of the *simple job-shop problem*, described as follows. As in the flow-shop problem $<$ is a set of chains, each of arbitrary length, called jobs. (In the *general* job-shop problem there is no constraint on $<$.) Each job J_i can be characterized by a sequence of pairs (a_{ij}, P_{ij}), where a_{ij} is the execution time of the jth task of J_i and P_{ij} is the processor on which it must execute. The general problem is NP-complete for all $m \geq 2$. This is not shown in Chapter 4, but later in this section we illustrate a technique that can be used for the purpose. However, there is an interesting special case, which we now describe, that admits of a polynomial-time solution for $m = 2$.

Each job J_i is characterized simply by a single operation on each machine (i.e., each J_i is a two-task chain): each J_i either executes a task first on P_1 then on P_2 or it executes a task first on P_2 then on P_1. Let (x_i, y_i) be the execution times for the tasks of J_i. Construct two ordered sets C_1 and C_2 such that all J_i whose first task executes on P_1 (respectively P_2) are elements of C_1 (respectively C_2) and such that if (x_i, y_i) and (x_j, y_j) are both in C_1, then $\min(x_i, y_i) < \min(x_j, y_j)$ implies that J_i precedes J_j in the ordering. (This is the rule used in problem 15.) Order C_2 in the same way.

According to this ordering, assign tasks on P_1 first from C_1 then C_2, observing precedence constraints. Similarly, assign tasks on P_2 first from C_2 then C_1. It is easily shown (see, e.g., Theorem 2.12) that this assignment produces a minimum-length schedule. Note that x_i or y_i can be zero, in which case we effectively account for jobs having only a single task for one machine or the other.

The basic intractability of problems in which there are additional resources is made clear in problems 12 to 14. Problem 11, not discussed later in the book, can be viewed as an application of the maximum-matching [E] problem. One may construct in less than $O(n^3)$ time an undirected graph G such that $(T_i, T_j) \in G$ if and only if T_i and T_j are compatible: that is, $R_k(T_i) + R_k(T_j) \leq m_k$, for all k; hence T_i and T_j can execute in parallel. A maximum matching of G provides a shortest-length schedule and can be found in $O(n^3)$ time.

Problem 18 is discussed in Section 1.5. Problem 7 with $< = \varphi$ has an $O(n)$ algorithm, which we reconsider later in the chapter. Chapter 2 also discusses this problem in connection with a study providing quantitative comparisons of the various scheduling disciplines.

We conclude this subsection with a brief description of recent results bearing on deadline problems relevant to the problems we have been discussing. Consider the problem of scheduling equal-execution-time tasks on two identical processors when there is an arbitrary partial order and each task has an individual deadline to meet. If the partial order is given in transitively closed form, it is known [GJ2] how to determine in time $O(n^2)$ whether a valid schedule exists which meets all the deadlines, and if so, generate one. If it is desired to know whether a valid schedule exists that violates at most k deadlines, where k is fixed, this can be done in time $O(n^{k+2})$. However, the problem of the existence of a valid schedule that violates at most k deadlines, k variable, is NP-complete, even for only one processor.

1.4.2   Mean Flow-Time Results

Chapter 3 deals with recent results generalizing those in the previous section for single-machine systems. Additional resources are not included because corresponding results do not exist. Discipline constraints are also not considered, since nonpreemptive scheduling is assumed throughout for the same reason. (Recall, however, that a preemptive capability does not accomplish anything more in the case of identical processors, non-negative weights, and an empty partial order.) Comments 1, 2, 4, and 5 describing Table 1.1 also apply to Table 1.2 in which we summarize most of the results of Chapter 3.

For problem 1 of Table 1.2 the existence of a polynomial-time algorithm

TABLE 1.2   RESULTS FOR MINIMIZING $\Sigma_i w_i f_i$

Problem Complexity	Parameters: n and				
	$<$	$\{w_i\}$	$\{\tau_{ij}\}$	m	References
1. $O(n^3)$	ϕ	Equal	—	—	[BCS2, Ho2]
2. NP-complete	Set of chains	Equal	Identical processors	—	[BSe]
3. $O(n^2)$	Forest	—	Identical processors	1	[Ho1] (See also [Ga, Si1])
4. Open	—	—	Identical processors	1	
5. NP-complete	φ	—	Identical processors	Fixed $m \geq 2$	[BCS1]
6. NP-complete	Flow shop			Fixed $m \geq 2$	[GJS]

is indicated for the most general case of independent tasks and equal deferral costs. Special cases of this result have been known for some time, in particular the result for SPT sequencing introduced in Section 1.3. The result of problem 1 is based on a formulation that identifies it as a special case of the general transportation problem.

The solution of problem 3 results from a general formulation that proceeds by identifying a locally computable cost function (sequencing criterion) to be associated with each vertex (subtree) of the forest. This function is in fact a generalization of the function τ_i / w_i introduced in Theorem 1.1. Using an ordering obtained from these computed costs, the optimal sequence is achieved by recursively identifying the subtrees of the forest that are to be executed next.

Problem 6 of Table 1.2 concerns a flow-shop problem that has received considerable attention. This NP-complete problem forms the basis of an illustration in Chapter 6 of enumerative and approximate techniques applied to sequencing problems.

A problem not covered in our general model, which naturally extends the results of problem 3, is also solved, yielding a polynomial-time algorithm. Once again a forest and a single processor are assumed, but each tree (called a job) in the forest is now regarded as a decision tree in the following sense. There is an arbitrary (discrete) probability distribution associated with each vertex governing the decision as to which task (vertex) is to be executed next in the job. Thus the eventual execution of a job consists of a sequence or chain of tasks beginning with the root and ending at a descendant vertex, and the chain can be interrupted only at task termination times. These sequences and their total execution times are random variables, hence the problem becomes one of minimizing the expected value of the mean weighted flow time. A sequencing criterion for deciding sequentially which job is next to have a task executed is again developed along the lines of problem 3. The complexity question is studied, with the result that an $O(n^2)$ algorithm is produced.

The problem of minimizing mean tardiness (see previous section) is also relevant to Table 1.2, with due dates also a parameter. It has been shown that the minimum mean weighted tardiness problem is NP-complete for all $m \geq 1$ [BLR]. An interesting open problem is the complexity of the minimum mean tardiness problem (equal weights) when $m = 1$.

1.4.3 Complexity of Sequencing Problems

In Chapter 4 a formal approach to the definition of problem complexity is introduced and used in demonstrations of the NP-completeness of a large variety of sequencing problems, either explicitly or implicitly. A distinguishing feature of the presentation is the avoidance of explicit use of a formal abstract theory of computation in which complexity results find their origin. The result of this treatment is an appeal to a much larger class of readers and a mechanism by which pragmatic issues are more easily appreciated.

The presentation begins with the description of a computer model by which algorithms for combinatorial problems can be commonly posed, in a manner that simplifies their analysis and comparison with respect to their complexity. We define the notion of polynomial-time nondeterministic algorithms, which identifies with problems admitting of an enumerative solution describable by a polynomial-depth search tree. As a matter of definition, the existence of such an algorithm is necessary for the NP-completeness of a sequencing problem. The subtleties necessary to an insight into the limitations and implications of the model are discussed. The concept of polynomial reducibility among combinatorial problems is defined, a definition used in deciding that a problem has a polynomial-time solution if and only if some NP-complete problem has such a solution.

In connection with Table 1.1, comment 4 is worth repeating at this point. Namely, the reader will be able to infer the NP-completeness of new problems from results shown in Chapter 4. For example, in Chapter 4 the NP-complete problem 6 of Table 1.1 is shown to have a polynomial-time solution if and only if a similar solution exists for the classical deadline problem; that is, given a deadline d common to all (independent) tasks, is there a schedule on m identical processors such that all tasks finish no later than d? The consequent NP-completeness of this problem in effect accounts in a straightforward manner for the NP-completeness of the general additional-resource ($s \geq 1$) and bin-packing problems in Chapter 5.

We can illustrate informally but effectively the process of reducing one combinatorial problem to another by the following examples, not given explicit treatment in Chapter 4. Consider as a basis the simple version of the knapsack problem, stated as follows. Given as parameters a set $X = \{a_1, \ldots, a_n\}$ of n positive integers and an additional integer b, is there a subset of X whose elements sum exactly to b? That is, does the equation $\Sigma_{i=1}^n c_i a_i = b$ have a 0–1 solution in the c_i's? This problem is well known to be NP-complete [Ka]. We now make use of this problem in assessing the complexity of the following sequencing problems.

1. Consider problem 7 of Table 1.1 with $< = \varphi$, for which it is readily verified that in general there can be $O(n!)$ solutions. Suppose we add in the "Discipline" column that the number of preemptions must be minimized. Call this the PM(m) problem for m processors.

An example of the case for $m = 2$ and $\max\{\tau_i\} < \Sigma_{i=1}^n \tau_i/2$ is shown in Fig. 1.5a. Note that any sequence of tasks can be used in carrying out the assignment; one simply must insert a preemption when necessary for the last task scheduled on P_1 (first task scheduled on P_2). Thus at most one preemption is necessary, and its necessity depends on finding a subset of $\{\tau_i\}$ that adds up to exactly $\Sigma_{i=1}^n \tau_i/2$. Therefore, we can reduce a knapsack problem to a PM(2) problem as follows. Let b and $\{a_i\}_{i=1}^n$ be an instance of the knapsack problem. Consider the instance of the PM(2) problem given by $\{\tau_i\}_{i=1}^{n+1}$ where $\tau_i = a_i$, $1 \leq i \leq n$, and $\tau_{n+1} = |2b - \Sigma_{i=1}^n a_i|$. It is easy to see that this PM(2) problem has a solution with no preemptions if and only if the original knapsack problem has a solution. Figure 1.5b provides examples. Clearly, because of the simplicity of the reduction (calculating $|2b - \Sigma_{i=1}^n a_i|$), we expect the PM(2) problem to be at least as hard as the knapsack problem. We make the same statement for the general case $m \geq 3$, since we can add $m - 2$ tasks of length $\Sigma_{i=1}^n \tau_i/2$ to reduce the PM(2) problem to the PM(m) problem.

2. Consider problem 16 of Table 1.1, and let the jobs (i.e., three-task chains) be specified by the triples (x_i, y_i, z_i), $1 \leq i \leq n$, where x_i (respectively, y_i and z_i) is the time required for the first (respectively, second and third) task to execute on P_1 (respectively, P_2 and P_3). We can provide as follows the basic observation in a proof of NP-completeness.

From an instance b, $\{a_i\}$ of the knapsack problem, let the execution times in an instance of problem 16 for $m = 3$ be given by $(0, a_1, 0), \ldots, (0, a_n, 0)$, $(b, 1, \Sigma_{i=1}^n a_i - b)$. Figure 1.6 gives an example

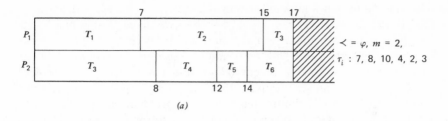

$\prec = \varphi$, $m = 2$,

τ_i : 7, 8, 10, 4, 2, 3

(a)

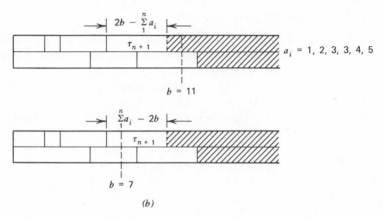

$2b - \overset{n}{\underset{1}{\Sigma}} a_i$

τ_{n+1}

$a_i = 1, 2, 3, 3, 4, 5$

$b = 11$

$\overset{n}{\underset{1}{\Sigma}} a_i - 2b$

τ_{n+1}

$b = 7$

(b)

Figure 1.5 Preemptive scheduling.

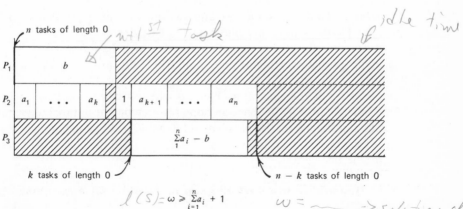

n tasks of length 0 $n+1^{st}$ task   idle time

P_1 b

P_2 a_1 $\cdots$ a_k 1 a_{k+1} $\cdots$ a_n

P_3 $\overset{n}{\underset{1}{\Sigma}} a_i - b$

k tasks of length 0   *n* − *k* tasks of length 0

$\ell(S) = \omega \geqslant \overset{n}{\underset{i=1}{\Sigma}} a_i + 1$

$\omega = \underline{\quad\quad} \Rightarrow$ solution of knapsack problem, since $\Sigma a_i = b$

Figure 1.6 A flow-shop schedule, $m = 3$.

27

schedule. Note that a minimal-length schedule is at least $\Sigma_{i=1}^{n} a_i + 1$ long. But as illustrated, we can know whether we have a minimal-length schedule only if we can answer the question: is there a subset of the a_i's which sum exactly to b? Thus by a simple algorithm we can transform an instance of the knapsack problem to an instance of the ($m = 3$) flow-shop problem such that an algorithm for the flow-shop problem finds a minimal solution if and only if the original knapsack problem has a solution. As before, it is not difficult to render a general case for $m > 3$ identical to a problem for $m = 3$. It follows that we can expect the problem to be at least as hard as the knapsack problem.

A similar type of argument can be easily constructed for the result of problem 17. The reader is encouraged to work one out, taking advantage of the absence of the "processor ordering" implicit in the flow-shop problem. It is important to note that the knapsack problem can be solved in time polynomial in the desired sum b (this does not contradict the NP-completeness of the knapsack problem since b can be expressed using $\log_2 b$ bits). Therefore, if the complexity parameter of interest is the sum of task execution times we can not infer from the above arguments that these problems are intractable. For example, Problem 6 in Table 1.1 can be solved in polynomial time for fixed $m \geq 2$ for this less stringent input measure. However, Problems 16 and 17 remain NP-complete even for the latter measure [GJS].

Clearly, we have only shown these problems to be at least as hard as NP-complete problems; we have not verified that they are no harder. At this point it is best to leave full proofs of NP-completeness to those who have read Chapter 4. We might note here, however, that the problem of showing reducibility has no generally applicable structure (thus the open problems of Tables 1.1 and 1.2), and solutions to these problems can be quite involved, as is amply illustrated in Chapter 4.

We conclude this discussion of complexity with the warning that having a specific problem in hand, one should be fully aware of any special features or constraints that might exist. For in this case the NP-completeness of the general problem to which it corresponds should not immediately cause us to abandon hope for an efficient optimal algorithm. Specific limitations on the problem may enable us to design an algorithm whose execution time is bounded by a polynomial in the basic characteristics of the problem.

1.4.4 Bounds on the Performance of Scheduling Algorithms

The results on complexity demonstrate rather clearly that much of the progress in the theory of scheduling is very likely to result from the study

of heuristics (approximate algorithms) and effective enumerative procedures. In Chapter 5, which we now discuss, the approach focuses on quite
simple procedures [usually of at most $O(n^2)$ execution time], and
performance bounds by which their worst-case behavior can be determined relative to optimal procedures. Initially, performance bounds are
derived for arbitrary (unstructured or random) sequencing rules, the
objectives being to demonstrate the importance of developing efficient
heuristics and to gain insight into the combinatorial structure of the
problem. Easily implemented heuristics are then proposed whose performance bounds show that even simple heuristics can be expected to
provide quite adequate performance for many sequencing problems
known to be NP-complete.

The analysis is restricted to the (nonpreemptive) list-scheduling rules
according to which processors are never allowed to remain idle when a
task is ready for execution. As we have pointed out, this is not in fact a
restriction when dealing with independent tasks and identical processors,
but it is not difficult to motivate in any case. As we have already seen, the
optimal nonpreemptive algorithms known to exist can be rendered as
list-scheduling rules. Moreover, not only are the simplest attractive
heuristics expressible in this form, but efficient extensions of these, which
are not list-scheduling rules, are difficult to envisage.

The presentation begins with a rather fully illustrated analysis of the
general problem of minimizing schedule length with no additional resources, identical processors, and m, $\{\tau_i\}$, and $<$ arbitrary. A number of
unexpected anomalies are revealed which show that individual *decreases*
in execution times, *increases* in the number of processors, and *removal* of
precedence constraints can in fact *lengthen* schedules. An anomaly in
which the total removal of a task from a system can increase schedule
length is illustrated in Fig. 1.7. An analysis is provided to demonstrate that
the new schedule length resulting from such changes can be no more than
$1 + (m - 1)/m'$ times larger than the original, where $m' \geq m$ is the new
number of processors. Moreover, the bound is shown to be best in the
sense that it is either achievable or asymptotically so.

A good description of critical path scheduling and its limitations is also
provided, along with many examples, thus complementing the presentation
in Chapter 2. Included here in particular is a full analysis of the (best)
schedule-length bound for LPT (or critical path) scheduling for independent tasks. Table 1.3 summarizes most of the results obtained or treated
for the material we have discussed thus far. (Unless otherwise noted, all
bounds shown in this section are best bounds.) Note that problem 1 of the
table follows from the analysis leading to the bound on list-scheduling
anomalies mentioned earlier.

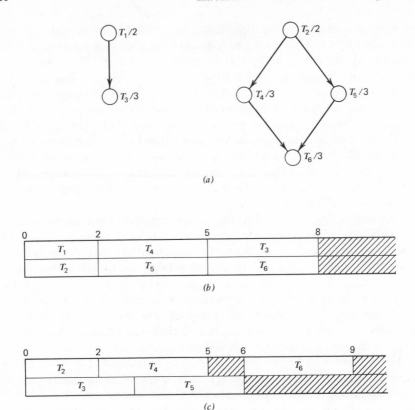

(a)

(b)

(c)

Figure 1.7   A list scheduling anomaly. (a) $\mathcal{T}$, $<$. (b) An optimal list schedule for $\mathcal{T}$, $<$. (c) An optimal list schedule for $\mathcal{T} - \{T_1\}$, $< - \{(T_1, T_3)\}$.

The analysis next turns to scheduling problems under the assumption of additional resources ($s \geq 1$). The principal objective is the presentation of worst-case performance bounds for arbitrary schedules. The value of the results lies in the insights one obtains into these very difficult problems, and because of the magnitude of these bounds, the need for further study of efficient heuristics. A fair amount of attention is also given to the performance of simple heuristics, particularly for the case when all $\tau_i = 1$. The major results are the best bounds given in Table 1.4, which except for the first, are somewhat surprising for the difficulty in their proof.

The final effort in the chapter is directed mainly at computing bounds for the bin-packing problem—the special case of the previous additional-resources model in which $s = 1$, $< = \varphi$, all $\tau_i = 1$, and $m \geq n$. Recall the significance of this problem in terms of deadline scheduling as illustrated in Fig. 1.4. Later in the chapter results are given when the restrictions

TABLE 1.3   LIST SCHEDULING BOUNDS

		Parameters: $n, m, \{\tau_i\}$, and		
		---	---	---
Problem	Bounds	$L(\omega')$	$<$	References
1.	$\dfrac{\omega'}{\omega} \le 2 - \dfrac{1}{m}$	—	—	[G1]
2.	$\dfrac{\omega'}{\omega} \le \dfrac{4}{3} - \dfrac{1}{3m}$	LPT(CP)	φ	[G2]
3.	$\dfrac{\omega'}{\omega} \le 1 + \dfrac{1 - \dfrac{1}{m}}{1 + \left\lfloor \dfrac{k}{m} \right\rfloor}$ *	First k elements produce an optimal schedule for k largest tasks	φ	[G2]
4.	$\dfrac{\omega'}{\omega} \le 1 + (m-1)\dfrac{\max\{\tau_i\}}{\sum\limits_{i=1}^{n} \tau_i}$	—	φ	[G2]
		CP	Tree	[K2]
6.	$\dfrac{\omega'}{\omega} \le 2 - \dfrac{1}{m}$	CP	—	(See Section 5.2.1)

* Best for $k = 0 \bmod m$.

Notation:

1. ω = length of optimal list schedule.
2.   CP = critical path.
3.   LPT = largest-processing-time-first.
4. $L(\omega')$ = list producing ω'.
5. $\lfloor x \rfloor$ = largest integer not greater than x.

$s = 1$ and $m \ge n$ are relaxed. For the simple bin-packing problem, four basic heuristics are examined; these are described in terms of the deadline problem as follows.

Given an arbitrary task list examined in a fixed, directed scan:

1. The first-fit (FF) rule assigns successively each task onto the lowest indexed processor on which it fits (i.e., does not cause the deadline to be exceeded).
2. The best-fit (BF) rule assigns successively each task onto the processor for which the resulting unused execution time (until the deadline) is minimal.

TABLE 1.4 BOUNDS FOR ADDITIONAL RESOURCES

		Parameters: $n, L, \{\tau_i\}$, and			
Problem	Bounds	s	m	$<$	References
1	$\dfrac{\omega'}{\omega} \le m$	1	—	—	[GG1], [GG2]
2	$\dfrac{\omega'}{\omega} \le s + 1$	—	$m \ge n$	φ	[GG1], [GG2]
3	$\dfrac{\omega'}{\omega} \le \min\left[\dfrac{m+1}{2}, s + 2 - \dfrac{2s+1}{m}\right]$	—	$m \ge 2$	φ	[GG2]

Notation:
1. ω' corresponds to arbitrary L.
2. ω corresponds to optimal L.

3. The first-fit-decreasing (FFD) rule proceeds as in item 1 but assumes that the given list is in nonincreasing order of execution times (with respect to the scanning order).

4. The best-fit-decreasing (BFD) rule is described as in item 3, with first-fit replaced by best-fit.

An example for each of these algorithms appears in Fig. 1.8. Table 1.5a summarizes the major results for these heuristics, and Table 1.5b presents additional results applying to certain cases when parameter restrictions are relaxed. The results for the basic bin-packing problem are shown as best asymptotic bounds. In terms of an additional-resource scheduling problem, these bounds are made more precise as functions of the largest resource requirement, assuming an amount $m_1 = 1$ of the additional resource, any fraction of which can be required for the execution of a given task. In particular, let $\omega_A(L)$ denote the schedule-length (number of bins) required in assigning the tasks of list L by rule A. In Table 1.5a A denotes one or more of the four rules mentioned above, where processors (bins) become time units in the schedule and task execution times (as in Fig. 1.8) become resource requirements. Let $\omega^*(L)$ denote the minimum schedule-length required for the tasks in L. Table 1.5a shows values for the asymptotic bound

$$R_A(\alpha) = \varlimsup_{\omega^*(L) \to \infty} \frac{\omega_A(L)}{\omega^*(L)}$$

where L ranges over all lists for which $\max\{R(T_i)\} \le \alpha \in I(\alpha)$, and $I(\alpha)$

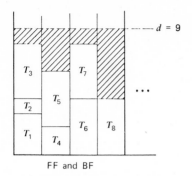

FF and BF

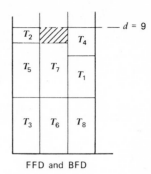

FFD and BFD

(a)

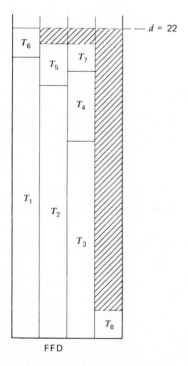

FFD

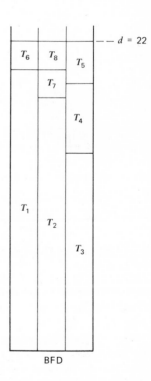

BFD

(b)

Figure 1.8 Bin-packing examples. (a) Example of ordering effect: lists: $(T_1, T_2, T_3, T_4, T_5, T_6, T_7, T_8)$ and $(T_3, T_5, T_6, T_7, T_8, T_1, T_4, T_2)$ $\tau_i = 3, 1, 4, 2, 4, 4, 4$ (b) Example showing advantage of BF and BFD: $\tau_i = 20, 18, 14, 5, 3, 2, 2, 2$.

TABLE 1.5a   BIN–PACKING BOUNDS

$\tau_i = 1, 1 \le i \le n, m \ge n, < = \varphi, s = 1, m_1 = 1\ (R_1(T_i) \le 1, 1 \le i \le n)$

Parameters: n and $\{R_1(T_i)\}$

Asymptotic bounds	$I(\alpha)$	A	References
$R_A(\alpha) = \dfrac{17}{10}$	$(\frac{1}{2}, 1)$	FF and BF	[U2], [GGU], [JDUGG]
$R_A(\alpha) = 1 + \lfloor \alpha^{-1} \rfloor^{-1}$	$(0, \frac{1}{2}]$		[GGU], [JDUGG]
$R_A(\alpha) = \dfrac{11}{9}$	$(\frac{1}{2}, 1]$	FFD and BFD	[JDUGG], [J1]
$R_A(\alpha) = \dfrac{71}{60}$	$(\frac{8}{29}, \frac{1}{2}]$		
$R_A(\alpha) = \dfrac{7}{6}$	$(\frac{1}{4}, \frac{8}{29}]$		
$R_A(\alpha) = \dfrac{23}{20}$	$(\frac{1}{5}, \frac{1}{4}]$		
$R_A(\alpha) = 1 + \dfrac{k-1}{k(k+1)}$ * $\quad k = \lfloor \alpha \rfloor^{-1}$	$(0, \frac{1}{4}]$		[J2], [JDUGG]

* Conjecture.

is an interval in $(0, 1)$. In Table 1.5b results for related problems appear in the form of asymptotic bounds that are not functions of max $\{R(T_i)\}$.

An impressive effort has been invested in the derivation of the results in Table 1.5. In fact, including proofs for all the results shown would likely have doubled the size of the book. However, the proofs given and outlined should guide the student of similar combinatorial problems.

The approach of Chapter 5 to combinatorial problems in which promising and very fast heuristics are analyzed for worst-case performance is relatively recent and is gaining momentum in other applications, such as storage allocation (see Chapter 5). It has been applied to other sequencing problems as noted in Section 1.5, and its application to job-shop problems seems to be inviting. For example, it can be shown quite readily that an arbitrary schedule for the flow-shop problem can be up to m times longer than the optimal. It would be of interest to consider

TABLE 1.5*b* FURTHER BOUNDS ON EXTENSIONS

| | $\tau_i = \tau_j$ for all i, j | | | | |
| | Parameters: n and | | | | |
Asymptotic bounds	A	s	$<$	m	References
$\dfrac{27}{10} - \dfrac{37}{10m} < R_A < \dfrac{27}{10} - \dfrac{24}{10m}$	—	1	φ	—	[Kr]
$R_A = 2 - \dfrac{2}{m}$	FFD	1	φ	$m \geq 2$	[Kr]
$R_A = s + \dfrac{7}{10}$	—	—	φ	$m \geq n$	[GGJY]
$R_A = \dfrac{17}{10} s + 1$	CP	—	—	$m \geq n$	[GGJY]

simple, superficially attractive heuristics for which performance bounds can be found, to see if worst-case performance can be brought down to an "acceptable" level. It appears somewhat more difficult to envision good heuristics with the simplicity of those considered in Chapter 5, for the bin-packing problem, for example. (For a recent survey comparing numerous heuristics for the flow-shop problem, see [D].) However, it is clearly not essential to have best (i.e., achievable) bounds, and the removal of this objective can simplify the mathematical effort greatly.

Perhaps the earliest work in bounding the performance of sequencing rules is that of [EEI], in which bounds are computed for mean weighted flow times. Specifically, for $< = \varphi$, $s = 0$, and identical machines one can show

$$\max\{\bar{\omega}(n), \frac{\bar{\omega}(1)}{m} + \frac{m-1}{2m}\bar{\omega}(n)\} \leq \bar{\omega}(m) < \frac{1}{m}\bar{\omega}(1) + \frac{m-1}{m}\bar{\omega}(n)$$

where $\bar{\omega}(k)$ is the mean weighted flow time on k machines. [Note that $\bar{\omega}(1)$ and $\bar{\omega}(n)$ can be easily calculated for the collection $\{w_i\}$ of deferral costs.]

1.4.5 Enumerative and Iterative Computational Approaches

In accordance with the sequence chosen, the book concludes with the chapter whose content is motivated by each of the preceding ones, addressing the realities of solving problems formulated directly from applications. The primary goal is an exposition of the principles in designing efficient, exact, and approximate algorithms (or heuristics) with the following detailed objectives:

1. A formulation sufficiently general to encompass virtually all applications dealing with problems of sequencing.

2. Emphasis on systematically deciding on an approach that takes into account the tradeoff between computational investment and the quality of the solution obtained.

3. An analysis by which one formally proves the correctness of branch-and-bound algorithm design and by which algorithm performance can be studied with changes in problem parameters.

The presentation is abstracted from specific applications and, as in previous chapters, is formal in its treatment. These limitations are not only consistent with the basic objectives of the book but are clearly inevitable in view of the following considerations: the existence of the large literature on enumerative and approximate algorithms for NP-complete problems, and the fact that these specific applications contain so many ad hoc techniques arising from the advantages taken of detailed properties of specific problems. However, the models, general techniques, and the principles governing their application are well illustrated in a detailed study of a specific flow-shop problem.

The chapter exploits a classification of computational approaches into exact, purely heuristic, and guaranteed accuracy methods (i.e., methods by which one organizes and implements an efficient algorithm for computing a solution whose desired accuracy has been prespecified). The first major effort is a generalization of previous work in a fully parameterized model of branch-and-bound techniques which is shown to encompass dynamic programming approaches as well. For those having some familiarity with branch-and-bound terminology, we can illustrate the scope of this undertaking by providing the list of algorithm parameters.

1. The *branching rule* defining the branching process vis-à-vis the search tree, whose specific function is to partition the space of solutions into disjoint subsets to be searched or eliminated in sequence.

2. The *selection rule* by which one chooses the next node of the tree from which to branch.

3. The *characteristic function* used in eliminating subtrees of the complete search tree which do not contain feasible solutions.

4. A node *dominance relation* used in connection with item 7, below.

5. A *lower bound function*, which assigns to each partial solution a lower bound cost for all complete solutions to which the partial solution can eventually lead.

6. An *upper bound cost*, which is the cost of some complete solution known at the outset or is effectively infinite if no such complete solution is known initially.

7. The *elimination rules*, which use the dominance relation and upper-bound cost to eliminate newly generated and currently active nodes in the search tree.

8. A *bracket* or real number in the interval [0, 1] representing the desired maximum relative deviation of the optimal cost from an acceptable solution.

9. A *resource bound* vector whose components are upper bounds on the total expendable execution time and the usable storage for active nodes and immediate descendants of the branching node.

A proof of the correctness of the general algorithm is provided along with studies of the (in some cases anomalous) variation in performance with changes in parameters. The local-neighborhood-search and limited backtracking branch-and-bound heuristics, which have proved successful in practice, are then described, again with a discussion of the all-important problem of deciding the desired tradeoff between computational costs and accuracy of the solution.

The chapter next presents an application of the major enumerative and approximate techniques to a nontrivial flow-shop problem in which mean flow time is to be minimized (problem 6 of Table 1.2). Numerical results are presented and conclusions drawn relative to different objectives.

The chapter concludes with a discussion of the close relationship between dynamic programming and branch-and-bound approaches to enumerative and approximate techniques. An example is worked out in detail to exhibit this relationship.

1.5 RELATED TOPICS

In this section we present some sequencing problems closely related to but different from those of subsequent chapters. We begin with theoretical results in real time, deadline scheduling for systems of cyclically executing tasks. Next, we consider sequencing problems in which more than one performance measure is addressed. An example is the problem defined by row 18 in Table 1.1. We conclude with some remarks on general issues surrounding but not including those contained in subsequent chapters concerned with problem formulation and solution.

1.5.1 Deadline Scheduling of Cyclic Tasks on One Processor

There are many, very important applications in process control and other real-time control or monitoring systems in which tasks consist of a computation that must be executed periodically, with each computation of the task having a fixed deadline for completion. The deadline of a given computation can be no later than the time of the request for executing the next computation of the task. We analyze below a model in which a number of such tasks share a single processor and all deadlines must be respected (the so-called hard real-time environment). Results in this area of scheduling are few, but current research motivated by the importance of these problems will no doubt produce many new results of the nature encompassed by this book.

Formally, we define the model to be analyzed as the system $\mathcal{S} = (\{T_i\}, \{\tau_i\}, \{I_i\}, \{d_i\}, \{t_{0i}\})$ where T_i, $1 \le i \le n$, is a task consisting of a periodic sequence of requests for execution of a computation such that

1. Execution of the kth computation is requested at $t_{0i} + (k-1)I_i$, $k = 1, 2, \ldots$; I_i is the period of T_i.
2. The kth computation requires τ_i units of execution time.
3. The kth computation must be completed no later than the deadline $t_{0i} + (k-1)I_i + d_i$, with $0 < \tau_i \le d_i \le I_i$.

Figure 1.9 shows an example. An algorithm A is said to *accept* the system $\mathcal{S}$ if it schedules (using preemptions if necessary) the n tasks on a single processor so that the deadlines of all task computations are respected.

For a given algorithm let

$$\mu_i(t) = \begin{cases} 1 & \text{if a computation of } T_i \text{ is executing} \\ & \text{at time } t \\ 0 & \text{otherwise} \end{cases}$$

For an acceptable schedule, $\sum_{i=1}^{n} \mu_i(t) \le 1$ for all t. A schedule is defined by a specification of the functions $\mu_i(t)$ for all i and $t \ge \min\{t_{0i}\}$. We say that a task T_i is *active* at time t if for some $k \ge 0$, $t_{0i} + kI_i \le t \le t_{0i} + kI_i + d_i$ and

$$\int_{t_{0i}+kI_i}^{t} \mu_i(t) \, dt < \tau_i$$

The relative urgency (RU) algorithm, analogous to the slack-time algorithm in Theorem 1.3, assigns the processor at each instant of time t to an active task whose deadline is closest to t; that is, for some i

$$\mu_i(t) = \begin{cases} 1 & \text{if } t_{0i} + k_iI_i + d_i - t \le t_{0j} + k_jI_j + d_j - t \\ & \text{for all active tasks } T_j \\ 0 & \text{otherwise} \end{cases}$$

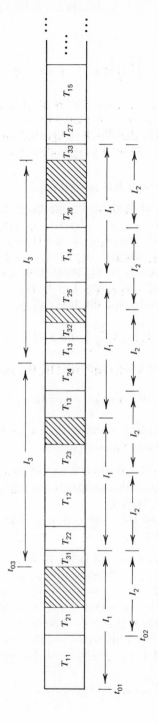

Figure 1.9 Example deadline schedule: $I_3 = 10$, $I_2 = 6$, $I_3 = 15$; $d_1 = 6$, $d_2 = 3$, $d_3 = 11$; $t_{01} = 0$, $t_{02} = 4$, $t_{03} = 9$; $\tau_1 = 4$, $\tau_2 = 2$, $\tau_3 = 1$; T_{ij} is jth computation of T_i.

where

$$k_r = \left\lfloor \frac{t - t_{0r}}{I_r} \right\rfloor, \qquad 1 \leq r \leq n$$

A subtlety arises if there exists a tie with respect to the RU criterion. Let us assume now that ties never occur; we will come back to this question later. We now want to show that the RU algorithm is optimal in the sense that if a system $\mathscr{S}$ is accepted by any algorithm A, it must also be accepted by RU.

Theorem 1.4   [L]   Algorithm RU is optimal.*

Proof   The eventual proof will be by contradiction; that is, we now suppose there exists a system $\mathscr{S}$ accepted by some algorithm A but not by RU. Our first objective is to characterize an RU schedule for the system $\mathscr{S}$ in which a deadline is not respected. We need a number of definitions.

Let $\min\{t_{0i}\} = 0$, without loss of generality, and suppose t_2 is the earliest deadline that is not respected. Let $W_e(t)$ be the amount of work done by the processor until t for the tasks of $\mathscr{S}$; that is,

$$W_e(t) = \sum_{i=1}^{n} \int_0^t \mu_i(x)\, dx$$

Let $W_r(t)$ be the amount of work requested by the same tasks; that is,

$$W_r(t) = \sum_{i=1}^{n} \left\lceil \frac{t - t_{0i}}{I_i} \right\rceil \tau_i$$

Now define t_0 as the latest time no later than t_2 at which $W_e(t) = W_r(t)$. Thus we can make the following statements.

1. $0 \leq t_0 < t_2$, since $W_e(0) = W_r(0) = 0$ and $W_e(t_2) < W_r(t_2)$.
2. The executions of all task computations requested prior to t_0 are completed, since $W_e(t_0) = W_r(t_0)$.
3. The processor must be fully utilized in $(t_0, t_2]$ by the RU algorithm, since $W_r(t) > W_e(t)$ for $t \in (t_0, t_2]$.

Next define t_1 as the last instant prior to t_2 at which the processor worked for a computation in $\mathscr{S}$ whose deadline exceeds t_2, if there is such a computation; $t_1 = t_0$, if not. We claim that no task computation requested prior to t_1 can be executed at any time in the interval $(t_1, t_2]$. Since this claim is trivially true if $t_1 = t_0$, suppose $t_1 > t_0$. Let T denote the computation of a task that executes in $(t_1, t_2]$ but whose request occurred before t_1. By definition of t_1 the deadline of T must precede t_2. But by

---

* For an earlier special case of this result, see [LL].

definition of RU, the computation executing at t_1 must have a deadline prior to that of T, hence prior to t_2; this immediately contradicts the definition of t_1 and the claim is proved.

Thus the interval $(t_1, t_2]$ has the following properties:

1. A computation may execute in $(t_1, t_2]$ only if it was requested in that interval and its deadline does not exceed t_2.

2. If a computation is requested in $(t_1, t_2]$ and if its deadline is strictly previous to t_2, that deadline is respected.

3. There is at least one computation requested in $(t_1, t_2]$ whose deadline is t_2 and is not respected.

It is now but a short step to a proof of the theorem. Let C_1 be the set of computations requested in $(t_1, t_2]$ whose deadlines are strictly previous to t_2 and let C_2 be the (nonempty) set of computations requested in this interval with the deadline t_2. If W_1 denotes the execution time devoted to computations in C_1 by RU, we have

$$W_1 = t_2 - t_1 - \delta$$

where δ is the execution time devoted to computations in C_2 in the interval $(t_1, t_2]$. The amount of work W_2 done in $(t_1, t_2]$ using the hypothetical algorithm A must be greater than W_1 by definition of C_1 and C_2; hence we can write

$$W_2 = W_1 + \delta'$$

where δ' represents the amount of execution time requested and therefore done for the computations of C_2 plus possibly some other work. Thus since algorithm A accepts $\mathscr{S}$, we have $\delta' > \delta$ and

$$W_2 = t_2 - t_1 + \delta' - \delta > t_2 - t_1$$

This contradiction proves the theorem. ∎

We now come back to the question of ties with the RU rule. The formal solution to this problem, which is consistent with the RU criterion, is to allow all the tasks with the nearest common deadline to share the processor equally in a "processor-sharing" mode of operation. That is, if T_i is one of the k tasks (computations) with the common closest deadline, set $\mu_i(t) = 1/k$ for as long as this condition persists. Pragmatically, and without sacrificing optimality, one can compute the earliest subsequent time instant at which this condition ceases to exist, divide the interval so defined into k equal subintervals, and distribute these subintervals, giving one to each of the "tied" tasks.

It is of obvious interest to determine necessary and sufficient acceptability conditions on the system parameters for the optimal RU algorithm.

Clearly, we can do no more than keep the processor busy all the time, which means that $\Sigma_{i=1}^{n} \tau_i / I_i \leq 1$ is a necessary condition. However, a sufficient condition for the general case is not known. But for the interesting subcase in which $d_i = I_i$, $1 \leq i \leq n$, the above-mentioned necessary condition is also sufficient. (Note that this subcase corresponds to those applications in which it is never too late to execute a computation unless it must finish after the next computation request.) For consider the processor-sharing algorithm A that for a given system assigns at each $t_{0i} + kI_i$ ($1 \leq i \leq n$, $k = 0, 1, 2, \ldots$) exactly the fraction τ_i / I_i of the processor to the corresponding computation of T_i. Obviously, each deadline is met exactly, since $d_i = I_i$. Moreover, since we are assuming $\Sigma_{i=1}^{n} \tau_i / I_i \leq 1$, it follows that A accepts the system. Since RU accepts any system A accepts, we have Theorem 1.5.

Theorem 1.5 The RU algorithm will accept a system $\mathcal{S}$ for which $d_i = I_i$, $1 \leq i \leq n$, if and only if $\Sigma_{i=1}^{n} \tau_i / I_i \leq 1$.

Assuming we retain $\tau_i / I_i \leq 1$, the natural generalization of the foregoing model to $m \geq 2$ processors leads, by means of the same arguments, to $\Sigma_{i=1}^{n} \tau_i / I_i \leq m$ as a necessary and sufficient condition for the existence of an accepting algorithm.

The question of processor utilization for arbitrary sequencing rules or task priority assignments has also been examined, but only for the special case $t_{0i} = t_{0j}$ and $d_i = I_i$ for all i and j [LL]. Let us say that a system fully utilizes a processor for a given sequencing rule if an increase in any of the τ_i causes the system to become unacceptable by the rule. Under these assumptions it has been shown that there exist systems of n tasks fully utilizing the processor for which processor utilization (percentage of time busy) can be at most $n(2^{1/n} - 1)$.

1.5.2 Sequencing with Secondary Performance Measures

Performance measures such as schedule length, mean flow time, mean number in system, and maximum and mean tardiness, are all desirable, but usually for different reasons. On the other hand, the motivations for more than one performance measure may coexist in one computer or job shop. For example, very commonly one desires minimum mean flow time (or waiting time) from the standpoint of, say, computer users, but minimum schedule lengths from the point of view of the system manager desiring maximum throughput. There is little work that can be reported on this kind of problem, despite its importance. In this section we examine three such efforts, all assuming $s = 0$, two of them very recent.

1.5.2.1   Due Date and Secondary Mean Flow-Time Performance.   Assume $<$ is empty, $w_i = 1$, for all i, and suppose we are given a set of due dates d_i as described in Section 1.2. A relatively early result considers the single-machine problem of minimizing mean flow time *given* that all due dates can be satisfied (i.e., maximum tardiness is zero). Theorem 1.2 gives a simple $O(n \log_2 n)$ procedure for determining whether this is possible. In this case the algorithm described below consists of SPT sequencing subject to the maintenance of the foregoing due-date performance [Sm].

   For a set $\mathcal{T}$ of tasks, the algorithm proceeds as follows. One first finds a largest task T in $\mathcal{T}$ whose deadline does not precede $\Sigma_{i=1}^{n} \tau_i$ (the schedule length for $\mathcal{T}$), assigning it as the last (nth) task to be executed. Then one finds the largest task in $\mathcal{T} - \{T\}$ whose deadline does not precede $\Sigma_{i=1}^{n} \tau_i - \tau$ (the schedule length for $\mathcal{T} - \{T\}$), assigning it as the $(n - 1)$st to be executed. The procedure continues recursively in this fashion until only one task remains. Thus we have a relatively simple polynomial-time algorithm for minimizing mean flow time when due dates can be (and are) satisfied. The proof of optimality is straightforward and again is subject to an interchange argument as illustrated in Section 1.2.

1.5.2.2   Schedule-Length and Secondary Mean Flow-Time Performance. The problem examined here was for $< = \varphi, m > 1$ identical processors and unit deferral costs. Since SPT sequencing is optimal for mean flow time, one can expect LPT sequencing to have very poor performance in this respect (in fact, worst for $m = 1$). On the other hand, LPT schedule lengths can be expected to be shorter on the average than SPT schedule lengths (Table 1.6 provides support for this statement). One solution to this dilemma is quite simply to use the reverse of the LPT schedule, to be called the RPT schedule. In this way, the schedule length remains unchanged, but the task lengths on individual processors now are placed in nondecreasing order. See Fig. 1.10 for an example.

   It is known that although examples can be found that make $\bar{\omega}_{LPT}/\bar{\omega}_{SPT}$ as large as desired, we have for RPT the bound $\bar{\omega}_{RPT}/\bar{\omega}_{SPT} \leq m$, which is best in the sense that it can be approached arbitrarily closely [BCS1]. Simulation studies have shown, however, that this bound is very uninformative, since RPT schedules having a mean flow-time performance more than a few percentage points worse than optimal were never found for any of a wide range of distributions for the task execution times.

1.5.2.3   Mean Flow-Time and Secondary Schedule-Length Performance. Again we make the assumptions $< = \varphi, m > 1$ identical processors and unit deferral costs. We now address the problem of finding a minimal-length schedule that minimizes mean flow time. First, let us verify that for

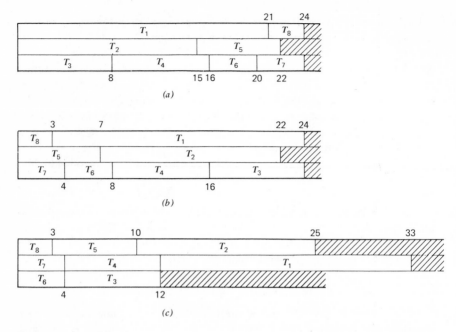

Figure 1.10   Example comparing (a) LPT, (b) RPT (reverse LPT), and (c) SPT schedules.

arbitrary m there are a large number of schedules that minimize mean flow time (all these schedules are called SPT schedules). Observe that the mean flow time of a schedule for a set $\mathcal{T}$ of n tasks can be written as

$$\bar{\omega} = \frac{1}{n} \sum_{i=1}^{n} k_i \tau_i \qquad (9)$$

where k_i is one greater than the number of tasks following T_i on its processor. This equation expresses the fact that T_i, for each i, contributes (its execution time) to its own finishing time and to the finishing times of each task that follows it on the same processor. Now suppose n is a multiple of m (we can always add zero-length tasks to assure this if necessary). Call the m tasks that are the jth to be scheduled on their respective processors, *rank-j* tasks. If a schedule minimizes mean flow time, the rank-1 tasks are the shortest m tasks, the rank-2 tasks are the next m shortest tasks, and so on. From (9) we see that for an m-processor problem we can permute the m tasks in a given rank of an SPT schedule in any way we choose without affecting $\bar{\omega}$; that is, we are still left with an SPT schedule. Thus there are $O(m!^{n/m})$ SPT schedules.

Strict SPT (list) scheduling is obtained from a list of tasks in nondecreasing order of execution times and produces the longest possible SPT schedule (to be called the $\overline{SPT}$ schedule); the largest tasks of each rank are on the same processor. Thus the problem is to find a set of rank permutations that produces a minimal-length SPT schedule (to be referred to as an $\underline{SPT}$ schedule). Unfortunately, this problem is known to be NP-complete as shown in row 18 of Table 1.1. A heuristic that has been studied is simply a rank-by-rank assignment in which rank j is assigned after rank $(j-1)$ such that the LPT rule applies (locally) to adjacent ranks, and such that $i < j$ implies that the tasks in the ith rank are all smaller than those in the jth rank. That is, after $j-1$ ranks have been assigned, the jth rank is assigned, one task to a processor, in LPT order to the finishing times of the rank $(j-1)$ tasks. Let us call this the SPT_L rule. Table 1.6 summarizes in the form of best bounds the known results comparing the $\underline{SPT}$, LPT, $\overline{SPT}$, and SPT_L rules.

The proofs of rows 1 and 2 are relatively straightforward, but those of rows 3 and 4 are fairly elaborate. The examples of Fig. 1.11 give an idea of the combinatorial nature of the problems by showing each of the latter two bounds to be achievable or asymptotically so.

1.5.2.4 Other Measures. Another primary or secondary performance measure is the mean number $\bar{N}$ in the system. As shown in Section 1.2 we have $\bar{N} = n\bar{\omega}/\omega$ for an n-task system. For $m = 1$, $\bar{N}$ is minimized by an SPT schedule. However, Fig. 1.12 gives examples for $m > 1$ restricted to list scheduling such that the schedule minimizing $\bar{N}$ is not an SPT schedule. In fact, for $m \geq 1$ and $< = \varphi$ it can be shown that strict SPT sequencing can be up to $2m/(m+1)$ times worse than optimal with respect

TABLE 1.6 BOUNDS FOR SPT SEQUENCING

Bounds	$< = \varphi, s = 0,$ parameters n, m, and $\{\tau_i\}$		
	$L(\omega)$	$L(\omega')$	References
$\dfrac{\omega'}{\omega} \leq 2 - 1/m$	LPT	$\underline{SPT}$	[BCS1]
$\dfrac{\omega'}{\omega} \leq \dfrac{3}{2}$	$\underline{SPT}$	$\overline{SPT}$	[CS]
$\dfrac{\omega'}{\omega} \leq \dfrac{5m-2}{4m-1}$	$\underline{SPT}$	LPT	[BCS2]
$\dfrac{\omega'}{\omega} \leq \dfrac{5m-4}{4m-3}$	$\underline{SPT}$	SPT_L	[CS]

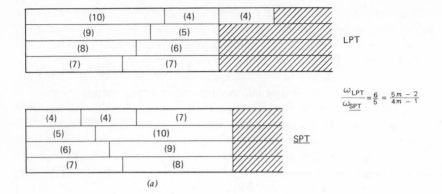

$$\frac{\omega_{LPT}}{\omega_{SPT}} = \frac{6}{5} = \frac{5m - 2}{4m - 1}$$

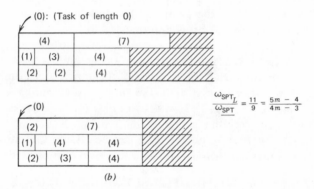

(a)

$$\frac{\omega_{SPT_L}}{\omega_{SPT}} = \frac{11}{9} = \frac{5m - 4}{4m - 3}$$

(b)

Figure 1.11 Worst-case examples for Table 1.6; execution times in parentheses. (a) Worst-case for row 4 and $m = 4$. (b) Worst case for row 5 and $m = 3$.

to $\bar{N}[CL]$. Taking the limit $k \to \infty$, $\epsilon \to 0$ while holding $k\epsilon$ fixed in Fig. 1.12b shows that the bound is best possible for $m = 2$. (The example is readily generalized to arbitrary m.) Inspection of the examples leads one to expect that the bound $2m/(m + 1)$ is not very informative. However, the problem of finding the schedule minimizing $\bar{N}$ is easily shown to be NP-complete; thus simulation studies assessing the performance of heuristics would be far more costly than those mentioned earlier with respect to the comparative mean flow-time performance of the SPT and RPT rules.

It is relevant in the context of the problems in this section to mention the class of so-called sequence-control or timing problems not covered in this book. With these problems the first objective is simply one of correct

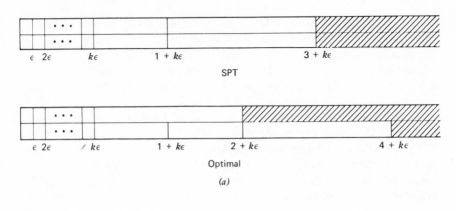

(a)

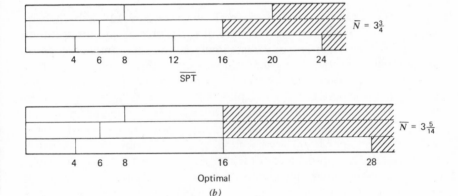

(b)

Figure 1.12   Minimizing $\bar{N}$.

performance, rather than the optimization of a performance measure. We refer in particular to the problems of deadlocks, mutual exclusion, determinacy, and synchronization. Textual material on these subjects can be found in [CD] and [BrH]. In fact, such problems provide primary performance criteria for systems in which mean or maximum flow times are secondary criteria. However, the latter three sequence-control problems are concerned primarily with correct design and specification of task systems, and hence can be taken for granted for our purposes.

The problem of deadlocks, on the other hand, also generalizes the model of additional resources studied in Chapter 5. In particular, with this generalization tasks are assumed to request and release additional resources in an arbitrary manner during their execution, natural constraints being (a) that at no time is a larger quantity of a resource type requested than exists in the system, and (b) that all resources used by a task are eventually released prior to termination. Note that if resources are not preemptible (not removable from tasks currently using them), situations naturally called deadlocks are possible, in which a set of two or more active tasks are all requesting additional resources to proceed, and are in possession of resources such that because of limited resource capacity, no one of the tasks can proceed.

This is, of course, an extensive generalization of the basic model, which is quite difficult already. At present, little is known about the related secondary-performance-measure problems, but their importance will no doubt motivate continuing research.

1.5.3 Final Remarks

As can be seen, the book deals with what is basically a branch of combinatorics. However, the structure of the problems and the methods used to analyze them extend substantially beyond the limited scope of deterministic sequencing problems. In support of this statement, Chapter 6 on approximate and enumerative techniques applies quite generally to combinatorial problems. The complexity results of Chapter 4, although directed at sequencing problems, can similarly be redirected in several cases to a large number of other assignment, allocation, or partitioning problems that appear in a very large variety of operations research applications. The approach to combinatorial problems given in Chapter 5 extends to many other applications in which very fast heuristics can be expected to be effective in practice. A brief discussion of this point is made in Chapter 5 before treating algorithms for the bin-packing problems. The results of Chapters 2 and 3 along with certain parts of Chapters 4 and 5 are perhaps the most specialized to scheduling problems. But here again one can be guided in the treatment of other combinatorial problems by the proof techniques and general approaches that have proved successful in deterministic scheduling theory.

From a mathematical point of view, the book is not light reading. Also, as we noted earlier, there was no hope for inclusion of the proofs of all the results. Although the proofs given or outlined in the book generally involve one or more astute observations, in the end, a fully rigorous proof very frequently amounts to laborious case analyses. In any case, the mathematical nature of the book faithfully reflects the nature of the problem area. It also accounts in part for the effort made in this chapter to summarize as well as possible the currently known results in scheduling theory; the intent is to provide the students and researchers in specific areas with a means of staying moderately up to date in scheduling theory as a whole, without having to peruse an extensive literature.

As a final remark on generalities, we note that queueing theory provides a complementary approach to the study of service systems. It is complementary in the sense that it is concerned primarily with the analysis of given algorithms in a stochastic environment; that is, service times and arrival times are taken as random variables governed by given probability distribution functions. As will be seen, our interest focuses on the synthesis or design of optimal or heuristic algorithms, the analysis being confined largely to derivations of simple descriptions of complexity and worst-case performance bounds. The models successfully studied by means of queueing theory are generally far simpler in structure—a necessity, in view of the greater demands on mathematical tractability. Indeed, if this were not the case, the more pragmatically useful approach to our analysis problems would be by means of probability models; for by the use of such models one is able to represent and determine the influence of the randomness in job and customer behavior in computer and job-shop environments.

The reader will have little difficulty in perceiving many generalizations and extensions to the material in this book. The approaches in Chapters 5 and 6, especially, open up a great variety of interesting and promising research problems. For example, important extensions of this work would concern inclusion of preemption and job set-up costs. In only very restricted cases are these sequence independent, in which case a simple augmentation of execution times will account for them. As did Conway, Maxwell, and Miller [CMM] in 1967, we must expect, in part, the success of the book to be based on the extent to which it motivates others in resolving the many open problems remaining in scheduling theory.

1.6 NOTATION

The following symbols are subsequently used as shown in the list below.

$\mathcal{T}$ a set of tasks

n the cardinality of $\mathcal{T}$

T_i the ith task in $\mathcal{T}$; T, T', and so on, are also used to refer to tasks in $\mathcal{T}$

$<$ an irreflexive partial order defined on $\mathcal{T}$. A typical element of $<$ is denoted (T_i, T_j), meaning that T_i must complete before T_j can begin execution. As described in Section 1.2, $<$ is represented frequently by a directed acyclic graph (dag).

P a set of processors or machines

m the cardinality of P

P_i the ith processor in P
τ_{ij} the execution time of T_j on P_i
τ_j the execution time of T_j assumed common to all P_i
w_j the deferral cost (rate) of T_j

The following symbols are in Chapters 1, 4, and 5 only.

$\mathcal{R}$ a set of resource types (additional to the processors)
s the cardinality of $\mathcal{R}$
R_i the ith resource type in $\mathcal{R}$
m_i the total number or amount of resource type R_i
$R_i(T_j)$ the amount of resource type R_i required by T_j during its execution
$r_i(t)$ the amount of resource type R_i allocated to executing tasks at time t
ω the schedule length or maximum flow time (often modified by subscripts or superscripts to indicate specific rules)

Other notations for schedule properties are defined in context (e.g., the mean flow time). The reader should be cautioned, however, that Chapters 3 and 4 deal with the unnormalized mean weighted flow time (i.e., only the weighted sum of the finishing times or $n\bar{\omega}$ as we have defined $\bar{\omega}$).

The Boolean operators $+$ and $\neg$ are used in Chapter 4 with the conventional meaning of "inclusive or" and "negation," respectively; the "and" operator is implicit in juxtaposition. The symbol τ is used in Chapter 5 to denote the "execution-time function"; that is, $\tau(T_i) = \tau_i$. The symbol $\triangleq$ is used in Chapter 6 to denote "is defined by."

Task systems or scheduling problems are variously represented. The five-tuple characterization of Section 1.2 is not used subsequently, since the simplifications of the general model treated in Chapters 2 through 6 are exploited in more abbreviated notations. In this regard, although "jobs" may occasionally be used synonymously with tasks, in Sections 3.5 through 3.8, and 6.4 they take on a special meaning as particular task subsystems. A good part of the required notation is briefly defined at the beginning of the individual chapters or just prior to use. All notation not presented in this chapter is defined when used.

CHAPTER TWO

ALGORITHMS FOR MINIMAL-LENGTH SCHEDULES

RAVI SETHI
THE PENNSYLVANIA STATE UNIVERSITY

2.1 INTRODUCTION

We are given a task system $(\mathcal{T}, <)$, where $\mathcal{T}$ is a set of tasks to be scheduled on m processors and $<$ is a partial order on $\mathcal{T}$ that specifies precedence constraints between tasks. Thus for tasks T and T' in $\mathcal{T}$, if $T < T'$, then task T must be finished before T' can be started. In general, the execution times of tasks in $\mathcal{T}$ are arbitrary. Given a schedule for $(\mathcal{T}, <)$, the time taken to execute all tasks in the system is called the *length* of the schedule. We are interested in efficient algorithms for determining minimal-length schedules. For our purposes, an efficient algorithm is one that starts with a system of n tasks and constructs a schedule in no more than time proportional to n^c, where c is a constant. Such an algorithm is called a *polynomial-time*, (or simply *polynomial*) algorithm.

In addition to finishing all tasks in a system as quickly as possible, a minimal-length schedule leads to maximal utilization of system resources. The length of a schedule depends on the total execution time of tasks and the total time for which the processors are idle. Minimizing the schedule length minimizes the idle time, leading to maximal utilization of processors. Such a cost criterion is useful when the order in which tasks are finished is unimportant. When the time at which a task finishes is important, a cost criterion like the "mean flow time" of a schedule (Chapter 3) may be more appropriate.

We are going to consider two kinds of schedules. In *preemptive* schedules, it is possible to suspend and at a later stage resume execution of a task at the point of suspension. In *nonpreemptive* schedules, a task once started is executed to completion. Figure 2.1 gives a common example illustrating the two kinds of schedules. A task system consisting of three independent tasks of length 2 is to be scheduled on two processors. A nonpreemptive schedule for the system takes 4 units of time. A shortest preemptive schedule on the other hand takes 3 units; a savings of 25%.

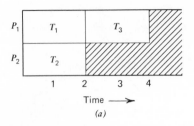 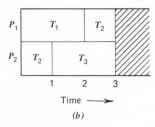

Figure 2.1 (*a*) Nonpreemptive and (*b*) preemptive schedules for a system of three independent tasks of length 2 scheduled on two identical processors.

The time savings are bought at the expense of moving a task off a processor before it is finished and saving information about the task while it is waiting. If the computer installation has a mass storage device like a high-speed drum, the transfer of information between main memory and mass storage is relatively efficient. The costs of preempting a task can then be ignored. Even if the costs are noticeable, the pressure to finish a task system may override considerations other than the length of a schedule.

There are notably few known polynomial algorithms for determining minimal-length schedules, even when severe restrictions are placed on the partial order and execution times in a task system. To begin with, we assume that all processors are identical; therefore task T executes at the same rate on any processor. Basically, there are two cases for which polynomial algorithms are known: (*a*) when the graph of the task system is a tree, and (*b*) when there are only two processors available.

When nonpreemptive schedules are to be constructed, we have the added restriction in both *a* and *b* that all tasks have the same execution time.

It is shown in Chapter 4 that most scheduling problems fall into a class of combinatorial problems that have long defied attempts to find a nonenumerative solution. This class of problems has been referred to as "NP-complete," "polynomial complete," or, when the context is clear, "complete." The interesting property of the class is that a polynomial solution for one member of the class implies the existence of a polynomial solution for all members of the class. Given the size of the class, and the kind of problems that are in it, we are pessimistic about the possibility of a polynomial solution to any "complete" problem.

Several results showing scheduling problems to be "complete" occur in Chapter 4. A couple of them are relevant to this discussion and are listed below. In each of the following cases, determining a minimal length nonpreemptive schedule is a "complete" problem.

1. The execution time of tasks is arbitrary; there are two or more processors available. (The result is true even if all tasks are independent.)

2. The execution time of tasks is restricted to one time unit or two time units, the partial order is arbitrary, there are two or more processors available.

The first result implies that within the constraints of a polynomial-time algorithm, we cannot permit the execution times of tasks to be arbitrary. If the execution times are not arbitrary, they must be chosen from some set of allowable values. The second result leads us to consider task systems in which all tasks have the same execution time, at least when the partial order is arbitrary.

In studying a task system in which all tasks have the same execution time, there is no loss in generality if we suppose the tasks all have unit execution times. Such systems are called unit-execution-time (UET) systems. Given an n-task, UET system $(\mathcal{T}, <)$ Section 2.2 contains an almost linear time algorithm to determine a minimal-length nonpreemptive schedule, when the graph of $(\mathcal{T}, <)$ is a tree. An arbitrary partial order can be represented by a directed acyclic graph (*dag*). In Section 2.3 dags are examined. An $O(n^2)$ algorithm that is optimal (i.e., determines a shortest nonpreemptive schedule) is given for the case when $m = 2$. For $m = 3, 4, 5, \ldots$, it is not known whether for that particular value of m, there is an optimal polynomial-time algorithm. This question is considered in more detail in Chapter 4.

We find in Section 2.6 that the nonpreemptive algorithms of Sections 2.2 and 2.3 lead very naturally to preemptive algorithms. Consider a task system $(\mathcal{T}, <)$ in which the execution times are arbitrary. We can split each task in $\mathcal{T}$ into a chain of equal execution time tasks. Then, modulo some details in Section 2.6, we are left with essentially a UET system. Not surprisingly, the only cases for which polynomial-time algorithms for determining minimal-length preemptive schedules are known are (*a*) when the graph of $(\mathcal{T}, <)$ is a tree, or (*b*) when $m = 2$ processors are available. The special case of independent tasks is considered in Section 2.5.

So far we have restricted attention to identical processors. In Section 2.8 it is assumed that there is a set of m processors $P = \{P_1, P_2, \ldots, P_m\}$ of speeds $b_1 \geq b_2 \geq \cdots \geq b_m$. A task with an execution requirement of τ units takes τ/b_j time units on processor P_j. It turns out that the preemptive algorithm of Section 2.6 extends immediately to the set of processors P. The new algorithm is optimal for independent tasks.

Finally in this chapter we consider the flow-shop problem. The task system consists of chains of m tasks in which task i must be executed on processor P_i. An interpretation for such chains might be the following: the first task corresponding to input must be done on a card reader, the second corresponding to execution on a processing unit, and a third corresponding to output must be done on a line printer. We give an algorithm for the two-processor flow-shop problem. For $m = 3, 4, \ldots,$ determining a minimal-length flow-shop schedule is a "complete" problem.

2.2 TREE-STRUCTURED TASK SYSTEMS

We assume in this section that the graph of the task system $(\mathcal{T}, <)$ is a forest. Each task has an execution time of one unit. And there are m identical processors, where m is arbitrary. We give an almost linear time algorithm for determining a minimal-length nonpreemptive schedule for such a task system.

Since all tasks have the same execution time and are scheduled nonpreemptively, it is convenient to treat time as being discrete rather than continuous. All schedules start at time 0. For all integers i, *time unit i* is the time interval $(i - 1, i)$.

For the moment, consider the tree in Fig. 2.2. Following the path from task 14 to the terminal, tasks 14, 12, 7, 3, and 1 are encountered. Since $14 < 12 < \cdots < 1$, regardless of the number of processors available, at least 5 time units will be required to execute all the tasks in the system. On a sufficiently large number of processors, an optimal strategy would be to start with the tasks farthest away from the terminal and work towards the terminal. It will become apparent that such a strategy works on any number of processors.

Let the *level* of a node x in a dag be the maximum number of nodes (including x) on any path from x to a terminal task. In a forest, there is exactly one such path. A terminal task is at level 1. Let a task be *ready* when all its predecessors have been executed. We can show that the following strategy leads to an optimal schedule for a forest on any number of processors:

Level strategy: *whenever a processor becomes available, assign it an unexecuted ready task at the highest level (farthest from a terminal).*
A schedule thus constructed is called a level schedule.

Initially, we restrict our discussion to trees; later the extension to forests is seen to be trivial.

Example 1   Using the level strategy on three processors, for the task system in Fig. 2.2 the schedule in the figure might be constructed. Tasks 14 and 13 at level 5 are assigned first. Task 12 at level 4 must await the

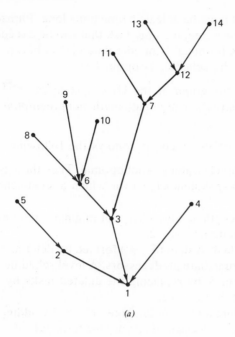

(a)

14	12	8	6	3	1
13	10	7	4		
11	9	5	2		

(b)

Figure 2.2 (*a*) A tree-structured task system. (*b*) A schedule for the task system on three processors.

completion of 14 and 13, thus 11 is assigned to the third processor during the first time unit. Tasks 12, 10, and 9 at level 4 are executed during the second time unit. The reader is encouraged to verify that the schedule given is indeed a level schedule.

The schedule in Fig. 2.2 illustrates an important property of minimal-length nonpreemptive schedules. Task 1 being the only terminal, must await the completion of all other tasks. And it takes at least 5 time units to execute 13 tasks nonpreemptively on three processors. Thus all schedules for the task system must be at least 6 time units long. Phrased differently, given a schedule for a tree, the only task that can be executed during the last time unit is the terminal. If no idle time occurs before the second to the last time unit, the schedule is optimal.

Theorem 2.1 Let the graph of the UET system $(\mathcal{T}, <)$ be a tree. The level strategy constructs a minimal-length nonpreemptive schedule for $(\mathcal{T}, <)$.

Proof The proof of this theorem follows the following plan:

1. Suppose the level strategy is not optimal. Then there is a smallest (in the number of tasks) system $(\mathcal{T}, <)$ for which a level schedule S is not minimal length.

2. Let S be of length ω. Since S is not minimal, there must be an idle processor during time unit $\omega - 2$.

3. Consider the task system $(\mathcal{T}', <')$ formed by deleting the terminal of $(\mathcal{T}, <)$ and all its immediate predecessors. A level schedule S' for $(\mathcal{T}', <')$ can be formed from S by replacing the deleted tasks by idle periods.

4. The length of S' is $\omega - 2$.

5. Convert the forest $(\mathcal{T}', <')$ to a tree $(\mathcal{T}'', <'')$ by adding a new task T_r that is an immediate successor of exactly the terminals of $(\mathcal{T}', <')$. A level schedule S'' for $(\mathcal{T}'', <'')$ is of length $\omega - 1$.

6. Since $(\mathcal{T}'', <'')$ has been formed from $(\mathcal{T}, <)$ by deleting two levels and adding one, $(\mathcal{T}'', <'')$ must have at least one less task than $(\mathcal{T}, <)$. But level schedule S'' for $(\mathcal{T}'', <'')$ can not be optimal. Since we have found a task system smaller than $(\mathcal{T}, <)$ for which a level schedule is not optimal, we have contradicted the assumption in 1. The theorem must therefore be true.

Before elaborating on the foregoing plan, note that in the level strategy, nodes at a given level may be assigned in any order. Thus schedules constructed by the level strategy are not unique. The strategy will be pronounced nonoptimal if there is at least one level schedule that is not optimal.

Let $(\mathcal{T}, <)$ be an n-task system with a minimal number of tasks such that a level schedule S for $(\mathcal{T}, <)$ is of length ω, where ω is greater than ω_0, the length of an optimal schedule for the task system.

Since the number of tasks to be executed is fixed, the length of the schedule S for $(\mathcal{T}, <)$ depends on the number of idle periods in S. As in the discussion preceding the statement of the theorem, there must be an idle period in S on some processor for a time unit t, $t \leq \omega - 2$.

Since there is an idle processor during t, from the level strategy it follows that none of the tasks executed after t can be ready in time unit t.

Therefore all tasks executed after t must have a predecessor on some processor during t. Since the graph of $(\mathcal{T}, <)$ is a tree, each task has at most one immediate successor; thus the number of tasks executed during $t + 1$ cannot exceed the number of tasks executed during t. Since there is an idle processor during t, it follows that there must be an idle processor for every time unit after t: in particular, there must be an idle processor during time unit $\omega - 2$.

The terminal T of $(\mathcal{T}, <)$ is executed during ω. Therefore an immediate predecessor R of the terminal must be on some processor during time unit $\omega - 1$. Since there is an idle processor during $\omega - 2$, it follows that a predecessor Q of R must be executed during $\omega - 2$.

Consider the task system $(\mathcal{T}', <')$ formed by deleting the terminal and all its immediate predecessors. We claim that the schedule S' formed by replacing all the deleted tasks in S' by idle periods is a level schedule for $(\mathcal{T}', <')$. The terminal T is executed during the last time unit; since it is a successor of all tasks, its replacement by an idle period cannot change the level structure of the remaining system.

Now consider an immediate predecessor U of T, such that U is executed during some time unit t. The only tasks that might be considered during t if U is deleted, are either at the same level as U or lower. If any higher level tasks are executed after t, they must have been considered before U and found not ready. Since all tasks at the same level or lower than U are deleted, no task can fill the idle period created by deleting U. Task Q at level 3 is executed during time unit $\omega - 2$. Thus there can be no time unit before $\omega - 2$ during which only level 2 tasks are executed. Thus the length of S' is $\omega - 2$. Since the level of tasks in $(\mathcal{T}', <')$ is uniformly 2 less than the level of the corresponding task in $(\mathcal{T}, <)$, S' is a level schedule for $(\mathcal{T}'. <')$.

Since the theorem applies to trees, we convert $(\mathcal{T}', <')$ into a tree by adding a new task T_r that is an immediate successor of exactly the terminals of $(\mathcal{T}', <')$. Let the new task system be called $(\mathcal{T}'', <'')$. A level schedule S'' for $(\mathcal{T}'', <'')$ can be constructed from S' by adding the task T_r onto some processor during time unit $\omega - 1$. Note that T_r cannot be executed before $\omega - 1$ because Q, a predecessor of T_r, is executed during $\omega - 2$. Thus the length of S'' is $\omega - 1$. Moreover $(\mathcal{T}'', <'')$ has at most $n - 1$ tasks.

The optimal-length schedule for $(\mathcal{T}, <)$ must execute the terminal during ω_0 and only immediate predecessors of the terminal during $\omega_0 - 1$. Thus deleting the terminal and its immediate predecessors leads to a minimal-length schedule no longer than $\omega_0 - 2$. Adding a new task T_r as we did earlier leads to a task system with a minimal-length schedule no longer than $\omega_0 - 1$.

Since $\omega_0 < \omega$, it follows that $\omega_0 - 1 < \omega - 1$, and we have found a smaller task system than $(\mathcal{T}, <)$ for which the level strategy is not optimal. Contradiction. The theorem must therefore be true. ∎

Corollary 2.1   Let the graph of the UET system $(\mathcal{T}, <)$ be a forest. The level strategy constructs a minimal-length nonpreemptive schedule for $(\mathcal{T}, <)$.

Proof   If the level strategy does not generate a minimal-length schedule for $(\mathcal{T}, <)$, the strategy cannot generate a minimal-length schedule for the tree $(\mathcal{T}', <')$ formed by adding a new task that is an immediate successor of exactly the terminals of $(\mathcal{T}, <)$. The result follows from Theorem 2.1 applied to $(\mathcal{T}', <')$. ∎

We have shown that the level strategy is optimal, but we have yet to deliver an algorithm to construct schedules. The algorithm we give assigns a priority to all tasks in a system. Tasks at higher levels have a higher priority. Henceforth, our discussion is extended to forests.

Since levels are measured from the terminals, the algorithm starts at the terminals and visits nodes level by level, assigning a *label* to each node. For an n-task system, the label for a node is an integer between 1 and n. In Fig. 2.2 the terminal is assigned label 1, the three tasks at level 2 get labels 2, 3 and 4, and so on, until 13 and 14 are assigned to the two tasks at level 5.

Once the labeling is completed, a list of tasks in order of decreasing label is created. As in Chapter 1, this list is used to construct a schedule as follows:

> **List Scheduling:** *whenever a processor becomes available, the list is scanned from left to right; the first unexecuted ready task encountered in the scan is assigned to the processor.*

The schedule in Fig. 2.2b is a list schedule formed from the tasks in Fig. 2.2a listed in order of decreasing label. Note that in the first time unit, task 12 is not ready because it must await the completion of 14 and 13. Thus the next task in the list, 11, is assigned to the third processor. Likewise, in the third time unit, task 6 is not ready, and task 5 is assigned to the third processor.

Algorithm 2.1   Let the graph of the system $(\mathcal{T}, <)$ be a forest. First a *label* is assigned to each task in $\mathcal{T}$. Labels are given* by the function $L_t(\cdot)$ from tasks into the set $\{1, 2, \ldots, n\}$. The labels are then used to construct

---

* We use the subscript t to distinguish this labeling function for trees from the labeling function of the next section.

a list for $(\mathcal{T}, <)$. The list leads to a minimal-length nonpreemptive schedule for $(\mathcal{T}, <)$ on m processors.

For the moment, suppose that $(\mathcal{T}, <)$ has a single terminal.

1. If T is the terminal of $(\mathcal{T}, <)$, assign T the label 1 (i.e., $L_t(T) = 1$).

2. Let labels $1, 2, .., j-1$ already be assigned. If T is a task with the lowest labeled immediate successor, define $L_t(T)$ to be j. (Note that the labeling proceeds level by level, assigning consecutive labels to tasks at the same level.)

3. Use list $(T_n, T_{n-1}, \ldots, T_1)$, where for all i, $1 \le i \le n$, $L_t(T_i) = i$, to schedule the task system.

A forest $(\mathcal{T}, <)$ can be scheduled by adding a dummy task that is an immediate successor of exactly the terminals of $(\mathcal{T}, <)$, then applying steps 1 through 3 to the augmented task system.

The labels in Fig. 2.2a have been assigned using Algorithm 2.1.

Theorem 2.2   Let the graph of the UET system $(\mathcal{T}, <)$ be a forest. Algorithm 2.1 constructs a minimal-length nonpreemptive schedule for $(\mathcal{T}, <)$.

Proof   From Corollary 2.1, we need only show that Algorithm 2.1 constructs a level schedule for $(\mathcal{T}, <)$. From step 3 of the algorithm we have to show that labels are assigned level by level by the algorithm. It is left to the reader to complete the proof. (One approach might be to show by induction on j that when label j is assigned to task T, no unlabeled task is at a lower level than T.)   ∎

In this section we showed that an optimal strategy for scheduling UET forests was to execute tasks at higher levels preferentially. An algorithm was given to label tasks level by level with higher labels being assigned to tasks at higher levels. Data structures for the algorithm are discussed in Section 2.4. Section 2.4 indicates that starting with the labeling $L_t(\cdot)$, an optimal schedule can be constructed in almost linear time.

In the forests we have considered, each task may have more than one immediate predecessor, but the immediate successor of each task is unique. The opposite orientation of precedence constraints is also of interest: the execution of a task may permit more than one task to begin executing, but the immediate predecessor of each task is unique. Such task systems are called *antiforests*. Informally, an antiforest is formed by reversing all the edges in a forest. The results in this section also apply to antiforests. Simply ignore the orientation of edges and generate a schedule using the level strategy. For an antiforest, the schedule has to be read backward (i.e., from right to left). In fact, such statements can be made about a number of algorithms in this chapter. (See Section 2.7 also.)

2.3 PARTIAL ORDERS ON TWO PROCESSORS

There are no known polynomial algorithms for scheduling UET task systems on a fixed number of processors, m, if $m > 2$. For $m = 2$ we give an $O(n^2)$ algorithm in this section. The approach is similar to that for forests: labels giving priority are assigned to tasks; a list for scheduling the task system is constructed from the labels. For the algorithm to work, the UET system must not have any transitive edges.

The level strategy—higher levels first—was found to be optimal for forests in the last section. Since trees are a special case of dags, in scheduling dags we expect levels to play a part in the algorithm. It would be nice if we could still assign priorities level by level, for then we would only have to worry about the order in which tasks at the same level are to be executed. So let us write down desirable property 1 (DP1) for a labeling $L(\cdot)$ for dags.

DP1: *If T is at a higher level than T', then $L(T) > L(T')$.*

Keeping in mind that we expect to schedule the task system on two processors, if each level has an even number of tasks, we will finish all tasks at one level before beginning another, and property DP1 is enough to grant an optimal schedule.

To indicate some of the factors considered in designing an optimal labeling, let us examine the task system in Fig. 2.3. At the highest level (7) we have placed 3 tasks O, P and Q so that in the second time unit we will have to find a task from a lower level to execute. Since Q has J as an immediate successor in addition to N, Q should have a priority higher than O and P. We are led to:

DP2: *If the set of immediate successors of a task T contains the set of immediate successors of T', then $L(T) > L(T')$.*

Property DP2 is not enough, but let us proceed. Since there are 17 tasks, label 17 is assigned to Q and 15 and 16 to O and P, respectively. The only task at level 6 is N, which gets label 14. We placed only one task at level 6 to demonstrate that even in an optimal schedule there may be some idle time for a processor.

Properties DP1 and DP2 suffice until we reach level 3 and have to label tasks G, H, I, and J. Since $G < A$, while $H < F$, tasks G and H can not be distinguished by DP2. The point to note is that A is at level 1, but F is at level 2. Since F, being at a higher level than A, will probably be executed sooner than A, we should assign a higher label to H than to G.

Two related points emerge: (a) we need a mechanism for comparing successors of tasks, and (b) the comparison must take into account the

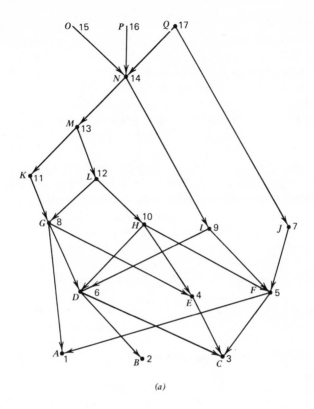

(a)

17	15	14	13	12	10	6	4	3	
16	7		9	11	8	5	2	1	

(b)

Figure 2.3 (a) Task system labeled according to labeling L. (b) List schedule for the task system on two processors.

priorities of the successors. Since priorities are given by the labels, we would like to be able to use labels in the comparison. If labels are to be used, we must label successors before their predecessors. It turns out that there is a level-by-level labeling algorithm that is optimal.

The labeling algorithm we use starts by assigning label 1 to one of the terminals. Suppose labels $1, 2, \ldots, j - 1$ have been assigned. Since labels give the priority of a task, label j is now assigned to the task that has the *lowest* priority from the set of tasks that are ready for labeling. To determine this task, we compare the sets of immediate successors of the tasks that are ready to be labeled. For each such task we form a decreasing sequence, using the labels of the immediate successors of the task. The smallest such sequence (lexicographically) determines the task to be assigned the label j.

More precisely, let $l = (n_1, n_2, \ldots, n_k)$ and $l' = (n'_1, n'_2, \ldots, n'_k)$ be sequences of integers, $k, k' \geq 0$. When $k = 0$, l is the empty list. We say that l is *lexicographically smaller* than l', written $l \leq l'$, if (1) the two sequences agree up to j, for some j, but $n_j < n'_j$ (i.e., there exists j, $1 \leq j \leq k$, such that for all i, $1 \leq i < j$, $n_i = n'_i$ and $n_j < n'_j$), or (2) the two sequences agree, but list l is shorter (i.e., $k \leq k'$ and $n_i = n'_i$ for all i, $1 \leq i \leq k$).

Algorithm 2.2 defines the labeling L discussed informally here.

Algorithm 2.2 Let $(\mathcal{T}, <)$ be an n-task unit execution time system. Labels from the set $\{1, 2, \ldots, n\}$ are assigned to each task in $\mathcal{T}$ by the function $L(\cdot)$. The labels are used to construct a list of tasks that will yield a minimal-length nonpreemptive schedule for $(\mathcal{T}, <)$ on two processors.

1. Assign label 1 to one of the terminals.
2. Let labels $1, 2, \ldots, j - 1$ have been assigned. Let S be the set of unassigned tasks with no unlabeled successors. We next select an element of S to be assigned label j.

For each node x in S define $l(x)$ as follows: Let $y_1, y_2, \ldots, y_k$ be the immediate successors of x. Then $l(x)$ is the decreasing sequence of integers formed by ordering the set $\{L(y_1), L(y_2), \ldots, L(y_k)\}$. Let x be an element of S such that for all x' in S, $l(x) \leq l(x')$. Define $L(x)$ to be j.

3. When all tasks have been labeled, use the list $(T_n, T_{n-1}, \ldots, T_1)$, where for all i, $1 \leq i \leq n$, $L(T_i) = i$, to schedule the task system.

Since each task is executed for one time unit, processors 1 and 2 both become available at the same time. By convention, we assume that processor 1 is scheduled before processor 2.

To prove that the schedule constructed by Algorithm 2.2 is optimal on two processors, we need to examine the relationship between a task system and the schedule for it. The basic idea behind the proof is the following:

Determine sets $F_k, F_{k-1}, \ldots, F_0$, $F_i \subseteq \mathcal{T}$, $k \geq i \geq 0$, such that all tasks in F_i precede all tasks in F_{i-1}. All tasks in F_i must therefore be finished before any task in F_{i-1} can be started. The sets will be such that any schedule that executes them in order takes at least as long as the schedule constructed by Algorithm 2.2 (see Fig. 2.4).

We want to make the definition of the sets F_i as intuitive as possible. Consider task 14, executed during the third time unit in the schedule in Fig. 2.3b. Since the second processor is idle during that time unit, task 14 must precede all tasks executed after it. This is because according to the definition of list scheduling, all other tasks were considered for the third time unit but were not ready.

However, we cannot divide the tasks into two sets S_1 and S_2, S_1 containing all tasks executed no later than 14 and S_2 containing all other tasks, hoping that all tasks in S_1 precede all tasks in S_2. Task 7 executed in the second time unit does not precede any tasks with labels higher than 7. We will look at tasks that are executed out of turn and show that if certain tasks like 7 are ignored, we can determine the sets $F_k, F_{k-1}, \ldots, F_0$ that we are after.

Definition Given a schedule for a task system, we use $\lambda(T)$ to give the time unit in the schedule during which task T is executed.

The convention of assigning a task to processor 1 before processor 2 leads to a useful property of schedules.

Lemma 2.1 Let S be the list schedule constructed for a task system $(\mathcal{T}, <)$ using labeling L of Algorithm 2.2. If task T is executed by processor 1, for all $T' \in \mathcal{T}$ if T' is executed no earlier than T, then T' has a lower label than T; that is, $\lambda(T) \leq \lambda(T')$ implies $L(T) > L(T')$.

Proof Since task T is assigned to processor 1 during $\lambda(T)$, task T is the highest labeled task that is ready for that time unit. All tasks that are not

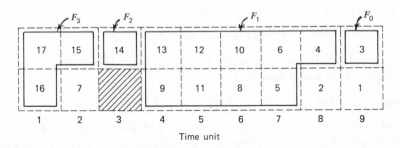

Figure 2.4 Follow-sets for the schedule in Fig. 2.3b.

ready must await a task that is. From labeling L, for all U, U' such that $U < U'$, it must be true that $L(U) > L(U')$. The lemma follows. ∎

In showing that Algorithm 2.2 is optimal, we examine schedules generated by it as in the discussion preceding Lemma 2.1.

Definitions Let S be a list schedule generated for a task system $(\mathcal{T}, <)$ by labeling L of Algorithm 2.2. We determine *follow-sets* $F_k, F_{k-1}, \ldots, F_0$, where k depends on the schedule, such that each task in F_i is a predecessor of all tasks in F_{i-1}. The follow-sets depend on tasks $D_k, D_{k-1}, \ldots, D_0$ and $J_k, J_{k-1}, \ldots, J_0$, where D_i "dominates" all tasks in the follow-set F_{i-1} and J_i "jumps ahead" of all tasks in F_{i-1}. Both D_i and J_i are executed in the same time unit. Figure 2.5 illustrates the following definitions.

1. Let tasks T and T' (where T' may represent an idle period) be executed during the last time unit in S by processors 1 and 2, respectively. Note that task T has the higher label of the two. D_0 represents the task T and J_0 represents the task T'.

2. Suppose $D_{k-1}, D_{k-2}, \ldots, D_0$ and $J_{k-1}, J_{k-2}, \ldots, J_0$ have been defined. We say that J_k is the (possibly idle) task T such that

    a. $L(T) < L(D_{k-1})$, where an idle task is treated as having label 0.

    b. $\lambda(T) < \lambda(D_{k-1})$ and $\lambda(T)$ is maximal.

Informally, T jumps ahead of D_{k-1}, and it is the nearest such task to D_{k-1}.

The task D_k is the task on the other processor while J_k is being executed; $\lambda(D_k) = \lambda(J_k)$. From Lemma 2.1, tasks $D_k, D_{k-1}, \ldots, D_0$ are on processor 1 and $J_k, J_{k-1}, \ldots, J_0$ are on processor 2.

3. Suppose $D_k, D_{k-1}, \ldots, D_0$ have been defined and D_{k+1} does not exist. For all i, $k > i \geq 0$, F_i is the set of all tasks executed after D_{i+1} and before D_i, along with task D_i. We therefore have

$$F_i = \{T \mid \lambda(D_{i+1}) < \lambda(T) < \lambda(D_i)\} \cup \{D_i\}.$$

Since D_{k+1} does not exist, F_k is defined separately

$$F_k = \{T \mid \lambda(T) < \lambda(D_k)\} \cup \{D_k\}$$

The next two lemmas show that for all i, $k \geq i \geq 1$, each task in F_i is a predecessor of every task in F_{i-1}.

Lemma 2.2 For all i, $k \geq i \geq 1$, $D_i < T$, for all T in F_{i-1}.

Proof As in Fig. 2.5, tasks D_i and J_i are executed during the same time unit. Recall that the task called J_i was selected to be called J_i because $L(J_i) < L(D_{i-1})$, and J_i was the nearest such task to D_{i-1}. It follows that

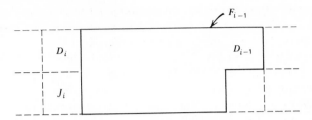

Figure 2.5 Proof of Lemma 2.2: J_i has a lower label than all tasks in F_{i-1}.

for all the other tasks T in F_{i-1}, $L(T) \geq L(D_{i-1})$. Since $L(J_i) < L(D_{i-1})$, by transitivity $L(J_i) < L(T)$. From the definition of list scheduling, since each task T in F_{i-1} has a label higher than J_i, task T was considered before J_i was assigned to a processor. Thus task T could not have been ready at that time unit. Thus D_i must be a predecessor of T. The reader might note that D_i need not necessarily be an immediate predecessor of T. ∎

The argument used in the proof of the next lemma is based on the reason why a given task is assigned a label higher than another task. Consider tasks 5 and 4 in Fig. 2.4. From Lemma 2.2 we know that task 4 precedes task 3. Thus when the list of immediate successors was constructed in step 2 of Algorithm 2.2, the first element in $l(4)$ must have been 3. Since task 5 has a higher label than 4, the first element in $l(5)$ must also be at least 3. The two possibilities are 3 and 4. In either case, task 5 is a predecessor of task 3.

Lemma 2.3 For all i, $k \geq i \geq 1$, if T is in F_i and T' in F_{i-1}, then $T < T'$.

Proof Suppose the lemma is false. Then for some i, $k \geq i \geq 1$, there is a task T in F_i that does not precede a task T' in F_{i-1}. Suppose for the moment that T has no successors in F_i.

From Lemma 2.2, D_i precedes T'. From the definition of F_i it must be true that T has a higher label than D_i, for otherwise T would be a candidate for J_{i+1} which is not in F_i. From the labeling L it follows that $l(D_i) \leq l(T)$.

Let $l(D_i) = (n_1, n_2, \ldots, n_r)$. We claim that the first few elements of $l(D_i)$ must be labels of tasks in F_{i-1}. From Lemma 2.1, D_{i-1} has a label higher than all tasks executed after D_{i-1}. By definition all other tasks in F_{i-1} have a label higher than D_{i-1}. Thus elements of the follow-set F_{i-1} have the highest labels of all tasks executed after $\lambda(D_i)$. Clearly then the largest elements of $l(D_i)$ must come from tasks in the set F_{i-1}. In particular if I is the maximal set of tasks in F_{i-1} that have no predecessors in F_{i-1}, the first $|I|$ elements of $l(D_i)$ must be the labels of tasks in I. (The last statement follows from the assumption in Chapter 1 that the graph of a task system $(\mathcal{T}, <)$ has no transitive edges. As Fig. 2.6 shows, Algorithm 2.2 is not optimal if the graph has transitive edges.)

We have chosen T so that it has no successors in F_i. To complete the proof, note that for $l(D_i)$ to be lexicographically smaller than $l(T)$, T must be an immediate predecessor of each element of I. Thus T must be a predecessor of all elements of F_{i-1}, which is a contradiction.

The remaining case, when T does have a successor in F_i, follows from transitivity because T will precede all tasks that the successor precedes. And sooner or later we will reach a successor of T in F_i that itself has no successors in F_i. The lemma follows. ■

Theorem 2.3   Let $(\mathcal{T}, <)$ be a UET system. Algorithm 2.2 generates a minimal-length nonpreemptive schedule for $(\mathcal{T}, <)$ on two processors.

Proof   Let S be the list schedule constructed by Algorithm 2.2 for $(\mathcal{T}, <)$. Let there be $k + 1$ follow-sets $F_k, F_{k-1}, \ldots, F_0$ in S. From Lemma 2.3, each task in F_k is a predecessor of all tasks in F_j, for all j, $k > j$. Thus

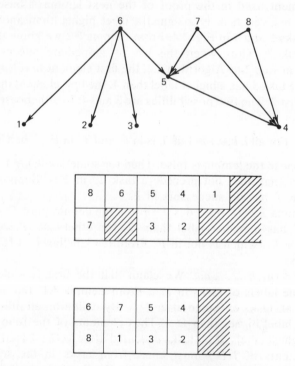

Figure 2.6   Example showing that transitive edges can lead to Algorithm 2.2 delivering a nonoptimal schedule.

all tasks in F_k must be finished before any task in F_j can be started. Since each follow-set has an odd number of tasks, by definition, let F_i have $2n_i - 1$ tasks. Clearly n_i time units are required to execute all tasks in F_i. Thus any schedule for $(\mathcal{T}, <)$ will take at least $\Sigma_{i=0}^k n_i$ time units. Since S takes $\Sigma_{i=0}^k n_i$ time units, schedule S must be optimal. $\blacksquare$

Forests are a special case of dags. The reader can show that labeling L assigns labels level by level. Thus it is possible, although not advisable, to use Algorithm 2.2 to construct optimal schedules for forests on m processors.

One of the points worth repeating is that Algorithm 2.2 constructs an optimal schedule only when there are no transitive edges in the graph of the given task system. Skeptical readers might look at Fig. 2.6. However, it is not difficult to verify that transitive edges can be deleted in $O(n^{2.8})$ time at worst [AGU].

Since labeling L leads to optimal schedules on two processors, it is natural to ask how well or badly it does on more processors. As Fig. 2.7 shows on three processors, a schedule constructed from the labeling is of length 5, and the optimal schedule is of length 4. In fact, if tasks 1 and 2 in

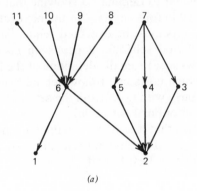

(a)

11	8	6	3	2
10	7	5	1	////
9	////	4	////	////

(b)

7	5	4	2
11	9	3	1
10	8	6	////

(c)

Figure 2.7 (*a*) Task system with labels assigned by labeling L. (*b*) List schedule from the labeling. (*c*) An optimal schedule.

Fig. 2.7 are deleted and the labeling done just wrong, the list schedule from the labeling will be of length 4, and the optimal schedule of length 3.

On six processors, consider the task system appearing in Fig. 2.8. Let labeling L assign labels in the order $A_{18}, B_1, \ldots, B_{18}, C_1, \ldots, C_{18}, D_1$. A list schedule based on the labeling would then take one unit for each level with 2 tasks and two units for each level with $m + 2$ tasks, where $m = 6$. The schedule length is therefore $\omega = 11$. An optimal schedule takes $\omega_0 = 8$ units. As the pattern is repeated, however, ω/ω_0 becomes $(5k + 1)/(3k + 2)$, which approaches 5/3. On m processors, a similar construction leads to ratios of $[(m - 1)k + 1]/(mk/2 + 2)$, which approaches $2 - 2/m$ as k increases.

From Fig. 2.8 it is evident that labeling L can fare quite poorly on a large number of processors. Why then is it optimal on two processors? An intuitive explanation might be as follows.

Consider the follow-sets that were constructed on two processors. On m processors we can define an analog of the follow-sets on two processors by looking for time units during which $m - 1$ processors are either idle, or executing tasks that jump ahead. For these new follow-sets we can prove a lemma similar to Lemma 2.3 showing that all tasks in one follow-set must be finished before any task in the next follow-set can be started. Since the follow-sets must be executed sequentially, the performance of a labeling L based schedule depends on how the schedule executes individual follow-sets. From the definition of the follow-sets, for every time unit during which tasks in a follow-set are being executed, at least two processors are busy with tasks from the set. If we have only two processors, we will get an optimal schedule.

It has been shown in [LS] that if ω is the length of a schedule based on labeling L, and ω_0 the length of an optimal schedule, $\omega/\omega_0 \leq 2 - 2/m$. As Fig. 2.8 indicates, $2 - 2/m$ is a best bound.

2.4 IMPLEMENTING THE NONPREEMPTIVE ALGORITHMS

The time complexity of Algorithms 2.1 and 2.2 depends on the data structures used to represent graphs and on the mechanisms for assigning labels and constructing list schedules. A matrix representation has $O(n^2)$ elements; thus $O(n^2)$ time is taken in just determining which entries in the matrix are nonzero. Representing a forest by a matrix is therefore inadvisable, since it contains only $O(n)$ edges.

In this section we first consider a linear time algorithm to label trees. The algorithm is extended to label dags, its time complexity going up to $O(n^2)$. In the worst case a dag may have $O(n^2)$ edges, but often the

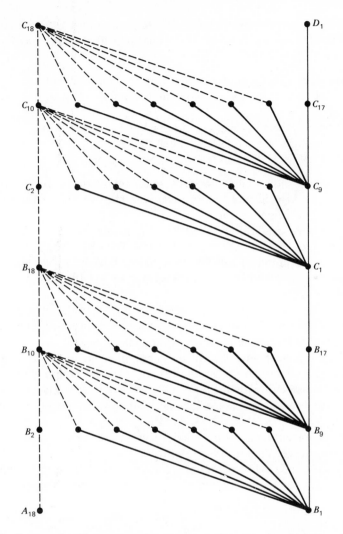

Figure 2.8   By repeating this pattern we can construct task systems for which the ratio of the lengths of a labeling L based schedule and an optimal schedule approaches $2 - 2/6 = 5/3$. For even m a similar construction leads to task systems for which the ratio approaches $2 - 2/m$. Some of the edges are dotted for clarity. All edges are directed downward.

number of edges is relatively small. A labeling algorithm that takes time linear in the number of edges may be found in [Se]. Later in this section we give an almost linear algorithm that constructs the schedule for a given labeling.

A data structure that is convenient for Algorithm 2.1 is a list of immediate predecessors of each node. In addition we have a queue Q of tasks that are ready to be labeled. The algorithm then consists of the following steps:

1. Starting with Q empty, enter the terminals of the forest into the queue. All level 1 tasks are now in the queue. No labels have been assigned.

2. Suppose labels $1, 2, \ldots, j - 1$ have been assigned. Take a task T out of the queue and assign it label j. Enter all immediate predecessors of T at the tail of Q. Stop if the queue is empty.

It is easy to show that these steps will label a forest level by level, and according to Algorithm 2.1. Moreover, the steps will take time linear in the number of nodes in the forest.

For dags, we can still use the lists of immediate predecessors and the queue of tasks that are ready to be labeled. The difference is that labeling a task does not at once ready its immediate predecessors for labeling. For example, in Fig. 2.9 when label 1 is assigned to A, both F and G still have unlabeled successors.

A point to note in implementing Algorithm 2.2 is that it is possible to avoid constructing the lists of labels in decreasing order. We illustrate the point by considering the labeling of the task system in Fig. 2.9. Suppose that labels 1 through 4 have been assigned. Since nodes D and F have not been labeled, all we can say about the lists for nodes G and H at this stage is that $l(G)$ will end with 4, 1, and $l(H)$ will end with 4. The reason is that all labels to be assigned later will be larger than 4. Instead of keeping track of the lists for G and H, all we need note is that H now has a smaller partial sequence than G. When label 5 is assigned, the partial sequence for H becomes larger than that for G, since 5 is an immediate successor of H but not of G. If 5 had been an immediate successor of both G and H, the relative order of their sequences would have remained the same.

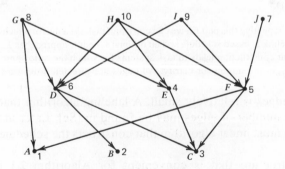

Figure 2.9   Task system for Example 2.

Algorithm 2.2 can be implemented by having a queue of tasks that are ready to be labeled and a list LEX that orders the other tasks relative to the labels that have already been assigned. Let LEX_i represent the list after the label i is assigned. When label $i + 1$ is assigned to some node x, the updated ordering LEX_{i+1} can be constructed from LEX_i by scanning LEX_i from the smallest to the largest element and picking out the immediate predecessors of x. These tasks have $i + 1$ as the largest label in their partial sequence. They are therefore the last few elements of LEX_{i+1}. We have not specifically mentioned predecessors of x that were not in LEX_i, nor have we said anything about tasks that are ready to be labeled. The following example indicates the actions taken.

Example 2 Consider the task system in Fig. 2.9. The contents of the ready queue Q and the list LEX during the process of labeling are as follows:

Label assigned	1	2	3	4	5	6
Queue	BC	C	EFD	FD	DJ	JGIH
LEX	GF	GFD	G	HG	GIH	—

The labels 7 through 10 are assigned to J, G, I, and H as they are removed from the queue.

It is left to the reader to translate the foregoing discussion into an algorithm to update the list LEX. Here we ponder on the time complexity of the overall labeling. If the test, "is y an immediate predecessor of x?" can be performed in constant time, then for each node labeled, updating LEX takes at most n steps for an n-task system. The time complexity is then $O(n^2)$. The test mentioned can be performed by setting up a 0–1 matrix that gives precedence information.

Once the task system has been labeled, the next step is to construct a schedule from the labeling. As Fig. 2.10 shows, list scheduling as we have considered it so far may sometimes be inefficient. Consider the list of tasks from which a schedule for the system in Fig. 2.10 is constructed. If the list is scanned from left to right to find the first ready task, successive scans will have to skip over $n - 1, n - 2, \ldots, 1$ tasks, respectively. The construction of the schedule will therefore take $O(n^2)$ steps.

We will show that it is possible to construct a list schedule in almost linear time. The algorithm exploits the following two facts. (1) Each task has an execution time of one unit. (2) In the lists we deal with, predecessors appear before their successors. Given the list $(T_n, T_{n-1}, \ldots, T_1)$, all the predecessors of task T_i appear before T_i in the list.

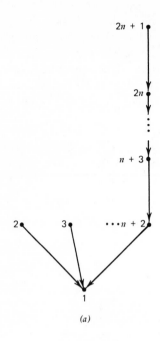

(a)

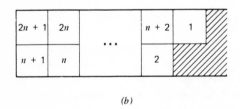

(b)

Figure 2.10 (a) Labeled task system. (b) Schedule on two processors constructed from the labeling of Fig. 2.10a.

Intuitively, the algorithm builds up a schedule by successively constructing schedules for the lists (T_n), (T_n, T_{n-1}), ... until the schedule for the entire list $(T_n, T_{n-1}, \ldots, T_1)$ is constructed.

Consider the task system in Fig. 2.3a. Schedules corresponding to some partial lists for the task system appear in Fig. 2.11. When the lists (17) and (17, 16) are considered, we get the schedules in Figs. 2.11a and b, with tasks 17 and 16 on processors 1 and 2. The next list to be considered is (17, 16, 15). Task 15 is ready to begin execution during the first time unit, but there is no free processor. Thus task 15 is assigned in the next time unit. As the next lemma shows, there is a simple algorithm for constructing the schedule for an augmented list.

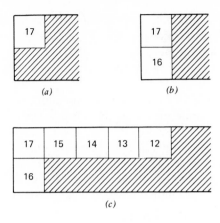

(a)

(b)

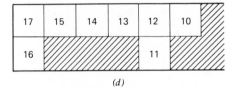

(c)

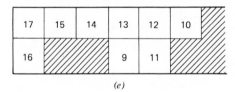

(d)

(e)

Figure 2.11 Schedule for the task system in Fig. 2.3a, constructed by successively considering the lists (17), (17, 16), ..., (17, 16, ..., 1).

Lemma 2.4 Let S_{i+1} be the list schedule for $(T_n, T_{n-1}, \ldots, T_{i+1})$. The list schedule S_i for $(T_n, T_{n-1}, \ldots, T_i)$ can be constructed from S_{i+1} as follows. Let t be the first time unit by which all predecessors of T_i have been executed. Assign T_i to a processor during the first time unit u, $u \geq t$ at which a processor is available.

Proof For all time units before t, the statement of the lemma assures us that T_i is not ready to be executed. Thus even if it is reached in a scan of the list $(T_n, T_{n-1}, \ldots, T_i)$, it cannot be assigned. Thus until time unit t, the two schedules will be the same. After time unit t, in constructing schedule S_i, task T_i will be reached when there is a processor free and no other task can be assigned. Clearly, this situation corresponds to the first idle time after t in schedule S_{i+1}. The lemma must therefore be true. ■

From Lemma 2.4 it seems that we can trade repeated scans of the list for scans to determine a time unit during which a processor is free. We show that by using an efficient algorithm for merging disjoint sets, we can cut down on the rechecking of time units during which all processors are busy.

Suppose all processors are busy during time unit i and will remain busy until j. Then for all t, $i \le t \le j$, the first time unit at which a processor is available is j. We collect all such t into a set identified by j. In general we choose names of sets so that if t is in set u, then u is the first time unit at or after t at which a processor is available. To construct schedules as outlined in Lemma 2.4, we therefore need to be able to determine the set that a time unit is in, as well as the first time unit at which a task becomes ready.

Algorithm 2.3   Let D be a dag labeled by Algorithm 2.2 or a tree labeled by Algorithm 2.1. This algorithm constructs a list schedule for the task system represented by D using the list of tasks in order of decreasing label.

By way of data structures we need a set for each time unit. Initially $\mathrm{SET}(t) = \{t\}$ for each time unit.

1. All initial tasks in D are said to be *ready* at time unit 1.
2. For all tasks x in D, do step 3 in order of decreasing label.
3. Consider task x. Let x be ready at time unit t. If t is in $\mathrm{SET}(u)$, assign x to a processor during time unit u. If u now has no free processors, look at time unit $u + 1$. Let $u + 1$ be in $\mathrm{SET}(v)$. Merge $\mathrm{SET}(u)$ and $\mathrm{SET}(v)$ calling the new set $\mathrm{SET}(v)$.

Examine all y such that y is an immediate successor of x. If all predecessors of y have now been examined, task y is said to become *ready* at $u + 1$.

In proving that Algorithm 2.3 is correct, we first show that the set operations are performed correctly.

Lemma 2.5   Let time unit t be in $\mathrm{SET}(u)$ at some stage. Then u is the first time unit, $u \ge t$ at which a processor is available.

Proof   Initially, time unit t is in $\mathrm{SET}(t)$, and all processors are free. Suppose that for some u, all processors have just been assigned tasks during u. Both u and $u + 1$ then have the same unit as the first free time unit. If $u + 1$ is in $\mathrm{SET}(v)$, the algorithm merges $\mathrm{SET}(u)$ and $\mathrm{SET}(v)$ and calls the new set $\mathrm{SET}(v)$. The reader is invited to construct a more rigorous proof based on the number of executions of step 3 of the algorithm.   ∎

Theorem 2.4   Algorithm 2.3 constructs a list schedule using the list of tasks in order of decreasing label.

Proof   Since tasks appear in order of decreasing label, when task x is considered, all predecessors of x have already been assigned. Thus the time unit at which x becomes ready is known. From Lemma 2.5, the algorithm correctly locates the next free time unit. Since schedules are augmented as in Lemma 2.4, the theorem must be true.   ∎

We avoid the details of how the set operations are performed, referring the reader to [T, HU]. We do note that step 3 of Algorithm 2.3 looks at each edge in the task system exactly once. And the number of set operations is proportional to n, the number of tasks. It has been shown in [T] that n set operations can be done in time almost linear in n. More precisely, n operations can be done in $O(n\alpha(n))$ time, where $\alpha(n)$ is a functional inverse of Ackermann's function.

The following table gives some idea of how slowly $\alpha(n)$ grows.

n	$\alpha(n)$
255	1
256	2
65535	2
65536	3
$2^{65536} - 1$	3
2^{65536}	4

Let $A(i, j)$ be a function on integers defined by

$$A(0, j) = 2j$$

For $i \geq 1$, $j \geq 2$, we have

$$A(i, 0) = 0, \qquad A(i, 1) = 2$$
$$A(i, j) = A(i - 1, A(i, j - 1))$$

Then

$$\alpha(n) = \min\{i \mid A(i, 3) > \lfloor \log_2 n \rfloor\}$$

2.5   PREEMPTION WITH INDEPENDENT TASKS

In the last few sections it has been assumed that a task once started is executed to completion. We noted in Section 2.1 that we expect a polynomial-time nonpreemptive scheduling algorithm only when all tasks have equal execution times. In two subcases—when the task system is a forest, and when only two processors are available—we provided polynomial-time algorithms to determine minimal-length schedules.

Let us now turn to preemptive schedules. Since tasks no longer have to be executed to completion, execution times can be allowed to be arbitrary. It turns out that the known polynomial-time preemptive algorithms are closely related to the nonpreemptive algorithms in Sections 2.2 and 2.3. In addition we have to consider the case when all tasks are independent, since execution times are now arbitrary. For independent tasks there is a simple algorithm for determining minimal preemptive schedules. Let independent tasks $T_1, T_2, \ldots, T_n$ with execution times $\tau_1, \tau_2, \ldots, \tau_n$ be scheduled on m processors. The shortest possible schedule is one with no idle time in it at all. The length of such a schedule is $\omega = X/m$, where $X = \sum_{i=1}^{n} \tau_i$. We see later that such a schedule can indeed be constructed as long as none of the tasks is longer than X/m. If one of the tasks is longer than X/m, then ω is given by the length of the longest task.

The algorithm works essentially as follows: first compute ω as in the last paragraph. For the tasks in Fig. 2.12 $\omega = 7$. Assign tasks to a processor until one of the tasks overflows past ω, the end of the schedule. Assign the overflow to the next processor starting at time 0. Thus in Fig. 2.12, 4 does not fit into the interval (6, 7), and the overflow is assigned to processor P_2. Notice that the times assigned to a task on two processors cannot overlap, since we have chosen ω to be at least as long as the longest task.

Algorithm 2.4 Let $(\mathcal{T}, <)$ be a task system consisting of independent tasks $T_1, T_2, \ldots, T_n$ with execution times $\tau_1, \tau_2, \ldots, \tau_n$. This algorithm determines a minimal-length preemptive schedule for the task system on m identical processors. The running time of the algorithm is clearly $O(n)$.

1. Let $X = \sum_{i=1}^{n} \tau_i$, and let τ be the length of the longest task in the

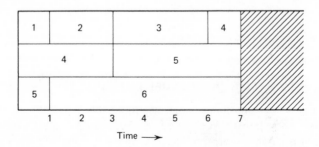

Figure 2.12 Independent tasks of length $1, 2, \ldots, 6$ scheduled on three processors by Algorithm 2.4.

system; ω, the length of the schedule to be constructed, is given by $\omega = \max(X/m, \tau)$.

2. Initially none of the processors has been assigned any tasks. Do step 3 for $T_1, T_2, \ldots, T_n$.

3. Let tasks $T_1, T_2, \ldots, T_{i-1}$ already be assigned to processors $P_1, P_2, \ldots, P_{j-1}$ in the interval $(0, \omega)$ and processor P_j in the interval $(0, t)$, for some $t < \omega$. Consider task T_i. If $t + \tau_i \leq \omega$, assign task T_i to P_j in the interval $(t, t + \tau_i)$. Otherwise assign T_i to P_j during (t, ω) and to P_{j+1} during $(0, \tau_i - (\omega - t))$.

Figure 2.1b has an example of a task system scheduled according to Algorithm 2.4. Figure 2.12 contains another example. We now show that Algorithm 2.4 does indeed determine optimal schedules.

Theorem 2.5   Algorithm 2.4 determines minimal-length preemptive schedules for systems of independent tasks on m identical processors.

Proof   Clearly a schedule can do no better than to finish all tasks in $\omega = \max(X/m,$ length of longest task$)$ time, where X is the sum of the execution times of all tasks. From step 3 of the algorithm, at no time is more than one task assigned to the same processor. Since ω is longer than the longest task in the system, at no time is the same task assigned to more than one processor. No task is assigned past time ω. Moreover, since $\omega \cdot m$ is at least as much as X, it is possible to fit all tasks into the interval $(0, \omega)$. Thus the schedule determined by Algorithm 2.4 is optimal.   ∎

Since a cost, however slight, is incurred every time a preemption occurs, we are interested in the number of preemptions that must take place in a minimal-length schedule. It was seen in Chapter 1 that determining minimal-length schedules with the fewest preemptions is difficult enough to be outside the scope of this discussion. Here we restrict ourselves to determining a bound on the number of preemptions. Relative to the bound, Algorithm 2.4 does fairly well.

Definitions   A task T is said to be *preempted* at time t if execution of T is suspended on some processor at time t, and T does not finish at t. A task is said to be *active* at time t if some processor is executing T at time t. If a task begins execution on processor P at time t, and is executed continuously by P until t', where t' is maximal, (t, t') is called an *active period* for the task on processor P.

Theorem 2.6   Let S be a schedule determined by Algorithm 2.4 for a system of independent tasks on m identical processors. Then S has at most $m - 1$ preemptions. Moreover, $m - 1$ is a best bound on the number of preemptions in that there exists a task system for which every minimal-length schedule has at least $m - 1$ preemptions.

Proof From Algorithm 2.4, each task has at most two active periods. When a task has two active periods, the first starts at time 0 on some processor and the second ends at the end of the schedule, on a lower numbered processor. There can be at most $m - 1$ such tasks, and each such task is preempted once. Hence a schedule determined by the algorithm has at most $m - 1$ preemptions.

Now we show that an optimal schedule for the task system consisting of $m + 1$ tasks of length m will have at least $m - 1$ preemptions. Suppose this task system can be scheduled optimally with less than $m - 1$ preemptions. Then the schedule will contain at least two processors that are never preempted. Let these be P_1 and P_2 without loss of generality. Since all tasks are of length m, these processors execute tasks, say T_1 and T_2, in the interval $(0, m)$. From Algorithm 2.4, an optimal preemptive schedule for this task system has no idle time and is of length $m + 1$. Thus P_1 and P_2 must be executing some tasks until time $m + 1$. For some t and t', $m \leq t < t' \leq m + 1$, let T_3 be on P_1 and T_4 on P_2 in the interval (t, t'), as in Fig. 2.13. (Note that resuming execution of T_3 and T_4 on P_1 and P_2 does not count as preemption.) During the interval (t, t'), the only tasks that can be executed on the remaining $m - 2$ processors are $T_5, T_6, ..., T_{m+1}$. Since we have only $m - 3$ tasks to be assigned to $m - 2$ processors in the interval (t, t'), there must be some idle time in the schedule. Since the schedule is therefore nonoptimal, the theorem must be true. ∎

2.6 EXTENDING THE NONPREEMPTIVE ALGORITHMS

Consider the task system $(\mathcal{T}, <)$ in Fig. 2.14a. An optimal nonpreemptive schedule for the task system has length 9. Let a set $\{U_1, U_2, \ldots, U_k\}$ of tasks be called a *chain* if $U_1 < U_2 < \cdots < U_k$. Let us examine the effect of

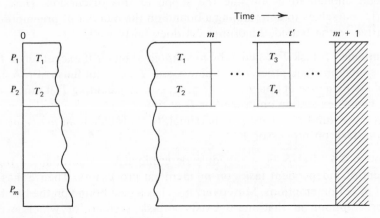

Figure 2.13 Proof of Theorem 2.6.

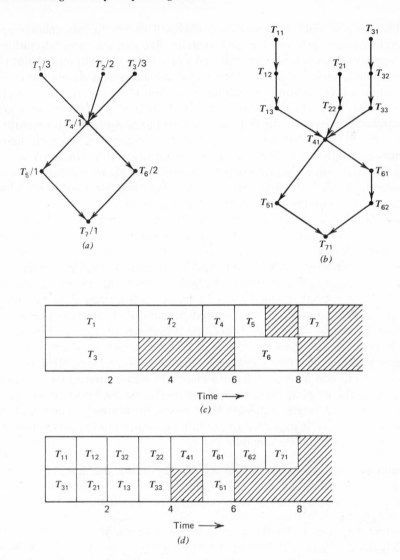

Figure 2.14 (*a*) A task system ($\mathcal{T}$, <). (*b*) The task system formed by splitting each task in ($\mathcal{T}$, <) into a chain of one-unit tasks. (*c*) Optimal nonpreemptive schedules for the two task systems.

splitting each task in ($\mathcal{T}$, <) into a chain of one-unit tasks. The optimal nonpreemptive schedule for the new task system is of length 8. At least in this example, splitting each task into a chain of smaller tasks leads to a better "nonpreemptive" approximation to an optimal preemptive schedule.

The nonpreemptive algorithms considered earlier in this chapter applied to equal-execution-time task systems. We can use those algorithms for approximations if we can split tasks of arbitrary length into chains of equal-length tasks. We therefore make the following assumption: let $(\mathcal{T}, <)$ be a task system in which the execution times are $\tau_1, \tau_2, \ldots, \tau_n$. If there exists a positive real number w such that all execution times are integral multiples of w, the tasks in $\mathcal{T}$ are said to be *mutually commensurable*. We assume that all systems under consideration have mutually commensurable tasks. This assumption is not restrictive, since any set of real numbers can be approximated arbitrarily closely by a set of rational numbers. Besides, the finite precision numbers that are used in entering data into a computer are mutually commensurable.

Let G be the directed acyclic graph representing the task system $(\mathcal{T}, <)$. Node x_i in G represents task T_i of length τ_i for all i, $1 \le i \le n$. Given the close correspondence between a task system and the graph for it, we use the terms "node" and "task" interchangeably. Moreover, we sometimes refer to G as if it were the task system being scheduled. Define G_w to be the graph formed from G by replacing node T_i by a chain $T_{i1}, T_{i2}, \ldots, T_{in_i}$, where $n_i = \tau_i / w$. Predecessors of T_i become predecessors of T_{i1} and successors of T_i become successors of T_{in_i} (see Fig. 2.14). Each node in G_w then represents a task of length w, permitting the nonpreemptive algorithms earlier in the chapter to be applied to G_w. Nodes in G_w can also be split into chains of equal-length tasks. Define $G_{w/k}$ to be the graph formed from G_w by replacing each node in G_w by a chain of k equal-length nodes. As k increases, the optimal nonpreemptive schedule for $G_{w/k}$ is expected to provide an improving approximation of the optimal preemptive schedule for G.

Definition Let $\omega(G, m)$ and $\omega'(G, m)$ represent the lengths of the optimal nonpreemptive and preemptive schedules, respectively, on m identical processors for the task system represented by G.

Theorem 2.7 Let G be the graph representing the task system $(\mathcal{T}, <)$ with tasks $T_1, T_2, \ldots, T_n$ having execution times $\tau_1, \tau_2, \ldots, \tau_n$. Let w be a positive real number that is a submultiple of each of the execution times. Then $\omega'(G, m) \le \omega(G_{w/k}, m) \le \omega'(G, m) + C/k$, $k = 1, 2, \ldots$, where C is a constant depending only on G.

Proof Let S be an optimal preemptive schedule for G. Since G has n tasks, there will be at most n instants in the schedule at which a task finishes. Let these times be $t_1 \le t_2 \le \cdots \le t_n$. (Note that the times need not all be distinct because more than one task may finish at the same time.) Let t_0 be the starting time of the schedule.

Consider the interval $I_i = (t_{i-1}, t_i)$, for all i, $1 \le i \le n$. Since no task finishes within the interval, all tasks executed in I_i must be independent. Since S can be *any* optimal preemptive schedule, there may be an arbitrary number of preemptions within interval I_i. Let tasks $T_{i_1}, T_{i_2}, \ldots, T_{i_{n_i}}$ be executed within interval I_i, and let the total time devoted to task T_{i_j} in I_i be λ_j. Treating T_{i_j} as a task of length λ_j, we can reassign interval I_i using Algorithm 2.4. Let the schedule formed by reassigning all intervals be called S'. The reassignment permits us to bound the number of active periods of each task within an interval. Note that the length of schedule S' is the same as that of S. Let $S'(t, t')$ denote that part of schedule S' between time t and t'. For all i, $1 \le i \le n$, $S'(t_{i-1}, t_i)$ corresponds to interval I_i in schedule S.

Since there are no restrictions on the times at which preemptions may occur, in general, the length of an active period for any task will not be a multiple of w/k. We can construct a new schedule S'' in which each active period is a multiple of w/k. In addition, S'' can be constructed in n segments S''_i, $1 \le i \le n$, which are concatenated to give S''. For all i, $1 \le i \le n$, construct S''_i as follows: lengthen each active period in $S'(t_{i-1}, t_i)$ so that it becomes a multiple of w/k; add dummy tasks at the end so that all processors finish at the same time.

We claim that S'' is at most $2n^2 w/k$ longer than S', and hence S. Consider $S'(t_{i-1}, t_i)$, which corresponds to interval I_i in S. At most, all tasks are present in the interval. From Algorithm 2.4, there can be at most two active periods for each task in $S'(t_{i-1}, t_i)$. Thus the length of S'' is at most $2nw/k$ more than $S'(t_{i-1}, t_i)$. Since there are no more than n segments of S'', the length of S'' is at most $2n^2 w/k$ more than the length of S and S'.

Every active period in S'' is a multiple of w/k. We can therefore use S'' to construct a nonpreemptive schedule for $G_{w/k}$. Since the times assigned to each task have been increased in S'', we may need to introduce some idle time within the schedule to get a nonpreemptive schedule for $G_{w/k}$. Clearly the optimal nonpreemptive schedule for $G_{w/k}$ can be no longer than S''. It follows that $\omega(G_{w/k}, m) \le \omega'(G, m) + 2n^2 w/k$. The lower bound in the theorem is obvious, since every nonpreemptive schedule is trivially a preemptive schedule. ∎

From Theorem 2.7, whenever we can construct an optimal nonpreemptive schedule for a task system consisting of equal execution time tasks, we can approximate arbitrarily closely an optimal preemptive schedule for a system of tasks of arbitrary length. The only cases for which such nonpreemptive algorithms are known were studied in Sections 2.2 and 2.3: trees on an arbitrary number of processors and partial orders on two processors.

Consider the labeling algorithm in Section 2.3 that was used to determine schedules for partial orders on two processors. It was seen that labels are assigned level by level. From Section 2.2, the level strategy schedules trees level by level. As tasks are split into chains of smaller tasks, the number of levels increases, reaching a continuous case in the limit where execution is proceeding level by level even for partial orders.

Let us translate level-by-level execution of $G_{w/k}$ into a schedule for G. Since levels are determined from the terminal tasks, we need a measure of the distance of a task from the terminals, in terms of the execution time that follows a task. Tasks at the same level get the same level of service. To illustrate diagrammatically how tasks get the same level of service, we introduce the notion of *processor sharing*. If there are more processors than tasks, each task gets a processor to itself. Otherwise, the tasks must share the available processors. Thus each task is assigned α "processors", where $0 < \alpha \le 1$. Instead of talking of a task T with execution time τ, we refer to T having a *service requirement* of τ processor-time units. An example of a task system scheduled using processor sharing is given in Fig. 2.15. If there are no preemptions, task T assigned α processors will execute for τ/α time units, where $\tau/\alpha \ge \tau$, since $0 < \alpha \le 1$. Thus, α may be regarded as the rate at which T executes.

Definition   Let $(\mathcal{T}, <)$ be a task system containing tasks $T_1, T_2, \ldots, T_n$ having service requirements $\tau_1, \tau_2, \ldots, \tau_n$. Let $T_{i_1}, T_{i_2}, \ldots, T_{i_{n_i}}$ be a chain in $\mathcal{T}$. The chain is said to *start* with task T_{i_1}. The *length* of the chain is given by $\Sigma_{j=1}^{n_i} \tau_{i_j}$. The *level* of task T in $\mathcal{T}$ is the maximum over the lengths of all chains starting with T. Note that this definition is consistent with that of levels in UET systems.

Algorithm 2.5   Let $(\mathcal{T}, <)$ be a task system where $\mathcal{T}$ contains mutually commensurable tasks. This algorithm first determines a processor-shared schedule for the task system, then converts that schedule into a preemptive schedule.

1. Let there be a processors available, and let there be b tasks at the highest level. If $b > a$, assign a/b processors to each of the b tasks. Otherwise assign one processor to each task. If there are any processors left, consider the tasks at the next highest level, and so on.

2. Reassign all processors to the unexecuted portion of the task system whenever one of the following occurs:
Event 1:   A task is finished.
Event 2:   A point is reached at which continuing with the present assignment implies that (in the unexecuted portion of the task system) a task at a lower level will be executed at a faster rate than a task at a higher level.

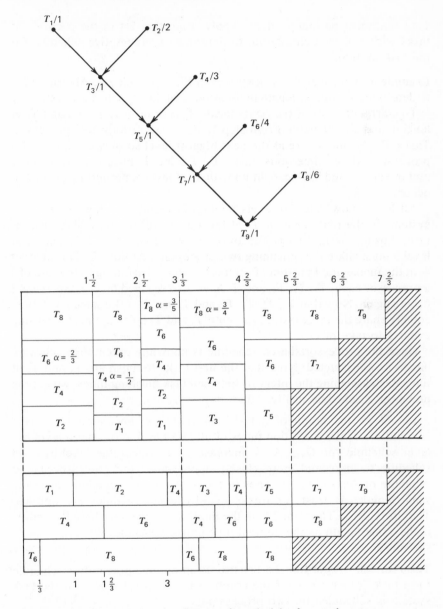

Figure 2.15   Processor-shared and preemptive schedules for a task system.

3. Let $t_1 \le t_2 \le \cdots \le t_n$ be the times at which a task is finished in the schedule constructed at the end of step 2. Note that $t_1, t_2, \ldots, t_n$ will be the times at which event 1 takes place. Let t_0 be the starting time of the schedule. Clearly all tasks executed within the interval (t_{i-1}, t_i), for all i,

$1 \le i \le n$, must be independent. Apply Algorithm 2.4 to the portions of tasks within each such interval to determine a preemptive schedule for the task system.

Example 3   Consider the task system in Fig. 2.15. We use Algorithm 2.5 to determine a minimal-length preemptive schedule for the task system.

To start, note that of the ready tasks, T_8 is at level 7, T_2, T_4, and T_6 at level 6, and T_1 at level 5. From step 1, T_8 is assigned a whole processor. Tasks T_2, T_4, and T_6 are at the next highest level so they each get $\frac{2}{3}$ of a processor. After $\frac{3}{2}$ time units, tasks T_2, T_4, and T_6 have each received 1 unit of service and have caught up with T_1 at level 5, permitting event 2 to occur.

All levels now refer to levels in the unexecuted portion of the task system. In the reassignment T_8 at level $5\frac{1}{2}$ is still the only highest level task; thus it is assigned a processor of its own. Tasks T_1, T_2, T_4, and T_6 at level 5 must share the remaining two processors. At time $2\frac{1}{2}$, T_8 is at level $4\frac{1}{2}$ in the unexecuted portion of the task system. Executing at the rate of $\frac{1}{2}$ a processor each, T_1, T_2, T_4, and T_6 have also reached level $4\frac{1}{2}$, so event 2 occurs again. Now that T_1, T_2, T_4, T_6, and T_8 are all at the same level, they equally share the three processors until T_1 and T_2 finish at time $3\frac{1}{3}$, causing event 1 to take place.

Once the processor-shared schedule is known, a preemptive schedule has to be constructed. Note that the first tasks to finish are T_1 and T_2 at time $3\frac{1}{3}$. Reassigning the intervals between task finishing times, we get the preemptive schedule in Fig. 2.15.   ∎

Let G be the graph of a task system $(\mathcal{T}, <)$ and suppose w is a submultiple of the execution times of all tasks in $\mathcal{T}$. Consider a level-by-level schedule for $G_{w/k}$. As k increases, we expect the level-by-level schedule to more and more closely approximate the processor-shared schedule of Algorithm 2.5. Thus in the limit the two schedules have the same length. At least for trees, level-by-level schedules are optimal. Therefore, from Theorem 2.7, in the limit, the processor-shared schedule is the same length as the optimal preemptive schedule. We can actually say more.

Theorem 2.8.   Algorithm 2.5 constructs an optimal preemptive schedule for a task system $(\mathcal{T}, <)$ if the graph of $(\mathcal{T}, <)$ is a forest or if the task system is scheduled on two processors.

Proof   We outline the proof, leaving some of the details to [MC1, MC2].

1. During each interval between events in the shared schedule, each task is executed for a rational amount of time.

2. In the process of showing statement 1, we can determine how finely

we need to divide each task. Since each task is executed for a rational amount of time, we can find a k such that a level by level schedule for $G_{w/k}$ "fits" into the intervals between events.

3. From Section 2.2, a level-by-level schedule is optimal for trees. For dags, as long as k is even, we can show that a level-by-level schedule is optimal for $G_{w/k}$ on two processors.

4. Now note that further subdividing $G_{w/k}$ cannot give a shorter schedule. In particular, for all j, $\omega(G_{w/k}, m) = \omega(G_{w/k \cdot j}, m)$. From Theorem 2.7, $\omega(G_{w/k \cdot j}, m)$ approaches the length of the optimal preemptive schedule for G. It follows that $\omega(G_{w/k}, m)$ must be equal to $\omega'(G, m)$. Since the shared schedule is the same length as $\omega(G_{w/k}, m)$ the theorem follows.   ∎

As was true in the nonpreemptive case, a level-by-level approach does not lead to optimal schedules for dags on more than two processors. See Fig. 2.16 for an example. It has recently been shown [LS] that $2 - 2/m$ is a worst-case bound for the ratio of the lengths of a level-by-level schedule to an optimal preemptive schedule.

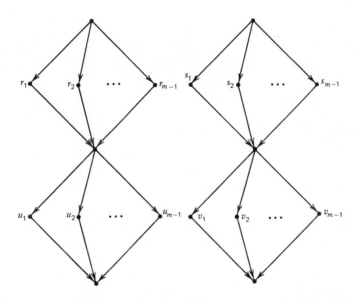

Figure 2.16   A level-by-level preemptive schedule for the task system illustrated is of length $2(3 - 2/m) + 1$, whereas an optimal schedule (nonpreemptive) is of length $2(2) + 2$. As levels are added to the task system, the ratio of the lengths of the level-by-level and optimal schedules approaches $3/2 - 1/m$.

2.7 ADVANTAGES OF PREEMPTION

Figure 2.1 demonstrates that a preemptive schedule may be shorter than a minimal-length nonpreemptive schedule for a given task system. In this section we compare the lengths of preemptive and nonpreemptive schedules.

In addition to the general class, a special class of nonpreemptive schedules is also of interest. Such schedules are called list schedules and are constructed by assigning priorities to all tasks, then assigning tasks to processors in order of priority. The essential difference between a list and a general nonpreemptive schedule is that in a list schedule a processor cannot remain idle as long as there is a task that is ready to execute. As we see later in this section, this restriction can lead to an optimal list schedule being longer than a general nonpreemptive schedule. Properties of list schedules are examined in more detail in Chapter 5.

Definition   Let $\omega_L(G, m)$ represent the length of a shortest list schedule* for the task system represented by the graph G on m identical processors. Recall that $\omega(G, m)$ and $\omega'(G, m)$ were defined in Section 2.6 as the lengths of the shortest nonpreemptive and preemptive schedules, respectively. When G and m are understood, we drop them and write ω_L, ω, and ω'.

Since every list schedule executes tasks nonpreemptively, we can state that $\omega \le \omega_L$. Moreover, the class of nonpreemptive schedules is contained in the class of preemptive schedules, which means that $\omega' \le \omega$. We can prove that $\omega_L/\omega' \le 2 - 1/m$. Since $\omega \le \omega_L$, it follows immediately that $\omega/\omega' \le 2 - 1/m$. Figure 2.17 shows that the bound of $2 - 1/m$ for ω_L/ω' can be approached arbitrarily closely. We do not have as tight a bound for ω/ω'. In the worst example we can construct, the ratio is $2m/(m + 1)$, which is somewhat smaller than $2 - 1/m$.

To prove the above-mentioned bounds, we need a lemma that appears in Chapter 5.

Lemma 2.6   Let S be a list schedule on m processors for a task system $(\mathcal{T}, <)$. If I is the sum of the times that each processor is idle in S, there exists a chain of tasks in $(\mathcal{T}, <)$ of length at least $I/(m - 1)$.

Proof   See Theorem 5.1.   ∎

Lemma 2.7   Let ω_L and ω' represent the lengths of the shortest list and preemptive schedules on m identical processors for a task system $(\mathcal{T}, <)$. Then $\omega_L/\omega' \le 2 - 1/m$.

---

* Shortest over all possible lists.

Proof Let S be the shortest list schedule (of length ω_L) for a task system $(\mathcal{T}, <)$ on m processors. If I is the idle time in S, we know from Lemma 2.6 that there is chain of tasks in $(\mathcal{T}, <)$ of length at least $I/(m-1)$. Any schedule for $(\mathcal{T}, <)$ must have length at least $I/(m-1)$. Thus $\omega' \geq I/(m-1)$, which leads to $I \leq \omega'(m-1)$.

Let X represent the sum of the execution times of all tasks in $\mathcal{T}$. No schedule, preemptive or otherwise, can do better than to have no idle time. Therefore $\omega' \geq X/m$, which yields $X \leq m\omega'$.

From the definition of I and X,

$$\omega_L = \frac{I + X}{m}$$

Substituting for I and X in terms of ω', we get

$$\omega_L \leq \frac{(m-1)\omega' + m\omega'}{m}$$

It follows immediately that $\omega_L/\omega' \leq 2 - 1/m$. ∎

It has been mentioned that the task system in Fig. 2.17 shows that $2 - 1/m$ is a best bound for ω_L/ω'. The figure also provides a comparison between a list and a general nonpreemptive schedule. Consider the task system in Fig. 2.17. Suppose task T is executed by processor 1, keeping processors 2 through m idle during $(0, \epsilon)$. At ϵ, the m processors can begin executing $V_1, V_2, \ldots, V_m$. At $1 + \epsilon$, the processors can begin execution of W and $U_1, U_2, \ldots, U_{m-1}$, finishing the entire task system at $m + \epsilon$. Thus from this example we see that ω_L/ω approaches $2 - 1/m$.

We summarize the bounds in the following theorem.

Theorem 2.9 Let ω_L, ω, and ω' represent the lengths of the shortest list, nonpreemptive and preemptive schedules, respectively, on m identical processors for a task system $(\mathcal{T}, <)$.

    1. $\omega' \leq \omega \leq \omega_L$.

    2. $\omega_L/\omega' \leq 2 - 1/m$.

    3. $\omega_L/\omega \leq 2 - 1/m$.

    4. There exists a task system for which ω_L/ω' and ω_L/ω approach $2 - 1/m$.

    5. There exists a task system for which $\omega/\omega' = 2m/(m+1)$.

Proof The only part that does not follow from the previous discussion is item 5. Consider a task system consisting of $m + 1$ identical tasks, each of length m. The shortest nonpreemptive schedule is of length $2m$; the shortest preemptive schedule of length $m + 1$. ∎

Consider the task system in Fig. 2.17. Let $(\mathcal{T}, <^R)$ be formed by

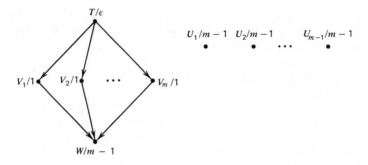

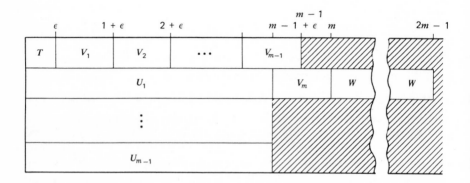

Figure 2.17 Task system with $\omega_L = 2m - 1$ and $\omega' = m + \epsilon$. The ratio ω_L/ω' approaches $2 - 1/m$ as ϵ decreases.

reversing all the edges giving the precedence constraints. Regardless of the list used, a list schedule for $(\mathcal{T}, <^R)$ is of length $m + \epsilon$. Thus reversing the edges has led to a shorter list schedule. Such an anomaly does not occur in the general nonpreemptive case.

Definition Let S be a schedule for a task system $(\mathcal{T}, <)$. Let $(\mathcal{T}, <^R)$ denote the task system formed by reversing all precedence constraints in $(\mathcal{T}, <)$ (i.e., $T <^R T'$ if and only if $T' < T$). Let S^R be the *reverse* (mirror image) of S (i.e., the completion time of S is the starting time of S^R and the processor assignment in S^R is given by reading S backward in time). Note that S^R may have a processor idle even if there is a task in $(\mathcal{T}, <^R)$ that is ready to execute.

Theorem 2.10 Let S be a preemptive or general nonpreemptive schedule for $(\mathcal{T}, <)$. Then S is a minimal-length schedule for $(\mathcal{T}, <)$ if and only if S^R is a minimal-length schedule for $(\mathcal{T}, <^R)$. (This theorem does not apply to list schedules.)

Proof From symmetry, we only need to prove the "if" part. First, note that S^R is a schedule for $(\mathcal{T}, <^R)$, since precedence constraints are obeyed and each task executes for a proper amount of time.

Suppose S is a minimal-length schedule for $(\mathcal{T}, <)$, but S^R is not a minimal-length schedule for $(\mathcal{T}, <^R)$. Then there exists S', shorter than S^R, which is minimal length for $(\mathcal{T}, <^R)$. Since $< = (<^R)^R$, $(S')^R$ must be a schedule for $(\mathcal{T}, <)$. Since $(S')^R$ is shorter than S, we have contradicted the minimality of S. The theorem must therefore be true. ∎

An interesting case that is not covered by Theorem 2.10 occurs when $(\mathcal{T}, <)$ is a UET forest. Although a list was used in Algorithm 2.1 to construct an optimal schedule S for $(\mathcal{T}, <)$, Theorem 2.1 assures us that S is a shortest general nonpreemptive schedule. Thus arguments similar to the proof of Theorem 2.10 apply to UET forests and antiforests.

2.8 PROCESSORS OF DIFFERENT SPEEDS

So far in this chapter we have considered processors that are equal in their processing capabilities. In general, processors may execute at different speeds. Even if the hardware is identical, processor P_1 may be spending some of its time attending to remote terminals for instance. If the proportion of time P_1 spends attending to other tasks is relatively constant, P_1 can be treated as a slower dedicated processor. And then, there is always the possibility that this year's budget can accommodate a fast processor.

The net result is that we have a set of m processors, $P = \{P_1, P_2, \ldots, P_m\}$ of speeds $b_1 \geq b_2 \geq \cdots \geq b_m$. We use the notation $P = (b_1, b_2, \ldots, b_m)$ to denote the processors and their speeds. In this section we consider the problem of determining a minimal-length preemptive schedule for a set of independent tasks. (The spectre of "hard" combinatorial problems precludes consideration of minimal-length non-preemptive schedules.) Consider a set of independent tasks with execution requirements $\tau_1 \geq \tau_2 \geq \cdots \geq \tau_n$. Just as for the processors, we use $\mathcal{T} = (\tau_1, \tau_2, \ldots, \tau_n)$ to denote the tasks and their service requirements. Task T_i executes at rate b_j on processor P_j.

Suppose we have to schedule $\mathcal{T} = (8, 7)$ on $P = (2, 1)$. Task T_1 requires 4 time units on P_1. If T_1 is assigned to P_1 and T_2 to P_2, as in Fig. 2.18a, we get a schedule of length 7. A shorter schedule can be obtained by slowing down execution of T_1 and speeding up T_2, as in Fig. 2.18b. An interesting special case is one in which $P = (b_1, b_2, \ldots, b_m)$ and we have m tasks each with execution requirement of τ. In some sense, having all tasks finish at the same time requires that they be executed at the same average rate. The approach in Fig. 2.18b can again be used.

Definition Since we now begin to discuss the collective processing capacity of a set of processors, define $B_j = \Sigma_{i=1}^{j} b_i$, for all j, $1 \leq j \leq m$. Similarly, let $X_j = \Sigma_{i=1}^{j} \tau_i$, for all j, $1 \leq j \leq n$.

Using the notation just defined, Algorithm 2.4 in Section 2.5 for scheduling independent tasks on identical processors, constructed a schedule of length $\omega = \max(\tau_1, X_n / B_m)$. Note that X_n / B_m corresponds to a schedule with no idle time and is still a lower bound on the schedule length. However, as Fig. 2.18 shows, we have to be careful in choosing the analog of τ_1 when the processors are not identical.

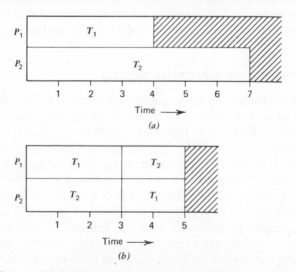

Figure 2.18 Processor P_1 is twice as fast as processor P_2. The execution times of T_1 and T_2 are 8 and 7 units, respectively.

Consider $\mathcal{T} = (\tau_1, \tau_2, \ldots, \tau_n)$ scheduled on $P = (b_1, b_2, \ldots, b_m)$. Since each task can be executed by at most one processor at a time, a schedule will be at least τ_1/b_1 time units long. Task T_1 would take longer on any other processor. If the second processor is significantly slower than the first, it is possible that τ_2/b_2 is longer than τ_1/b_1. As in Fig. 2.18b, we can average the execution of the two tasks. The total execution requirement is $X_2 = \tau_1 + \tau_2$. The processing capacity is $B_2 = b_1 + b_2$. Thus the average schedule will be at least X_2/B_2 units long. In general we have to consider $\max_j X_j/B_j$ as a lower bound on the schedule length, since τ_3/b_3 may be longer than X_2/B_2, and so on.

The algorithm we give constructs a schedule of length ω,

$$\omega = \max \left[\max_{1 \le j \le m} \left(\frac{X_j}{B_j} \right), \frac{X_n}{B_m} \right]$$

From the foregoing discussion, this value of ω can be seen to be optimal. The algorithm is a slight modification of Algorithm 2.5 in Section 2.6 that constructed processor-shared schedules for trees on m identical processors.

Algorithm 2.6   Consider a set of independent tasks $\mathcal{T} = (\tau_1, \tau_2, \ldots, \tau_n)$ to be scheduled on $P = (b_1, b_2, \ldots, b_m)$. Recall that $\tau_1 \ge \tau_2 \ge \cdots \ge \tau_n$ and $b_1 \ge b_2 \ge \cdots \ge b_m$. This algorithm determines a minimal-length preemptive schedule for the tasks on P. The algorithm may also be used to construct schedules for arbitrary task systems.

1. The *level* of a task at any point is the execution requirement of the unexecuted portion of the task. Let j be the number of unassigned processors, and let k be the number of tasks at the highest level. If $k \le j$, assign the k tasks to be executed at the same rate on the fastest k processors. Otherwise assign the k tasks onto the j processors. If there are any processors left, consider the tasks at the next highest level, and so on.

2. Reassign all processors to the unexecuted portion of the task system whenever one of the following occurs:

Event 1:   A task is finished.

Event 2:   A point is reached at which continuing with the present assignment implies that (in the unexecuted portion of the task system) a task at a lower level is being executed at a faster rate than a task at a higher level.

3. To construct a preemptive schedule from the shared schedule, reassign the portion of the schedule between every pair of events. If k tasks have been sharing k processors, assign the tasks to execute at the same average rate in the k processors (see Fig. 2.19).

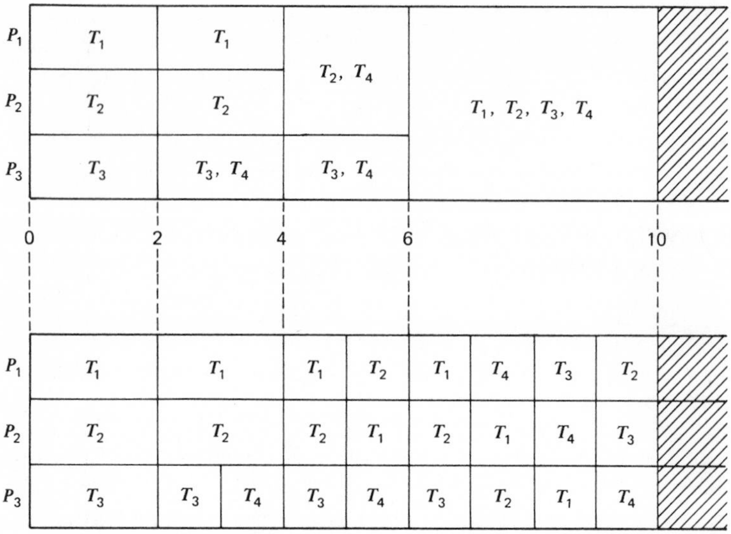

Figure 2.19   Task system $\mathcal{T} = (41, 25, 13, 11)$ scheduled on $\mathbf{P} = (6, 2, 1)$.

If k tasks have been sharing j processors, $k > j$, let each of the k tasks have an execution requirement of τ in the interval. Let b be the speed of the slowest among the j processors. If τ/b is less than the length of the interval, the tasks can be assigned as in Algorithm 2.4, ignoring the different speeds of the processors. Otherwise divide the interval into k equal subintervals. Assign the k tasks so that each task occurs in exactly j intervals, each time on a different processor. An example of four tasks assigned to three processors occurs in the time interval $(6, 10)$ in Fig. 2.19.

Figure 2.19 gives an example of a task system scheduled according to Algorithm 2.6.

Theorem 2.11   Algorithm 2.6 constructs a minimal-length preemptive schedule for the set of independent tasks $\mathcal{T} = (\tau_1, \tau_2, \ldots, \tau_n)$ on the processing system $\mathbf{P} = (b_1, b_2, \ldots, b_m)$.

Proof   If there is no idle time in the shared schedule constructed by the algorithm, it is optimal, and $\omega = X_n/b_m$.

Suppose P_i is the fastest processor on which there is idle time. Then the last task to finish on P_i is at a lower level than the tasks that have yet to finish on $P_1, P_2, \ldots, P_{i-1}$. It follows from the algorithm that as time increases, the level of tasks being executed decreases. Hence $P_1, P_2, \ldots, P_{i-1}$ have been executing $T_1, T_2, \ldots, T_{i-1}$ from the beginning of the schedule. Since there is no idle time on $P_1, P_2, \ldots, P_{i-1}$, tasks $T_1, T_2, \ldots, T_{i-1}$ finish at the same time. It follows that the length of the schedule is X_{i-1}/B_{i-1}. Note that if any of the tasks $T_1, T_2, \ldots, T_{i-1}$ is ever assigned to a processor slower than P_{i-1}, the schedule becomes even longer.

It is easy to see that the shared schedule is transformed into a valid preemptive schedule. The algorithm therefore constructs an optimal schedule for $\mathcal{T}$ on P.   ◼

Note that Algorithm 2.6 can also be applied to trees and dags. On two processors it is expected to construct optimal schedules, since idle time can only occur on the slow processor. With trees on three or more processors, Algorithm 2.6 is not optimal. Consider a tree with tasks at three levels as in Fig. 2.20, scheduled on a processing system with $b_1 = \sqrt{m} + 1$ and $b_i = 1$ for all i, $2 \le i \le m$. Let there be $\sqrt{m}$ tasks $V_1, V_2, \ldots, V_{\sqrt{m}}$ at the level just above the root. In Fig. 2.20 $m = 9$, thus $\sqrt{m} = 3$. The execution times are chosen so that the resultant schedules look like the ones in Fig. 2.20. As m increases, the ratio of the level by level to an optimal schedule becomes 2 in the limit.

2.9   THE FLOW-SHOP PROBLEM

During its passage through a computer system, a program is processed by a number of distinct machines. Since all programs pass through the input, execution, and output phases, a task system can be viewed as a set of chains of m tasks, where the ith task in the chain must be executed on processor P_i. Determining a minimal-length schedule in such a situation is referred to as the *flow-shop problem*. We give an algorithm to determine minimal-length schedules when $m = 2$. For larger values of m the problem is known to be NP-complete. (See Chapter 1.)

For the two-processor flow-shop problem let the task system $(\mathcal{T}, <)$ consist of n chains $C_1, C_2, \ldots, C_n$, where each chain C_i has two tasks A_i and B_i, $A_i < B_i$. Task A_i must be executed for α_i time units on processor P_1, and once A_i has finished, task B_i must be executed for β_i units on processor P_2. Figure 2.21 contains an example.

In Fig. 2.21 tasks $B_1, B_2, \ldots, B_n$ are executed on P_2 in the same order as $A_1, A_2, \ldots, A_n$ are executed on P_1. We show that in general we can restrict attention to schedules in which if A_i is executed before A_j, then B_i is executed before B_j.

Definition   Let S be a flow-shop schedule on two processors for a set of chains $C_1, C_2, \ldots, C_n$. Chain C_i is said to *precede* chain C_j if and only if A_i is executed before A_j and B_i is executed before B_j.

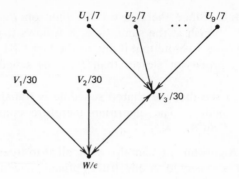

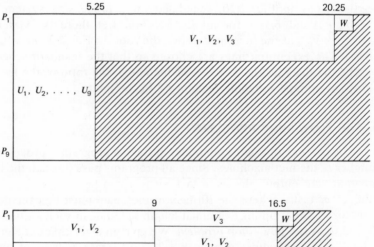

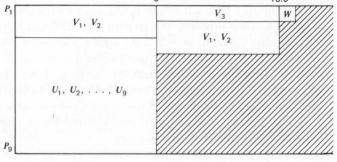

Figure 2.20 Algorithm 2.6 is not optimal for trees on three or more processors. In this example, $b_1 = 4$, $b_2 = b_3 = \cdots b_9 = 1$.

Lemma 2.8 Let S be a flow-shop schedule on two processors for a set of chains $C_1, C_2, \ldots, C_n$. Then we can construct a schedule no longer than S in which for each pair of chains C_i and C_j either C_i precedes C_j or C_j precedes C_i.

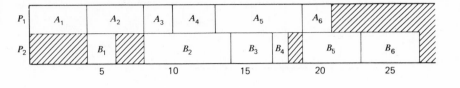

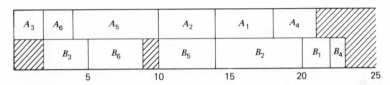

Figure 2.21 Two flow-shop schedules for the chains $C_1, C_2, \ldots, C_6$ as given. The best order is 362514.

Proof Suppose the lemma is false. Then there exist two chains C_i and C_j as in Fig. 2.22a, such that A_i is executed before A_j, but B_j is executed before B_i. Let B_j and B_i be the last such tasks on processor P_2. Clearly we can defer execution of A_i until just after A_j, at the same time executing all tasks between A_i and A_j (including A_j) α_i units earlier, as in Fig. 2.22b. A transformation on schedules that causes tasks to be executed earlier on processor P_1 does not violate the precedence constraints between tasks in a chain. Moreover, A_i is still executed before B_i and we have not lengthened the schedule. The proof follows by induction on the number of such interchanges necessary to produce the desired schedule. ∎

From Lemma 2.8 we have shown that attention can be restricted to schedules that execute tasks $A_1, A_2, \ldots, A_n$ on processor P_1 in the same order as $B_1, B_2, \ldots, B_n$ are executed on P_2. All we have to specify now is the relative order in which the chains $C_1, C_2, \ldots, C_n$ are to be executed.

To acquire a feeling for how to approach the problem, let us examine two chains C_i and C_j. If C_i is executed before C_j as in Fig. 2.23, ω_{ij}, the length of time for which at least one of C_i and C_j is being executed, is given by

$$\omega_{ij} = \alpha_i + \max(\alpha_j, \beta_i) + \beta_j$$

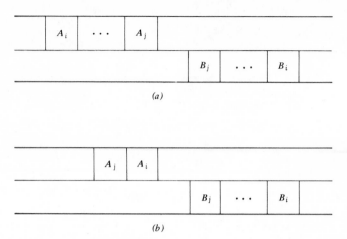

Figure 2.22 If B_j is executed before B_i, we can ensure that A_j is executed before A_i.

Similarly, if ω_{ji} gives the length of the schedule for C_i and C_j when C_j is executed before C_i, we have

$$\omega_{ji} = \alpha_j + \max\,(\alpha_i, \beta_j) + \beta_i$$

The following lemma shows that the condition under which ω_{ji} is shorter than ω_{ij} is $\min\,(\alpha_j, \beta_i) < \min\,(\alpha_i, \beta_j)$.

Lemma 2.9 Let S be a flow-shop schedule on two processors for a set of chains $C_1, C_2, \ldots, C_n$. Let C_i be executed just before chain C_j in S. If $\min\,(\alpha_i, \beta_j) \leq \min\,(\alpha_i, \beta_j)$, the schedule formed by interchanging the order in which C_i and C_j are executed, is no longer than S.

Proof First suppose that C_i and C_j are the first two chains to execute in S. Processor P_1 is free after $\alpha_i + \alpha_j$ units, regardless of the order in which C_i and C_j are executed. Thus we have only to consider the time at which processor P_2 becomes available.

Let ω_{ij} and ω_{ji} be as in the discussion preceding this lemma. We have to show that $\omega_{ij} \geq \omega_{ji}$.

Given $\min\,(\alpha_j, \beta_i) \leq \min\,(\alpha_i, \beta_j)$, we conclude $\max\,(-\alpha_j, -\beta_i)$ $\geq \max\,(-\alpha_i, -\beta_j)$. Adding $\alpha_i + \alpha_j + \beta_i + \beta_j$ to both sides, we get

$$\alpha_i + \beta_j + \max\,(\beta_i, \alpha_j) \geq \alpha_j + \beta_i + \max\,(\beta_j, \alpha_i)$$

The foregoing expressions stand for ω_{ij} and ω_{ji}, giving $\omega_{ij} \geq \omega_{ji}$, which is what we set out to prove.

If C_i and C_j are not the first two chains in the schedule, then as in Fig. 2.23c, d there may be some time interval x, such that B_i may not begin

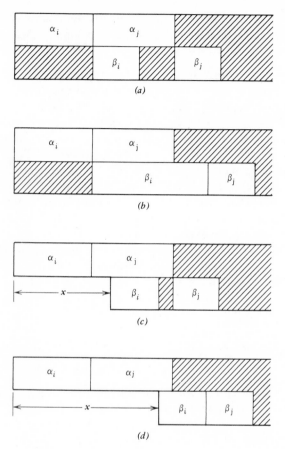

Figure 2.23   Possibilities in executing chains C_i and C_j. In (c) and (d) task β_i may not begin until x time units have elapsed.

until x units have elapsed from the initiation of A_i. If x is small, B_j finishes ω_{ij} units after A_i starts. If x is large, B_j finishes $x + \beta_i + \beta_j$ units later.

Similarly, if C_j is executed before C_i, then B_i finishes max $(\omega_{ji}, x + \beta_i + \beta_j)$ units later. Thus even if the two chains are not the first ones to be executed, interchanging C_j and C_i does not lengthen the schedule.   ∎

As might be expected, the condition in Lemma 2.9 is the basis for an algorithm to determine minimal-length schedules.

Theorem 2.12   Consider a system of n chains $C_i = (A_i, B_i)$, $1 \le i \le n$, for a two-processor flow-shop problem. Let α_i and β_i be the execution times of A_i and B_i on processors P_1 and P_2, respectively. Now a minimal-length schedule can be constructed for the system with chain C_i executed before chain C_j if $\min(\alpha_i, \beta_j) < \min(\alpha_j, \beta_i)$.

Proof Let S be a minimal-length schedule for the system. From Lemma 2.8 we can assume without loss of generality that for all chains C_i and C_j, if A_i is executed before A_j, then B_i is executed before B_j.

If there are any two adjacent chains in S that violate the conditions of the theorem, we can interchange them using Lemma 2.9. We simply need to show that interchanges yield a desired schedule.

Using the condition $\min(\alpha_i, \beta_j) < \min(\alpha_j, \beta_i)$, we can partially order the chains. Ties can be broken at will to yield a total order. It can be shown that interchanging chains as specified by the total order transforms S into a schedule as specified by the theorem. ∎

The two-processor flow-shop problem that we have considered does not encompass the input, execution, and output phases of a computation. Although the three-processor flow-shop problem is NP-complete, there are special cases in which meaningful statements can be made. Let chain C_i now have three tasks with execution times α_i, β_i, and γ_i. Consider, for example, an input-output (I/O) bound system in which the second processor is expected to have a certain amount of idle time. In particular, if $\min(\alpha_i, \alpha_j) \geq \max(\beta_i, \beta_j)$, or if $\min(\gamma_i, \gamma_j) \geq \max(\beta_i, \beta_j)$, we can use

$$\min(\alpha_i + \beta_i, \beta_j + \gamma_j) < \min(\alpha_j + \beta_j, \beta_i + \gamma_i)$$

to place C_i before C_j. Experimental studies [CMM] have shown that even if the system is not I/O bound, the foregoing condition is a reasonable heuristic.

For an application of Theorem 2.12 to the simple job-shop problem see section 1.4.1.

BIBLIOGRAPHICAL NOTES

The level strategy in Section 2.2 is due to T. C. Hu [H]. Fujii, Kasami, and Ninomiya [FKN], Muraoka [Mur], and Coffman and Graham [CG] have given algorithms for determining minimal-length nonpreemptive schedules on two processors for UETs. In [FKN] an undirected graph G is constructed for a task system. An edge (T, T') in G denotes the fact that $T < T'$ and $T' < T$ are both false. A schedule on two processors is then determined from a maximal matching of G. The algorithm does not generalize conveniently to provide heuristics for more than two processors. In [Mur] the problem is approached by first considering "tight" graphs: task systems in which for all tasks T, the sum of the maximal path length from an initial node to T and the level of T is a constant. The algorithm is then extended to general task systems. The exposition is rather long. Algorithm

2.2 follows [CG] since the labelling used to construct optimal schedules on two processors immediately provides a heuristic for $m > 2$ processors.

A different proof for the Coffman-Graham algorithm is given by Misra [M]. In general, the minimal-length schedules constructed by Algorithms 2.1 and 2.2 are not unique. Schindler and Simonsmeier are interested in characterizing the class of all optimal schedules on two processors [SS].

The preemptive scheduling of independent tasks in Section 2.5 follows McNaughton [Mc] and Rothkopf [R]. The notion of processor sharing and level-by-level schedules is due to Muntz and Coffman [MC1, MC2], as are Theorems 2.7 and 2.8. The comparison of the lengths of preemptive and nonpreemptive schedules appears in [CG].

Several authors have considered processors of different speeds. Baer [B2] examines nonpreemptive schedules for two processors of different speeds. He gives an algorithm to determine minimal-length schedules for UET trees when one processor is twice as fast as the other. Liu and Liu [LiL1] give an algorithm for determining minimal-length preemptive schedules for independent tasks on a system with one fast processor. The expression for minimal schedule length in Theorem 2.11 is also due to them. See also [LiL2]. Section 2.8 follows [HSe].

The solution of the two-processor flow-shop problem was discovered by Johnson [Jo]. See also Jackson [Ja1].

CHAPTER THREE

MEAN WEIGHTED FLOW-TIME CRITERION

J. L. BRUNO
THE PENNSYLVANIA STATE UNIVERSITY

3.1 INTRODUCTION

In this chapter we consider scheduling problems for which the cost criterion is the weighted sum of the finishing times of all the tasks receiving service, that is, the mean weighted finishing (or flow) time.*
We treat three versions of this problem:

1. In the first model there is a single machine and a task system with each task having an associated processing time and deferral cost. We obtain efficient algorithms for determining optimal schedules when we restrict the precedence constraints to be a forest.

2. A *job* in the second model consists of an ordered sequence of tasks generated probabilistically by a task system, and a problem is composed of a collection of jobs to be scheduled on a single machine. The processing times and deferral costs are given by random variables, and the cost criterion is the expected value of the sum of the weighted finishing times of all the tasks obtaining service.

3. In the final model we allow more than one machine. The machines themselves are not necessarily identical. We take the deferral costs to be unity and show how this scheduling problem reduces to a transportation problem.

For complexity results concerning flow-time problems, see Chapters 1 and 4.

---

* Note that here, in contrast to the definition for $\bar{\omega}$ in Chapter 1, the weighted sum is not divided by the number n of tasks. It is easily seen that the results for our simpler definition also apply to the definition for $\bar{\omega}$ in Chapter 1.

3.2 THE MODEL

A scheduling problem $\mathscr{P}$ consists of:

1. A task system $(\mathscr{T}, <)$ where $\mathscr{T}$ is an indexed set of $n \geq 0$ tasks and $<$ is a partial order on $\mathscr{T}$. The index set of $\mathscr{T}$ is denoted by $I(\mathscr{P})$ and for each j in $I(\mathscr{P})$, T_j is an element of $\mathscr{T}$.

2. For each j in $I(\mathscr{P})$, a positive number τ_j, which gives the service-time requirement of T_j.

3. For each j in $I(\mathscr{P})$ a real number w_j, called the deferral cost of T_j. There is no restriction on w_j; in particular, it may be negative as well as positive.

Since we assume a single processor, we may restrict our attention to schedules determined by permutations of the task indices. A permutation $\alpha = \alpha_1, \alpha_2, \ldots, \alpha_n$ of the members of $I(\mathscr{P})$ is said to be *consistent* with $<$ (or $\mathscr{P}$) if $T_j < T_{j'}$, implies that $k < k'$ where $\alpha_k = j$ and $\alpha_{k'} = j'$.

The schedule determined by a permutation $\alpha = \alpha_1, \ldots, \alpha_n$ of $I(\mathscr{P})$ is the natural one; that is, task T_{α_1} is processed first, T_{α_2} second, T_{α_3} third, and so on. The mean weighted flow time (mwft) of the schedule determined by α is

$$\text{mwft}(\alpha) = \sum_{j=1}^{n} w_{\alpha_j}\left(\sum_{i=1}^{j} \tau_{\alpha_i}\right)$$

A permutation (sequence, or schedule) α is said to be *optimal* if α is consistent with $\mathscr{P}$ and minimizes the mwft over all permutations consistent with $\mathscr{P}$.

In the absence of any precedence constraints, we can easily characterize optimal permutations. Let $\rho_j = w_j/\tau_j$ for j in $I(\mathscr{P})$.

Theorem 3.1 [Sm] Let $\mathscr{P}$ be a scheduling problem such that $< = \varphi$. Then $\alpha = \alpha_1, \ldots, \alpha_n$ is an optimal permutation with respect to $\mathscr{P}$ if and only if $\rho_{\alpha_1} \geq \rho_{\alpha_2} \geq \cdots \geq \rho_{\alpha_n}$.

Proof This result is obtained by considering any permutation $\beta = \beta_1, \ldots, \beta_n$ and calculating the effect on the mwft of interchanging two adjacent terms β_j and β_{j+1}. The result is to decrease the mwft if and only if $\rho_{\beta_j} < \rho_{\beta_{j+1}}$ and to leave it unchanged if and only if $\rho_{\beta_j} = \rho_{\beta_{j+1}}$. Thus we can conclude Theorem 3.1. (See Section 1.3 for greater detail.) ■

The idea of defining the ratios ρ_j can be extended to the case where $<$ is an arbitrary precedence relation. This leads to an interesting characterization of optimal schedules [Si] and efficient algorithms for constructing optimal schedules for problems with suitably restricted precedence constraints [Ho1, Si].

In the next section we define a function ρ that is a generalization of the ratios ρ_j. The function ρ is defined on nonempty subsets of task indices and is used to determine an ordering on collections of tasks. We also introduce the notions of an initial set and a ρ-maximal set of task indices. The ρ-maximal sets are important since, as the next section demonstrates, the indices in such a set must appear as an uninterrupted sequence in every optimal permutation. Finally, we give a "dual" formulation in terms of final sets and ρ-minimal sets that is used to justify a scheduling algorithm.

3.3 SOME PRELIMINARIES

In this section we generalize the ratios ρ_i of the preceding section to include nonempty subsets of task indices.

Let $U \subseteq I(\mathcal{P})$ and $U \neq \varphi$. Define $\tau(U)$, $w(U)$, and $\rho(U)$ as

$$\tau(U) = \sum_{j \in U} \tau_j$$

$$w(U) = \sum_{j \in U} w_j$$

$$\rho(U) = \frac{w(U)}{\tau(U)}$$

A set $U \subseteq I(\mathcal{P})$ is called an *initial set* with respect to $\mathcal{P}$ if

1. $U \neq \varphi$, and
2. if $T_j < T_{j'}$, then $j \notin U$ implies $j' \notin U$.

For example, the sets $\{1\}$, $\{1, 2, 3\}$, $\{1, 2, 4\}$, and $\{1, 2, 3, 4, 6\}$ are some of the initial sets with respect to the task system in Fig. 3.1. Let $\mathcal{I}$ denote the

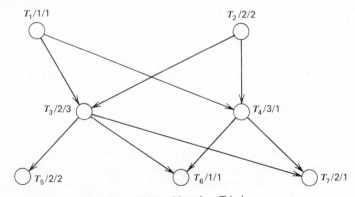

Figure 3.1 Scheduling problem: Notation $T_j/\tau_j/\omega_j$.

class of initial sets (with respect to $\mathcal{P}$). Define the number ρ^* as

$$\rho^* = \max_{U \in \mathcal{I}} \rho(U)$$

We say that a set $U \subseteq I(\mathcal{P})$ is a ρ-*maximal set* with respect to $\mathcal{P}$ if

1. $U \in \mathcal{I}$,
2. $\rho(U) = \rho^*$, and
3. if $V \in \mathcal{I}$, $\rho(V) = \rho^*$ and $V \subseteq U$, then $V = U$.

The value of ρ^* for the scheduling problem depicted in Fig. 3.1 is 6/5 and this value is attained by $U = \{1, 2, 3\}$; U is also a ρ-maximal set.

Very often we must restrict our attention to a subset of the tasks in a scheduling problem $\mathcal{P}$ and calculate ρ-maximal sets for the restricted problem. Let $U \subseteq I(\mathcal{P})$ and define $\mathcal{T}/U$ and $</U$ as

$$\mathcal{T}/U = \{T_j | T_j \in \mathcal{T} \qquad \text{and} \quad j \in U\}$$

and

$$</U = \{(T_i, T_j) | (T_i, T_j) \in <, i \in U \text{ and } j \in U\}$$

The scheduling problem $\mathcal{P}/U$ is obtained from $\mathcal{P}$ by restricting our attention to the task system $(\mathcal{T}/U, </U)$ where $(\mathcal{T}, <)$ is the task system for $\mathcal{P}$.

In this regard we also have occasion to consider permutations of subsets of $I(\mathcal{P})$. Let $U \subseteq I(\mathcal{P})$ and $\alpha = \alpha_1, \ldots, \alpha_k$ be a permutation of a subset of $I(\mathcal{P})$. Then α/U is the permutation of the subset of U formed by taking the subsequence of α consisting of only those terms in U. For example, if $U = \{2, 3, 4, 5\}$ and $\alpha = 1, 2, 8, 5, 6, 3$, then $\alpha/U = 2, 5, 3$. Let λ denote the null permutation; that is, if α is any permutation, $\alpha/\varphi = \lambda$.

The restriction of permutations is commutative. Thus if U and V are any two subsets of $I(\mathcal{P})$ and α any permutation of a subset of $I(\mathcal{P})$, then $\alpha/U/V = \alpha/V/U = \alpha/U \cap V$.

Let α and β be two permutations. Then the composition α, β of α and β is just the sequence consisting of α followed by β. Suppose $\alpha = 2, 3, 7$ and $\beta = 4, 5, 6, 1$, then $\alpha, \beta = 2, 3, 7, 4, 5, 6, 1$; $\beta, \alpha = 4, 5, 6, 1, 2, 3, 7$; and $\alpha, \lambda = \lambda, \alpha = 2, 3, 7$.

In evaluating expressions of the form $\alpha/U, \beta/V$, the operator $/$ takes precedence over composition of permutations and thus $\alpha/U, \beta/V = \alpha/U, (\beta/V)$.

We now give a series of lemmas expounding the properties of the function ρ and the ρ-maximal sets that are needed in subsequent sections.

If $U \subseteq I(\mathcal{P})$, let $\bar{U}$ denote the set $I(\mathcal{P}) - U$. If α is a permutation that is consistent with $\mathcal{P}$, then $\mathrm{mwft}(\alpha/U)$ is the mean weighted flow time of α/U with respect to $\mathcal{P}/U$.

Lemma 3.1 Let $\mathcal{P}$ be a scheduling problem and α a permutation of $I(\mathcal{P})$ consistent with $\mathcal{P}$. If U is a subset of $I(\mathcal{P})$ such that $\alpha = \alpha/U, \alpha/\bar{U}$, then $\mathrm{mwft}(\alpha) = \mathrm{mwft}(\alpha/U) + \mathrm{mwft}(\alpha/\bar{U}) + w(\bar{U})\tau(U)$.

Proof Let $k = |U|$.

$$
\begin{aligned}
\mathrm{mwft}(\alpha) &= \sum_{j=1}^{n} w_{\alpha_j}\left(\sum_{i=1}^{j} \tau_{\alpha_i}\right) \\
&= \sum_{j=1}^{k} w_{\alpha_j}\left(\sum_{i=1}^{j} \tau_{\alpha_i}\right) + \sum_{j=k+1}^{n} w_{\alpha_j}\left(\sum_{i=1}^{j} \tau_{\alpha_i}\right) \\
&= \mathrm{mwft}(\alpha/U) + \sum_{j=k+1}^{n} w_{\alpha_j}\left(\sum_{i=k+1}^{j} \tau_{\alpha_i} + \sum_{i=1}^{k} \tau_{\alpha_i}\right) \\
&= \mathrm{mwft}(\alpha/U) + \mathrm{mwft}(\alpha/\bar{U}) + w(\bar{U})\tau(U)
\end{aligned}
$$

It follows from Lemma 3.1 that if α is optimal with respect to $\mathcal{P}$ and $\alpha = \alpha/U, \alpha/\bar{U}$, then α/U is optimal with respect to $\mathcal{P}/U$ and $\alpha/\bar{U}$ is optimal with respect to $\mathcal{P}/\bar{U}$. The converse is not necessarily true.

Lemma 3.2 Let $\mathcal{P}$ be a scheduling problem and U, U_1, and U_2 be subsets of $I(\mathcal{P})$ such that $U = U_1 \cup U_2$, $U_1 \cap U_2 = \varphi$, $U_1 \neq \varphi$ and $U_2 \neq \varphi$. Then

$$
\rho(U) = \frac{\tau(U_1)}{\tau(U)}\rho(U_1) + \frac{\tau(U_2)}{\tau(U)}\rho(U_2)
$$

Proof

$$
\begin{aligned}
\rho(U) &= \frac{w(U)}{\tau(U)} \\
&= \frac{w(U_1) + w(U_2)}{\tau(U)} \\
&= \frac{\tau(U_1)}{\tau(U)}\rho(U_1) + \frac{\tau(U_2)}{\tau(U)}\rho(U_2) \quad \blacksquare
\end{aligned}
$$

Lemma 3.2 tells us that $\rho(U)$ is a convex combination of $\rho(U_1)$ and $\rho(U_2)$; that is, $\rho(U) = \eta\rho(U_1) + (1 - \eta)\rho(U_2)$, where $0 < \eta < 1$. Therefore, if $\rho(U_1) < \rho(U_2)$ then $\rho(U_1) < \rho(U) < \rho(U_2)$; if $\rho(U_2) < \rho(U_1)$, then $\rho(U_2) < \rho(U) < \rho(U_1)$; and if $\rho(U_1) = \rho(U_2)$, then $\rho(U) = \rho(U_1)$.

Lemma 3.3 (Adjacent interchange) Let $\mathcal{P}$ be a problem and α and β two permutations of $I(\mathcal{P})$ consistent with $\mathcal{P}$, such that $\alpha = \alpha/U, \alpha/V_1, \alpha/V_2, \alpha/W$ and $\beta = \alpha/U, \alpha/V_2, \alpha/V_1, \alpha/W$, where U, V_1, V_2 and W are disjoint sets, $V_1 \neq \varphi$ and $V_2 \neq \varphi$. Then $\mathrm{mwft}(\alpha) \leq \mathrm{mwft}(\beta)$ if and only if $\rho(V_1) \geq \rho(V_2)$.

Proof It is easy to calculate $\mathrm{mwft}(\beta)$ in terms of $\mathrm{mwft}(\alpha)$, namely:

$$
\begin{aligned}
\mathrm{mwft}(\beta) &= \mathrm{mwft}(\alpha) + w(V_1)\tau(V_2) - w(V_2)\tau(V_1) \\
&= \mathrm{mwft}(\alpha) + \tau(V_2)\tau(V_1)[\rho(V_1) - \rho(V_2)]
\end{aligned}
$$

Accordingly, $\mathrm{mwft}(\beta) - \mathrm{mwft}(\alpha) = \tau(V_2)\tau(V_1)[\rho(V_1) - \rho(V_2)]$

and the theorem follows, since $\tau(V_2)\tau(V_1) > 0$. ∎

Lemma 3.4   Let U and V be two distinct ρ-maximal sets with respect to $\mathcal{P}$. Then $U \cap V = \varphi$.

Proof   Let $W = U \cap V$ and assume $W \neq \varphi$. W is an initial set and since U is ρ-maximal, we conclude by Lemma 3.2 that $\rho(W) < \rho^*$. Therefore by Lemma 3.2 we find that $\rho(U - W) > \rho^*$. Again by Lemma 3.2 we write $\rho(U \cup V) = \eta\rho(U - W) + (1 - \eta)\rho(V)$, where $0 < \eta < 1$; therefore $\rho(U \cup V) > \rho^*$. This is a contradiction, since $U \cup V$ is an initial set. ∎

The following lemmas show that ρ-maximal sets provide an insight into the structure of optimal schedules.

Lemma 3.5   If U is a ρ-maximal set with respect to $\mathcal{P}$, then U occurs as an uninterrupted sequence in every optimal permutation for $\mathcal{P}$.

Proof   We first show that U must appear as an uninterrupted sequence in every optimal permutation of a related problem $\mathcal{P}'$, chosen such that the optimal permutations with respect to $\mathcal{P}$ form a subcollection of the optimal permutations with respect to $\mathcal{P}'$; thus the lemma will follow.
   Let

$$<' = < - \{(T_i, T_j) | (T_i, T_j) \in <   \quad \text{and} \quad T_i \in U \quad \text{and} \quad T_j \notin U\}$$

The specification of $\mathcal{P}'$ is exactly the same as $\mathcal{P}$ except we replace $<$ by $<'$. Clearly every permutation compatible with $\mathcal{P}$ is compatible with $\mathcal{P}'$. Later we show that there is an optimal permutation with respect to $\mathcal{P}'$ which is compatible with $\mathcal{P}$; thus every optimal permutation for $\mathcal{P}$ will be optimal for $\mathcal{P}'$.
   Let α be an optimal permutation with respect to $\mathcal{P}'$. We can show that U appears as an uninterrupted sequence in α. Assume the contrary; that is, α is of the form

$$\alpha = \alpha/V_1, \alpha/U_1, \alpha/V_2, \alpha/U_2, \ldots, \alpha/V_r, \alpha/U_r, \alpha/V_{r+1}$$

where all the sets V_i, U_i are pairwise disjoint, $r > 1$, none are empty except possibly for V_1 and V_{r+1}, and $U = \bigcup_{i=1}^{r} U_i$.
   Let $k = \min\{j | \text{ for all } 1 \leq i \leq r, \rho(U_j) \geq \rho(U_i)\}$. The value of k must be greater than 1, since otherwise, using Lemma 3.2, we obtain a contradiction of the ρ-maximality of U. Thus we are able to write $\rho(U_{k-1}) < \rho(U_k)$. Furthermore, $\rho(V_k) \geq \rho(U_k)$, since if we assume the contrary, we could use Lemma 3.3 to show that α is not optimal with respect to $\mathcal{P}'$. Using these facts and Lemma 3.3, we can exchange α/U_{k-1} and α/V_k in α to obtain a new permutation α' such that $\mathrm{mwft}(\alpha') < \mathrm{mwft}(\alpha)$. This con-

tradicts the optimality of α with respect to $\mathcal{P}'$, allowing us to conclude that U must appear as an uninterrupted sequence in every optimal permutation for $\mathcal{P}'$.

It remains to show that there is an optimal permutation of $\mathcal{P}'$ that is also optimal for $\mathcal{P}$. Let α be an optimal permutation with respect to $\mathcal{P}'$, where $\alpha = \alpha/V, \alpha/U, \alpha/W$. If $V = \varphi$, we are done. Therefore, assume $V \neq \varphi$. Clearly, $\alpha' = \alpha/U, \alpha/V, \alpha/W$ is compatible with $\mathcal{P}$ and $\mathcal{P}'$. By Lemma 3.3 and the optimality of α, we can assume that $\rho(V) \geq \rho(U)$. Assume $\rho(V) > \rho(U)$. Using Lemma 3.2, we get $\rho(U \cup V) > \rho(U)$. But this is impossible, since $U \cup V$ is an initial set with respect to $\mathcal{P}$. Consequently, we can assume that $\rho(V) = \rho(U)$ and thus, by Lemma 3.3, $\text{mwft}(\alpha') = \text{mwft}(\alpha)$. ∎

Lemma 3.6 If U is a ρ-maximal set with respect to $\mathcal{P}$, there is an optimal permutation α for $\mathcal{P}$ such that $\alpha = \alpha/U, \alpha/\bar{U}$.

Proof See proof of Lemma 3.5. ∎

Lemma 3.7 If α is an optimal permutation with respect to $\mathcal{P}$, then α can always be expressed in the form $\alpha = \alpha/U, \alpha/\bar{U}$, where U is some ρ-maximal set with respect to $\mathcal{P}$.

Proof Let U be the ρ-maximal set which occurs earliest in α. Then by Lemma 3.5 we can write α as $\alpha/V, \alpha/U, \alpha/W$. If $V \neq \varphi$, since V is an initial set, $\rho(V) \leq \rho(U)$. Using Lemma 3.3, we can rule out $\rho(V) < \rho(U)$. Consequently, $\rho(V) = \rho(U)$ and either V is a ρ-maximal or it contains ρ-maximal set. This contradicts our choice of U; thus $V = \varphi$. ∎

The developments of this section may be carried out in a dual manner, as follows.

A set $U \subseteq I(\mathcal{P})$ is called a *final set* with respect to $\mathcal{P}$ if

1. $U \neq \varphi$, and
2. if $T_j < T_{j'}$, then $j' \notin U$.

Let $\mathcal{F}$ denote the class of final sets with respect to $\mathcal{P}$ and define ρ_* as

$$\rho_* = \min_{U \in \mathcal{F}} \rho(U)$$

We say that a set U is a ρ-*minimal* set with respect to $\mathcal{P}$ if

1. $U \in \mathcal{F}$,
2. $\rho(U) = \rho_*$, and
3. if $V \in \mathcal{F}$, $\rho(V) = \rho_*$ and $V \subseteq U$ then $V = U$.

All the lemmas of this section which refer to ρ-maximal sets have appropriate dual formulations in terms of ρ-minimal sets. In addition we have Lemma 3.8.

Lemma 3.8 Let U be a ρ-maximal set and V a ρ-minimal set with respect to $\mathcal{P}$. If $U \neq V$, then $U \cap V = \varphi$.

Proof Let $W = U \cap V$. Assume $W \neq \varphi$. Then

$$\rho(U) = \eta\rho(U - W) + (1 - \eta)\rho(W)$$

where $0 < \eta < 1$, and

$$\rho(V) = \gamma\rho(V - W) + (1 - \gamma)\rho(W),$$

where $0 < \gamma < 1$. Since W is contained in both an initial and a final set, the sets $U - W$ and $V - W$ are initial and final sets, respectively. Accordingly, $\rho(U - W) < \rho^*$ and $\rho(V - W) > \rho_*$. Thus $\rho(W) > \rho^* \geq \rho_* > \rho(W)$. We are forced to conclude that $W = \varphi$. In the proof we have assumed both $U - V$ and $V - U$ are non-empty. The proof goes through if just one is empty. ◼

3.4 ALGORITHMS

A precedence relation $<$ is a *terminally rooted forest* (trf) if each vertex in the precedence graph for $<$ has no more than one immediate successor. We say that $<$ is an *initially rooted forest* (irf) if each vertex in the precedence graph for $<$ has no more than one immediate predecessor. In this section we give efficient algorithms that find optimal schedules for problems with either trf or irf precedence constraints. The trf problem is treated first and then we use duality to justify the scheduling algorithm in the irf case. We also give an algorithm for the case of a scheduling problem that may be decomposed into two or more "independent" problems.

Let $\mathcal{P}$ be a scheduling problem such that $<$ is a terminally rooted forest (more simply, we say that $\mathcal{P}$ is trf). Using Lemma 3.2 and the definition of a ρ-maximal set, it can be shown that we need not consider all the initial sets of $\mathcal{P}$ to determine a ρ-maximal set with respect to $\mathcal{P}$; in fact, we need only consider n of them, where n is the number of tasks.

Let H_j be the set consisting of j and all task indices i such that $T_i < T_j$.

Lemma 3.9 Let $\mathcal{P}$ be a trf scheduling problem and let U be a ρ-maximal set with respect to $\mathcal{P}$. Then $U = H_j$ for some $j \in I(\mathcal{P})$.

Proof Let l be the index of a task in U such that no successor task of T_l has its index in U. We claim that $U = H_l$. Clearly, $H_l \subseteq U$. Let $V = U - H_l$ and suppose $V \neq \varphi$. Now we claim that V is an initial set. Suppose the contrary. Then $H_l < V$.* But this is impossible because there are no successors of T_l in U, and by the trf property and the definition of H_l, no member of H_l has a successor in U. Therefore V is an initial set and U is the union of two disjoint initial sets. This contradicts the ρ-maximality of U; therefore $V = \varphi$. ∎

Informally, the construction of an optimal permutation for a trf scheduling problem $\mathcal{P}$ can be organized as follows: associate with each task T_j the number $\rho(H_j)$ and determine an index l such that $\rho(H_l) \geq \rho(H_j)$ for $j \in I(\mathcal{P})$ and for all indices $j \neq l$ in H_l, $\rho(H_l) > \rho(H_j)$. Since T_l is a successor of every other task with index in H_l, there exists an optimal permutation α with respect to $\mathcal{P}$ such that

$$\alpha = \alpha/(H_l - \{l\}), l, \alpha/(I(\mathcal{P}) - H_l).$$

Thus our problem may be "factored" into two smaller problems $\mathcal{P}/(H_l - \{l\})$ and $\mathcal{P}/(I(\mathcal{P}) - H_l)$.

Algorithm 3.1

Input: $\mathcal{P}$, a trf scheduling problem
Output: an optimal permutation for $\mathcal{P}$
Method:
procedure TRF($\mathcal{P}$)
begin
   if $\mathcal{P}$ is empty **then return** λ
   else
   begin
      Let l be an index of a task in $\mathcal{P}$ such that H_l is a ρ-maximal set for $\mathcal{P}$
      $U := H_l - \{l\}$; $V := I(\mathcal{P}) - H_l$
      return TRF($\mathcal{P}/U$), l, TRF($\mathcal{P}/V$)
   end
end TRF

Procedure TRF is recursive—it has one input parameter, a trf scheduling problem, and it returns a value, namely, an optimal permutation with respect to the input scheduling problem. Execution of the statement **return** ⟨expression⟩ in a procedure causes ⟨expression⟩ to be evaluated and this value to be returned to the point of call of the procedure. The computation evoked by TRF may not be unique because there may be more than one ρ-maximal set to choose from. Regardless of the choice, however, TRF obtains an optimal permutation.

Theorem 3.2   Let $\mathcal{P}$ be a trf scheduling problem. Then α is an optimal permutation for $\mathcal{P}$ if and only if α can be obtained by applying TRF to $\mathcal{P}$.

* Let U and V be subsets of $I(\mathcal{P})$. We write $U < V$ if there exists a pair of tasks T_i and T_j such that $T_i < T_j$, $i \in U$ and $j \in V$.

Proof We proceed by induction on n, the number of tasks in $\mathcal{P}$. The theorem is easily seen to be true when $n = 1$. Let n be some integer greater than 1 and assume the theorem is true for all scheduling problems smaller than n. Let $\mathcal{P}$ be a scheduling problem with n tasks and let α be generated by TRF. We can write α as $\alpha = \alpha/U, l, \alpha/V$, where U, V, and l are determined by TRF and $U \cup \{l\}$ is a ρ-maximal set. And by Lemma 3.6 there is an optimal permutation $\beta = \beta/(U \cup \{l\}), \beta/V$. Since T_l is a successor of all tasks with indices in U, we may write $\beta = \beta/U, l, \beta/V$, where β/U is an optimal permutation for $\mathcal{P}/U$ and β/V is an optimal permutation for $\mathcal{P}/V$. By induction, α/U and α/V are optimal permutations for $\mathcal{P}/U$ and $\mathcal{P}/V$, respectively. Therefore α is an optimal permutation for $\mathcal{P}$.

Let β be any optimal permutation for $\mathcal{P}$. By Lemma 3.7, we can write β in the form $\beta = \beta/U, \beta/\bar{U}$ where U is a ρ-maximal set with respect to $\mathcal{P}$. By Lemma 3.9 there exists an l such that $H_l = U$. Therefore TRF can generate a permutation α of the form $\mathrm{TRF}(\mathcal{P}/U - \{l\}), l, \mathrm{TRF}(\mathcal{P}/\bar{U})$. Clearly, β can be written as $\beta = \beta/(U - \{l\}), l, \beta/\bar{U}$. Finally, using the inductive hypothesis, we conclude that TRF is capable of producing the permutation β. ∎

The asymptotic running time of any reasonable implementation of TRF is easily analyzed: let T_j be a task in $\mathcal{P}$ and let $T_{i_1}, \ldots, T_{i_k}$ be the immediate predecessors of T_j. We have

$$\rho(H_j) = \frac{w(H_j)}{\tau(H_j)} = \frac{w_j + \sum_{p=1}^{k} w(H_{i_p})}{\tau_j + \sum_{p=1}^{k} \tau(H_{i_p})}$$

We can arrange to traverse the precedence graph of $<$ in such a way that for each task T_j, the values of w and τ are known for the sets $H_{i_1}, \ldots, H_{i_k}$ before we visit T_j[Kn]. Therefore in $O(n)$ time $\rho(H_j)$ can be calculated for all tasks in $\mathcal{P}$. This determines the position of at least one task in an optimal schedule, and since it takes no more than $O(n)$ time to determine the position of each of the remaining tasks, the worst-case time complexity of TRF is $O(n^2)$.

Let $\mathcal{P}$ be an irf scheduling problem and K_j be the set consisting of j and all task indices i such that $T_j < T_i$. The following lemma shows that the irf scheduling problems are dual to the trf scheduling problems.

Lemma 3.10 Let $\mathcal{P}$ be an irf scheduling problem and let U be a ρ-minimal set with respect to $\mathcal{P}$. Then $U = K_j$ for some $j \in I(\mathcal{P})$.

Proof The argument is dual to that given for Lemma 3.9. ∎

Algorithm 3.2

Input: $\mathscr{P}$, an irf scheduling problem
Output: an optimal permutation for $\mathscr{P}$
Method:
procedure IRF($\mathscr{P}$)
begin
  if $\mathscr{P}$ is empty, **return** λ
  else
  begin
    Let l be an index of a task in $\mathscr{P}$ such that K_l is a ρ-minimal set for $\mathscr{P}$
    $U := K_l - \{l\};\ \ V := I(\mathscr{P}) - K_l$
    return   IRF($\mathscr{P}/V$), l, IRF($\mathscr{P}/U$)
  end
end IRF

Theorem 3.3 Let $\mathscr{P}$ be an irf scheduling problem. Then α is an optimal permutation for $\mathscr{P}$ if and only if it can be obtained by applying IRF to $\mathscr{P}$.

Proof The argument is dual to that given for Theorem 3.2. ◼

Let $\mathscr{P}$ be a scheduling problem and suppose there exists a partition of $I(\mathscr{P})$ into two nonempty sets U_1 and U_2 such that $< = </U_1 \cup </U_2$. Then we write $\mathscr{P} = \mathscr{P}_1 \| \mathscr{P}_2$ where $\mathscr{P}_i = \mathscr{P}/U_i, i = 1, 2$. Informally, $\mathscr{P}$ can be viewed as consisting of two independent (parallel) task systems $\mathscr{P}_1$ and $\mathscr{P}_2$.

The following lemmas reveal some of the important properties of the foregoing decomposition and form the basis of the correctness of the next algorithm.

Lemma 3.11 Let $\mathscr{P}$ be a scheduling problem such that $\mathscr{P} = \mathscr{P}_1 \| \mathscr{P}_2$. If U is a ρ-maximal (minimal) set with respect to $\mathscr{P}$, then U is a ρ-maximal (minimal) set with respect to either $\mathscr{P}_1$ or $\mathscr{P}_2$. Moreover, if V_1 and V_2 are ρ-maximal (minimal) sets for $\mathscr{P}_1$ and $\mathscr{P}_2$, respectively, at least one of V_1 or V_2 is a ρ-maximal (minimal) set for $\mathscr{P}$.

Proof The lemma is easily established using Lemma 3.2 as the main tool. ◼

Lemma 3.12 Let $\mathscr{P}$ be a scheduling problem such that $\mathscr{P} = \mathscr{P}_1 \| \mathscr{P}_2$. Let U_1 and U_2 be the sets of task indices for $\mathscr{P}_1$ and $\mathscr{P}_2$, respectively. If α is an optimal permutation with respect to $\mathscr{P}$, then α/U_1 and α/U_2 are optimal permutations with respect to $\mathscr{P}_1$ and $\mathscr{P}_2$, respectively. Moreover, if α_1 and α_2 are optimal for $\mathscr{P}_1$ and $\mathscr{P}_2$, there exists an optimal permutation α with respect to $\mathscr{P}$ such that $\alpha/U_1 = \alpha_1$ and $\alpha/U_2 = \alpha_2$.

Proof By induction on n, the number of tasks in $\mathcal{P}$. The theorem is trivially true for $n = 1$. Let $n > 1$ and α be an optimal permutation with respect to $\mathcal{P}$. By Lemma 3.7, we can write α as $\alpha = \alpha/U, \alpha/\bar{U}$ where U is a ρ-maximal set for $\mathcal{P}$ and by the previous lemma, U is a ρ-maximal set for either $\mathcal{P}_1$ or $\mathcal{P}_2$, say $\mathcal{P}_1$. By induction, α/U_2 is optimal with respect to $\mathcal{P}_2$, and $\alpha/(U_1 - U)$ is optimal with respect to $\mathcal{P}_1/(U_1 - U)$. Using Lemma 3.6 we conclude that $\alpha/U, \alpha/(U_1 - U) = \alpha/U_1$ is optimal with respect to $\mathcal{P}_1$.

Let α_1 and α_2 be optimal permutations with respect to $\mathcal{P}_1$ and $\mathcal{P}_2$, respectively. Without loss of generality, assume $\alpha_1 = \alpha_1/U, \alpha_1/(U_1 - U)$ and U is a ρ-maximal set with respect to $\mathcal{P}$. By Lemma 3.6 there exists an optimal permutation α with respect to $\mathcal{P}$ such that $\alpha = \alpha/U, \alpha/(I(\mathcal{P}) - U) = \alpha_1/U, \alpha/(I(\mathcal{P}) - U)$, using the inductive hypothesis we can further assume that $\alpha/(I(\mathcal{P}) - U)/U_2 = \alpha_2$ and $\alpha/(I(\mathcal{P}) - U)/U_1 = \alpha_1/(U_1 - U)$. ■

The lemmas can easily be generalized to the case where $\mathcal{P}$ can be "decomposed" into more than two problems. The following algorithm capitalizes on such a decomposition to simplify the determination of an optimal permutation.

Algorithm 3.3

Input: a scheduling problem $\mathcal{P}$ such that $\mathcal{P} = \mathcal{P}_1\|\mathcal{P}_2\| \cdots \|\mathcal{P}_k$, where $k > 1$
Output: α an optimal permutation with respect to $\mathcal{P}$
Notation: $<_i$ denotes the precedence relation for $\mathcal{P}_i$, $1 \le i \le k$
Method:
procedure PAL
begin
  for $i := 1$ **until** k **do**
  begin
    $\alpha := $ optimal permutation with respect to $\mathcal{P}_i$
    $<_i := <_i \cup \{(T_r, T_s)|r$ appears before s in $\alpha\}$
    end;
    $< := \cup_{i=1}^{k} <_i$; $\alpha := \text{TRF}(\mathcal{P})$
end PAL

It follows from the preceding lemmas that PAL constructs an optimal permutation for $\mathcal{P}$ and, furthermore, if α is any optimal permutation for $\mathcal{P}$, one can evoke a computation of PAL that results in α.

Theorem 3.4 Let $\mathcal{P}$ be a scheduling problem such that $\mathcal{P} = \mathcal{P}_1\|\mathcal{P}_2\| \cdots \|\mathcal{P}_k$, where $k > 1$. Then α is an optimal permutation with respect to $\mathcal{P}$ and if and only if it can be generated by procedure PAL.

3.5   THE MODEL WITH NONDETERMINISM

In this section we extend previous results on deterministic chains of tasks by introducing a probability model governing execution times, deferral costs and the sequences of tasks which make up each job. In particular, each job may be viewed as a decision tree whose vertices correspond to tasks. For each task T there is an arbitrary but known joint probability distribution governing the execution time, deferral cost, and the decision as to the next task, if any, to be executed following T. Thus, execution of a job consists of the execution of some chain of tasks in the tree beginning with the initial (root) task and ending with some descendant task in the tree.

It is only at task terminations where job executions can be interrupted (preempted) in order to assign the processor to another job. Mean weighted flow times for schedules of a collection of independent jobs (called a job-system) are computed as a weighted sum of task finishing times. Our main result is an efficient algorithm for deciding at each task termination time the job to be assigned the processor in order that the expected value of the mean weighted flow-time of the entire schedule be minimized [BCJ].

A *job-system* $\mathcal{J}$ consists of:

1. A task system $(\mathcal{T}, <)$, where $\mathcal{T}$ is an indexed set of $n \geq 0$ tasks and $<$ is a partial order on $\mathcal{T}$. The index set of $\mathcal{T}$ is denoted $I(\mathcal{J})$, and for each j in $I(\mathcal{J})$, T_j is an element in $\mathcal{T}$. The partial order is restricted to be an *initially rooted forest* (recall that $<$ is an irf if each vertex in the precedence graph for $<$ has no more than one immediate predecessor).

2. For each j in $I(\mathcal{J})$, a random variable S_j which takes on positive values and gives the service time requirement of T_j. Let τ_j denote the expected value of S_j.

3. For each j in $I(\mathcal{J})$, a random variable C_j which gives the deferral cost of T_j. The range of C_j is unrestricted. Let w_j denote the expected value of C_j.

4. For each j in $I(\mathcal{J})$, a random variable D_j which takes on values corresponding to the indices of the immediate successors of T_j or zero (zero is never a task index). We impose the restriction that if T_i is an immediate successor of T_j, then $\Pr\{D_j = i\} > 0$; that is, there are no tasks whose probability of executing is zero.

5. For each j in $I(\mathcal{J})$, a trivariate probability distribution function F_j which governs the mutual behavior of S_j, C_j, and D_j. For all i and j, the triples (S_i, C_i, D_i) and (S_j, C_j, D_j) are independent.

A job-system with one initial task is called a *job*. If $\mathcal{J}$ is a nonempty job-system, $\mathcal{J}$ may be expressed as

$$\mathcal{J} = J_1 \| \cdots \| J_r$$

where J_i is a job for $1 \le i \le r$.

Let $T_{j_1}, \ldots, T_{j_r}$ be the initial tasks of $J_1, \ldots, J_r$, respectively. The processor must be assigned to one of the tasks $T_{j_1}, \ldots, T_{j_r}$. Assuming the processor is assigned at time $t \ge 0$ to task T_{j_i}, the initial task of J_l, the processor may not be reassigned until time $t + S_{j_i}$. When T_{j_i} finishes, the contribution of T_{j_i} to the mean weighted flow time is $(t + S_{j_i})C_{j_i}$. The value of D_{j_i} determines the "subjob" of J_l to replace J_l in $\mathcal{J}$, namely: if $D_{j_i} = 0$, then J_l is removed from $\mathcal{J}$; if $D_{j_i} = i \ne 0$, then J_l/K_i replaces J_l in $\mathcal{J}$ (recall that K_i is the index set consisting of i and all indices j such that $T_i < T_j$).

We define a transition function δ which takes as arguments a job-system $\mathcal{J}$, an initial task T_j of $\mathcal{J}$, and value i where i is either zero or the index of an immediate successor of T_j. The value "returned" by δ is a (possibly empty) job-system $\delta(\mathcal{J}, T_j, i)$ determined by: if $i = 0$, then $\delta(\mathcal{J}, T_j, i) = \mathcal{J}/(I(\mathcal{J}) - K_j)$; if $i \ne 0$, then $\delta(\mathcal{J}, T_j, i) = \mathcal{J}/(I(\mathcal{J}) - (K_j - K_i))$.

In Fig. 3.2 we give a job-system consisting of two jobs J_1 and J_2. The

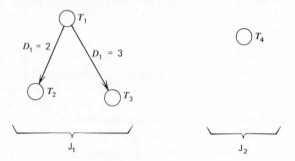

Figure 3.2   A job system: $\mathcal{J} = J_1 \| J_2$.

initial task T_1 of J_1 has two possible "outcomes" $D_1 = 2$ or $D_1 = 3$. The random variables S_1, C_1, and D_1 are governed by

$$\Pr\{S_1 = 1 \quad \text{and} \quad C_1 = \tfrac{1}{2} \quad \text{and} \quad D_1 = 2\} = p$$

and

$$\Pr\{S_1 = 2 \quad \text{and} \quad C_1 = 1 \quad \text{and} \quad D_1 = 3\} = 1 - p$$

where $0 \le p \le 1$. The remaining variables are governed by

$$\Pr\{D_i = 0\} = 1 \quad \text{for} \quad i = 2, 3, 4$$
$$\Pr\{S_i = 1\} = 1 \quad \text{for} \quad i = 2, 3, 4$$
$$\Pr\{C_i = 1\} = 1 \quad \text{for} \quad i = 2, 4$$

and

$$\Pr\{C_3 = 5\} = 1$$

Therefore job J_1 has two possible realizations, namely,

$$T_1/1/\tfrac{1}{2} \text{ followed by } T_2/1/1$$

or

$$T_1/2/1 \text{ followed by } T_3/1/5$$

where the notation corresponds to task/execution time/deferral cost. The former realization occurs with probability p and the latter with probability $1 - p$. Job J_2 has exactly one realization, $T_4/1/1$.

If we assign the processor to task T_1 at $t = 0$, there are only two possibilities:

1. T_1 finishes at $t = 1$, contributing $\tfrac{1}{2}$ to the mean weighted flow time and resulting in the job-system $\delta(\mathcal{J}, T_1, 2) = \mathcal{J}/\{2, 4\}$, *or*
2. T_1 finishes at $t = 2$, contributing 2 to the mean weighted flow time and resulting in the job-system $\delta(\mathcal{J}, T_1, 3) = \mathcal{J}/\{3, 4\}$.

A *scheduling rule* ξ is a mapping that associates with each nonempty job-system $\mathcal{J}$ an initial task $\xi(\mathcal{J})$ of $\mathcal{J}$.

The mean weighted flow time criterion for the scheduling rule ξ applied to job-system $\mathcal{J}$ at time $t \geq 0$ is determined by procedure mwft applied to ξ, $\mathcal{J}$, and t.

Algorithm 3.4

Input: ξ a scheduling rule, $\mathcal{J}$ a job-system, and t a nonnegative number
Output: the mean weighted flow-time criterion of ξ applied to $\mathcal{J}$, assuming the processor is unavailable until $t \geq 0$
Method:
procedure mwft($\xi, \mathcal{J}, t$)
begin
  if $\mathcal{J}$ is empty **then return** 0
  else
  begin
    Let j be such that $T_j = \xi(\mathcal{J})$; $(\tau, w, i) := (S_j, C_j, D_j)$
    return $(t + \tau)w + \text{mwft}(\xi, \delta(\mathcal{J}, T_j, i), t + \tau)$
  end
end mwft

The assignment statement $(\tau, w, i) := (S_j, C_j, D_j)$ is executed by obtaining samples of the random variables S_j, C_j, and D_j according to F_j and assigning these to τ, w, and i, respectively. Thus mwft($\xi, \mathcal{J}, t$) is a random variable taking on values depending on the outcomes of the experiments carried out during the execution of Algorithm 3.4.

If ζ is a random variable, $\bar{\zeta}$ denotes the expected value of ζ. We say that a scheduling rule ξ is *optimal* if for all scheduling rules ξ' and all job-systems $\mathscr{J}$ we have

$$\overline{\text{mwft}}(\xi, \mathscr{J}, 0) \leq \overline{\text{mwft}}(\xi', \mathscr{J}, 0)$$

Let $\mathscr{J}$ be the job-system in Fig. 3.2 and let ξ be a scheduling rule such that $\xi(\mathscr{J}) = T_1$, $\xi(\mathscr{J}/\{2, 4\}) = T_4$ and $\xi(\mathscr{J}/\{3, 4\}) = T_3$. It is easy to see that $\text{mwft}(\xi, \mathscr{J}, 0)$ takes on two possible values depending on the outcome of D_1. These two values are $\frac{1}{2} + 2 + 3 = \frac{11}{2}$ and $2 + 15 + 4 = 21$, the former occurring with probability p and the latter with probability $1 - p$. Therefore $\overline{\text{mwft}}(\xi, \mathscr{J}, 0) = 21 - (31/2)p$.

There is only one other strategy we need consider, namely, a scheduling rule ξ' that initially assigns T_4 instead of T_1. There are again only two possible outcomes, and we find that $\text{mwft}(\xi', \mathscr{J}, 0) = 24 - 19p$. From this we conclude that ξ gives the best results for $0 \leq p \leq \frac{6}{7}$ and ξ' is best when $\frac{6}{7} \leq p \leq 1$.

3.6 A RANK FUNCTION

Our aim in this section is to define a rank function ρ that associates with each job J a number $\rho(J)$ called the rank of J. This rank function has the property that optimal schedules are obtained by assigning the processor to the initial task of a job with the largest rank. In the next section we prove that scheduling according to a largest-rank-first strategy is optimal and, conversely, that every optimal scheduling rule corresponds to such a strategy.

Let J be a job, T_j the initial task of J, and U a subset of the task indices of J. We define the random variables $s(J, U)$ and $c(J, U)$ as

$$s(J, U) = \begin{cases} 0 & \text{if } j \notin U \\ S_j + s(\delta(J, T_j, D_j), U) & \text{if } j \in U \end{cases}$$

and

$$c(J, U) = \begin{cases} 0 & \text{if } j \notin U \\ C_j + c(\delta(J, T_j, D_j), U) & \text{if } j \in U \end{cases}$$

Let $\tau(J, U)$ and $w(J, U)$ denote the expected values of $s(J, U)$ and $c(J, U)$, respectively.

Let U be an initial set with respect to J. We define $\rho(J, U)$ as

$$\rho(J, U) = w(J, U)/\tau(J, U)$$

We define $\rho(J)$, the *rank of job* J, as $\rho(J) = \max\{\rho(J, U) | U$ is an initial set with respect to J$\}$.

We say a set $U \subseteq I(J)$ is ρ *maximal* with respect to J if

1. U is an initial set with respect to J,
2. $\rho(J, U) = \rho(J)$, and
3. if V is an initial set with respect to J, $V \subseteq U$ and $\rho(J, V) = \rho(J)$ then $V = U$.

In the remainder of this section we develop some of the properties of the rank function ρ.

Let T_j be a task in J and $T_{i_1}, \ldots, T_{i_k}$ be the sequence of tasks (i.e., path) in J such that $T_{i_{l+1}}$ is an immediate successor of T_{i_l} for $l = 1, \ldots, k - 1$, T_{i_1} is the initial task of J, and $T_{i_k} = T_j$. We define the number p_j, the probability of "reaching" T_j, as

$$p_j = \prod_{l=1}^{k-1} \Pr\{D_{i_l} = i_{l+1}\}$$

The empty product ($k - 1 = 0$) is 1. It follows from our definition of a job that $p_j > 0$ for all $j \in I(J)$.

Lemma 3.13   Let J be a job and U an initial set with respect to J. Then

$$\tau(J, U) = \sum_{j \in U} p_j \tau_j$$

and

$$w(J, U) = \sum_{j \in U} p_j w_j$$

Proof   The proof is by induction on the number of tasks in U. The basis $|U| = 1$ is easy, since $\tau(J, U) = \tau_j$ and $w(J, U) = w_j$, where T_j is the initial task of J.

Let U be an initial set of J such that $|U| \geq 2$, and assume the lemma holds for any job and a corresponding initial set with fewer than $|U|$ elements.

Let T_i be the initial task of J and $T_{i_1}, \ldots, T_{i_k}$ the immediate successors of T_i. Let $U_{i_l} = K_{i_l} \cap U$ for $l = 1, \ldots, k$. The set U_{i_l} is either empty or an initial set of J/K_{i_l} for $l = 1, \ldots, k$. We can write $\tau(J, U)$ as

$$\tau(J, U) = \tau_i + \sum_{l=1}^{k} \Pr\{D_i = i_l\} \tau(J/K_{i_l}, U_{i_l})$$

By applying the induction hypothesis to $\tau(J/K_{i_l}, U_{i_l})$ and using the definition of the p_j's, it is not too difficult to see that

$$\tau(J, U) = \sum_{j \in U} p_j \tau_j$$

A similar argument applies to $w(J, U)$. ■

We define the quantities $\tau(U)$, $w(U)$, and $\rho(U)$, where U is any nonempty subset of the indices of job J.

$$\tau(U) = \sum_{j \in U} p_j \tau_j$$

$$w(U) = \sum_{j \in U} p_j w_j$$

and

$$\rho(U) = w(U)/\tau(U)$$

Lemma 3.14 Let J be a job and U a nonempty subset of $I(J)$. If l is an index in $I(J)$ such that $U \subseteq K_l$, we have

$$\tau(U) = p_l \sum_{j \in U} p'_j \tau_j$$

and

$$w(U) = p_l \sum_{j \in U} p'_j w_j$$

where p_l is defined with respect to J and p'_j is defined with respect to J/K_l for $j \in U$.

Proof The proof follows directly from the definitions of the quantities involved. ■

The next lemma relates the rank of certain "subjobs" of a given job to the rank of the job. We use this result in the next section.

Lemma 3.15 Let U be ρ-maximal set with respect to job J and l an index in U such that T_l is not the initial task of J. Then $\rho(J/K_l) > \rho(J)$.

Proof Let $U_1 = U - K_l$ and $U_2 = K_l \cap U$. Applying Lemma 3.2, we have

$$\rho(J) = \eta \rho(U_1) + (1 - \eta)\rho(U_2)$$

where $0 < \eta < 1$. Since U_1 is an initial set of J, we have $\rho(U_1) < \rho(J)$; therefore $\rho(U_2) > \rho(J)$.

Since $\rho(J/K_l) \geq \rho(J/U_2, U_2)$, it remains to show that $\rho(J/U_2, U_2) = \rho(U_2) = w(U_2)/\tau(U_2)$, where $w(U_2)$ and $\tau(U_2)$ are both defined with respect to J. This follows directly from Lemma 3.14. ■

3.7 OPTIMAL SCHEDULES

Let ξ be a scheduling rule and $\mathcal{J} = J_1 \| \cdots \| J_r$ a nonempty job-system where J_i is a job for $i = 1, \ldots, r$. Let l be such that $\xi(\mathcal{J})$ is the initial task of job J_i. We say that $\xi(\mathcal{J})$ is a largest rank (LR) *assignment* if $\rho(J_1) \geq \rho(J_i)$ for $i = 1, \ldots, r$. A scheduling rule ξ is called an *LR scheduling rule* if for all job-systems $\mathcal{J}$, $\xi(\mathcal{J})$ is an LR assignment.

Theorem 3.5 A scheduling rule ξ is optimal if and only if ξ is an LR scheduling rule.

Proof A scheduling rule ξ is called an *n-optimal scheduling rule* if for all scheduling rules ξ' and all job-systems $\mathcal{J}$, if $|I(\mathcal{J})| \leq n$ then $\overline{\text{mwft}}(\xi, \mathcal{J}, 0) \leq \overline{\text{mwft}}(\xi', \mathcal{J}, 0)$. A scheduling rule ξ is called an *n-LR scheduling rule* if for all job-systems $\mathcal{J}$, if $|I(\mathcal{J})| \leq n$, then $\xi(\mathcal{J})$ is an LR assignment. To prove the theorem, we show for each $n \geq 1$ that ξ is an n-optimal scheduling rule if and only if it is an n-LR scheduling rule. The proof is by induction on n, and the case $n = 1$ is obvious.

Let $n \geq 2$ and assume there exists an n-optimal scheduling rule ξ and a job-system $\mathcal{J} = J_1 \| \cdots \| J_r$ such that $|I(\mathcal{J})| = n$ and $\xi(\mathcal{J})$ is not an LR assignment. Let $T_{j_1} = \xi(\mathcal{J})$ be the initial task of job J_{l_1}. By assumption, $r \geq 2$ and there exists an initial task T_{l_2} of job J_{l_2} such that T_{l_2} is an LR assignment with respect to $\mathcal{J}$ and $\rho(J_{l_2}) > \rho(J_{l_1})$. Our goal is to obtain a contradiction by constructing a scheduling rule ξ' such that $\overline{\text{mwft}}(\xi', \mathcal{J}, 0) < \overline{\text{mwft}}(\xi, \mathcal{J}, 0)$.

We describe ξ applied to $\mathcal{J}$ by a labeled tree* E. Each vertex v of E has two labels $T(v)$, a task, and $\mathcal{J}(v)$, a nonempty job-system, satisfying $T(v) = \xi(\mathcal{J}(v))$. The root of E is v_0 and $\mathcal{J}(v_0) = \mathcal{J}$. Each vertex v in E has one subtree for each nonempty job-system, which may result from $\mathcal{J}(v)$, given the assignment of the processor to $T(v)$.

The tree in Fig. 3.3 describes a scheduling rule as applied to the problem

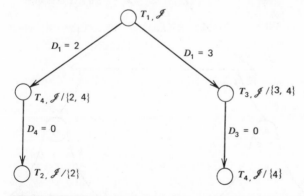

Figure 3.3 Schedule depicted as a tree: Notation $T(v)$, $\mathcal{J}(v)$.

* A *tree* E is a finite set of elements called *vertices* having a distinguished element, called the *root*, and a partition $E_1, \ldots, E_k$ of the remaining elements (if any) into $k \geq 1$ trees. The trees $E_1, \ldots, E_k$ are called the *subtrees* of the root.

given in Fig. 3.2. This is one of the scheduling rules we analyzed in a previous section.

If V is a subset of the vertices of E, we write

$$I(V) = \{i \,|\, v \in V \qquad \text{and} \qquad T(v) = T_i\}$$

Let A be a *maximal* subset of the vertices of E such that

1. v_0 is in A.
2. If $v \in A$, $v \neq v_0$, then the immediate predecessor of v is in A.
3. If $v \in A$, then $T(v)$ belongs to J_{l_1}.

Clearly, the set A is unique, and $I(A)$ is an initial set of J_{l_1}.

A vertex v is said to be an *immediate successor* of a subset V of vertices if v does not belong to V and the immediate predecessor of v is contained in V.

Let $v_1, \ldots, v_a$ be the immediate successors of A. And $\mathscr{J}_i = \mathscr{J}(v_i)$ for $i = 1, \ldots, a$. Since $|I(\mathscr{J}_i)| \leq n - 1$, we may employ the inductive hypothesis to conclude that the assignments made by ξ in $\mathscr{J}_i$ are LR assignments and moreover, we may alter these assignments, as long as they remain LR, without changing the expected mean weighted flow time.

Let E_i be the subtree of E according to $\mathscr{J}_i$; the root of E_i if v_i for $i = 1, \ldots, a$ (see Fig. 3.4). Since all assignments in A are in J_{l_1}, $\rho(J_{l_2})$ has

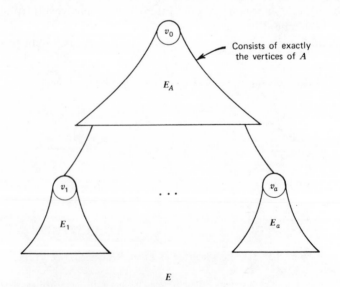

Consists of exactly the vertices of A

Figure 3.4 ξ depicted as the tree E.

largest rank among all jobs in $\mathcal{J}_i$ (there may be ties) for $i = 1, \ldots, a$. Let U be the ρ-maximal set for J_{l_2}. Using the inductive hypothesis and Lemma 3.15, we may take E_i to be of the form appearing in Fig. 3.5, where $I(B) = U$. We show no dependency of B on i since, by Lemma 3.15, assignments to tasks in J_{l_2} with indices in U are LR assignments. Therefore, the initial "structure" of E_i can be taken to be E_B for $i = 1, \ldots, a$.

Figure 3.6 presents the structure of E and the structure of E' obtained from E by an "interchange." We shall not give all the details of the

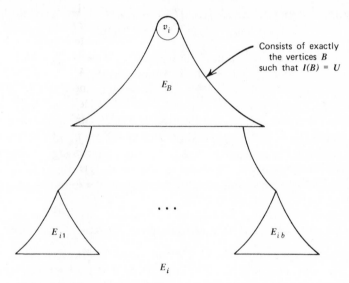

Figure 3.5 The structure of E_i.

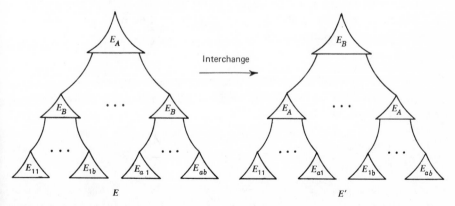

Figure 3.6 Interchange.

interchange; the idea is simply to execute the tasks with indices in $I(B)$ before those with indices in $I(A)$. The labels $\mathcal{J}(\cdot)$ of the vertices in E_A and E_B in the tree E' are different than those in E because of the change in processing order. Let ξ' denote the scheduling rule depicted by E'. It is easy to calculate the change in the expected mean weighted flow time in going from ξ to ξ':

$$\overline{\text{mwft}}(\xi', \mathcal{J}, 0) = \overline{\text{mwft}}(\xi, \mathcal{J}, 0) + \overline{s(J_{l_2}, I(B))c(J_{l_1}, I(A))}$$
$$- \overline{s(J_{l_1}, I(A))c(J_{l_2}, I(B))}$$

Using the independence of $s(J_{l_2}, I(B))$ and $c(J_{l_1}, I(A))$ and the independence of $s(J_{l_1}, I(A))$ and $c(J_{l_2}, I(B))$, we obtain

$$\overline{\text{mwft}}(\xi', \mathcal{J}, 0) = \overline{\text{mwft}}(\xi, \mathcal{J}, 0) + \tau(J_{l_2}, I(B))w(J_{l_1}, I(A))$$
$$- \tau(J_{l_1}, I(A))w(J_{l_2}, I(B))$$
$$= \overline{\text{mwft}}(\xi, \mathcal{J}, 0) + \gamma(\rho(J_{l_1}, I(A)) - \rho(J_{l_2}))$$

where $\gamma > 0$. Since $\rho(J_{l_2}) > \rho(J_{l_1}) \geq \rho(J_{l_1}, I(A))$, we obtain a contradiction.

To finish the proof we must show that if $I(\mathcal{J}) = n$, all n-LR schedules for $\mathcal{J}$ produce the same cost. The foregoing "interchange" argument can be used to reduce n-LR schedules to one another without increasing the expected value of the mean weighted flow time. We omit the details. ∎

3.8 ALGORITHMS FOR THE MODEL WITH NONDETERMINISM

In this section we consider the computational questions that arise when we implement the LR scheduling rule. Algorithm 3.5 is an LR scheduling algorithm that takes a job-system $\mathcal{J}$ as input and determines a sequence of LR assignments and the resultant mean weighted flow time. This algorithm is similar in structure to Algorithm 3.4; however, here we ensure that all assignments are LR.

Algorithm 3.5

Input: $\mathcal{J} = J_1 \| \cdots \| J_r$
Output: sequence of LR assignments and the mean weighted flow-time of resultant schedule
Method:

1. **procedure** LR($\mathcal{J}$)
2. **begin**
3. $t := 0$
4.   mwft $:= 0$
5. $l[i] :=$ index of the initial task of J_i for $i = 1, \ldots, r$

6.   **while** not $(l[i] = 0$ for $i = 1, \ldots, r)$ **do**
7.   **begin**
8.   let j be such that $l[j] \neq 0$ and $\rho(\mathrm{J}_j/K_{l[j]}) \geq \rho(\mathrm{J}_i/K_{l[i]})$, for all
          $1 \leq i \leq r$ and $l[i] \neq 0$
9. $U := \rho$-maximal set with respect to $\mathrm{J}_j/K_{l[j]}$
10.   **while** $l[j] \in U$ **do**
11.   **begin**
12. $(\tau, w, d) := (S_{l[j]}, C_{l[j]}, D_{l[j]})$
13. $\mathrm{mwft} := \mathrm{mwft} + (t + \tau) \cdot w$
14. $t := t + \tau$
15. $l[j] := d$
16.   **end**
17.   **end**
18.   **return** mwft
19. **end** LR

As in Algorithm 3.4, LR($\mathcal{J}$) is a random variable whose outcome is dependent on the choice of j in line 8 and the outcome of the assignment statement in line 12. This random variable is seen to be equal to the mean weighted flow time of the resultant schedule as a comparison of lines 13 and 14 of LR($\mathcal{J}$) with the "return" statement in procedure mwft will show.

Theorem 3.6 Let $\mathcal{J}$ be a job-system and ξ a scheduling rule. Then $\overline{\mathrm{LR}(\mathcal{J})} \leq \overline{\mathrm{mwft}}(\xi, \mathcal{J}, 0)$.

Proof This result is an immediate consequence of Theorem 3.5 and Lemma 3.15. ∎

Line 8, in procedure LR, determines a job with largest rank and can be computationally burdensome if no precautions are taken. A similar remark applies to the determination of the ρ-maximal set U in line 9. The following preprocessing algorithm, if applied to a given job, provides information that can be used to obtain an efficient implementation of lines 8 and 9 in procedure LR.

Let J be a job. We say that a partition $B_1, \ldots, B_q$ of $I(\mathrm{J})$ is *complete* with respect to J if for each i in $\{1, \ldots, q\}$ we have the following conditions.

1. The B_i contains a unique element, say l, such that if T_j is a predecessor of T_l in J, then j is not a member of B_i. The index l is called the *initial index* of B_i.

2. If j is an index in B_i and j is not the initial index of B_i, then j' is in B_i where $T_{j'}$ is the immediate predecessor of T_j.

3. If l is the initial index of B_i, then B_i is a ρ-maximal set with respect to J/K_l.

It is not too difficult to demonstrate that a complete partition with respect to J exists and is unique. The algorithm that follows gives a strategy for computing the complete partition of a job.

Algorithm 3.6

Input: J a job
Output: $B_1, \ldots, B_q$ a complete partition with respect to J and numbers $R_1, \ldots, R_q$, such that $R_i = \rho(J/K_{l_i})$, where l_i is the initial index of B_i for $i = 1, \ldots, q$
Method:
1. **procedure** RANK
2. **begin**
3. $q := 0$
4. $U := I(J)$
5.   **while** $U \neq \varphi$ **do**
6.   **begin**
7.   let l be an index in U such that $\rho(K_l \cap U) \leq \rho(K_i \cap U)$ for all i in U and $\rho(K_l \cap U) < \rho(K_j \cap U)$ for all j in $K_l \cap U$ and $j \neq l$
8. $q := q + 1$
9. $B_q := K_l \cap U$
10. $R_q := \rho(K_l \cap U)$
11. $U := U - K_l$
12.   **end**
13. **end** RANK

Lemma 3.16 Let J be a job and $B_1, \ldots, B_q$ and $R_1, \ldots, R_q$ be the sets and the numbers, respectively, determined by procedure RANK applied to J. Then $B_1, \ldots, B_q$ is a complete partition of J and if l_i is the initial index of B_i, then $\rho(J/K_{l_i}) = R_i$.

Proof Lemma 3.8 and induction are the natural tools to use in proving Lemma 3.16. The whole matter is routine; and we leave the details of the proof to the concerned reader. ∎

Assuming that for each task T_j in J we have available the numbers τ_j, w_j and $\Pr\{D_j = i\}$ for each i such that T_i is an immediate successor of T_j, a reasonably straightforward implementation of Algorithm 3.6 will have an $O(n^2)$ worst-case time complexity, where $n = |I(J)|$. The idea is to calculate for each j in $I(J)$ the numbers $\tau'_j = p_j \tau_j$ and $w'_j = p_j w_j$. This can be accomplished by a single traversal of the precedence graph of J and takes $O(n)$ time. The minimizations in line 7 may also be done using a "bottom-up" traversal of the precedence graph of J, namely: If T_j is a task with immediate successors $T_{i_1}, \ldots, T_{i_k}$, and $\tau(K_{i_l})$ and $w(K_{i_l})$ are known for T_{i_l} for $l = 1, \ldots, k$, we can write

$$\rho(K_j) = \frac{w(K_j)}{\tau(K_j)} = \frac{w'_j + \sum_{l=1}^{k} w(K_{i_l})}{\tau'_j + \sum_{l=1}^{k} \tau(K_{i_l})}$$

Therefore, if we "visit" tasks $T_{i_1}, \ldots, T_{i_k}$ before we visit task T_j, we will be able to calculate $\rho(K_j)$ from local information.

Since line 7 is executed $O(n)$ times, we obtain a worst-case time complexity of $O(n^2)$ for Algorithm 3.6.

The initial computation of the products $p_j w_j$ and $p_j \tau_j$ may be eliminated by recognizing that a cancellation takes place when we compute the ratios $w(K_j)/\tau(K_j)$. The exact cancellation is given by Lemma 3.14. Thus if instead of computing $w(K_j)$ and $\tau(K_j)$, we compute $\tilde{w}(K_j) = (1/p_j)w(K_j)$ and $\tilde{\tau}(K_j) = (1/p_j)\tau(K_j)$, the ratios would be unaffected; that is,

$$\rho(K_j) = \frac{w(K_j)}{\tau(K_j)} = \frac{\tilde{w}(K_j)}{\tilde{\tau}(K_j)}$$

The point is that $\tilde{w}$ and $\tilde{\tau}$ may be obtained without having to perform the initial computation of w'_j and τ'_j for each task T_j, namely:

$$\tilde{w}(K_j) = w_j + \sum_{l=1}^{k} \Pr\{D_j = i_l\}\tilde{w}(K_{i_l})$$

and

$$\tilde{\tau}(K_j) = \tau_j + \sum_{l=1}^{k} \Pr\{D_j = i_l\}\tilde{\tau}(K_{i_l}).$$

We return now to procedure LR and the use of complete partitions in obtaining efficient realizations of the LR scheduling rule. Let J be a job and $\mathcal{B}(J) = \{(B_1, R_1), \ldots, (B_q, R_q)\}$, where $B_1, \ldots, B_q$ is a complete partition of J and $R_i = \rho(J/K_{l_i}) = \rho(B_i)$, where l_i is the initial index of B_i for $i = 1, \ldots, q$.

Lemma 3.17 Let $\mathcal{J} = J_1 \| \cdots \| J_r$ be a job-system and $l_1, \ldots, l_r$ be the values of the program variables $l[1], \ldots, l[r]$, respectively, just prior to some execution of line 6 in procedure LR applied to $\mathcal{J}$. If $l_i \neq 0$, there exists a $(B, R) \in \mathcal{B}(J_i)$ such that l_i is the initial index in B.

Lemma 3.17 guarantees that the information in $\mathcal{B}(J_1), \ldots, \mathcal{B}(J_r)$ is relevant (i.e., that it can be used to efficiently implement steps 8 and 9 in procedure LR). In effect, we have precomputed all the ranks and the

ρ-maximal sets we will ever need during procedure LR($\mathcal{J}$). Clearly, the determination of j in line 8 may be accomplished in constant time if the ranks of the jobs are stored in a priority queue. The management of the priority queue itself can be done in $O(\log_2 r)$ steps per access to the queue [AHU]. Therefore, assuming we have $\mathcal{B}(J_1), \ldots, \mathcal{B}(J_r)$, the LR scheduling rule may be implemented in $O(n \log_2 r)$ time, where $n = |I(\mathcal{J})|$ and r is the number of jobs in $\mathcal{J}$.

3.9 MULTIPLE–PROCESSOR SCHEDULING

In this section we consider deterministic scheduling problems in which we allow the number of processors to be greater than 1. To make the problem tractable, we impose two restrictions: (1) tasks are independent (i.e., $< = \varphi$), and (2) the deferral costs are all unity. Thus the specification of a scheduling problem consists of a matrix of processing times. Let $[\tau_{ij}]$ denote an $m \times n$ matrix where τ_{ij} is the time to process task T_j on processor i for $1 \le j \le n$ and $1 \le i \le m$ [Ho 2, BCS 1, BCS 2].

A schedule ξ consists of a partition of the set $\{1, \ldots, n\}$ into m blocks $B_1, \ldots, B_m$, some of which may be empty, and a permutation α_i of the elements of B_i for $i = 1, \ldots, m$. Block B_i gives the indices of those tasks to be scheduled on processor i and α_i determines the order of task executions on the ith processor for $1 \le i \le m$.

Suppose $n = 8$, $m = 3$, $[\tau_{ij}]$ is given by

$$[\tau_{ij}] = \begin{bmatrix} 2 & 3 & 1 & 4 & 6 & 5 & 2 & 3 \\ 1 & 4 & 1 & 5 & 5 & 4 & 3 & 4 \\ 3 & 2 & 3 & 2 & 3 & 5 & 1 & 2 \end{bmatrix}$$

and ξ consists of blocks $B_1 = \{3, 5, 8\}$, $B_2 = \varphi$, and $B_3 = \{1, 2, 4, 6, 7\}$, and permutations $\alpha_1 = 3, 8, 5$, $\alpha_2 = \lambda$, and $\alpha_3 = 7, 4, 2, 6, 1$. We calculate

$$\text{mwft}(\xi) = \sum_{j=1}^{n} f_j(\xi) = 47$$

In the following sections we show how to reduce a scheduling problem to a minimal-cost flow problem [FF] and give an efficient algorithm that takes $[\tau_{ij}]$ as input and constructs an optimal schedule ξ^*.

3.10 A REDUCTION

Let $[\tau_{ij}]$ be an $m \times n$ matrix of processing times and ξ be some schedule. Suppose ξ specifies that T_j be run on the ith processor and that there are exactly k tasks that follow T_j on processor i, $0 \leq k < n$. The execution time τ_{ij} contributes to the finishing time of T_j and to the k tasks that follow T_j. With this in mind, we can write $mwft(\xi)$ in such a way that all the terms depending on τ_{ij} are isolated, that is,

$$mwft(\xi) = (k + 1) \cdot \tau_{ij} + \text{other terms not containing } \tau_{ij}$$

If T_j runs last on the ith processor, the coefficient of τ_{ij} is 1; if T_j runs next-to-last on the ith processor, the coefficient of τ_{ij} is 2, and so on. This observation leads to the following reformulation of our problem.

Form the $m' \times n$ matrix C as follows:

$$C = \begin{bmatrix} [1\tau_{ij}] \\ [2\tau_{ij}] \\ \cdot \\ \cdot \\ \cdot \\ [n\tau_{ij}] \end{bmatrix}$$

where $[r\tau_{ij}]$ denotes the matrix obtained from $[\tau_{ij}]$ by multiplying each element of $[\tau_{ij}]$ by r. The elements of C are denoted by c_{ij}, where $1 \leq i \leq m'$, $1 \leq j \leq n$, and $m' = mn$.

Intuitively, the elements in $[1\tau_{ij}]$ represent the possible contributions to the mwft from tasks scheduled last on their respective processors, $[2\tau_{ij}]$ represents the possible contributions from tasks scheduled next-to-last on their respective processors, and so on.

Using the matrix C as a cost matrix, we formulate a minimal-cost network "flow" problem where the i, jth entry of the matrix C gives the per-unit cost of flow (of some commodity) from location x_i to location y_j. After setting up this problem, we show how an "optimal" flow pattern determines an optimal schedule.

In the transportation network $\mathcal{N}$ [FF] of Fig. 3.7, each arc in $\mathcal{N}$ has a capacity of one unit of flow in the direction of the arrow except for the return arc, which has a capacity of n units. Let (z, z') be an arc in $\mathcal{N}$ and $c(z, z')$ denote the per-unit cost of flow from z to z'. We have $c(x_i, y_j) = c_{ij}$ for $1 \leq i \leq m'$ and $1 \leq j \leq n$, and all other costs are zero.

A *flow pattern* for $\mathcal{N}$ is specified by giving a function h from the arcs of $\mathcal{N}$ into the set $\{0, 1, \ldots\}$. Let (z, z') be an arc in $\mathcal{N}$ and $h(z, z')$ denote the flow from z to z'. We say a flow pattern h is *feasible* if for all arcs (z, z') in $\mathcal{N}$, $h(z, z')$ is less than or equal to the capacity of arc (z, z') and flow is conserved at each vertex in $\mathcal{N}$. The *value* of a feasible flow pattern h is equal to $h(y_0, x_0)$.

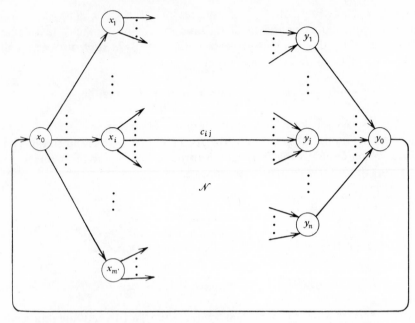

Return arc

Figure 3.7 Transportation network $\mathcal{N}$.

Vertices of $\mathcal{N}$ $x_0, \ldots, x_{m'}, y_0, \ldots, y_n$
Arcs of $\mathcal{N}$ (x_i, y_j) $1 \le i \le m', 1 \le j \le n$
                    (x_0, x_i) $1 \le i \le m'$
                    (y_j, y_0) $1 \le j \le n$
                    (y_0, x_0) return arc

A feasible flow pattern h is called an *optimal flow pattern* if the value of h is n and

$$\text{cost}(h) = \sum_{i=1}^{m'} \sum_{j=1}^{n} c(x_i, y_j) h(x_i, y_j)$$

is a minimum among all feasible flow patterns with value n.

A schedule ξ is easily interpreted as a feasible flow pattern for the network $\mathcal{N}$. For all tasks T_j, if task T_j is scheduled on the ith processor and there are k tasks following T_j on processor i, set $h(x_{i'}, y_j) = h(x_0, x_{i'}) = 1$ where $i' = km + i$. Also set $h(y_0, x_0) = n$ and $h(y_j, y_0) = 1$ for $1 \le j \le n$. All the remaining variables are set to zero. It is easy to see that h is a feasible flow pattern and that $\text{mwft}(\xi) = \text{cost}(h)$.

On the other hand, if $\tau_{ij} > 0$ for $1 \le i \le m$ and $1 \le j \le n$, any optimal flow pattern h can be interpreted as an optimal schedule. If $h(x_{i'}, y_j) = 1$, then T_j is scheduled on processor i and there are k tasks following T_j on processor i, where i and k are determined by the following system of equations.

$$i' = km + i$$
$$0 \le k < n \tag{1}$$
$$1 \le i \le m$$

Equations (1) uniquely determine k and i. The contribution of task T_j to the mwft is $(k + 1)\tau_{ij}$, and this is precisely the coefficient of $h(x_{i'}, y_j)$ in cost (h). It is not difficult to show that the schedule obtained in this manner from the optimal flow pattern h is well formed in the sense that h determines k additional tasks that follow T_j. The restriction on the τ_{ij}'s supports this result. If there is a task T_j with $\tau_{ij} = 0$ for some value of i, then T_j may be scheduled on the ith processor at $t = 0$ without contributing to the mwft of the schedule. Thus we can ignore all such tasks in any scheduling algorithm.

Theorem 3.7 Let $\mathscr{P}$ be a scheduling problem determined by an $m \times n$ matrix $[\tau_{ij}]$ of processing times where $\tau_{ij} > 0$ for $1 \le i \le m$ and $1 \le j \le n$. If h is an optimal flow pattern for the network $\mathscr{N}$ corresponding to $\mathscr{P}$, then the schedule ξ determined by h using (1) is an optimal schedule for $\mathscr{P}$.

3.11 MULTIPLE-PROCESSOR ALGORITHMS

A feasible flow pattern h for $\mathscr{N}$ is called *extreme* if it has cost equal to the minimum among all feasible flow patterns with value $h(y_0, x_0)$. A well-known method for finding an optimal flow pattern is successively to find flow patterns $h_0, h_1, \ldots, h_n$ such that h_p is extreme and the value of h_p is p for $0 \le p \le n$ [FF]. The initial pattern h_0 assigns zero flow to every arc in $\mathscr{N}$. Suppose we have determined h_p for some p less than n. To find h_{p+1} we locate a path from x_0 to y_0 in $\mathscr{N}$ along which the flow may be "increased" by one unit and such that the per-unit cost of the increase is minimal over all such paths. Such a path is called a *minimal-cost flow-augmenting path* and may be found using a shortest-path algorithm. It is known that if h_p is extreme and h_{p+1} is obtained by increasing the flow by one unit along a minimal-cost flow-augmenting path, h_{p+1} is extreme [FF].

Let $X = \{x_1, \ldots, x_m\}$ and $Y = \{y_1, \ldots, y_n\}$. A *flow-augmenting path* with respect to a feasible flow pattern h is a sequence of distinct vertices $\nu = x_0, x_{i_1}, y_{j_1}, \ldots, x_{i_r}, y_{j_r}, y_0$ satisfying: $r \ge 1$; $x_{i_k} \in X$ and $y_{j_k} \in Y$ for $1 \le k \le r$; $h(x_0, x_{i_1}) = h(y_{j_r}, y_0) = 0$; $h(x_{i_k}, y_{j_k}) = 0$ for $1 \le k \le r$; $h(x_{i_{k+1}}, y_{j_k}) = 1$ for $1 \le k < r$.

The following algorithm takes as input a flow-augmenting path $\nu = z_1, z_2, \ldots, z_r$ and produces a new flow pattern h' from h by increasing the flow by one unit along ν.

Algorithm 3.7

Input: a feasible flow pattern h and a flow augmenting path $\nu = z_1, \ldots, z_r$ with respect to h
Output: a feasible flow pattern h obtained from the input flow pattern by increasing the flow by one unit along ν
Method:
procedure AUGMENT FLOW
begin
    $h(y_0, x_0) := h(y_0, x_0) + 1$
    $h(z_{r-1}, y_0) := 1$
    $h(x_0, z_2) := h(z_2, z_3) := 1$
    $k := 4$
    while $k \le r - 2$ **do**
    begin
        $h(z_k, z_{k-1}) := 0$
        $h(z_k, z_{k+1}) := 1$
        $k := k + 2$
    end
end AUGMENT FLOW

The flow pattern we obtain from AUGMENT FLOW is easily seen to be feasible. If we let h' denote this flow pattern and h the original flow pattern, we find

$$\text{cost}(h') = \text{cost}(h) + \sum_{k \in Ev} c(z_k, z_{k+1}) - \sum_{k \in Od} c(z_{k+1}, z_k)$$

where $Ev = \{2, 4, \ldots, r - 2\}$, $Od = \{3, 5, \ldots, r - 3\}$. The positive terms result from increasing the flow from zero to one unit in arcs (x, y), where $x \in X$, $y \in Y$, and $h(x, y) = 0$. The negative terms correspond to the arcs in which we decrease the flow from one unit to zero units.

A minimal-cost flow-augmenting path may be found by applying a shortest-path labeling algorithm to the network $\mathcal{N}$ where the distance function d is chosen to isolate only the flow-augmenting paths in $\mathcal{N}$. Let $X_1 = \{x_i | h(x_i, y_j) = 1 \text{ for some } j\}$ and $Y_1 = \{y_j | h(x_i, y_j) = 1 \text{ for some } i\}$. Let π be a function from the vertices of $\mathcal{N}$ into the nonnegative integers. The distance function d is defined as

$$d(z, z') = \begin{cases} \pi(z) + c(z, z') - \pi(z') & z \in X, z' \in Y & \text{and} & h(z, z') = 0 \\ \pi(z) - c(z', z) - \pi(z') & z' \in X, z \in Y & \text{and} & h(z', z) = 1 \\ \pi(x_0) - \pi(z') & z = x_0 & \text{and} & z' \in X - X_1 \\ \pi(z) - \pi(y_0) & z \in Y - Y_1 & \text{and} & z' = y_0 \\ \infty & \text{otherwise} \end{cases}$$

The function π has been introduced to insure that d is nonnegative. Let $\nu = z_1, \ldots, z_r$ be a flow-augmenting path with respect to h and let h' be the flow pattern that results when we apply AUGMENT FLOW to ν and h. The length of ν is given by

$$\text{length}(\nu) = \sum_{i=2}^{r} d(z_{i-1}, z_i)$$

It is easy to show that $\text{length}(\nu) = \pi(x_0) - \pi(y_0) + \text{cost}(h') - \text{cost}(h)$. Therefore the flow-augmenting path with shortest length corresponds to a minimal-cost flow-augmenting path. Thus we can use a labeling algorithm to locate a shortest-length flow-augmenting path ν. As we mentioned earlier, the role of the function π is to keep d nonnegative, thereby allowing us to use an efficient shortest-path algorithm.

Algorithm 3.8 is basically the algorithm proposed by Edmonds and Karp [EK] for finding minimal-cost flows.

Algorithm 3.8

Input: a network $\mathcal{N}$ corresponding to a scheduling problem $\mathcal{P}$
Output: an optimal flow pattern h
Data structures: X_1 and Y_1 are sets, h is defined on $X \times Y$, and π is defined on $X \cup Y \cup \{x_0, y_0\}$, and σ and β are defined on $X_1 \cup Y \cup \{y_0\}$
Method:

  1. **procedure** MFT
  2. **begin**
  3. $X_1 := \varphi$; $Y_1 := \varphi$
  4.   **for each** $u \in X \cup Y \cup \{x_0, y_0\}$ **do** $\pi(u) := 0$
  5.   **for each** $(x, y) \in X \times Y$ **do** $h(x, y) := 0$
  6. $p := 0$
  7.   **while** $p < n$ **do**
  8.   **begin**
  9.   **call** FIND PATH
10.   **call** UPDATE FLOW
11. $p := p + 1$
12.   **end**
13. **end** MFT

The subroutines used by MFT are given in Algorithms 3.9 to 3.11.

The flow pattern h in MFT is defined only on arcs (x, y), where $x \in X$ and $y \in Y$. The flow pattern in arcs (x_0, x) and (y, y_0) for $x \in X$ and $y \in Y$ is easily deduced from h, and the flow in the return arc (y_0, x_0) is equal to p. When we refer to the flow pattern h in MFT we assume that it is extended in the appropriate manner to all the arcs in $\mathcal{N}$.

The correctness of MFT rests on the following theorem.

Theorem 3.8 [FF]   Let h be an extreme flow pattern of $\mathcal{N}$ and let ν be a minimal-cost flow-augmenting path with respect to h. If h' is the flow pattern that results when AUGMENT FLOW is applied to h and ν, then h' is extreme.

Algorithm 3.9

```
procedure FIND PATH
begin
   call INITIALIZE LABELS
   S := Y
   while S ≠ φ do
   begin
      select y* ∈ S such that σ(y*) ≤ σ(y) for all y ∈ S
      S := S − {y*}
      if y* ∈ Y₁ then
      begin
         let x* be such that h(x*, y*) = 1
         σ(x*) := σ(y*)
         β(x*) := y*
         for each y ∈ S do
         if σ(x*) + d(x*, y) < σ(y) then
         begin
            σ(y) := σ(x*) + d(x*, y)
            β(y) := x*
         end
      end
      else
      if σ(y*) + d(y*, y₀) < σ(y₀) then
      begin
         σ(y₀) := σ(y*) + d(y*, y₀)
         β(y₀) := y*
      end
   end
end FIND PATH
```

Algorithm 3.10

procedure INITIALIZE LABELS
begin
  for each $y \in Y$ **do**
  begin

   $\sigma(y) := \min_{x \in (X - X_1)} d(x, y)$
   $\beta(y) := x$, where x is such that $d(x, y) = \sigma(y)$
  end
   $\sigma(y_0) := \infty$
end INITIALIZE LABELS

Algorithm 3.11

procedure UPDATE FLOW
begin
  $y := \beta(y_0)$
  $x := \beta(y)$
  while $x \in X_1$ **do**
  begin
    $y' := \beta(x)$
    $h(x, y) := 1$
    $h(x, y') := 0$
    $y := y'$
    $x := \beta(y)$
  end
  $h(x, y) := 1$
  $Y_1 := Y_1 \cup \{\beta(y_0)\}$
  for each $u \in X_1 \cup Y \cup \{y_0\}$ **do** $\pi(u) := \pi(u) + \sigma(u)$
  $X_1 := X_1 \cup \{x\}$
end UPDATE FLOW   ■

In line 5 of MFT, h is set identically equal to zero; accordingly h is the extreme flow pattern with value $p = 0$ (line 6). The inductive assertion at line 7 in MFT is:

A1.   *The flow pattern h is an extreme flow pattern with value p.*

Another key factor in the correctness of MFT is the distance function d. Initially (line 4) π is set to zero on all the vertices of $\mathcal{N}$. This means that for all $x \in X$ and $y \in Y$ $d(x, y) = c(x, y)$ and $d(x_0, x) = d(y, y_0) = 0$. The inductive assertions at line 7 in MFT with regard to d are:

A2. *For all* $x \in X$ *and* $y \in Y$, *if* $h(x, y) = 0$ *then* $d(x, y) \geq 0$ *and if* $h(x, y) = 1$ *then* $d(y, x) = 0$.

A3. *For all* $x \in (X - X_1)$ *and* $y \in (Y - Y_1)$ $d(x_0, x) = 0$ *and* $d(y, y_0) \geq 0$.

Procedure FIND PATH is a shortest-path labeling algorithm that locates shortest paths with respect to d from x_0 to all vertices in $X \cup Y \cup \{y_0\}$. Since $d(x_0, x)$ is zero for all $x \in (X - X_1)$, MFT records path information in the labels σ and β associated only with the vertices in $X_1 \cup Y \cup \{y_0\}$. As with the function h, we assume that σ and β are extended to the vertices in $(X - X_1) \cup \{x_0\}$ in the following manner: for all $x \in (X - X_1) \cup \{x_0\}$, $\sigma(x) = 0$ and $\beta(x) = x_0$.

FIND PATH is nothing more than the well-known method for finding shortest paths with respect to a nonnegative distance function. We have taken advantage of the properties of d (A2 and A3) to speed up the labeling process. The first instance of this is in INITIALIZE LABELS. Since $d(x_0, x) = 0$ for all $x \in X - X_1$, we know that the vertices in $X - X_1$ will be "scanned" first. It is easy to see that after scanning all the vertices in $X - X_1$, we have for all $y \in Y$, $\sigma(y) = \min_{x \in X - X_1} d(x, y)$ and $\beta(y) = x$, where x is such that $d(x, y) = \sigma(y)$. Furthermore, all the vertices in Y are candidates for scanning.

In another instance we have taken advantage of A2 to perform a 2-ply labeling step: if y^* is in Y_1, we know that $d(y^*, x^*) = 0$ and that x^* is the only vertex reachable from y^* with respect to d. Therefore we immediately set the labels $\sigma(x^*) = \sigma(y^*)$ and $\beta(x^*) = y^*$ and proceed to scan x^*. We summarize the foregoing discussion in the following lemma.

Lemma 3.18 If A2, A3, and $p < n$ hold prior to the execution of FIND PATH, then after executing FIND PATH the variables σ and β satisfy:

1. For all vertices u in $\mathcal{N}$ and $u \neq x_0$, $\sigma(u)$ is the length of a shortest path from x_0 to u with respect to d.

2. For all vertices u in $\mathcal{N}$ and $u \neq x_0$, $\beta(u)$ is the immediate predecessor vertex on a shortest path from x_0 to u with respect to d.

Procedure UPDATE FLOW uses the shortest-path information to augment the flow along a minimal-cost flow-augmenting path and to adjust the values of the variables h, X_1, Y_1, and π in preparation for the next cycle of the "while" statement in MFT. It is easy to see that given the properties of σ and β (Lemma 3.18), UPDATE FLOW correctly alters the flow pattern h, thus verifying the inductive assertion A1. Assertions A2 and A3 remain true with respect to the new flow pattern because of the adjustments made to π at the end of UPDATE FLOW.

The correctness of MFT follows from Theorem 3.8 and the validity of the inductive assertions A1, A2, and A3.

Theorem 3.9   Given a network $\mathcal{N}$ corresponding to a scheduling problem $\mathcal{P}$, procedure MFT correctly computes h, an optimal flow pattern.

The worst-case time complexity of MFT can be taken to be $O(mn^2 + n^3)$. The n^3 term is obvious and the mn^2 derives from INITIALIZE LABELS. At first glance the minimization for each $y \in Y$ over all x in $X - X_1$ takes $O(mn^2)$ time, and since this minimization occurs n times, the total time devoted to this minimization is $O(mn^3)$. However, we may take advantage of the structure of the matrix C to reduce the *total* cost of INITIALIZE LABELS to $O(mn^2)$. The idea is to observe that $c_{ij} < c_{i+mj}$; therefore the minimization for each y can be restricted to only m different vertices in $X - X_1$.

Algorithm MFT can be used to calculate an optimal schedule when we delay the availability of each processor. Let $\tau_1, \ldots, \tau_m$ be m nonnegative numbers and assume that the ith processor may not be assigned to any task before time τ_i for $i = 1, \ldots, m$. Therefore, for any given schedule each of the tasks on the ith processor is delayed by τ_i time units.

Let $[\tau_i]$ denote the $m \times n$ matrix formed as follows:

$$[\tau_i] = \begin{bmatrix} \tau_1 & \tau_1 & \cdots & \tau_1 \\ \tau_2 & \tau_2 & \cdots & \tau_2 \\ \cdot & & & \cdot \\ \cdot & & & \cdot \\ \cdot & & & \cdot \\ \tau_m & \tau_m & \cdots & \tau_m \end{bmatrix}$$

and let D be the $m' \times n$ matrix defined by

$$D = \begin{bmatrix} [\tau_i] \\ [\tau_i] \\ \cdot \\ \cdot \\ \cdot \\ [\tau_i] \end{bmatrix}$$

If we take $C + D$ to be the cost matrix of the transportation network $\mathcal{N}$ (rather than C), an optimal flow pattern for $\mathcal{N}$ determines an optimal schedule with respect to $[\tau_{ij}]$ and the delays $\tau_1, \ldots, \tau_m$.

3.12 SPECIAL CASES

In many instances there is no necessity for the generality permitted in the previous section. It may be more likely that the m processors are essentially identical except for their relative speeds—line printers, for example. One way to model this is to associate with each processor a positive number $\gamma_i \geq 1$, and with each task T_j a processing time $\tau_j > 0$. The time taken for processor i to service task T_j is given by $\gamma_i \cdot \tau_j$ [CMM].

Clearly, by defining $\tau_{ij} = \gamma_i \cdot \tau_j$ we may use MFT to determine an optimal schedule. However, a more economical method for finding an optimal schedule is based on the following lemma.

Lemma 3.19 Let $a_1 \geq a_2 \geq \cdots \geq a_n$ and $b_1, \ldots, b_n$ be two sequences of numbers. A permutation $\alpha = \alpha_1, \ldots, \alpha_n$ minimizes the quantity

$$\sum_{i=1}^{n} a_i b_{\alpha_i}$$

if and only if $b_{\alpha_1} \leq b_{\alpha_2} \cdots \leq b_{\alpha_n}$.

Proof   An interchange argument will suffice.   ∎

Form the $m \times n$ matrix Γ

$$\Gamma = \begin{bmatrix} \gamma_1 & 2\gamma_1 & 3\gamma_1 & \cdots & n\gamma_1 \\ \gamma_2 & 2\gamma_2 & 3\gamma_2 & \cdots & n\gamma_2 \\ \cdot & & & & \cdot \\ \cdot & & & & \cdot \\ \cdot & & & & \cdot \\ \gamma_m & 2\gamma_m & 3\gamma_m & \cdots & n\gamma_m \end{bmatrix}$$

We denote the ijth entry of Γ as γ_{ij} and let

$$\gamma_{i_1 j_1}, \ldots, \gamma_{i_{m'} j_{m'}}$$

be an enumeration of the elements of Γ ($m' = mn$) such that

$$\gamma_{i_1 j_1} \leq \gamma_{i_2 j_2} \leq \cdots \leq \gamma_{i_{m'} j_{m'}}$$

We also assume that the τ_j's satisfy

$$\tau_1 \geq \tau_2 \geq \cdots \geq \tau_n$$

We "match" τ_k with $\gamma_{i_k j_k}$ for $k = 1, \ldots, n$. If τ_k is matched with $\gamma_{i_k j_k}$, then T_k is scheduled on processor i_k and there are $j_k - 1$ tasks that follow T_k on processor i_k.

The justification for this approach is based on the observation that any schedule can be interpreted as a "matching" of the τ_j's with the elements of Γ. Moreover, Lemma 3.19 directs us to an optimal matching that associates τ_k with $\gamma_{i_k j_k}$. Finally, we observe that this optimal matching of terms produces a valid schedule, since $\gamma_{i,j}$ appears before $\gamma_{i,j+1}$ in the sequence $\gamma_{i_1 j_1}, \ldots, \gamma_{i_{m'} j_{m'}}$.

Using an efficient algorithm for implementing priority queues [AHU], we can construct an algorithm for building optimal schedules with $O(n \log n + n \log m + m)$ worst-case time complexity. The $O(n \log n)$ term is the cost of sorting of the processing times and the $O(n \log m + m)$ is the cost of using a priority queue to obtain the terms $\gamma_{i_1 j_1}, \ldots, \gamma_{i_n j_n}$.

Specializing further we take the γ_i to be all equal. This is the case of identical machines and the optimal schedules are commonly called shortest processing time (SPT) first schedules. The class of SPT schedules is rather large, and much is known about the maximum finishing time properties of these schedules. See Section 1.5.2.3 in Chapter 1 for a summary of results.

CHAPTER FOUR

COMPLEXITY OF SEQUENCING PROBLEMS

J. D. ULLMAN
PRINCETON UNIVERSITY

4.1 INTRODUCTION

In the field of scheduling theory, as in many other areas, we come across numerous problems that can be solved relatively easily, while other, similar problems appear quite hard. For example, as shown in Chapter 2, the optimal scheduling on two processors of n unit-execution-time tasks can be done in $O(n^2)$ steps. However, the same problem with three processors appears to require time that is exponential in n. That is, with three processors it appears that we must try virtually all schedules before we can be sure of having the best.

There is no way known to prove that exponential time is required for the three-processor, unit-execution-time problem, or for any other scheduling problem, for that matter. What we can do, however, is show that there is a large class of problems, called "NP-complete" problems, and either all or none of them have polynomial-time solutions. The NP-complete problems include many well-known problems [Ka] such as the traveling salesman problem or the general m-processor, n-job-scheduling problem, for which mathematicians and computer scientists have vainly searched for less than exponential solutions over a period of decades. There is thus strong evidence that no NP-complete problem has a polynomial-time solution.

As a consequence, it becomes important to determine whether a problem is NP-complete, for if so, we very likely need a heuristic to get approximations to the optimal solution. It is no surprise, therefore, that heuristics for scheduling problems have received such attention (see Chapters 5 and 6). If a problem has a polynomial-time solution, on the other hand, we are very likely to attempt an exact solution. Now an $O(n^{10})$ problem is really no easier to solve than an $O(2^n)$ problem, at least for reasonable n. But as a practical matter, the problems that arise

---

* $O(f(n))$ means "at most $cf(n)$" for some constant c and any $n \geq 1$.

139

naturally and have polynomial-time solutions tend to be $O(n^2)$ or $O(n^3)$ at the worst.

Thus, as a rule of thumb we can regard problems with a polynomial-time solution as "tractable"—subject to exact solution; those that are NP-complete, or worse, are "intractable"—not subject to exact solution. As the reader may expect, there is a grey area of problems that have not been shown to be NP-complete (or worse) but for which polynomial-time solutions are not known. Examples are three-processor, unit-execution-time scheduling and one-processor, minimum mean-flow-time with arbitrary precedence constraints (see Tables 1.1 and 1.2).

4.2 PROBLEMS AND THEIR POLYNOMIAL REDUCIBILITY

As a point of departure, let us define a *problem* formally as a question that has a "yes" or "no" answer. Normally, the question has several "parameters," that is, free variables. A selection of values for the parameters is termed an *instance* of the problem. The *size* of an instance is the length of the string used to represent the values of the parameters. The alphabet used for strings representing instances must be fixed for the problem and independent of the instances.

Example 1 We can couch the general scheduling problem as follows: "is there a schedule for the set of n tasks $T_1, T_2, \ldots, T_n$ with precedence constraint $<$ and execution times $\tau_1, \tau_2, \ldots, \tau_n$, on m processors with finishing time ω or less?" The parameters are $n, m, \omega, <, \tau_1, \tau_2, \ldots, \tau_m$. It is plausible to represent instances of this problem by using the five symbols 0, 1, left and right parentheses, and comma. The numbers n, m, and ω can be represented in binary. Separated by commas, they begin the string. Then follow pairs of the form (i, j), where i and j are binary numbers. There is a pair (i, j) if and only if task T_i precedes T_j according to precedence constraint $<$. Finally, we list the n execution times $\tau_1, \tau_2, \ldots, \tau_n$, in binary, separated by commas.

For example, suppose $n = 5$, $m = 2$, $\omega = 8$, $<$ is given by $1 < 4 < 5$ and $2 < 3$, and $\{\tau_i\}$ is given by

i	τ_i
1	4
2	5
3	4
4	2
5	1

Then the string representing this instance is

$$n \quad m \quad \omega \quad 1 < 4 \qquad 4 < 5 \qquad 2 < 3 \quad \tau_1 \quad \tau_2 \quad \tau_3 \quad \tau_4 \quad \tau_5$$
$$101, \ 10, 1000(1, \ 100) \ (100, \ 101) \ (10, \ 11) \ 100, \ 101, \ 100, \ 10, \ 1$$

The answer to this instance is "no."

One might naturally ask whether we are throwing something away by settling for a yes-no answer rather than insisting that a question be phrased as an optimization problem. That is, one might suggest that the yes-no scheduling problem of Example 1 may have a polynomial-time solution, yet the corresponding optimization problem—"given n, m, $<$ and the τ's, what is the smallest t for which the instance $n, m, t, <, \tau_1, \ldots, \tau_n$ of the yes-no problem has answer 'yes'?"—may not have a polynomial solution. The reply in this case is that such a situation is not possible, nor is it possible for any of the other known NP-complete problems.

In proof, suppose there is a polynomial-time algorithm for solution of the yes-no scheduling problem. Say the algorithm takes time $p(s)$ on an instance of size s. We could use the following algorithm to minimize t given $n, m, <$ and the τ's.* First, if $m = 0$, there is no such t, and we are done. If $m \geq 1$, the minimum t is no greater than $\Sigma_{i=1}^{n} \tau_i$. Since each τ_i is written in binary in the string encoding this instance of the optimization problem, we see that s, the size of the instance, is at least $\Sigma_{i=1}^{n} \log_2 \tau_i$. It follows that the optimum value of t does not exceed 2^s.

Our algorithm will call the assumed algorithm for the yes-no problem up to s times, each time with a different value of t. We begin by answering the instance $n, m, 2^{s-1}, <, \tau_1, \ldots, \tau_n$ of the yes-no problem. If the answer is "yes", answer the instance $n, m, 2^{s-2}, <, \tau_1, \ldots, \tau_n$; if not, answer $n, m, 3(2^{s-2}), <, \tau_1, \ldots, \tau_n$. We proceed in this manner, with each call halving the range in which the optimum t is known to lie.

The string representing each considered instance of the yes-no problem is of length no greater than $2s + 2$, since these strings are essentially the string for the optimization problem with the number t inserted. The binary representation of t requires at most $s + 1$ bits plus a comma, since $t \leq 2^s$. Thus each call to the assumed yes-no algorithm requires time at most $p(2s + 2)$, and there are s calls at most, for a total time of $sp(2s + 2)$. The time taken by our algorithm is just this time plus the time spent constructing the strings to pass to the various calls or deciding what instance to call next. Since the arithmetic involved in these decisions is easy, the reader may convince himself that at most cs^2 steps, for some constant c, are required. Thus our algorithm takes time $sp(2s + 2) + cs^2$.

---

* Let us assume instances $n, m, <, \tau_1, \ldots, \tau_n$ of the optimization version of the scheduling problem are encoded as in Example 1, but with ω omitted.

Since p is a polynomial, so is $sp(2s+2)+cs^2$. Hence our algorithm, too, is polynomial in time.

The foregoing argument is a good example of the principal tool used in the theory of NP-complete problems—the "polynomial reduction" of one problem to another. An instance of one problem (optimization, in this case) was converted to one or more instances of another problem (the yes-no version of scheduling), and an assumed algorithm for the second problem was used to solve these instances. The resulting solutions were used to solve the first problem. An essential feature was that the instance of the first problem was converted to instances of the second quickly—in polynomial time—hence the instances of the second were not too long, at most a polynomial function of the length of the original instance. We are thus moved to make the following definition.

Definition We say problem $\mathcal{P}_1$ *polynomially reduces to* problem $\mathcal{P}_2$, written $\mathcal{P}_1 \propto \mathcal{P}_2$, if problem $\mathcal{P}_1$ can be solved by an algorithm A having the following properties:

1. A calls a subroutine A' to solve problem $\mathcal{P}_2$ zero or more times.
2. Exclusive of the time spent in calls to A', algorithm A takes time that is polynomial in the size of that instance of $\mathcal{P}_1$ which is input to A.

We should make the following observation about polynomial reducibility. If $\mathcal{P}_1 \propto \mathcal{P}_2$ and $\mathcal{P}_2$ has a polynomial-time algorithm, so does $\mathcal{P}_1$. To understand this, suppose algorithm A' takes time $p_1(n)$. Algorithm A spends time $p_2(n)$ exclusive of calls to A', for some polynomial p_2. Then surely there are no more than $p_2(n)$ calls to A', and no argument to A' can have length greater than $p_2(n)$, since a larger argument could not even be written down in time $p_2(n)$. Thus the calls to A' each take no more than $p_1(p_2(n))$ time. Since there are no more than $p_2(n)$ of them, the total time taken by A on input of length n is no more than $p_2(n)+p_2(n)p_1(p_2(n))$, which is a polynomial if p_1 and p_2 are. Note that the time taken by algorithm A may be much greater than that taken by A', but it is still polynomial if the time taken by A' is.

In what follows we show that there are various "NP-complete" problems $\mathcal{P}$, including many kinds of scheduling problems, having the property that every problem in a huge class (called **NP**) polynomially reduces to $\mathcal{P}$. Thus if an NP-complete problem $\mathcal{P}$ had a polynomial-time solution, so would every problem in **NP**.

4.3 A COMPUTER MODEL

We must now fix on a model of a computer. We make a model that is simple, yet general enough that the reader should believe that any real computer is modeled thereby. First any computer, including its registers, control units, and primary and secondary storage devices can be represented at any time by a sequence of bits, called the *state*. A fixed finite number of bits serve to represent the contents of primary (core) memory and all the circuitry usually called the "control." Only the number of bits stored on secondary storage devices such as tapes can be regarded as potentially unbounded, since although a tape is of finite capacity, a program could call for an indefinite number of tape mountings, and all tapes ever used by the program can be considered part of the state, since even if a particular tape is currently dismounted, it could be mounted later at the request of the program. Let us now state the assumptions we make about the operation of a computer.

1. The state of the computer changes at fixed time intervals, called *steps*. Between steps, the state remains the same.

2. The value of each bit after a step depends on the values of some fixed set of bits just before that step.

3. For any integer n, the particular bits used by the program when given an input of length n bits does not depend on the input itself. Moreover, there is a constant c such that if a program runs for t steps, at most ct bits of the computer are used.

Condition 1 requires no justification. Condition 2 may not be immediately obvious. To begin an explanation, we name each bit on secondary storage devices such as tapes according to the bit's position relative to the read head on that storage device. Thus if a tape shifts left at a step, the value of a bit depends only on the value of its right-hand neighbor in its track at the previous step. Thus in general, the value of a bit on a secondary storage device can be determined by examining the finite-sized main memory to see whether motion of its storage device is called for (in the case of a permanently rotating disk or drum, this test is unnecessary) and determining the value of the appropriate neighbor bit if motion is required. The value of all the bits in the main memory and control unit of the computer depend only on themselves and on the secondary storage bits currently under read heads. Note that the size of main memory is large but invariably finite.

Condition 3 is more subtle still. We can imagine a pathological program that on reading an input of n decimal digits, requests that the ith disk pack be mounted, where i is the decimal number input. Since i can range from 0 to $10^n - 1$, the number of bits of storage utilized for some input of length n is exponential in n, although the program takes very little time to execute, certainly polynomial (in fact linear) time as a function of n.

We would like to know whether if a program ran for a polynomial amount of time, its storage would be polynomial as well. Fortunately, given any polynomial-time program, we can simulate it on any input of length n in at most the square of the necessary time, using a fixed set of storage elements. The amount of time and space used by the simulating program could be as high as the square of the time used by the simulated program, but if the latter is polynomial time, the former will be polynomial in time and space. We shall not go into the simulation details here. Further information can be found in Cook and Rechkow [CR] or Aho, Hopcroft, and Ullman [AHU], or the reader may convince himself that only in pathological cases would he want to use many different and disjoint regions of memory for different inputs of the same size.

4.4 NONDETERMINISTIC COMPUTATION

Having fixed a reasonable model of a deterministic computer, we now add a purely abstract feature—nondeterminism. Imagine an ordinary computer to have an instruction

CHOICE L1, L2

The effect of executing this instruction is that two copies of the computer in its present state are instantaneously made. Then each copy changes state, one by making L1 the next instruction to be executed, the other by making L2 the next instruction. Thus after n CHOICE instructions are executed, there would be 2^n copies of the computer, perhaps all in different states.

A nondeterministic computer can be used (abstractly, of course) to solve a yes-no problem if we declare that the answer given by the computer will be taken to be "yes" if one or more of the copies created give that answer, independently of how many give the answer "no."

We can abstractly define the time taken by a nondeterministic computer to be the length of the longest sequence of state transitions made.

Example 2 Consider the history of a nondeterministic computer portrayed in Fig. 4.1. At time $t = 0$, the computer begins in state s_0. It executes a CHOICE instruction with the two copies entering states s_1 and s_2 at time 1. In s_2, the computer executes an instruction other than CHOICE, entering state s_5. In s_1, however, a CHOICE is made, and s_3 and s_4 are the two next states. In s_4, there is no next state, and its answer is "no" (i.e., "yes" has not been printed out). In s_3, a transition to s_6 is made at time 3. Presumably the last step was to print "yes," because that is the answer indicated for s_6. We now know that this nondeterministic computer answers "yes" for whatever input is present for s_0.

We can follow the transitions made up to time 4 when we see that all

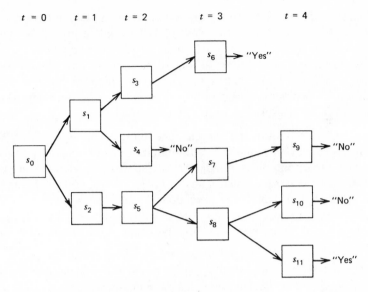

Figure 4.1 History of a nondeterministic computer.

copies of the computer have made an output and no further transitions are possible. That is, all copies of the computer have halted. We thus say that this nondeterministic computer, started in state s_0, takes time 4.

It should be emphasized that the "time taken" by a nondeterministic computer can be far less than the time required to simulate one deterministically. As was mentioned, a nondeterministic computer taking time n can, if it executes only CHOICE instructions, reach 2^n different states. The obvious way to simulate such a device with a real computer would thus take at least time 2^n.

It thus appears that at least some problems that can be solved by a nondeterministic computer in polynomial time require exponential time on a real computer, although no one has been able to prove this statement (or alternatively, to show that nondeterministic computers can be efficiently simulated by real ones).

Definition We may define the class **NP** to consist of all problems that can be solved by a nondeterministic computer in polynomial time. Define **P** to be the class of problems solved by a deterministic computer in polynomial time. Define a problem $\mathcal{P}$ to be *NP-complete* if every problem in **NP** polynomially reduces to $\mathcal{P}$.

As a consequence of the definitions already given, if any NP-complete problem has a deterministic polynomial-time algorithm, all problems in **NP** do (i.e., $\mathbf{P} = \mathbf{NP}$). Thus if one NP-complete problem has a polynomial-time solution, they all do. Since the class of NP-complete problems includes such problems as the traveling salesman, knapsack, and general scheduling problems, and no polynomial-time algorithm has been found for any of them (not for lack of trying), we are entitled to believe that all NP-complete problems require more than polynomial time deterministically, and in fact, probably require exponential time.

Example 3   Let us show the general scheduling problem to be in **NP**. The problem is in fact NP-complete, although more work is required to show that. The algorithm on a nondeterministic machine can be stated as follows. Assume we are given n tasks $T_1, T_2, \ldots, T_n$ to be scheduled on m processors, and that $<$, the precedence constraint is given as a list of pairs $T_i < T_j$. Suppose also that the execution times $\tau_1, \tau_2, \ldots, \tau_n$ are given as a list of binary numbers. Finally, suppose time limit ω is given in binary.

1. Using CHOICE repeatedly, assign to each T_i a processor P_{j_i} and a starting time $t_i < \omega$. That is, we guess a schedule.

2. For each k and l with $1 \leq k < l \leq n$, check that either $P_{j_k} \neq P_{j_l}$ or $t_k + \tau_k \leq t_l$ or $t_l + \tau_l \leq t_k$. That is, we check that no two tasks are scheduled for the same processor at the same time.

3. For each k, $1 \leq k \leq n$, check that $t_k + \tau_k \leq \omega$. That is, we check that all jobs finish before the ωth time step.

To analyze the time spent by the foregoing nondeterministic algorithm, let us first establish a lower bound on the input length N, assuming that the input is encoded as in Example 1. Since ω, n, m and the τ_i's must be written in binary separated by commas, and there are n execution times, we see* that

$$N \geq n + \log m + \log \omega + \sum_{i=1}^{n} \log \tau_i \qquad (1)$$

Now let us upper bound the time T taken by the algorithm. Assume conservatively that k time units are required to write down, add, or subtract k-bit numbers. Then step 1 requires at most $O(n(\log \omega + \log m))$ time to write down the processor and starting time for each of the n tasks. Note that an enormous number of copies of the computer are in existence by the time step 1 ends. However, the length of any path in the tree of copies (as in Fig. 4.1) is quite limited in comparison.

In step 2 at most n^2 [actually $n(n-1)/2$] pairs (k, l) are examined. The arithmetic required for the three tests of step 2 is at most $O(\log \tau_k +$

---

* All logarithms are base 2.

$\log \tau_l + \log \omega + \log m$). It is thus easy to show that the total time spent in step 2 is at most $O(\log \tau_k + \log \tau_l + \log \omega + \log m)$. It is thus easy to show that the total time spent in step 2 is at most $O(n^2(n + \log \omega + \log m + \Sigma_{i=1}^n \log \tau_i))$. Finally, step 3 clearly requires $O(n \log \omega + \Sigma_{i=1}^n \log \tau_i))$ time.

Hence the time spent is dominated by step 2, and we may establish that

$$T \le cn^2 \left(n + \log \omega + \log m + \sum_{i=1}^n \log \tau_i \right)$$

for some constant c. Putting (1) and (2) together, we have $T \le cN^3$. Thus since (1) is a lower bound on the input length and (2) an upper bound on running time, we can be sure that this nondeterministic computer program solving the general scheduling problem has running time that is at most a third-degree polynomial in its input length. Hence the general scheduling problem is in **NP**. ▣

4.5 AN NP-COMPLETE PROBLEM

We can now show to be NP-complete the *satisfiability problem for Boolean expressions*, which, given a Boolean expression, is as follows: does there exist an assignment of truth values 0 and 1 (**false** and **true**, respectively) to its propositional variables that makes the expression true?

To show satisfiability to be NP-complete, recall the need to show that for every problem $\mathcal{P}$ in **NP**, a deterministic polynomial-time solution to the satisfiability problem implies a deterministic polynomial-time solution to $\mathcal{P}$. That is, $\mathcal{P}$ polynomially reduces to satisfiability. Note that the polynomial amount of time spent reducing $\mathcal{P}$ to satisfiability need not be the same for every $\mathcal{P}$.

Theorem 4.1 Satisfiability of Boolean expressions is NP-complete.

Proof First we observe that satisfiability is in **NP**. Using CHOICE, we can generate all possible assignments of truth values to the variables. One copy of the computer is created for each of the 2^n possible assignments of truth and falsehood to the n variables. Only $O(n)$ steps are needed, since the process is nondeterministic. Then the value of the Boolean expression can be evaluated by each copy of the computer using its assignment of truth values. The reader should be able to construct a deterministic algorithm to do the evaluation in $O(N^2)$ steps, where N is the length of the input Boolean expression (note $n \le N$).* In fact, an $O(N)$ algorithm is

---

* We are assuming here that the "length" of a Boolean expression is the number of symbols $+$, $\cdot$, $\neg$, parentheses and propositional variables in the string denoting the expression. Actually, since all problems must be written in a fixed alphabet, propositional variables must be given numbers and encoded in binary or some other notation. Thus we can actually show $n \log n \le N$ if n variables appear in an expression.

possible. Thus the nondeterministic computer can answer whether its input is satisfiable in time polynomial in the length of the expression. Note that a nondeterministic computer answers "yes" whenever any of its copies does: this property is crucial here, as is the computer's ability to proliferate copies of itself.

Now we must show the hard part, that every problem $\mathcal{P}$ in **NP** polynomially reduces to satisfiability. Recall from Section 4.3 our assumptions about our computer model. Suppose we are given a nondeterministic computer loaded with a program to solve $\mathcal{P}$, and this program takes time $p(n)$ on an input of length n, for some polynomial $p_{\mathcal{P}}$. Given a supposed deterministic polynomial-time algorithm A to solve satisfiability, say one requiring $p(n)$ time, we can construct a deterministic polynomial-time algorithm $A_{\mathcal{P}}$ for $\mathcal{P}$ as follows: $A_{\mathcal{P}}$ works by taking any input I of any length n and constructing in polynomial time a Boolean expression B_I that is satisfiable if and only if the nondeterministic computer answers "yes" when presented with input I. The expression B_I will have on the order of $[p_{\mathcal{P}}(n)]^2$ variables X_{it} for $1 \le i \le cp_{\mathcal{P}}(n)$ and $0 \le t \le p_{\mathcal{P}}(n)$, where c is an upper bound on the ratio of the number of bits used to the number of steps executed. Constant c exists by the assumptions of our computer model. Intuitively, $X_{it} = 1$ if and only if the ith bit used by the program is 1 at time t. Note that since the program computes nondeterministically for no more than $p_{\mathcal{P}}(n)$ steps, we need only worry about $0 \le t \le p_{\mathcal{P}}(n)$. Also, we have assumed that at most c bits per step find use and there are at most $p_{\mathcal{P}}(n)$ steps; thus there are at most $cp_{\mathcal{P}}(n)$ bits that we need worry about. By our assumptions, the computer uses the same bits on any input of length n.

The expression B_I can now be written as the Boolean product ("and") of three expressions C, D, and E, which assert the following.

1. Expression C asserts that the initial configuration of the computer is correct. That is, the input is loaded with I, the program appears in the machine with the location counter set to its first instruction, and all unused bits are set to 0. Thus C is just the Boolean product of X_{i0} or $\neg X_{i0}$ for all i, $1 \le i \le cp_{\mathcal{P}}(n)$, and C is of length $O(p_{\mathcal{P}}(n))$.

2. Expression D asserts that at each time $t \ge 1$, the contents of each bit i is what it should be, based on the values at time $t - 1$ of the fixed number of bits on which the ith bit depends. If the move made by the computer at time $t - 1$ is not a choice move, the value of bit i at time t is uniquely determined from the value of bits at time $t - 1$. If the move at time $t - 1$ is a CHOICE, only the location counter bits change, and there are two legal assignments of values to the fixed number of bits of the location counter at time t.

We may thus write D as the product of expressions D_t for $1 \le t \le p_{\mathscr{P}}(n)$ and D_{it} for all i and t, $1 \le t \le p_{\mathscr{P}}(n)$, $1 \le i \le cp_{\mathscr{P}}(n)$. Moreover, D_{it} asserts either that the move at time $t - 1$ is CHOICE or that it is not and X_{it} has its proper value at time t; D_t asserts either that the move made at time $t - 1$ is not CHOICE, or that it is and the location counter at time t has one of the two permissible values, all other bits having the same value at time t as they had at time $t - 1$. By our assumptions about the computer, the D_{it}'s can each be written down in a fixed length, independent of n. Thus their total length is $O(p_{\mathscr{P}}^2(n))$, and we can write them down in this time by an obvious algorithm. The D_t's each require a string of length $O(p_{\mathscr{P}}(n))$ and can be easily written down. $O(p_{\mathscr{P}}^2(n))$ time and space suffices for these as well. Thus expression D can be written down in time and space $O(p_{\mathscr{P}}^2(n))$.

3. Expression E asserts that the sequence of configurations represented by the X_{it}'s causes the answer "yes" to be printed. We lose nothing in assuming that there is a particular bit j that is set to 1 by the program if and only if it answers "yes." Thus E is just the sum of X_{jt}'s for $0 \le t \le p_{\mathscr{P}}(n)$. Clearly the length of E is $O(p_{\mathscr{P}}(n))$.

It is easy to check that the answer to $\mathscr{P}$ on input I is "yes" if and only if $B_I = C \cdot D \cdot E$ is satisfiable. The satisfying set of truth values can easily be determined given a computation leading to the printing of "yes," and such a computation can easily be determined given a set of values for the X_{it}'s that satisfy B_I.

We have seen that B_I is of length $c_1 p_{\mathscr{P}}^2(n)$ for some constant c_1 and that B_I can be constructed from I in time $O(p_{\mathscr{P}}^2(n))$. We can now apply the supposed algorithm A to B_I and determine whether B_I is satisfiable. Since A takes $p(c_1 p_{\mathscr{P}}^2(n))$ time on input B_I, the entire algorithm A takes $O(p_{\mathscr{P}}^2(n) + p(c_1 p_{\mathscr{P}}^2(n)))$ time and is deterministic because A and the construction of B_I from I are deterministic. Since p and $p_{\mathscr{P}}$ are polynomials, the running time of $A_{\mathscr{P}}$ is clearly polynomial in n, the length of its input I.

We have thus shown that an arbitrary problem $\mathscr{P}$ in **NP** polynomially reduces to satisfiability. ∎

In fact, we can show more than was given in Theorem 4.1. Let us define the *conjunctive normal form (CNF)-satisfiability* problem to be the question of whether a Boolean expression in conjunctive normal form (product of sums of literals*) is satisfiable. Define *k-satisfiability* to be the question of whether a Boolean expression in CNF with exactly k literals per term (*in k-CNF*) is satisfiable.

* A *literal* is a variable or a negated variable (i.e. x or $\lnot x$).

Example 4 $(x + y + z)(\neg x + w + \neg z)$ is in 3-CNF. The expression $(x + y + z)(\neg w + \neg x)(z + \neg y)$ is in CNF but not in k-CNF for any k.

It is not hard to show that 2-satisfiability is in **P**; in fact, it has a deterministic linear-time solution. However, the situation appears to change at $k = 3$, since we can prove the following.

Theorem 4.2 3-satisfiability is NP-complete.

Proof First we observe that the expression B_I constructed in the proof of Theorem 4.1 is almost in CNF. In fact, expression C is in CNF, since it is the product of many "sums" of one literal. Expression E is in CNF because it is the "product" of one sum of literals. Expression D is the product of many expressions, the D_t's and D_{it}'s introduced in the proof of Theorem 4.1. Each of these expressions is of fixed length, independent of the length of the input I. Thus using the laws of Boolean algebra we can manipulate these expressions into CNF, perhaps increasing the length of D by a constant factor, but no more. Thus the proof of Theorem 4.1 could just as well have been used to show that CNF-satisfiability is NP-complete, and we can take this result as proven.

Now, to show 3-satisfiability to be NP-complete, we show that CNF-satisfiability reduces to it. Suppose we are given an expression $E = E_1 E_2 \cdots E_k$ in CNF, where each of the E_i's is a sum of literals. We can construct a new expression F in 3-CNF such that F is satisfiable if and only if E is. The time to construct F will be polynomial in the length of E, giving a polynomial reduction of CNF-satisfiability to 3-satisfiability.

We treat each term E_i separately, depending on how many literals it has.

Case 1 E_i has one literal x. Introduce two new variables y and z and replace E_i by $(x + y + z)(x + y + \neg z)(x + \neg y + z)(x + \neg y + \neg z)$. Then an assignment of values to the original variables (including x) makes E_i true if and only if there is an assignment of values to the original variables and y and z (any assignment for y and z will do) that makes the modified expression true.

Case 2 E_i has two literals. This case is similar to case 1.

Case 3 E_i has three literals. No modification is necessary.

Case 4 E_i has $k > 3$ literals, say $E_i = x_1 + x_2 + \cdots + x_k$. Introduce new variables $y_1, y_2, \ldots, y_{k-3}$ and replace E_i by $(x_1 + x_2 + y_1)(x_3 + \neg y_1 + y_2)(x_4 + \neg y_2 + y_3) \cdots (x_{k-2} + \neg y_{k-4} + y_{k-3})(x_{k-1} + x_k + \neg y_{k-3})$. If $k = 4$, the replacement for E_i is just $(x_1 + x_2 + y_1)(x_3 + x_4 + \neg y_1)$. It is left to the reader to check that for all and only the assignments of truth values that satisfy E_i are there assignments to the variables including the introduced y's that make the constructed product of expressions true.

We let F be the product of the expressions constructed from all the E_i's. Observe that in no case is the modified expression more than 32 times as long as the original,* and F can easily be constructed from E, certainly in time polynomial in the length of E. Thus CNF-satisfiability has been polynomially reduced to 3-satisfiability. ▣

4.6 NP-COMPLETENESS OF THE SCHEDULING PROBLEM

We are now ready to polynomially reduce 3-satisfiability to the general scheduling problem, thus showing the latter to be NP-complete.

Theorem 4.3 The scheduling problem is NP-complete.

Proof We show how to construct in polynomial time from any Boolean expression E in 3-CNF an instance S of the scheduling problem such that S can be scheduled to complete within its time limit if and only if E is satisfiable. The instance S will have a null precedence constraint and only two processors. The execution times of the jobs in S will be huge—in fact, exponential in the length of E. However, since the execution times are encoded in binary, the length of the representation of S will still be polynomial in the length of E, and S can be written down in time that is polynomial in the length of E.

To begin, let $E = E_1 E_2 \cdots E_k$ and let $E_j = (x_j + y_j + z_j)$, where each x_j, y_j, and z_j is a literal (i.e., a variable or a negated variable). Let there be p variables mentioned in the expression E, say, $v_1, v_2, \ldots, v_p$. We construct a set of tasks, each of whose execution times is a $(k + p + 1)$-place decimal number. The low-order places correspond to the sums E_i, and the high-order places, except for the highest, correspond to the variables. We explain the use of the highest-order place later.

1. For each variable $v_i, 1 \le i \le p$, construct tasks T_i and T'_i, with execution times τ_i and τ'_i. The decimal representations of τ_i and τ'_i have 0's in all positions except as follows.

   a. Each has 1 in position $i + 1$ from the left, the position corresponding to v_i.

   b. τ_i has a 1 in position j from the right (the position corresponding to E_j) if setting $v_i = 1$ makes E_j true. That is, one of x_j, y_j, or z_j is v_i.

   c. τ'_i has 1 in position j from the right if one of x_j, y_j, or z_j is $\neg v_i$ (i.e., setting $v_i = 0$ makes E_j true).

2. For each $j, 1 \le j \le k$ construct two tasks U_j and U'_j. Let the execution times of U_j and U'_j be $\sigma_j = \sigma'_j = 10^{j-1}$. That is, σ_j and σ'_j are all 0's with a single 1 in the position for E_j.

---

* Assume that each variable counts as one symbol. If we encode variable names in binary, we should include a factor of the logarithm of the input length; but the reduction is still polynomial.

3. Let V_0 be a task with execution time $\rho_0 = \Sigma_{i=k}^{p+k} 10^i$. That is, ρ_0 has 1 in the leftmost position and each of the positions corresponding to the variables and has 0 in the positions for the E_j's.

4. Let V_1 be a task with execution time $\rho_1 = \Sigma_{i=0}^{p+k} 10^i$.

The pattern of nonzero digits for the execution times of the various tasks appears in Fig. 4.2.

Tasks	Execution times	1	p		k	
T_i, T_i'	τ_i, τ_i'		1		1...1...11	
U_j, U_j'	σ_j, σ_j'				1	
V_0	ρ_0	1	11...1			
V_1	ρ_1	1	11...1		11...	1
ω		1	22...2		33...	3

Figure 4.2   Nonzero digit patterns for execution times.

To complete the specification of scheduling problem S, we let

$$\omega = 10^{p+k} + 2 \sum_{i=k}^{p+k-1} + 3 \sum_{i=0}^{k-1} 10^i$$

The digit pattern of ω also appears in Fig. 4.2. Note that the sum of all the execution times is exactly 2ω; thus the answer to S is "yes" if and only if the execution times can be partitioned into two equal sets. We can show that S has answer "yes" if and only if E is satisfiable.

if: Suppose E is satisfied if v_i is assigned the value a_i (0 or 1) for each i. Based on this assignment, we select a set of tasks whose execution times total exactly ω. These will be executed on one processor in any order, and the remaining jobs will be executed on the other processor, thus meeting the time limit ω.

First we select T_i if $a_i = 1$ and T_i' if $a_i = 0$. Since E is satisfied by the assignment, we know that in the decimal representation of the sum of the execution times of those tasks so far selected, there is a 1, 2, or 3 in each of the k rightmost positions. No 0's can appear there. Thus we can select from zero to two of U_j and U_j' for each j, which means that the sum of the execution times will have 3 in each of the k rightmost positions. Note also that since we have selected T_i or T_i' but not both, we have in the sum of execution times a 0 in the leftmost position and 1 in each of the next p positions. Thus selecting V_0 gives us tasks with execution times totaling exactly ω.

only if: First we observe that V_0 and V_1 must be executed on different processors, since their execution times together exceed ω. Consider the other tasks executed by the processor executing V_0, say processor P_1. Then to ensure that the sum of the execution times of all tasks executed by P_1 will have 2 in the second through $(p + 1)$st places, exactly one of T_i and T_i' must be executed by P_1 for each i. The execution times of those of the T_i's and T_i''s selected must together have at least one 1 in each of the k rightmost places. This is because if there were no 1 in place j from the right, execution of the two tasks U_j and U_j' by P_1 would be insufficient to cause a 3 in that place of the total execution time for processor P_1.

At this point we can easily construct a satisfying assignment of values to variables for the expression E. Specifically, assign x_j the value 1 if T_j is executed by P_1 and assign it the value 0 if T_j' is executed by P_1. The foregoing analysis assures that each E_j is given the value 1 by this assignment.

In fact, we have proved more than stated in Theorem 4.3, since we made no use of precedence and used only two processors.

Corollary 4.1   The scheduling problem restricted to have an empty precedence constraint and only two processors is still NP-complete.

Put in more abstract terms, we can say the following.

Corollary 4.2   The problem of determining, given a list of integers, whether the list can be partitioned into two parts so that the sum of the integers in one part is the same as the sum of the integers in the other, is NP-complete.

It should be noted that the foregoing proof makes heavy use of large execution times in the proof of NP-completeness of the scheduling problem. One might argue that the true "size" of the problem depends not on the length of the execution times written out, but on the sum of the magnitudes of those execution times. For the case of a fixed number of processors and no precedence constraints, the reader should have little trouble discovering an algorithm that runs in time proportional to the sum of the execution times (but exponential in the sum of the lengths of the decimal encodings of the execution times)!

Unquestionably, this situation exposes a potential shortcoming in the theory of NP-complete problems. The ability of different aspects of a problem to make that problem hard is not always proportional to the length of the encoding for that aspect. In the case at hand, one has the intuitive feeling that for their length, numbers written in decimal have much more power to defy efficient analysis than do other aspects of the scheduling problem. For example, the writing of precedence constraints requires at least that we use a few symbols for each constraint; thus the representation of precedence constraints will be relatively lengthy for the amount of complication they appear to introduce into the problem.

Fortunately in the case of scheduling, we can show that special cases in which the execution times are limited to 2 or even to 1 (but precedence constraints are permitted) are still NP-complete. Thus in a sense, the structure of precedence constraints contains all the combinatorial complexity that is contained by large execution times.

4.7 NP-COMPLETENESS OF THE MINIMUM MEAN WEIGHTED FLOW-TIME PROBLEM

Before proceeding to the results alluded to earlier, let us consider another kind of scheduling problem in which the size of execution times does appear to help make the problem NP-complete.

Definition The *minimum mean weighted flow-time problem* (stated in "yes"-"no" form) is the following: given a set of m processors for n tasks with execution times $\tau_1, \tau_2, \ldots, \tau_n$, *weights* $w_1, w_2, \ldots, w_n$, *limiting cost L*, and precedence constraint $<$, does there exist a schedule so that $\Sigma_{i=1}^n w_i f_i \le L$, where f_i is the finishing time of the ith task?

Theorem 4.4 The minimum mean weighted flow-time problem is NP-complete.

Proof We can polynomially reduce to this problem the problem mentioned in Corollary 4.2 to Theorem 4.3. That is, we know it is NP-complete to determine, given a list of integers $a_1, a_2, \ldots, a_n$, whether there exist two subsets S_1 and S_2 of integers such that

1. $S_1 \cup S_2 = \{1, 2, \ldots, n\}$.
2. $S_1 \cap S_2 = \varphi$.
3. $\displaystyle\sum_{i \in S_1} a_i = \sum_{i \in S_2} a_i$.

Given an instance $a_1, a_2, \ldots, a_n$ of this problem (the *partition problem*), we construct in polynomial time an instance of the minimum mean weighted flow-time problem as follows. Let there be two processors P_1 and P_2, a null precedence constraint, and n tasks $T_1, T_2, \ldots, T_n$, such that the ith task has both execution time and weight equal to a_i. Let the limit L be $\frac{1}{4}[\Sigma_{i=1}^n a_i]^2 + \frac{1}{2}\Sigma_{i=1}^n a_i^2$.

Suppose a particular schedule for this set of tasks causes processor P_1 to execute in sequence tasks with execution times (therefore weights)

$\sigma_1, \sigma_2, \ldots, \sigma_j$, and P_2 to execute the remaining tasks, with execution times $\rho_1, \rho_2, \ldots, \rho_k$, in that order. Note that there is a one-to-one correspondence between the a_i's and the union of the σ_i's and the ρ_i's. The mean weighted flow time of this schedule is

$$F = \sum_{i=1}^{j} \sigma_i \sum_{l=1}^{i} \sigma_l + \sum_{i=1}^{k} \rho_i \sum_{l=1}^{i} \rho_l \tag{3}$$

since the ith task executed by P_1 has weight σ_i and finishing time $\sum_{l=1}^{i} \sigma_l$, and similarly for the tasks executed by P_2. Algebraic manipulation on (3) yields

$$F = \frac{1}{2}\left[\sum_{i=1}^{j} \sigma_i\right]^2 + \frac{1}{2}\left[\sum_{i=1}^{k} \rho_i\right]^2 + \frac{1}{2}\left[\sum_{i=1}^{n} a_i^2\right] \tag{4}$$

Let $A = \sum_{i=1}^{n} a_i$ and $B = \sum_{i=1}^{n} a_i^2$. Then the limit L is $\frac{1}{4}A^2 + \frac{1}{2}B$. Also, let $A_1 = \sum_{i=1}^{j} \sigma_i$. Then $\sum_{i=1}^{k} \rho_i = A - A_1$, and (4) can be expressed as

$$F = \frac{1}{2}[A_1^2 + (A - A_1)^2 + B] = L + \left(\frac{A}{2} - A_1\right)^2 \tag{5}$$

Since in (5) we have $F > L$ unless $A_1 = A/2$, in which case $F = L$, we see that the answer to the constructed instance of the minimum mean weighted flow-time problem is "yes" if and only if the instance $a_1, a_2, \ldots, a_n$ of the partition problem has answer "yes." That is, given a solution to the partition problem instance, we can execute the tasks corresponding to one half on processor P_1, in any order. Conversely, given a solution to the instance of the minimum mean weighted flow-time problem, we may put a_i's corresponding to tasks executed by P_1 in one set S_1 and the remainder in S_2 to form a solution to the partition problem. ■

Corollary 4.3 The minimum weighted finishing-time problem with two processors and null precedence constraint is NP-complete.

4.8 NP-COMPLETENESS OF THE UNIT-EXECUTION-TIME SCHEDULING PROBLEM

Definition The *unit-execution-time (UET) scheduling problem*, in yes-no form, is to determine whether there exists a schedule for n tasks on m processors, with $\tau_i = 1$ for $1 \leq i \leq n$, time limit ω, and precedence constraint $<$.

It is easier to work with a modified version of this problem, in which a varying number of processors are available at each time unit.

Definition The *modified UET problem* is to determine whether there exists a schedule for n tasks, with $\tau_i = 1$ for $1 \le i \le n$, given time limit ω, precedence constraint $<$, and with $m(i)$ processors available at time i for $0 \le i < \omega$.*

We first show the modified UET problem to be NP-complete by polynomially reducing 3-satisfiability to it. We then show UET scheduling NP-complete by reducing modified UET scheduling to UET scheduling.

Lemma 4.1 The modified UET scheduling problem is NP-complete.

Proof We reduce 3-satisfiability to the modified UET problem. Let $E = E_1 E_2 \cdots E_k$ be a Boolean expression in 3-CNF, and let $F_j = x_j + y_j + z_j$ for $1 \le j \le k$, where x_j, y_j, and z_j are literals. Let $v_1, v_2, \ldots, v_p$ be the variables appearing in E. We construct an instance of the modified UET problem as follows. The tasks are:

1. T_{ij} and $\bar{T}_{ij}$ for $1 \le i \le p$ and $0 \le j \le p$.
2. S_i and $\bar{S}_i$ for $1 \le i \le p$.
3. D_{ij} for $1 \le i \le k$ and $1 \le j \le 7$.

The T and S tasks represent the variables, and the D tasks represent the factors of E.

The precedence constraint $<$ is given by

1. $T_{ij} < T_{i,j+1}$ and $\bar{T}_{ij} < \bar{T}_{i,j+1}$ for $1 \le i \le p$ and $0 \le j < p$.
2. $T_{i,i-1} < S_i$ and $\bar{T}_{i,i-1} < \bar{S}_i$ for $1 \le i \le p$.
3. Let us consider D_{ij}, where $a_1 a_2 a_3$ is the binary representation of j (note that the case $a_1 = a_2 = a_3 = 0$ cannot occur). Recall that E_i is $x_i + y_i + z_i$. Let literals x_i, y_i, and z_i be complemented or uncomplemented versions of variables v_{r_1}, v_{r_2}, and v_{r_3}, respectively. Let $T_{r_1,p} < D_{ij}$ if x_i is v_{r_1} (rather than $\neg\, v_{r_1}$) and $a_1 = 1$, or $x_i = \neg\, v_{r_1}$ and $a_1 = 0$. Otherwise, let $\bar{T}_{r_1,p} < D_{ij}$. Similarly, $T_{r_2,p} < D_{ij}$ if $y_i = v_{r_2}$ and $a_2 = 1$ or $y_i = \neg\, v_{r_2}$ and $a_2 = 0$; otherwise, $\bar{T}_{r_2,p} < D_{ij}$. Finally, $T_{r_3,p} < D_{ij}$ if $z_i = v_{r_3}$ and $a_3 = 1$ or $z_i = \neg\, v_{r_3}$ and $a_3 = 0$; otherwise, $\bar{T}_{r_3,p} < D_{ij}$.

The latest finishing time is $\omega = p + 3$. The numbers of processors $m(i)$ available at time i are given by:

$$m(0) = p$$
$$m(1) = 2p + 1$$
$$m(i) = 2p + 2 \qquad \text{for} \qquad 2 \le i \le p$$
$$m(p + 1) = k + p + 1$$
$$m(p + 2) = 6k$$

* A processor available at time i can be used to complete a task beginning at time i and completing at time $i + 1$.

We can show that the instance just given of the modified UET problem has a solution if and only if the given instance of 3-satisfiability is solvable. The intuitive idea behind the proof is that we may imagine v_i (or $\neg v_i$) to be **true** if and only if T_{i0} (or $\bar{T}_{i0}$, respectively) is executed beginning t time 0. We shall see that the presence of the S's and $\bar{S}$'s forces exactly one of T_{i0} and $\bar{T}_{i0}$ to be executed beginning at time 0 and the other to be executed beginning at time 1. Then the requirement that $k + m + 1$ tasks be executed beginning at time $p + 1$ is tantamount to the requirement that for each i there be one j such that D_{ij} can be executed beginning at that time (there cannot be more than one). But this condition is equivalent to saying that the sum of terms represented by D_i has truth value **true** when those of the v_i's and $\bar{v}_i$'s such that T_{i0} or $\bar{T}_{i0}$, respectively, was executed at time 0, are given the value **true**.

We first show that in any solution to the instance of the modified UET problem we may not execute both T_{i0} and $\bar{T}_{i0}$ beginning at time 0 for any i. Suppose we did. Then since $i_0 = p$, there would be some j such that neither T_{j0} nor $\bar{T}_{j0}$ was executed beginning at time 0. Then neither S_j nor $\bar{S}_j$ would be executed beginning at or before time j because, for example, S_j must be preceded by $T_{j0}, T_{j1}, \ldots, T_{j,j-1}$, each executed strictly before the next in the sequence. The total number of tasks that could be executed beginning at or before time j is thus seen to be:

1. At most $p(2j + 1)$ of the T's and $\bar{T}$'s; that is, $T_{i0}, T_{i1}, \ldots, T_{ij}$ if T_{i0} was executed at time 0 and $T_{i0}, T_{i1}, \ldots, T_{i,j-1}$ if not.
2. At most $2(j - 1)$ of the S's, specifically $S_1, \bar{S}_1, S_2, \bar{S}_2, \ldots, S_{j-1}, \bar{S}_{j-1}$.

The total number of tasks that may be begun by time j is thus at most $2pj + 2j + p - 2$. However, for $1 \leq j \leq p$,

$$\sum_{i=0}^{j} m(i) = 3p + 1 + (j - 1)(2p + 2) = 2pj + 2j + p - 1$$

We can conclude that in any solution to this instance of the modified UET problem, exactly one of T_{i0} and $\bar{T}_{i0}$ is executed beginning at time 0. Moreover, we can determine the exact tasks that are executed beginning at each time between 1 and p, given which of T_{i0} and $\bar{T}_{i0}$ is executed at time 0. That is, at time j we must commence T_{ij} if T_{i0} was executed beginning at time 0, and $T_{i,j-1}$ if not. Moreover, we must execute S_j (respectively $\bar{S}_j$) beginning at time j if T_{j0} (respectively $\bar{T}_{j0}$) was executed beginning at time 0 and execute S_{j-1} (respectively $\bar{S}_{j-1}$) at time j if T_{j0} (respectively $\bar{T}_{j0}$) was executed beginning at time 1.

Beginning at time $p + 1$ we can execute the p remaining T's and $\bar{T}$'s and the one remaining S or $\bar{S}$. Since $m(p + 1) = p + k + 1$, we must be able to execute k of the D's if we are to have a solution. We observe that for each pair D_{ij} and $D_{ij'}$, $j \neq j'$, there is at least one l such that $T_{lp} < D_{ij}$

and $\bar{T}_{lp} < D_{ij'}$, or vice versa. Since we have already proved that exactly one of T_{lp} and $\bar{T}_{lp}$ can commence by time p, it follows that for each i, at most one of $D_{i1}, D_{i2}, \ldots, D_{i7}$ can be executed beginning at time $p + 1$.

Moreover, if we assign the truth value **true** to v_j (respectively $\neg v_j$) if and only if T_{j0} (respectively $\bar{T}_{j0}$) was executed beginning at time 0, we can execute one of $D_{i1}, D_{i2}, \ldots, D_{i7}$ beginning at time $p + 1$ if and only if E_i takes the value **true** under this assignment of values to the variables. We conclude that a solution to the instance of the modified UET problem exists if and only if the original product of sums is satisfiable. ∎

Example 5 Let us consider the Boolean expression $(x_1 + \neg x_2 + x_3)$ $(\neg x_1 + \neg x_3 + x_4)$. That is, $k = 2$, $p = 4$, $E_1 = (x_1 + \neg x_2 + x_3)$, $E_2 = (\neg x_1 + \neg x_3 + x_4)$, and $m(0), \ldots, m(6)$ are, respectively, 4, 9, 10, 10, 10, 7, 12. One possible solution to the corresponding instance of the modified UET problem, which is based on the assignment of **true** to x_1, x_2, $\neg x_3$, and x_4 is shown in Fig. 4.3. Lines represent the relation $<$, except at time 6, when the many lines necessary are omitted.

Theorem 4.5 The UET scheduling problem is NP-complete.

Proof We polynomially reduce an instance of the modified UET problem to the UET problem. The construction is simple. If the instance of the modified problem has time limit ω and $m(i)$ processors available at time i for $0 \le i < \omega$, we let m be 1 plus the maximum of the $m(i)$'s. Then for $0 \le i < \omega$, create $m - m(i)$ new tasks $R_{i1}, R_{i2}, \ldots, R_{i,m-m(i)}$. Let $R_{i-1,j} < R_{ik}$

Beginning at time	Number of tasks												
0	4						T_{10}	T_{20}	$\bar{T}_{30}$	T_{40}			
1	9	$\bar{T}_{10}$	$\bar{T}_{20}$	T_{30}	$\bar{T}_{40}$	S_1	T_{11}	T_{21}	$\bar{T}_{31}$	T_{41}			
2	10	$\bar{S}_1$	$\bar{T}_{11}$	$\bar{T}_{21}$	T_{31}	$\bar{T}_{41}$	T_{12}	S_2	T_{22}	$\bar{T}_{32}$	T_{42}		
3	10	$\bar{T}_{12}$	$\bar{S}_2$	$\bar{T}_{22}$	T_{32}	$\bar{T}_{42}$	T_{13}	T_{23}	$\bar{S}_3$	$\bar{T}_{33}$	T_{43}		
4	10	$\bar{T}_{13}$	$\bar{T}_{23}$	S_3	T_{33}	$\bar{T}_{43}$	T_{14}	T_{24}	$\bar{T}_{34}$	S_4	T_{44}		
5	7	$\bar{T}_{14}$	$\bar{T}_{24}$	T_{34}	$\bar{S}_4$	$\bar{T}_{44}$	D_{14}	D_{23}					
6	12	D_{11}	D_{12}	D_{13}	D_{15}	D_{16}	D_{17}	D_{21}	D_{22}	D_{24}	D_{25}	D_{26}	D_{27}

Figure 4.3 Solution to instance of modified UET scheduling problem.

for all $0 < i < \omega$ and any j and k. Then if the original instance of the modified UET problem had a schedule, there will be a schedule for the system augmented by the new tasks using m processors at each time, and conversely.   ◾

Corollary 4.4   The preemptive scheduling problem is NP-complete.

Proof   It is easy to check that if any preemption occurs, it is impossible for the modified UET problem constructed in Lemma 4.1 to finish on time. Thus the constructed instance has a schedule allowing preemption if and only if the given Boolean expression is satisfiable.   ◾

4.9   SCHEDULING TWO PROCESSORS WITH EXECUTION TIMES OF 1 AND 2

In the previous section we saw that a subcase of the general scheduling problem could be NP-complete even though the possibility of specifying large execution times was not present. Only the time limit and number of processors were numerical parameters of the UET problem. In fact, the ability to encode the parameters m and ω of the UET problem in binary is not essential. The reader may check the reductions of Lemma 4.1 and Theorem 4.5 to see that if m, the $m(i)$'s, and ω are represented in unary, the reductions still require time that is only polynomial in the length of the input.

We now present an NP-complete subcase of the scheduling problem in which the number of processors and time limit are not parameters, and the execution times, although parameters, are limited to 1 and 2. This result shows clearly that the combinatorial structure of the precedence constraint is sufficient to make the problem hard; we do not have to rely on the complexity inherent in large integers.

Definition   The problem $S12$ is to determine whether a set of n tasks, with τ_i equal to 1 or 2 for $1 \le i \le n$, and with latest finishing time $\omega = \frac{1}{2}\sum_{i=1}^{n} \tau_i$ has a schedule on two processors. Note that if there is such a schedule, it has no idle time.

To prove $S12$ to be NP-complete, we need an easy strengthening of Theorem 4.5.

Lemma 4.2   The UET scheduling problem with $n = \omega m$ (i.e., constrained so that if there is a solution it has no idle time) is NP-complete.

Proof   Inspection of the proofs of Lemma 4.1 and Theorem 4.5 shows that in each case, if a solution exists it has no idle time. Thus we could have restricted the UET and modified UET problems in this way from the beginning and the same proofs would have gone through.   ◾

Theorem 4.6 $S12$ is NP-complete.

Proof   By Lemma 4.2 it suffices to reduce UET scheduling with $n = \omega m$ to the $S12$ problem. Suppose we are given an instance of UET scheduling with time limit ω, number of processors m, and precedence constraint $<$ on a set $\mathcal{T}$ of ωm tasks. We construct the following instance of $S12$. The tasks are:

1. X_i for $0 \le i < \omega'$, where $\omega' = (4m + 1)\omega$.
2. Y_{ij} for $0 \le i < \omega$ and $0 \le j \le m$.
3. T and T' for each T in $\mathcal{T}$.

The execution time is 2 for T in $\mathcal{T}$ and is 1 for all other tasks. The relation $<'$ is specified by:

a. $X_i <' X_{i+1}$ for $0 \le i < \omega' - 1$.
b. $X_u <' Y_{ij} <' X_{u+2}$, where $u = (4m + 1)i + 2j - 1$ (in the case $i = j = 0$, where $u = -1$, we have only the relation $Y_{00} <' X_1$).
c. $T' <' T$ for all T in $\mathcal{T}$.
d. $S <' T'$ for S and T in $\mathcal{T}$ if and only if $S < T$.

The latest finishing time is ω', defined in item 1.

We first observe by a that one processor must be devoted to processing an X at each time unit if the time limit is to be met. We may assume the first processor P_1 is used exclusively for this purpose. By b, the Y's must be executed on the second processor P_2 at very specific times, as in Fig. 4.4.

That is, progressing in time, we have an alternation of *breaks*, in which there is one time unit available on P_2 every other time unit, and *bands*, in which $2m$ consecutive time units are available on P_2. Since the unprimed tasks T in $\mathcal{T}$ require two time units each in our instance of $S12$, it is clear that they must be executed in the bands only. Since there are ωm unprimed tasks, they must completely fill the bands, which means that the primed tasks T' for T in $\mathcal{T}$ must be executed exclusively during the breaks.

As a consequence, if tasks S and T are executed in the same band, it is not possible that $S < T$. For if so, since we have $S <' T' <' T$, it follows that T' would also be executed in that band, violating what we have just concluded. Thus if our instance of $S12$ has a solution, we can find a solution to the original instance of UET scheduling by executing beginning at time unit i exactly those tasks executed in the ith band.

Conversely, if we have a solution to the given instance of UET scheduling, we can find a solution to the constructed instance of $S12$ by executing T' in break i and T in band i whenever T is executed beginning at time unit i in the original problem.   ∎

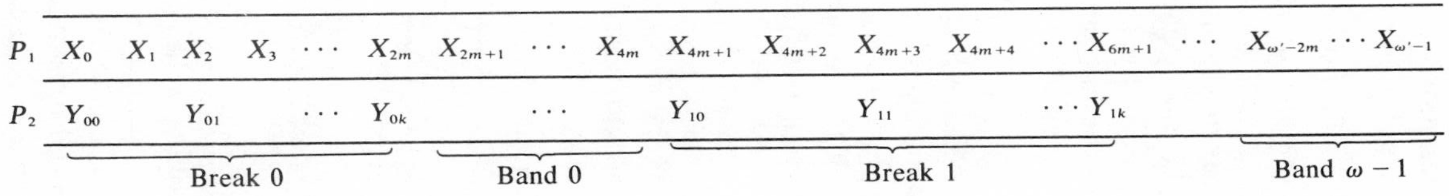

P_1 X_0 X_1 X_2 X_3 $\cdots$ X_{2m} X_{2m+1} $\cdots$ X_{4m} X_{4m+1} X_{4m+2} X_{4m+3} X_{4m+4} $\cdots X_{6m+1}$ $\cdots$ $X_{\omega'-2m}$ $\cdots$ $X_{\omega'-1}$

P_2 Y_{00} Y_{01} $\cdots$ Y_{0k} $\cdots$ Y_{10} Y_{11} $\cdots$ Y_{1k}

Break 0 Band 0 Break 1 Band $\omega - 1$

Figure 4.4 Times for execution of the X's and Y's.

4.10　SCHEDULING WITH RESOURCE CONSTRAINTS

If we introduce resource constraints into a scheduling problem, we can show NP-completeness under even more restrictive conditions than were set in the previous two sections.

Definition　A *scheduling problem with resource constraints* consists of a set of n tasks with given execution times, m processors, time limit ω, and precedence constraint $<$, all as usual, together with a set $\mathcal{R} = \{R_1, R_2, \ldots, R_s\}$ of *resource constraints* and *resource limits* m_i, $1 \le i \le s$. Each R_i maps the tasks into the nonnegative integers, indicating the amount of the ith resource required by the task.* The problem is to determine whether there exists a schedule meeting the time limit and such that at no time do the tasks in execution require more than m_i units of resource i for any i.

It is easy to show that the general scheduling problem with resource constraints is in **NP** by the technique used in Example 3 for the scheduling problem without resource constraints. That is, guess a schedule and check that it meets the time limit and all the resource constraints. Two strong theorems about NP-complete subcases of the scheduling problem with resource constraints have been shown by Garey and Johnson [GJ1]. We state them here.

Theorem 4.7　Scheduling with two processors, unit execution times, one resource, and precedence constraint restricted to being a forest is NP-complete.

Theorem 4.8　Scheduling with three processors, unit execution times, one resource, and empty precedence constraint is NP-complete.

Although we do not prove either of these theorems, we can give an easy proof of a result similar to Theorem 4.7.

Theorem 4.9　Scheduling with two processors, unit execution times, and one resource with limit 1 is NP-complete.

Proof　In a manner similar to the proof of Theorem 4.6 we can polynomially reduce UET scheduling with $\omega m = n$ to the stated subcase of scheduling with resource constraints. Instead of forcing tasks with execution time 2 to be executed in bands, we can force tasks that do not require a unit of the resource to be executed in bands.

Formally, suppose we are given an instance of UET scheduling with a

---

* Typical resources might be computer memory or input/output devices. Processors are not considered resources here, although they might have been treated as such.

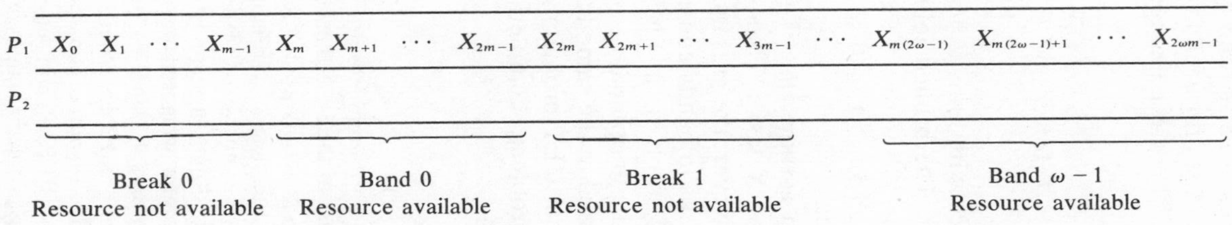

P_1 X_0 X_1 $\cdots$ X_{m-1} X_m X_{m+1} $\cdots$ X_{2m-1} X_{2m} X_{2m+1} $\cdots$ X_{3m-1} $\cdots$ $X_{m(2\omega-1)}$ $X_{m(2\omega-1)+1}$ $\cdots$ $X_{2\omega m-1}$

P_2

Break 0
Resource not available

Band 0
Resource available

Break 1
Resource not available

Band $\omega-1$
Resource available

Figure 4.5 Availability of resource.

set of n tasks $\mathcal{T}$, precedence constraints $<$, latest finishing time ω, and m processors, where $n = \omega m$. We construct an instance of UET scheduling with two processors and one resource as follows. There is a sequence of $2\omega m$ tasks $X_0, X_1, \ldots, X_{2\omega m - 1}$. Also, for each task T in $\mathcal{T}$ there are tasks T and T' in the new system. The precedence constraint $<'$ is:

1. $X_i <' X_{i+1}$ for $0 \le i < 2\omega m - 2$.
2. $T' <' T$ for all T in $\mathcal{T}$.
3. $S <' T'$ if and only if $S < T$ for S and T in $\mathcal{T}$.

The time limit is $\omega' = 2\omega m$.

Finally, there is one resource with limit 1. The unprimed jobs T in $\mathcal{T}$ require a unit of this resource. The primed jobs T', for T in $\mathcal{T}$, do not require any of the resource. The X_i's with i in the ranges 0 through $m - 1$, $2m$ through $3m - 1$, $4m$ through $5m - 1$, and so on, require a unit of the resource; the other X's do not.

As in Theorem 4.6, we can assume that if there is a schedule, one processor P_1 is used for all the X tasks. Then the T's and T''s can be executed on processor P_2. However, the presence of the resource forces us to execute the unprimed tasks in bands consisting of time m through $2m$, then $3m$ through $4m$, and so on, as in Fig. 4.5. The argument then proceeds as in Theorem 4.6. The unprimed tasks must all be executed in bands, and no two tasks executed in the same band can be related by $<$. Thus a schedule for the original UET problem exists if and only if one exists for the constructed problem, completing the polynomial-time reduction.   ∎

BIBLIOGRAPHIC NOTES

The originator of the concept of an NP-complete problem is Cook [Coo], and he also demonstrated NP-completeness of the 3-CNF problem (Theorems 4.1 and 4.2 were proved by him). Karp [Ka] is generally granted a large portion of the credit for demonstrating the richness of the class of NP-complete problems. See Aho, Hopcroft, and Ullman [AHU] for a synopsis of results in the area.

Theorem 4.3 that the general scheduling problem is NP-complete, is implicit in Karp [Ka]. Theorem 4.4 on minimum weighted finishing time is from Bruno, Coffman, and Sethi [BCS1]. Theorems 4.5 and 4.6 on UET scheduling and on scheduling with execution times of 1 and 2 are from Ullman [U1]. Theorems 4.7 and 4.8 regarding scheduling under resource constraints are from Garey and Johnson [GJ1]. The recent papers [BLR], [GJ2], and [GJS] provide additional results on NP-complete scheduling problems, many of which are summarized in section 1.4.

CHAPTER FIVE

BOUNDS ON THE PERFORMANCE
OF SCHEDULING ALGORITHMS

R. L. GRAHAM
BELL LABORATORIES, MURRAY HILL, NEW JERSEY

In this chapter we investigate the worst-case behavior of a number of scheduling algorithms for the general multiprocessor-with-resources model, as well as numerous important special cases. The model and notation are defined in Chapter 1. We begin in Section 5.1 by studying, under the framework of list scheduling, the rather unpredictable dependence of the schedule length ω on the various parameters of the problem, even for the case of no additional resource constraints. In Sections 5.2 and 5.3 the performance of critical path scheduling is examined, and in Section 5.4 bounds for the extended model including additional resource constraints are derived. In Section 5.5 heuristics are covered for the (bin-packing) problem of minimizing the number of processors to meet a given deadline. Finally, in Section 5.6, bounds for a number of related problems are presented. The complexity of the various problems studied in this chapter has been analyzed in the preceding chapter.

5.1 MULTIPROCESSOR SCHEDULING ANOMALIES

We begin with an example that illustrates, using a single-task system, the anomalies that can arise in varying any one of the parameters, including the priority list.

Example 1 The graph $G(<, \tau)$ of a task system appears in Fig. 5.1a. Holding the parameters fixed, we see in Figs. 5.2 through 5.5, the effects of changing the priority list, increasing the number of processors, reducing execution times, and weakening the precedence constraints, respectively. The basis for comparison is the optimal schedule in Fig. 5.1b.

Note that in Figs. 5.3, 5.4, and 5.5, although we would intuitively expect that the changes made would cause ω to decrease, in fact, an *increase* in ω occurred.

165

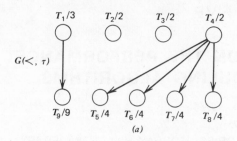

(a)

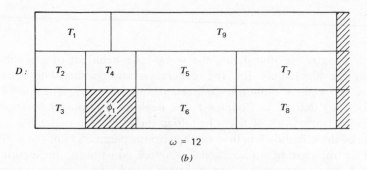

$\omega = 12$

(b)

Figure 5.1 A task system and optimal schedule. (a) $m = 3$, $L = (T_1, T_2, T_3, T_4, T_5, T_6, T_7, T_8, T_9)$. Figures 5.2 through 5.5 indicate effects of changes in L, m, τ, and $<$.

The next example shows that such an increase in ω is not necessarily caused by a poor choice of the list L but in fact is inherent in the model itself.

Example 2 Figure 5.6a shows a task system for which we assume $m = 2$ and the list as shown. An optimal schedule appears in Fig. 5.6b. Now consider the same task system except for execution times given by the new function $\tau' = \tau - 1$. We find that *no matter what list is assumed for*

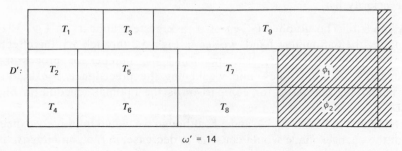

$\omega' = 14$

Figure 5.2 Priority list changed: L becomes $L' = (T_1, T_2, T_4, T_5, T_6, T_3, T_9, T_7, T_8)$.

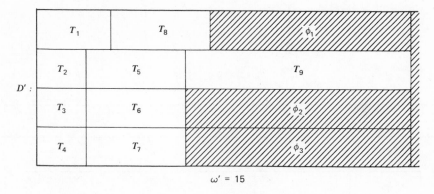

$$\omega' = 15$$

Figure 5.3 Number of processors increased: m is changed to $m' = 4$.

the new system, we cannot obtain a schedule whose length is less than that in Fig. 5.7.

We now derive a general bound on the relative effects on schedule length of changes in one or more problem parameters. Suppose we are given a set $\mathscr{T}$ of tasks, which we execute twice. The first time we use an execution time function τ, a partial order $<$, a priority list L, and a system composed of m identical processors. The second time we use a time function $\tau' \leq \tau$, a partial order $<' \subseteq <$, a priority list L' and a system composed of m' identical processors. As usual, ω and ω' denote the corresponding finishing times.

Theorem 5.1 [G1] Under the assumptions already stated, we have

$$\frac{\omega'}{\omega} \leq 1 + \frac{m-1}{m'}$$

Proof Consider the timing diagram D' obtained by executing the tasks T_i of $\mathscr{T}$ using the primed parameters. Define a partition of $[0, \omega')$ into two

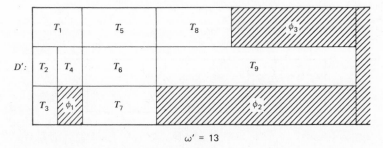

$$\omega' = 13$$

Figure 5.4 Execution times reduced: τ is changed to $\tau' = \tau - 1$.

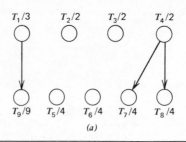

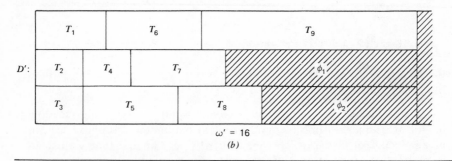

Figure 5.5 Precedence constraints weakened: $<$ is changed to $<' = < - \{(T_4, T_5), (T_4, T_6)\}$. (a) $m = 3$, $L = (T_1, T_2, T_3, T_4, T_5, T_6, T_7, T_8, T_9)$.

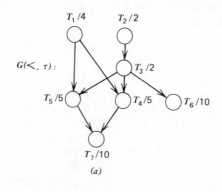

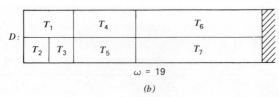

Figure 5.6 A task system and optimal schedule. (a) $m = 2$, $L = (T_1, T_2, T_3, T_4, T_5, T_6, T_7)$.

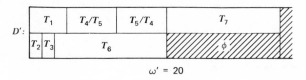

Figure 5.7 An optimal schedule assuming $\tau' = \tau \overline{\oplus} 1$.

subsets A and B as follows:

$$A = \{t \in [0, \omega')| \text{ all processors are busy at time } t\}$$
$$B = [0, \omega') - A$$

Note that A and B are both the unions of disjoint half-open intervals. Let T_{j_1} denote a task that finishes in D' at time ω' (i.e., such that $f_{j_1} = \omega'$). There are two possibilities.

1. If s_{j_1}, the starting time of T_{j_1}, is an *interior* point of B, then by the definition of B there is some processor P_i which for some $\varepsilon > 0$ is idle during the time interval $[s_{j_1} - \varepsilon, s_{j_1})$. The only way this can happen, however, is if for some task T_{j_2} we have $T_{j_2} <' T_{j_1}$ and $f_{j_2} = s_{j_1}$.

2. On the other hand, suppose s_{j_1} is not an interior point of B. Furthermore, suppose $s_{j_1} \neq 0$. Let $x_1 = \text{l.u.b.}\{x \,|\, x < s_{j_1} \text{ and } x \in B\}$, or 0 if the set is empty. By the construction of A and B, we see that $x_i \in A$, and for some $\varepsilon > 0$, P_i is idle during the time interval $[x_1 - \varepsilon, x_1)$. But again, this can occur only because of some task $T_{j_2} <' T_{j_1}$ which is being executed during this time interval.

Thus we have seen that *either* there exists a task $T_{j_2} <' T_{j_1}$ so that $y \in [f_{j_2}, s_{j_1})$ implies $y \in A$ *or* we have $x < s_{j_1}$ implies either $x \in A$ or $x < 0$.

We can repeat this procedure inductively, forming $T_{j_3}, T_{j_4}, \ldots$, until we reach a task T_{j_r} for which $x < s_{j_r}$ implies either $x \in A$ or $x < 0$. Hence we have shown the existence of a chain of tasks

$$T_{j_r} <' T_{j_{r-1}} <' \cdots <' T_{j_2} <' T_{j_1} \tag{1}$$

such that in D' at every time $t \in B$, some T_{j_k} is being executed. This implies that

$$\sum_{\emptyset' \in D'} \tau'(\emptyset') \leq (m' - 1) \sum_{k=1}^{r} \tau'_{j_k} \tag{2}$$

where the sum of the left-hand side is taken over all empty tasks $\emptyset'$ in D'. But by (1) and the hypothesis $<' \subseteq <$ we have

$$T_{j_r} < T_{j_{r-1}} < \cdots < T_{j_2} < T_{j_1} \tag{3}$$

Therefore,

$$\omega \geq \sum_{k=1}^{r} \tau_{j_k} \geq \sum_{k=1}^{r} \tau'_{j_k} \tag{4}$$

Consequently, by (2) and (4), we have

$$\omega' = \frac{1}{m} \left\{ \sum_{k=1}^{n} \tau'_k + \sum_{\emptyset' \in D'} \tau'(\emptyset') \right\}$$

$$\leq \frac{1}{m'} (m\omega + (m'-1)\omega) \tag{5}$$

From this we obtain

$$\frac{\omega'}{\omega} \leq 1 + \frac{m-1}{m'} \tag{6}$$

and the theorem is proved. ∎

The following examples show not only that the bound of Theorem 5.1 is best possible, but in fact it can be achieved (asymptotically) by varying any *one* of the parameters.

Example 3 In this example L varies, $<$ is empty, and m is arbitrary. The task/execution times are given by

$$T_1/1, T_2/1, \ldots, T_{m-1}/1, T_m/m-1, T_{m+1}/m-1, \ldots, T_{2m-2}/m-1, T_{2m-1}/m$$

Figure 5.8 presents the first list to be used and the resulting schedule. The second list and the resulting longer schedule are given in Fig. 5.9. As can be seen,

$$\frac{\omega'}{\omega} = 2 - \frac{1}{m}$$

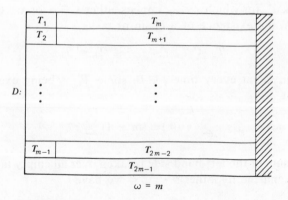

Figure 5.8 An optimal schedule: $L = (T_1, T_2, \ldots, T_{m-1}, T_m, T_{m+1}, \ldots, T_{2m-2})$.

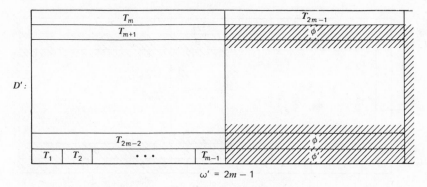

Figure 5.9 A bad schedule: $L' = (T_m, T_{m+1}, \ldots, T_{2m-2}, T_1, T_2, \ldots, T_{m-1}, T_{2m-1})$.

Example 4 In this example τ decreases. Here, as in the remainder of the chapter, ε denotes a suitably small positive number. A task system and corresponding optimal schedule are illustrated in Fig. 5.10. Figure 5.11 shows the effect of the following change in execution times

$$\tau' = \begin{cases} \tau_i - \varepsilon & \text{for } 1 \le i \le m - 1 \\ \tau_i & \text{otherwise} \end{cases}$$

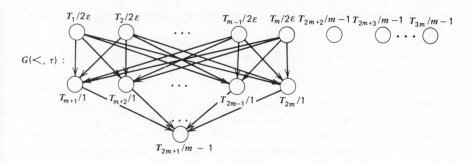

Figure 5.10 An optimal schedule.

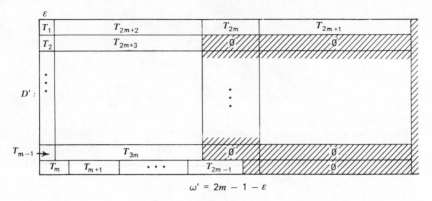

$$\omega' = 2m - 1 - \varepsilon$$

Figure 5.11 A bad schedule.

Inspecting the figures, we find

$$\frac{\omega'}{\omega} = \frac{2m - 1 + \varepsilon}{m + 2\varepsilon} \to 2 - \frac{1}{m} \qquad \text{as} \quad \varepsilon \to 0$$

Example 5 We weaken the precedence constraint $<$ in this example. Compare the task system and an optimal schedule (Fig. 5.12) with the results when all the precedence constraints are removed (Fig. 5.13). From the figures, we have

$$\frac{\omega'}{\omega} = \frac{2m - 1}{m + \varepsilon} \to 2 - \frac{1}{m} \qquad \text{as} \quad \varepsilon \to 0$$

Example 6 Finally, we consider increases in the number of processors. Suppose we are given the task system represented in Fig. 5.14a whose optimal schedule on m processors appears in Fig. 5.14b. Now let $m' > m$. We obtain the longer schedule given in Fig. 5.14c. Forming the ratio of schedule lengths, we obtain

$$\frac{\omega'}{\omega} = \frac{m' + m - 1 + \varepsilon}{m' + 2\varepsilon} \to 1 + \frac{m - 1}{m'} \qquad \text{as} \quad \varepsilon \to 0$$

For the case $m' < m$, a similar example exists, but we do not give it here.

The following example, due to M. Kaufman [K1], shows that (6) can be achieved by varying L, even if $<$ is a forest and all $\tau_i = 1$.

Example 7 Consider the graph shown in Fig. 5.15a and suppose we have unit execution times for all tasks. The optimal schedule and corresponding list is shown in Fig. 5.15b. If we change the list to that given in Fig.

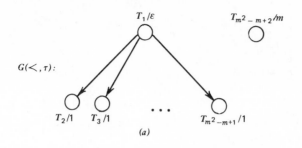

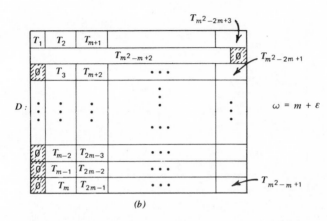

Figure 5.12 An optimal schedule. (a) $L = (T_1, T_2, \ldots, T_{m^2-m+2})$.

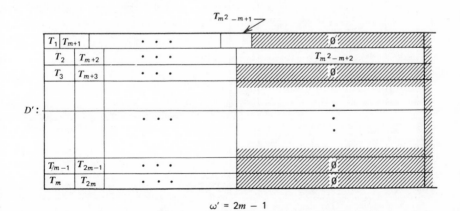

$$\omega' = 2m - 1$$

Figure 5.13 A bad schedule.

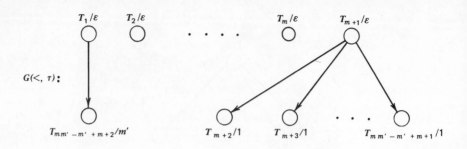

$G(<, \tau)$:

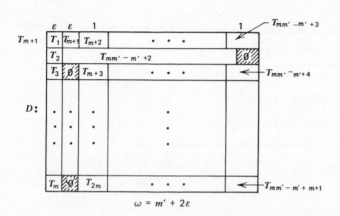

$$\omega = m' + 2\varepsilon$$

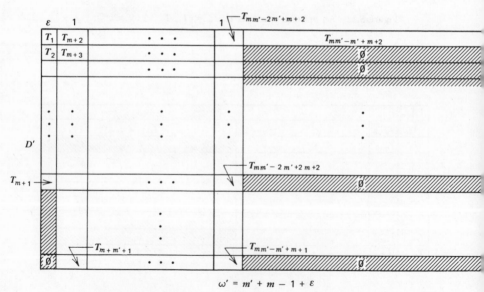

$$\omega' = m' + m - 1 + \varepsilon$$

Figure 5.14 Task system (a) for whose optimal schedule m varies (L) and (c).

174

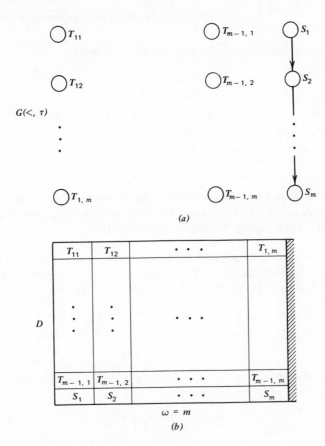

(a)

(b)

Figure 5.15 A task system and optimal schedule. (a) $L = (T_{11}, \ldots, T_{m-1,1}, S_1, T_{12}, \ldots, T_{m-1},$
$S_2, T_{21}, \ldots, S_m)$.

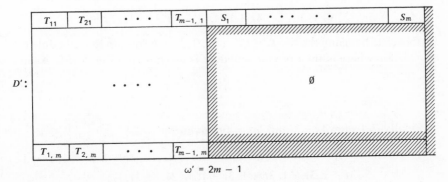

$\omega' = 2m - 1$

Figure 5.16 A very bad schedule. $L' = (T_{11}, \ T_{12}, \ldots, T_{1,m}, \ldots, \ T_{m-1,1}, \ldots, \ T_{m-1,m},$
$S_1, \ldots, S_m)$.

5.16 we obtain the longer schedule shown. Evidently,

$$\frac{\omega'}{\omega} = 2 - \frac{1}{m}$$

Finally, we give an example that again achieves the bound of $2 - 1/m$ by varying L, this time with $<$ empty and

$$\frac{\max\{\tau_i\}}{\min\{\tau_i\}} \leq 4$$

Whether the constant 4 is best possible here is not known. In any case, we see that the occurrence of the worst possible behavior does not depend on having tasks with widely disparate execution times.

Example 8   Let $<$ be empty and suppose the maximum ratio of execution times is no greater than 4. We consider three cases depending on $m \pmod 4$. For $m = 2r$, let $\tau = (\tau_1, \ldots, \tau_{2m+1})$ be given by

$$(r, r, r + 1, r + 1, \ldots, 2r - 2, 2r - 2, 2r - 1, 2r - 1,$$
$$3r - 2, 3r - 2, 3r - 3, 3r - 3, \ldots, 2r - 1, 2r - 1, 4r)$$

Then, by using the corresponding list $L = (T_1, \ldots, T_{2m+1})$, we obtain the schedule shown in Fig. 5.17a. Since the optimal schedule is as shown in Fig. 5.17b, when ω_0 is m, we have,

$$\frac{\omega_L}{\omega_0} = 2 - \frac{1}{2r} = 2 - \frac{1}{m}$$

For $m = 4r + 1$, *let* τ be given by

$$(2r + 1,\ 2r + 1,\ 2r + 1,\ 2r + 1,\ 2r + 3,\ 2r + 3,\ 2r + 3,\ 2r + 3, \ldots, 4r - 1,$$
$$4r - 1,\ 4r - 1,\ 4r - 1,\ 4r,\ 6r - 1,\ 6r - 1,\ 6r - 1,\ 6r - 1,\ 6r - 3,\ 6r - 3,$$
$$6r - 3,\ 6r - 3,\ \ldots,\ 4r + 1,\ 4r + 1,\ 4r + 1,\ 4r,\ 8r + 2)$$

In this case by using the list $L = (T_1, \ldots, T_{2m+1})$ we obtain the schedule of Fig. 5.18a whereas the optimal schedule is as shown in Fig. 5.18b. Again we obtain

$$\frac{\omega_L}{\omega_0} = 2 - \frac{1}{4r + 1} = 2 - \frac{1}{m}$$

Finally, let $m = 4r + 3$ and let τ be given by

$$(r + 1, r + 1, r + 1, r + 1, r + 2, r + 2, r + 2, r + 2, \ldots, 2r + 1, 2r + 1, 2r + 1,$$
$$3r + 1, 3r + 1, 3r + 1, 3r + 1, 3r, 3r, 3r, 3r, \ldots,$$
$$2r + 2, 2r + 2, 2r + 2, 2r + 2, 2r + 1, 2r + 1, 2r + 1, 4r + 3)$$

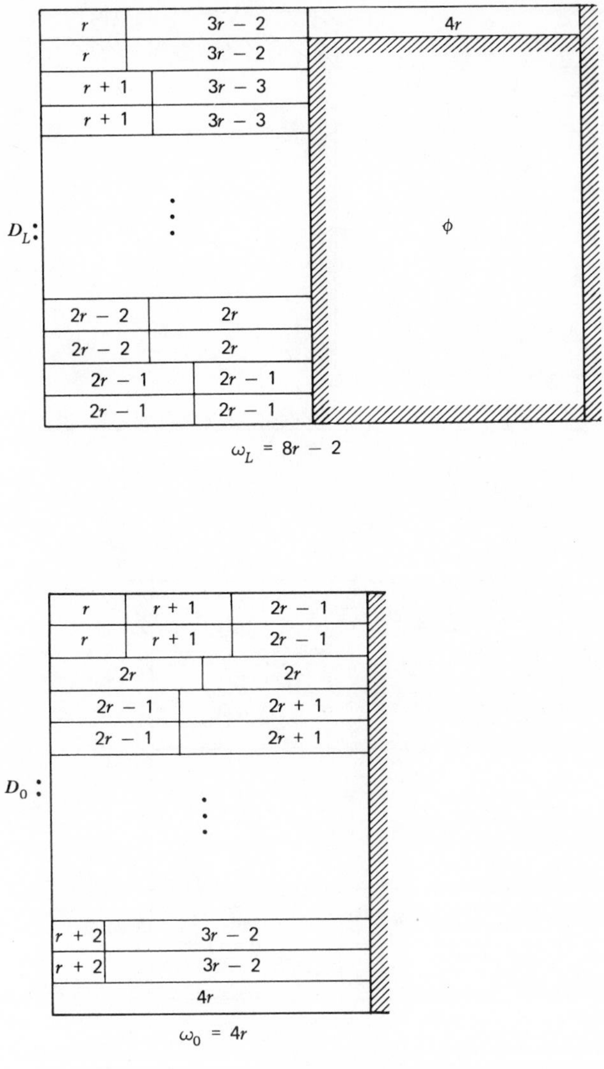

Figure 5.17 An extremal example for $m = 2r$.

The schedule in Fig. 5.19a is produced with these parameters using the list $L = (T_1, \ldots, T_{2m+1})$. The optimal schedule is given in Fig. 5.19b and shows that

$$\frac{\omega_L}{\omega_o} = 2 - \frac{1}{4r+3} = 2 - \frac{1}{m}$$

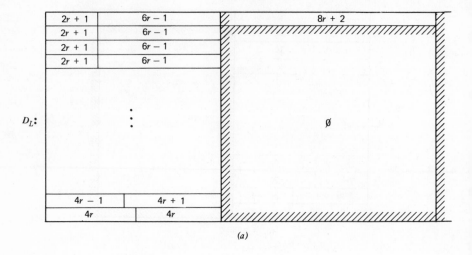

(a)

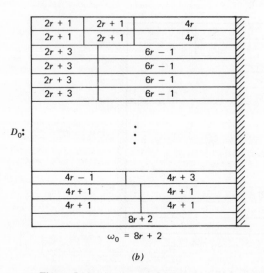

$\omega_0 = 8r + 2$

(b)

Figure 5.18   An extremal example for $m = 4r + 1$.

5.2   BOUNDS FOR INDEPENDENT TASKS AND NO ADDITIONAL RESOURCES

In this section we examine the special case in which the partial order $<$ is empty and, as before, $s = 0$ (i.e., there are no resource constraints). As shown in Example 3, a poor choice of the list L can still result in the worst

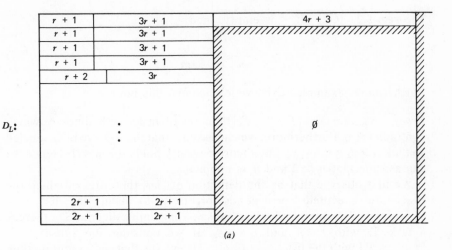

(a)

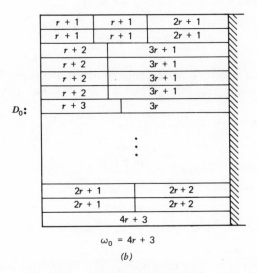

$$\omega_0 = 4r + 3$$

(b)

Figure 5.19   An extremal example for $m = 4r + 3$.

possible finishing time ω, that is, $\omega = (2 - 1/m)\omega_0$. However, if a little care is taken to prepare L, the bounds on ω can be improved considerably.

The first algorithm we consider for scheduling $\mathcal{T}$ is an example of a *critical path* algorithm (see Chapter 1). In this case, we simply form L by arranging the T_i in order of decreasing τ_i. Denote the corresponding finishing time by ω_{CP}.

Theorem 5.2   [G2]   If $<$ is empty, then

$$\frac{\omega_{CP}}{\omega_0} \le \frac{4}{3} - \frac{1}{3m} \tag{7}$$

Furthermore, examples exist which achieve this bound.

Proof   Assume $\mathcal{T} = \{T_1, \ldots, T_n\}$ is a set of tasks with times τ_i which contradicts (7). Furthermore, we can assume that the T_i have been labeled so that $\tau_1 \ge \tau_2 \ge \cdots \ge \tau_n$. The theorem clearly holds for $m = 1$. Hence we can assume that $m \ge 2$ and n is minimal.

We first observe that by the definition of ω_{CP}, the order in which the tasks are executed corresponds precisely to using the list $L = (T_1, T_2, \ldots, T_n)$. Suppose in the corresponding timing diagram D_L, there is a task T_r with $r < n$ and $f_r = \omega_{CP}$. If we consider the subset $\mathcal{T}' = \{T_1, \ldots, T_r\}$ with the list $L' = (T_1, \ldots, T_r)$, we see that the execution time ω' for $\mathcal{T}'$ using L' is just ω_{CP}. On the other hand, the optimal value ω_0' for $\mathcal{T}'$ certainly satisfies $\omega_0' \le \omega_0$. Hence we have

$$\frac{\omega'}{\omega_0'} \ge \frac{\omega_{CP}}{\omega_0} > \frac{4}{3} - \frac{1}{3m}$$

so that $\mathcal{T}'$ forms a smaller counterexample to the theorem. However, this contradicts the minimality of n. Thus we can assume that $f_k < \omega_{CP}$ for $k < n$.

It is clear that

$$\omega_0 \ge \frac{1}{m} \sum_{i=1}^{n} \tau_i \tag{8}$$

Also, it follows that

$$\sum_{i=1}^{n-1} \tau_i \ge m s_n, \qquad \omega_L = s_n + \tau_n \tag{9}$$

where s_n denotes the starting time of T_n, since no processor is idle before T_n starts being executed. Therefore, we can write

$$\frac{\omega_L}{\omega_0} = \frac{s_n + \tau_n}{\omega_0} \le \frac{\tau_n}{\omega_0} + \frac{1}{m\omega_0} \sum_{i=1}^{n-1} \tau_i$$

$$= \frac{(m-1)\tau_n}{m\omega_0} + \frac{1}{m\omega_0} \sum_{i=1}^{n} \tau_i \le \frac{(m-1)\tau_n}{m\omega_0} + 1$$

Since (7) does not hold for $\mathcal{T}$ by hypothesis, we have

$$1 + \frac{(m-1)\tau_n}{m\omega_0} \geq \frac{\omega_L}{\omega_0} > \frac{4}{3} - \frac{1}{3m}$$

$$\frac{(m-1)\tau_n}{m\omega_0} > \frac{1}{3} - \frac{1}{3m} = \frac{m-1}{3m} \tag{10}$$

$$\tau_n > \frac{\omega_0}{3}$$

Hence if (7) is false, in an optimal solution (with timing diagram D_0), no processor can execute more than two tasks.

Suppose the configuration shown in Fig. 5.20 occurs in D_0, where $\tau_i > \tau_j$, $\tau_{i'} > \tau_{j'}$. If we interchange $\tau_{i'}$ and $\tau_{j'}$ to form the configuration shown in Fig. 5.21, the (possibly) new finishing time ω' in D_0' certainly satisfies $\omega' \leq \omega_0$. Also, if the configuration in Fig. 5.22 occurs, where $\tau_i > \tau_j$, moving $T_{i'}$ from the processor executing T_i to the processor executing T_j cannot increase the finishing time. Let us call either of the two preceding operations a *type I* operation.

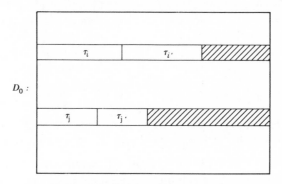

Figure 5.20   A portion of D_0.

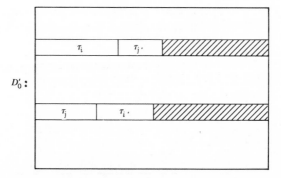

Figure 5.21 D_0 is modified.

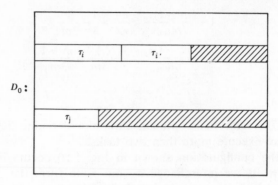

Figure 5.22   Another portion of D_0.

By a *type II* operation on D_0 we mean changing any occurrence of an "inversion" as illustrated in Fig. 5.23 to the "normalized" form in Fig. 5.24. Clearly, this operation does not affect ω_0.

For any timing diagram D we define a function $\mathscr{S}(D)$ as follows: if τ_i^* denotes the *least* time t such that for every time $t' \geq t$, the processor P_i is idle in D, then

$$\mathscr{S}(D) = \sum_{1 \leq i < j \leq m} |\tau_i^* - \tau_j^*|$$

It is not difficult to check:

1. If D' is obtained from D by a type I operation, $\mathscr{S}(D') < \mathscr{S}(D)$.
2. If D' is obtained from D by a type II operation, $\mathscr{S}(D') = \mathscr{S}(D)$.

Now we start from D_0 and apply all possible type I and type II operations until the resulting timing diagram D^* has no internal configurations to which either type of operation can be applied. That such a D^*

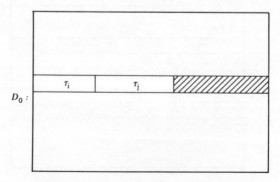

Figure 5.23   An inversion in D_0 with $\tau_i < \tau_j$.

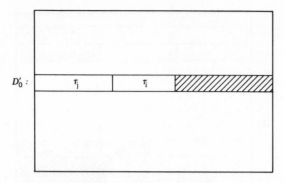

Figure 5.24 Normalized form.

exists follows because (a) there are only a finite number of possible arrangements of the n tasks on the m processors, (b) between any two type I operations only a finite number of type II operations can be performed, and (c) only a finite number of type I operations can be performed because of condition 1. Hence in D^* it follows that for any configuration of the form shown in Fig. 5.25, we have

$$\tau_i > \tau_j \quad \text{implies} \quad \tau_{j'} \geq \tau_{i'}, \ \tau_i \leq \tau_k, \text{ and } \tau_i > \tau_{i'} \tag{11}$$

Thus by a suitable rearrangement of the processors of D^*, we can bring D^* into the form of Fig. 5.26, where

$$\tau_{k_1} \geq \tau_{k_2} \geq \cdots \geq \tau_{k_s}$$
$$\tau_{i_1} \geq \tau_{i_2} \geq \cdots \geq \tau_{i_t}$$

and, by (11),

$$\tau_{i_1} \leq \tau_{i_2} \leq \cdots \leq \tau_{i_t}$$

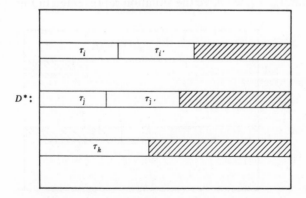

Figure 5.25 After operations are performed.

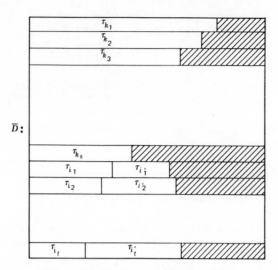

Figure 5.26 Further normalization of D^*.

But (11) also implies $\tau_{k_s} \geq \tau_{i_1}$ and $\tau_{i_t} \geq \tau_{i'_t}$. Hence combining these inequalities, we obtain

$$\tau_{k_1} \geq \cdots \geq \tau_{k_s} \geq \tau_{i_1} \geq \cdots \geq \tau_{i_t} \geq \tau_{i'_t} \geq \cdots \geq \tau_{i'_1} \tag{12}$$

Since none of the operations applied to D_0 causes an increase in ω_0, by the optimality of ω_0, the finishing time of $\bar{D}$ must also be ω_0. But $\bar{D}$ now looks very much like the timing diagram D_L obtained by using the decreasing-length list $L = (T_1, \ldots, T_n)$ (up to relabeling the tasks of equal length). In fact, the only way in which D_L could differ from $\bar{D}$ is in the assignment of the second-layer tasks T_{ik}. Specifically, a difference could occur only if for some pair T_{ik}, T_{ik}, we have the situation represented in Fig. 5.27, where

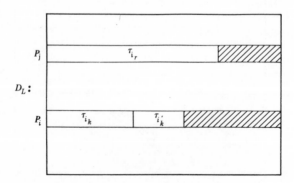

Figure 5.27 D_L differs from D_0.

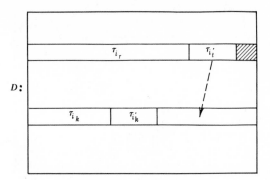

Figure 5.28   An unstable $\bar{D}$.

$\tau_{i_k} + \tau_{i_k} \leq \tau_{i_r}$ for $r < k$. In this case, in D_L, T_{i_r} with length τ_{i_r} might be assigned to P_j instead of P_i. However, if this situation were possible, we would have in $\bar{D}$ the situation illustrated in Fig. 5.28. Hence it would be possible to move T_{i_r} from P_i to P_j. Also, since the finishing time is not increased, it is still ω_0. But this is a *contradiction*, since we have an optimal solution in which a processor has three tasks assigned to it. Hence we conclude that D_L and $\bar{D}$ are isomorphic (in the obvious sense) and $\omega_0 = \omega_{\mathrm{CP}}$. But this contradicts the hypothesis that $\omega_{\mathrm{CP}}/\omega_0 > 4/3 - 1/(3m)$; hence (7) is proved.

To see that (7) is best possible, consider the following set of task lengths:

$$(\tau_1, \ldots, \tau_n) = (2m - 1, 2m - 1, 2m - 2, 2m - 2, \ldots, m + 1, m + 1, m, m, m)$$

where $n = 2m + 1$. That is,

$$\tau_k = 2m - \left\lfloor \frac{k+1}{2} \right\rfloor, \; 1 \leq k \leq 2m, \text{ and } \tau_{2m+1} = m$$

The corresponding timing diagrams for ω_{CP} and ω_0 appear in Fig. 5.29. As can be seen, we have

$$\frac{\omega_L}{\omega_0} = \frac{4}{3} - \frac{1}{3m}$$

as asserted.   ■

The following result verifies one's intuition in the following respect: as the proportion of the total execution time required by any one task tends to zero, the ratio ω/ω_0 tends to 1.

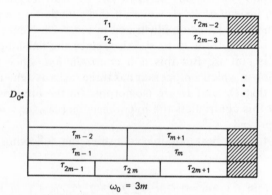

Figure 5.29   An extremal example.

Theorem 5.3   Suppose $<$ is empty. Then we have

$$\frac{\omega}{\omega_0} \leq 1 + (m - 1)\frac{\max \tau_i}{\sum\limits_i \tau_i} \tag{13}$$

Proof   Let τ^* denote $\max_i \tau_i$. Because of the rules under which the system operates, no processor is idle before time $\omega - \tau^*$. Since at least one processor is busy for ω units of time, we see that

$$\sum_i \tau_i \geq \omega + (m - 1)(\omega - \tau^*)$$

Thus we have

$$\omega_0 \geq \frac{1}{m}(\omega + (m - 1)(\omega - \tau^*))$$

that is,

$$\frac{\omega}{\omega_0} \le 1 + \frac{(m-1)}{m} \frac{\tau^*}{\omega_0} \le 1 + (m-1) \frac{\max \tau_i}{\sum_i \tau_i}$$

and the theorem is proved. ∎

The next result helps quantify the tradeoff between the cost of computing "partially" optimal schedules and the corresponding decreases in the ratio ω/ω_0.

Theorem 5.4 [G2] Assume $<$ is empty and L_k is a list of the k tasks T_i having largest τ_i, $1 \le i \le k$, which is *optimal* for this set of k tasks. Form a list $L(k)$ by adjoining the remaining tasks arbitrarily and let $\omega(k)$ denote the finishing time using $L(k)$. Then we have

$$\frac{\omega(k)}{\omega_0} \le 1 + \frac{1 - \frac{1}{m}}{1 + \left\lfloor \frac{k}{m} \right\rfloor} \tag{14}$$

This is best possible if $k \equiv 0 \pmod{m}$.

Proof If $\omega(k) = \omega_k$, the finishing time using $L(k)$, then $\omega(k) = \omega_0$ and the theorem holds. Therefore, we can assume $\omega(k) > \omega_k$. Also, we can assume $n > k$. Let τ^* denote $\max_{k+1 \le j \le n}\{\tau_j\}$. As in the proof of the preceding theorem, when using the list $L(k)$ no processor can be idle before time $\omega(k) - \tau^*$. Hence

$$\sum_{j=1}^{n} \tau_j \ge m(\omega(k) - \tau^*) + \tau^*$$

and

$$\omega_0 \ge \frac{1}{m} \sum_{j=1}^{n} \tau_j \ge \omega(k) - \left(\frac{m-1}{m}\right)\tau^*$$

There are at least $k + 1$ tasks having length $\ge \tau^*$. Thus some processor must execute at least $1 + \lfloor k/m \rfloor$ of these "long" tasks. This implies

$$\omega_0 \ge \left(1 + \left\lfloor \frac{k}{m} \right\rfloor\right)\tau^*$$

Combining the preceding inequalities, we obtain

$$\omega(k) \le \omega_0 + \left(\frac{m-1}{m}\right)\tau^* \le \omega_0 \left(1 + \frac{1 - \frac{1}{m}}{1 + \left\lfloor \frac{k}{m} \right\rfloor}\right)$$

and (14) is proved.

To see that (14) is best possible when $k \equiv 0 \pmod{m}$, consider the following example.

Example 9   Define τ_i for $1 \le i \le k + 1 + m(m - 1)$ by

$$\tau_i = \begin{cases} m & \text{for} \quad 1 \le i \le k + 1 \\ 1 & \text{for} \quad k + 2 \le i \le k + 1 + m(m - 1) \end{cases}$$

For this set of task lengths and the list

$$L(k) = (T_1, \ldots, T_k, T_{k+2}, \ldots, T_{k+1+m(m-1)}, T_{k+1})$$

we have $\omega(k) = k + 2m - 1$. Since $\omega_0 = k + m$, then

$$\frac{\omega(k)}{\omega_0} = \frac{k + 2m - 1}{k + m} = 1 + \frac{1 - 1/m}{1 + \lfloor k/m \rfloor} \qquad \text{since} \quad k \equiv 0 \pmod{m}$$

and the bound in (14) is achieved. This proves Theorem 5.4.   ∎

For k sufficiently large, we will thus have a better bound on $\omega(k)$ than we have in (7) on ω_{CP}. However, finding an optimal list for the largest k tasks may itself be a hard problem when k is large. One might instead try to work from a *near*-optimal priority list for the largest k tasks.

If L'_k denotes a list formed from the k largest τ_i such that for some $\alpha \ge 0$ we have

$$\frac{\omega'_k}{\omega_0} \le 1 + \alpha$$

and $L'(k)$ is formed from L'_k by adjoining the remaining tasks, the preceding arguments can be used to prove the following generalization of Theorem 5.4.

Theorem 5.4′   For L'_k defined as previously,

$$\frac{\omega'(k)}{\omega_0} \le 1 + \max \left(\alpha, \frac{m - 1}{m \lceil (k + 1)/m \rceil} \right) \tag{15}$$

A more specific application of finding near optimal priority lists for the largest τ_i is given in [J3]. Here a guess ω'_0 is made as to the value of ω_0, and a partial schedule is constructed as follows: order the tasks by nonincreasing values of τ_i. Assign the first (largest) task to be the first task executed on the first processor. In general, assign the ith task to be the next task executed on the lowest indexed processor to which it can be added without violating the deadline ω'_0. If it cannot be added to *any* processor without violating the deadline, halt. Let L_1 be the list of tasks assigned when the above procedure halts and L_2 the remaining portion of the list. Let L_1' be a permutation of L_1 which as a priority list will generate the same schedule as constructed above, and let L' be the list obtained from L_1' by appending L_2 to it. The following result has been proved.

Theorem   [J3]   For L' and ω_0' defined as above, $\omega_0' \geqslant \omega_0$ implies

$$\frac{\omega_{L'}}{\omega_0'} \leqslant \frac{5}{4}$$

This does not directly give us a bound on $\omega_{L'}/\omega_0$. However, the closer our guess ω_0' is to ω_0, the better the ratio $\omega_{L'}/\omega_0$ will be. Moreover, one can use repeated applications of the algorithm to *obtain* better guesses, using binary search techniques. If $L'(j)$ is the list obtained by the jth iteration, we have the following result.

Theorem   [J3]

$$\frac{\omega_{L'(j)}}{\omega_0} \leqslant \frac{5}{4}\left(1 + \frac{1}{2^{j-1}}\right)$$

This bound will be better than that given in (7) for ω_{CP} if $m \geqslant 5$ and $j \geqslant 8$.

One might remark, however, that critical path scheduling for independent tasks (i.e. $<$ is empty) can itself obey bounds better than (7), if different measures of performance are used. In particular, a natural alternative that has been considered (see [CW]) is $\omega^*(L)$, which is defined for a list L by

$$\omega^*(L) = \sum_{i=1}^{n} \omega_i^2(L)$$

where $\omega_i(L)$ denotes the time at which processor P_i finishes using the list L. This performance measure has arisen in a study of partitioning information on secondary storage with the aim of minimizing access times. The following result has been proved.

Theorem   [CW]

$$\frac{\omega_{CP}^*}{\omega_0^*} \leqslant \frac{25}{24}$$

On the other hand, examples exist [CW] for which

$$\frac{\omega_{CP}^*}{\omega_0^*} \geqslant \frac{37}{36} - \frac{1}{36m}$$

The complexity of the proof prohibits us from including it here.

In another secondary storage problem, a similar performance measure was considered; in particular, the function $(m - 2)/2 + (m/2)\omega^*$ was to be minimized. It has been shown that in this case [CC]

$$\frac{(m-2)/m + \omega^*_{\text{CP}}}{(m-2)/m + \omega^*_0} \le 1 + \frac{1}{16(m-1)}$$

which again illustrates the increased effectiveness of CP assignments when the "second moment" measure is involved.

Finally, CP sequencing has also been specialized to the problem of obtaining reasonably "short" schedules that guarantee minimum mean flow time (see Chapter 3). In particular, suppose independent tasks are assigned as follows. The m smallest (rank 1) tasks are assigned first, one to a processor. The next m smallest (rank 2) tasks are then assigned, one to a processor and largest-task-first to the finishing times of the rank-1 tasks. This process continues with subsequent ranks until all tasks are assigned and each processor has a task from each rank (we assume that n is a multiple of m). With the largest-first (CP) criterion, one can show [CS] that

$$\frac{\omega'_{\text{CP}}}{\omega'_0} \le \frac{5m-4}{4m-3}$$

is an optimal bound, where the prime signifies the restriction to schedules in the class of mean-flow-time-minimizing schedules.

5.3   REMARKS ON CRITICAL PATH SCHEDULING

As Example 7 shows, even if $<$ is a tree and all $\tau_i = 1$, it is still possible to have $\omega_L/\omega_0 = 2 - (1/m)$ for a suitably bad list L. If critical path scheduling is used in this case, it is known (see Chapter 2) that $\omega_{\text{CP}} = \omega_0$. The following example, due to G. S. Graham [Gr], shows that if the τ_i are allowed to be arbitrary, even though $<$ is a tree, the ratio $\omega_{\text{CP}}/\omega_0$ can still be very close to 2.

Example 9   Consider the tree and the critical path schedule illustrated in Figs. 5.30a and b, respectively. An optimal list can produce the schedule shown in Fig. 5.31. These diagrams show that

$$\frac{\omega_{\text{CP}}}{\omega_0} = \frac{2m+\epsilon}{(m+1)(1+\epsilon)}$$

which approaches $2 - 2/(m+1)$ as $\varepsilon \to 0$. Conceivably, this is the asymptotic worst-case behavior of ω_{CP} in the case that $<$ is a tree.

M. Kaufman [K2] has shown that if $<$ is a tree,

$$\frac{\omega_{\text{CP}}}{\omega_0} \le 1 + (m-1)\frac{\max \tau_i}{\sum_i \tau_i}$$

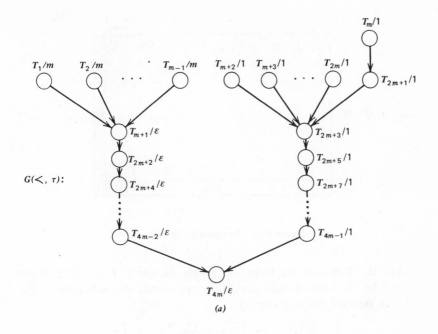

$G(<, \tau):$

(a)

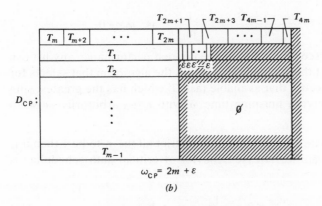

$\omega_{CP} = 2m + \varepsilon$

(b)

Figure 5.30   (a) Tree. (b) Critical path schedule.

which is analogous to the bound of Theorem 5.3 for $<$ empty and L arbitrary.

However, for general partial orders $<$ and arbitrary τ_i, critical path scheduling can result in the worst possible schedules, as the following example shows.

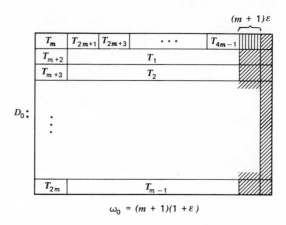

$$\omega_0 = (m + 1)(1 + \varepsilon)$$

Figure 5.31   An optimal schedule.

Example 10   Suppose we have the graph shown in Fig. 5.32a. When executed by the critical path algorithm, we obtain the schedule in Fig. 5.32b. An optimal list is given by

$$L = (\varepsilon_1, \ldots, \varepsilon_m, U_1, \ldots, U_m, T_1, \ldots, T_m)$$

with the corresponding schedule given in Fig. 5.33. Evidently,

$$\frac{\omega_{CP}}{\omega_0} = \frac{2m - 1 - 2\varepsilon}{m} \rightarrow 2 - \frac{1}{m} \qquad \text{as} \quad \varepsilon \rightarrow 0$$

which, as we have seen, is as bad as the poorest performance any list can ever give. Note that this example also shows the algorithm that selects for the next task to execute that available task T which has the greatest sum $\Sigma_{T < T_i} \tau_i$ also can have a finishing time $\bar{\omega}$ with $\bar{\omega}/\omega_0$ arbitrarily close to $2 - (1/m)$.

If we allow $<$ to be arbitrary but now restrict all the τ_i to be 1 then it is known [CLi] that the worst-case behavior of critical path scheduling is given by

$$\frac{\omega_{CP}}{\omega_0} \leq 2 - \frac{1}{m - 1}, \quad m \geq 3 \tag{16}$$

Also examples can be given [CLi] which show that this bound is best possible. We give such an example for $m = 3$.

Example 11   Let all $\tau_i = 1$ for the graph shown in Fig. 5.34a. One possible list resulting from critical path scheduling (in which the worst possible choices are made for breaking ties) is $L = (T_1, T_2, T_3, \ldots, T_{12})$. The

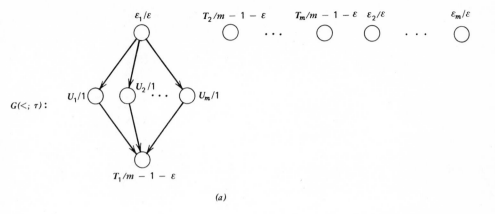

$$\omega_{CP} = 2m - 1 - 2\varepsilon$$

(b)

Figure 5.32 A graph and critical path schedule.

corresponding schedule is shown in Fig. 5.34*b*. An optimal schedule is
shown in Fig. 5.34*c* which corresponds to the list $L_0 = (T_4, T_8, T_1, T_2, T_3, T_5, T_6, T_7, T_9, T_{10}, T_{11}, T_{12})$. From the two schedules we find

$$\frac{\omega_{CP}}{\omega_0} = \frac{3}{2}$$

which is just the bound of (16) for $m = 3$.

Finally, we give a surprising example indicating that even when all
$\tau_i = 1$, there may be *no* list L that is optimal for executing $\mathcal{T}$ with both
$m = 2$ and $m = 3$.

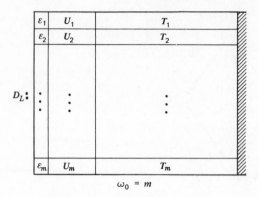

Figure 5.33 An optimal schedule.

Example 12 Consider the graph of Fig. 5.35, in which we suppose all τ_i to be 1. In any optimal list for $m = 2$, T_0 must precede *some* T_i, $1 \le i \le 6$. In any optimal list for $m = 3$, *all* T_i, $1 \le i \le 6$ must precede T_0!

5.4 SCHEDULING WITH MANY RESOURCES

We next examine the general case in which s, the number of resources, is nonzero. We recall that $\mathcal{R} = \{R_1, \ldots, R_s\}$ denotes the set of resources, $R_i(T_j)$ denotes the amount of resource R_i required by task T_j at all times during its execution, and for a fixed schedule, $r_i(t)$ denotes the total usage of resource R_i at time t. As might be expected, by allowing s to be nonzero, the ratio of ω/ω_0 can be much larger than before. We see this most clearly in the following result and example.

Theorem 5.5 [GG1] For $s = 1$, L, $<$, τ, m arbitrary, we have

$$\frac{\omega}{\omega_0} \le m \tag{17}$$

Proof The proof of (17) is immediate. We need only observe that

$$\omega \le \sum_{i=1}^{n} \tau_i \le m\omega_0$$

since at no time before time ω are all processors idle when using list L, and the number of processors busy at any time never exceeds m. ∎

To see that (17) is best possible, consider the following example.

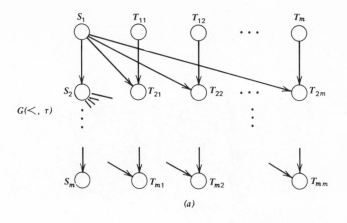

$G(<, \tau)$

(a)

D_{CP}

T_{11}	S_1	T_{21}	S_2					S_m
T_{12}		T_{22}						
$\vdots$	$\emptyset$	$\vdots$	$\emptyset$					$\emptyset$
T_{m1}		T_{m2}						

$\omega_{CP} = 2m$

(b)

D_0

S_1	$T_{1,\,m}$	$T_{2,\,m-1}$	$\cdots$		$T_{m,\,1}$
T_{11}	S_2	$T_{2,\,m}$	$\cdots$		$T_{m,\,2}$
T_{12}	T_{21}	S_3	$\cdots$		$T_{m,\,3}$
$\vdots$	$\vdots$	$\vdots$	$\vdots$		
$T_{1,m-1}$	$T_{2,m-2}$			S_m	T_{mm}

$\omega_0 = m + 1$

(c)

Figure 5.34 Conjectured worst case for CP scheduling.

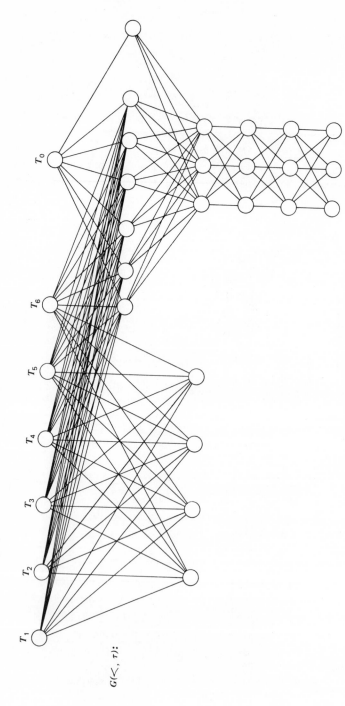

$G(<, \tau):$

Figure 5.35 List scheduling example.

Example 13   Let $\mathcal{T} = \{T_1, \ldots, T_m, T'_1, \ldots, T'_m\}$, and let

$$s = 1, \; R_1(T_i) = \frac{1}{m}, \; R(T'_i) = 1, \; 1 \le i \le m$$

$$\tau_i = 1, \quad \tau'_i = \varepsilon > 0$$

Let $<$ be defined by $T'_i < T_i$ for $1 \le i \le m$. For the lists

$$L = (T_1, \ldots, T_m, T'_1, \ldots, T'_m)$$
$$L' = (T'_1, \ldots, T'_m, T_1, \ldots, T_m)$$

we have, respectively, Figs. 5.36 and 5.37. Thus from the figures we have

$$\frac{\omega}{\omega'} = \frac{m + m\varepsilon}{1 + m\varepsilon} \to m \quad \text{as} \quad \varepsilon \to 0$$

A more interesting bound is given by the following theorem.

Theorem 5.6   [GG2]   If $<$ is empty, $m \ge n$, s, L, τ arbitrary, then

$$\frac{\omega}{\omega_0} \le s + 1$$

Proof   The proof requires several preliminary results.

Let G denote a graph with vertex set $V = V(G)$ and edge set $E = E(G)$. By a *valid labeling* λ of G, we mean a function $\lambda : V \to [0, \infty)$ satisfying

$$\lambda(a) + \lambda(b) \ge 1 \qquad \text{for all } e = \{a, b\} \in E \tag{18}$$

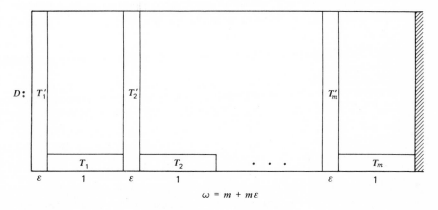

$$\omega = m + m\varepsilon$$

Figure 5.36   A bad schedule.

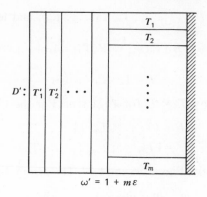

$$\omega' = 1 + m\varepsilon$$

Figure 5.37   An optimal schedule.

Define the *score of G*, denoted by $\tau^*(G)$, by

$$\tau^*(G) = \inf_{\lambda} \sum_{v \in V} \lambda(v)$$

where the inf is taken over all valid labelings λ of G.

Lemma 5.1   For any graph G, there exists a valid labeling $\lambda : V \to \{0, \frac{1}{2}, 1\}$ such that

$$\tau^*(G) = \sum_{v \in V} \lambda(v)$$

Proof   For the case that G is a bipartite graph (i.e., G has no odd cycles), a well-known theorem of König states that the number of edges in a maximum matching equals the cardinality of the minimum set of vertices of G incident to every edge of G. Thus for any bipartite graph G, there exists a valid labeling $\lambda : V \to \{0, 1\}$ such that

$$\tau^*(G) = \sum_{v \in V} \lambda(v)$$

For an arbitrary graph G, we construct a bipartite graph G_B as follows: for each vertex $v \in V(G)$ we form two vertices $v_1, v_2 \in V(G_B)$; for each edge $\{u, v\} \in E(G)$ we form two edges $\{u_1, v_2\}, \{u_2, v_1\} \in E(G_B)$. It is not difficult to verify that $\tau^*(G_B) = 2\tau^*(G)$ and furthermore, if $\lambda_B : V(G_B) \to \{0, 1\}$ is a valid labeling of G_B, then $\lambda : V(G) \to \{0, \frac{1}{2}, 1\}$ by $\lambda(v) = \frac{1}{2}(\lambda(v_1) + \lambda(v_2))$ is a valid labeling of G.   ∎

For positive integers k and s, let $G(k, s)$ denote the graph with vertex set $\{0, 1, \ldots, (s + 1)k - 1\}$ and edge set consisting of all pairs $\{a, b\}$ for which $|a - b| \geq k$.

Lemma 5.2 Suppose $G(k, s)$ is partitioned into s spanning subgraphs H_i, $1 \le i \le s$. Then we have

$$\max_{1 \le i \le s} \{\tau^*(H_i)\} \ge k \tag{19}$$

Proof Assume the lemma is false i.e., there exists a partition of $G(k, s)$ into H_i, $1 \le i \le s$, such that $\tau^*(H_i) < k$ for $1 \le i \le s$. Thus by Lemma 5.1, for each i there exists a valid labeling $\lambda_i : V(H_i) \to \{0, \frac{1}{2}, 1\}$ such that

$$\sum_{v \in V(H_i)} \lambda_i(v) = \tau^*(H_i) < k \tag{20}$$

Let $A = \{a_1 < \cdots < a_p | \lambda_i(a_j) \le \frac{1}{2}$ for all i, $1 \le i \le s\}$ and let $\hat{\tau}$ denote $\sum_{i=1}^{s} \tau^*(H_i)$.

There are three cases.

1. $p \le k$. In this case we have

$$\hat{\tau} \ge k(s + 1) - p \ge k(s + 1) - k = ks$$

which contradicts (20).

2. $k < p < 2k + 1$. For each edge $\{a_j, a_{j+k}\}$, $1 \le j \le p - k$, there must exist an i such that $\lambda_i(a_j) + \lambda_i(a_{j+k}) \ge 1$. Thus

$$\hat{\tau} \ge k(s + 1) - p + (p - k) = ks$$

again contradicting (20).

3. $p \ge 2k + 1$. We first note that for each vertex $v \in V(G(k, s))$, there exists an i such that $\lambda_i(v) \ge \frac{1}{2}$. For suppose $\lambda_i(v) = 0$ for $1 \le i \le s$. There must be some a_j such that $|a_j - v| \ge k$. But since $\lambda_i(a_j) \le \frac{1}{2}$ for all i, $\lambda_i(a_j) + \lambda_i(v) \le \frac{1}{2}$ for all i, which is a contradiction.

For each i, let n_i denote the number of vertices v such that $\lambda_i(v) = 1$. Then we have

$$|\{v | \lambda_i(v) > 0\}| \le 2k - 1 - n_i$$

since otherwise we would have

$$\sum_{v \in V(H_i)} \lambda_i(v) \ge n_i \cdot 1 + (2k - 2n_i) \cdot \frac{1}{2} = k$$

which contradicts (20). Therefore,

$$\sum_{i=1}^{s} |\{v | \lambda_i(v) > 0\}| \le (2k - 1)s - \sum_{i=1}^{s} n_i \tag{21}$$

Let q denote the number of vertices v such that there is exactly one i for which $\lambda_i(v) > 0$. Then we have

$$\sum_{i=1}^{s} |\{v | \lambda_i(v) > 0\}| \ge 2(k(s + 1) - q) + q \tag{22}$$

Combining (21) and (22) we obtain

$$q \geq 2k + s + \sum_{i=1}^{s} n_i \tag{23}$$

Of course we can assume without loss of generality that if $\lambda_i(v) = 1$, then $\lambda_j(v) = 0$ for all $j \neq i$. Hence by the definition of n_i, there must be at least $2k + s$ vertices, say, $b_1 < \cdots < b_{2k+s}$, such that

$$\sum_{i=1}^{s} \lambda_i(b_j) = \frac{1}{2}$$

that is, for each b_j there is a unique λ_i such that $\lambda_i(b_j) = \frac{1}{2}$ and $\lambda_l(b_j) = 0$ for all $l \neq i$. Thus if $|b_j - b_l| \geq k$, for some i, $\lambda_i(b_j) = \lambda_i(b_l) = \frac{1}{2}$. Since $|b_1 - b_{2k+s}| \geq k$, there exists i_0 such that $\lambda_{i_0}(b_1) = \lambda_{i_0}(b_{2k+s}) = \frac{1}{2}$. But by the same reasoning we must also have $\lambda_{i_0}(b_{k+j}) = \lambda_{i_0}(b_1) = \frac{1}{2}$ and $\lambda_{i_0}(b_{2k+s}) = \lambda_{i_0}(b_j) = \frac{1}{2}$ for $1 \leq j \leq k + s$. Therefore,

$$\tau^*(H_{i_0}) = \sum_{v \in V(H_{i_0})} \lambda_{i_0}(v) \geq (2k + s) \cdot \frac{1}{2} \geq k$$

which is a contradiction. This completes the proof of Lemma 5.2. ■

Recall that when $\mathcal{T}$ is executed using a fixed list L, s_i denotes the time at which T_i starts to be executed. Because of the way the system is defined, each s_i is a sum of a subset of the τ_j's.

We can assume without loss of generality that $\omega_0 = 1$. Assume now that $\omega > s + 1$. Furthermore, suppose that for some k, each τ_i can be written as $\tau_i = l_i/k$, where l_i is a positive integer. Thus $l_i \leq k$, since $\tau_i \leq \omega_0 = 1$. Also, for $1 \leq i \leq s$, each $r_i(t)$ is constant on each interval $[l/m, (l + 1)/m)$, this value being $r_i(l/m)$. It is important to note that since $<$ is empty and $m \geq n$, then for $t_1, t_2 \in [0, \omega)$ with $t_2 - t_1 \geq 1$, we must have

$$\max_{1 \leq i \leq s} \{r_i(t_1) + r_i(t_2)\} > 1$$

Otherwise, any task being executed at time t_2 should have been executed at time t_1 or sooner. Thus for each i, $1 \leq i \leq s$, we can define a graph H_i as follows:

$$V(H_i) = \{0, 1, \ldots, (s + 1)k - 1\}$$

$\{a, b\}$ is an edge of H_i iff

$$r_i\left(\frac{a}{k}\right) + r_i\left(\frac{b}{k}\right) > 1 \tag{24}$$

Note that if $|a - b| \geq k$, then $\{a, b\}$ is an edge of at least one H_i. Hence it is not difficult to see that

$$G(k, s) \subseteq \bigcup_{1 \leq i \leq s} H_i$$

Note that by (24), the mapping $\lambda_i : V(H_i) \to [0, \infty)$ defined by $\lambda_i(a) = r_i(a/k)$ is a valid labeling of H_i. Since $G \subseteq G'$ implies $\tau^*(G) \leq t^*(G')$ and the condition on the r_i in (24) is a strict inequality, it follows by Lemma 5.2 that

$$\max_i \left\{ \sum_{l=0}^{(s+1)k-1} r_i\left(\frac{l}{k}\right) \right\} = \max_i \left\{ \sum_{v \in V(H_i)} \lambda_i(v) \right\} > \max_i \{\tau^*(H_i)\} \geq k$$

But we must have

$$\frac{1}{k} \sum_{l=0}^{(s+1)k-1} r_i\left(\frac{l}{k}\right) \leq \int_0^\infty r_i(t)\, dt \leq 1, \quad 1 \leq i \leq s$$

that is,

$$\sum_{l=0}^{(s+1)k-1} r_i\left(\frac{l}{k}\right) \leq k, \quad 1 \leq i \leq s$$

Since this is a *contradiction*, Theorem 5.6 is proved in the case that $\tau_i = l_i/k$ for positive integers k and l_i. Of course it follows immediately that Theorem 5.6 holds when all the τ_i are rational. The proof of the theorem can be completed by establishing the following lemma.

Lemma 5.3 Let $\tau = (\tau_1, \ldots, \tau_n)$ be a sequence of positive real numbers. Then for any $\varepsilon > 0$, there exists $\tau' = (\tau'_1, \ldots, \tau'_n)$ such that:

1. $|\tau'_i - \tau_i| < \varepsilon$ for $1 \leq i \leq n$
2. For all $A, B \subseteq \{1, \ldots, n\}$,

$$\sum_{a \in A} \tau_a \leq \sum_{b \in B} \tau_b \quad \text{iff} \quad \sum_{a \in A} \tau'_a \leq \sum_{b \in B} \tau'_b$$

3. All τ'_i are positive rational numbers.

Remark The importance of condition 2 is that it guarantees that the order of execution of the T_i using the list L is the same for τ_i and τ'_i. Thus if L is used to execute $\mathcal{T}$, once using execution times τ_i and once using execution times τ'_i, the corresponding finishing times ω and ω' satisfy

$$|\omega - \omega'| \leq n\varepsilon$$

Hence if there were an example $\mathcal{T}$ with $\omega/\omega_0 > s + 1$ and some of the τ_i irrational, we could construct another example $\mathcal{T}^*$ by slightly changing the τ_i to rational τ'_i, permitting the corresponding new finishing ω^* and $\omega^{*\prime}$ to satisfy

$$|\omega - \omega^*| \le n\varepsilon, \qquad |\omega' - \omega^{*\prime}| \le n\varepsilon$$

and, therefore, if ε is sufficiently small, we still have $\omega^*/\omega^{*\prime} > s + 1$. However, this would contradict what has already been proved.

Lemma 5.3 is implied by the following slightly more general result. The proof here is due to V. Chvátal [C].

Lemma 5.3' Let $\mathscr{S}$ denote a finite system of inequalities of the form

$$\sum_{i=1}^{n} a_i x_i \ge a_0 \qquad \text{or} \qquad \sum_{i=1}^{n} a_i x_i > a_0$$

where the a_k are rational. If $\mathscr{S}$ has a real solution $(x_1, \ldots, x_n)$, then for any $\varepsilon > 0$, $\mathscr{S}$ has a *rational* solution $(x'_1, \ldots, x'_n)$ with $|x_i - x'_i| < \varepsilon$ for all i.

Proof We proceed by induction on n. For $n = 1$ the result is immediate. Now, let $\mathscr{S}$ be a system of inequalities in $n > 1$ variables, which is solvable in real numbers. $\mathscr{S}$ splits naturally into two classes: $\mathscr{S}_0$, the subset of inequalities involving x_n, and $\mathscr{S}_1$, the remaining inequalities of $\mathscr{S}$. Each inequality in $\mathscr{S}_1$ can be written in one of the following four ways:

a. $\alpha_0 + \displaystyle\sum_{i=1}^{n-1} \alpha_i x_i \le x_n$

b. $\alpha_0 + \displaystyle\sum_{i=1}^{n-1} \alpha_i x_i < x_n$

c. $\beta_0 + \displaystyle\sum_{i=1}^{n-1} \beta_i x_i \ge x_n$

d. $\beta_0 + \displaystyle\sum_{i=1}^{n-1} \beta_i x_i > x_n$

For each pair of inequalities, one of type a and one of type c, we consider the inequality

e. $\alpha_0 + \displaystyle\sum_{i=1}^{n-1} \alpha_i x_i \le \beta_0 + \sum_{i=1}^{n-1} \beta_i x_i$

Similarly, the pairs of types $\{a, d\}$, $\{b, c\}$, and $\{b, d\}$ give rise to inequalities

f. $\alpha_0 + \displaystyle\sum_{i=1}^{n-1} \alpha_i x_i < \beta_0 + \sum_{i=1}^{n-1} \beta_i x_i$

Let $\mathscr{S}^*$ be the set of all inequalities of types e and f we obtain from $\mathscr{S}_1$. Since by hypothesis, $\mathscr{S} = \mathscr{S}_0 \cup \mathscr{S}_1$ has a real solution $(x_1, \ldots, x_n)$, then

$\mathscr{S}_0 \cup \mathscr{S}^*$ has the real solution $(x_1, \ldots, x_{n-1})$. But $\mathscr{S}_0 \cup \mathscr{S}^*$ involves only $n - 1$ variables, so that by the induction hypothesis, $\mathscr{S}_0 \cup \mathscr{S}^*$ has a rational solution $(x'_1, \ldots, x'_{n-1})$ with $|x_i - x'_i| < \varepsilon'$ for all i and any preassigned $\varepsilon' > 0$. Substituting the x'_i into a, b, c, and d, we obtain a set of inequalities

g. $a' \leq x_n, \quad b' < x_n, \quad c' \geq x_n, \quad d' > x_n$

where a', b', c', and d' are rational. Since the x_i satisfy inequalities e and f, we have $a' \leq c'$, $b' < c'$, $a' < d'$, $b' < d'$. Thus for any $\varepsilon > 0$, if ε' is chosen to be suitably small, there is a rational x'_n satisfying g and with $|x_n - x'_n| < \varepsilon$, completing the proof of Lemma 5.3'. This proves Lemma 5.3 and Theorem 5.6. ∎

The following example shows that the bound in the preceding theorem cannot be improved.

Example 14 Let $\mathscr{T} = \{T_1, T_2, \ldots, T_{s+1}, T'_1, T'_2, \ldots, T'_{sN}\}$, $m \geq s(N + 1) + 1 = n$, and suppose $<$ is empty. Define

$$\tau_i = 1, \quad 1 \leq i \leq s + 1, \quad \tau'_i = \frac{1}{N}, \quad 1 \leq i \leq sN$$

$$R_i(T_i) = 1 - \frac{1}{N}, \quad R_i(T_j) = \frac{1}{Sn}, \quad j \neq i, \quad 1 \leq i \leq s$$

$$R_i(T_j) = \frac{1}{N}, \quad 1 \leq j \leq sN, \quad 1 \leq i \leq s$$

$$L = (T_1, T'_1, \ldots, T'_N, T_2, T'_{N+1}, \ldots, T'_{2N}, T_3, \ldots,$$

$$T_{k+1}, T'_{kN+1}, T'_{kN+2}, \ldots, T'_{(k+1)N}, T_{k+2}, \ldots, T'_{sN}, T_{s+1})$$

$$L' = (T'_1, T'_2, \ldots, T'_{sN}, T_1, T_2, \ldots, T_{s+1})$$

It is easily checked that for this example

$$\omega = s + 1, \quad \omega' = 1 + \frac{s}{N}$$

Thus ω / ω' and consequently ω / ω_0 are both arbitrarily close to $s + 1$ for N sufficiently large.

The last result in this section shows exactly the effect a processor constraint can have on the ratio ω / ω_0 (i.e., we do not assume $m \geq n$).

Theorem 5.7 [GG2] For $<$ empty, $m \geq 2$, s, L, τ arbitrary, we have

$$\frac{\omega}{\omega_0} \leq \min \left\{ \frac{m + 1}{2}, s + 2 - \frac{2s + 1}{m} \right\} \tag{25}$$

Proof The proof consists of two main lemmas, each of which gives a bound on ω/ω_0 that is best possible for certain values of s and m. If X is a finite union of disjoint intervals in $[0, \omega)$, we let $\mu(X)$ denote the sum of the lengths of these intervals.

Lemma 5.4 If $<$ is empty and s, L, τ, m arbitrary, we have

$$\frac{\omega}{\omega_0} \le \frac{m+1}{2}$$

Proof Let $I = \{t \mid |f(t)| = 1\}$, where we recall that $f(t)$ is defined to be that subset of tasks T_i which are being executed at time t (where we have a fixed list L under consideration). We first show

$$\mu(I) \le \omega_0 \qquad\qquad\qquad (26)$$

Consider the set T of tasks defined by

$$T = \bigcup_{t \in I} f(t)$$

For any pair of tasks T_i, T_j, belonging to T, there must exist some k, $1 \le k \le s$, such that

$$R_k(T_i) + R_k(T_j) > 1$$

since otherwise, one of those tasks should have been started earlier (unless $m = 1$, in which case the lemma is trivial). But this implies that in the optimal schedule no two members of T can be executed simultaneously. Therefore we have

$$\omega_0 \ge \sum_{T_i \in T} \tau_i \ge \mu(I)$$

which proves (26).

To complete the proof of Lemma 5.4, observe that at least two processors must be active at all times $t \in \bar{I} = [0, \omega) - I$. Thus,

$$m\omega_0 \ge \sum_{i=1}^{n} \tau_i \ge 2\mu(\bar{I}) + \mu(I)$$
$$= 2\omega - \mu(I)$$
$$\ge 2\omega - \omega_0$$

and so

$$(m+1)\omega_0 \ge 2\omega \qquad \blacksquare$$

Lemma 5.5 If $<$ is empty, $m \ge 3$ and s, L, τ arbitrary, then

$$\frac{\omega}{\omega_0} \le s + 2 - \frac{2s+1}{m} \qquad\qquad\qquad (27)$$

Proof Suppose we have a counterexample to the lemma. By Lemma 5.3 we can assume all the τ_i are rational; that is, there exists a positive integer k such that for each i, $1 \le i \le n$, there exists an integer l_i satisfying $\tau_i = l_i/k$. Without loss of generality we can also assume that $\omega_0 = 1$. Thus $\omega > s + 2 - (2s + 1)/m$ and each l_i satisfies $1 \le l_i \le k$.

Consider the operation of the system using the list L. As before, let $I = \{t \in [0, \omega) \mid |f(t)| = 1\}$, $I' = \{t \in [0, \omega) \mid |f(t)| = n\}$ and let $\bar{I} = [0, \omega) - I$. By the proof of Lemma 5.4, $\mu(I) \le 1$. Since at least two processors are active at each time $t \in \bar{I}$,

$$m \ge \sum_{i=1}^{n} \tau_i \ge m \cdot \mu(I') + \mu(I) + 2(\omega - \mu(I) - \mu(I'))$$
$$\ge (m - 2)\mu(I') + 2\omega - 1$$

or

$$\mu(I') \le \frac{m + 1 - 2\omega}{m - 2} \tag{28}$$

Since $\omega > s + 2 - (2s + 1)/m$, we have

$$\mu(\bar{I}) = \omega - \mu(I')$$
$$\ge \omega - \frac{m + 1 - 2\omega}{m - 2}$$
$$> s + 2 - \frac{2s + 1}{m} - \frac{m + 1 - 2\left(s + 2 - \dfrac{2s + 1}{m}\right)}{m - 2}$$
$$= s + 1 \tag{29}$$

Now, observe that for any $t_1, t_2 \in \bar{I}$ satisfying $t_2 - t_1 \ge 1$, there must exist an i, $1 \le i \le s$, such that

$$r_i(t_1) + r_i(t_2) > 1 \tag{30}$$

Otherwise, some task being executed at time t_2 should have been started at time t_1 or sooner. Recalling that $\bar{I}$ is a collection of intervals, each having the form $[l/k, (l + 1)/k)$ for some integer l, let $a_0 < a_1 < \cdots < a_p$ be integers such that

$$\bar{I} = \left\{ \left[\frac{a_i}{k}, \frac{a_i + 1}{k}\right) : 0 \le i \le p \right\}$$

Notice that (29) implies that $p \ge (s + 1)k$. For each i, $1 \le i \le s$, we construct a graph H_i as follows:

$$V(H_i) = \{0, 1, 2, \ldots, (s + 1)k - 1\}$$

$\{u, v\}$ is an edge of H_i iff

$$r_i\left(\frac{a_u}{k}\right) + r_i\left(\frac{a_v}{k}\right) > 1$$

Note that $|u - v| \geq k$ implies $|a_u - a_v| \geq k$, which, by (30), implies that $\{u, v\}$ is an edge of at least one H_i, $1 \leq i \leq s$. Hence it is not difficult to see that $G(k, s) \subseteq \cup_i H_i$. The same reasoning used in the proof of Theorem 5.6 can now serve to show that for some i, $1 \leq i \leq s$,

$$\int_0^\omega r_i(t)\, dt > 1$$

which contradicts the assumption that $\omega_0 = 1$. This completes the proof of Lemma 5.5. Theorem 5.7 follows by combining Lemmas 5.4 and 5.5.　■

We now give examples to show that the bound given in the preceding theorem is best possible. These examples are slightly more complicated than those previously presented. We leave the verification of the asserted values of ω and ω' to the reader.

Example 15　We consider three cases.

(i) $2 \leq m \leq s + 1$, where $\mathcal{T} = \{T_0, T_1, T_2, \ldots, T_{m-1}, T'_1, T'_2, \ldots, T'_{m-1}\}$, $<$ is empty, s arbitrary, and

$$\tau_0 = 1, \qquad \tau_j = \tau'_j = \frac{1}{2}, \qquad 1 \leq j \leq m - 1$$

$$R_i(T_0) = \frac{1}{2m}, \qquad 1 \leq i \leq s$$

$$R_i(T_i) = R_i(T'_i) = \frac{1}{2}, \qquad 1 \leq i \leq m - 1$$

$$R_i(T_j) = R_i(T'_j) = \frac{1}{2m}, \qquad i \neq j, \qquad 1 \leq i \leq s, \qquad 1 \leq j \leq m - 1$$

$$L = (T_1, T'_1, T_2, T'_2, \ldots, T_{m-1}, T'_{m-1}, T_0)$$

$$L' = (T_0, T_1, T_2, \ldots, T_{m-1}, T'_1, T'_2, \ldots, T'_{m-1})$$

Then

$$\omega = \frac{m + 1}{2}, \qquad \omega_0 = \omega' = 1$$

(ii) $s + 1 < m \geq 2s + 1$. For a suitably small $\varepsilon > 0$ and an arbitrary positive integer k, define $\varepsilon_i = \varepsilon (m - 1)^{i - 2k}$, $1 \leq i \leq 2k$.

$$\mathcal{T} = \{T_0\} \cup \{T_{i,j} \mid 1 \leq i \leq m - 1, 1 \leq j \leq k\} \cup \{T'_{i,j} \mid 1 \leq i \leq m - 1, 1 \leq j \leq k\}$$

Also, $<$ is empty, s arbitrary, and

$\tau_0 = 2k, \ \tau_{i,j} = \tau'_{i,j} = 1, \qquad 1 \le i \le m - 1, 1 \le j \le k$

$R_i(T_0) = \varepsilon_1, \ 1 \le i \le s$

$R_i(T_{i,j}) = 1 - (m - 1)\varepsilon_{2j-1}, \qquad 1 \le i \le s, 1 \le j \le k$

$R_l(T_{i,j}) = \varepsilon_{2j-1}, \qquad l \ne i, 1 \le l \le s, 1 \le i \le m - 1, 1 \le j \le k$

$R_i(T'_{s+i,j}) = 1 - (m - 1)\varepsilon_{2j}, \qquad 1 \le i \le m - s - 1, 1 \le j \le k$

$R_l(T'_{i,j}) = \varepsilon_{2j}, \qquad l \ne i - s, 1 \le l \le s, 1 \le i \le m - 1, 1 \le j \le k$

$L = (A_1, A_2, \ldots, A_k, A'_1, A'_2, \ldots, A'_{k-1}, A_0)$

where

$A_i = (B_{1,i}, B_{2,i}, \ldots, B_{s,i}), \qquad 1 \le i \le k$

$B_{j,i} = (T_{j,i}, T'_{j,i}), \qquad 1 \le i \le k, 1 \le j \le s$

$A'_i = (B'_{1,i}, B'_{2,i}, \ldots, B'_{m-1,i}), \qquad 1 \le i \le k - 1$

$B'_{j,i} = (T'_{s+j,i}, T_{s+j,i+1}), \qquad 1 \le i \le k - 1, 1 \le j \le m - 1$

$A_0 = (T_0, T_{s+1,1}, T_{s+2,1}, \ldots, T_{m-1,1}, T'_{s+1,k}, T'_{s+2,k}, \ldots, T'_{m-1,k})$

$L' = (C_0, C_1, C'_1, C_2, C'_2, \ldots, C_k, C'_k)$

where

$C_0 = (T_0)$

$C_i = (T_{1,i}, T_{2,i}, \ldots, T_{m-1,i}), \qquad 1 \le i \le k$

$C'_i = (T'_{1,i}, T'_{2,i}, \ldots, T'_{m-i,i}), \qquad 1 \le i \le k$

Then

$$\omega = k(m + 1) - (m - s - 1)$$
$$\omega' = \omega_0 = 2k$$

and

$$\frac{\omega}{\omega_0} = \frac{m + 1}{2} - \frac{(m - s - 1)}{2k} \to \frac{m + 1}{2} \qquad \text{as} \quad k \to \infty$$

(iii) $m > 2s + 1$.   For a suitably small $\varepsilon > 0$ and an arbitrary positive integer k', let $k = k'm$ and define $\varepsilon_i = \varepsilon(m - 1)^{i-k}$, $1 \le i \le k$.

$$\mathcal{T} = \{T_0\} \cup \{T_{i,j} : 1 \le i \le m - 1, 1 \le j \le k\}$$

$<$ is empty, s arbitrary

$$\tau_0 = k, \qquad \tau_{i,j} = 1, \qquad 1 \le i \le m-1, \, 1 \le j \le k$$
$$R_i(T_0) = \varepsilon_1, \qquad 1 \le i \le s$$
$$R_i(T_{i,j}) = 1 - (m-1)\varepsilon_j, \qquad 1 \le i \le s, \, 1 \le j \le k$$
$$R_l(T_{i,j}) = \varepsilon_j, \qquad l \ne i, \, 1 \le l \le s, \, 1 \le i \le m-1, \, 1 \le j \le k$$
$$L = (A_1, A_2, \ldots, A_{m-2s-1}, B_1, B_2, \ldots, B_s, C)$$

where

$$A_i = (T_{2s+i,1}, T_{2s+i,2}, \ldots, T_{2s+i,k}), \qquad 1 \le i \le m-2s-1$$
$$B_i = (T_{i,1}, T_{s+i,2}, T_{i,2}, T_{s+i,3}, \ldots, T_{i,k-1}, T_{s+1,k}), \qquad 1 \le i \le s$$
$$C = (T_0, T_{s+1,1}, T_{s+2,1}, \ldots, T_{2s,1}, T_{1,k}, T_{2,k}, \ldots, T_{s,k})$$
$$L' = (T_0, D_1, D_2, \ldots, D_k)$$

where

$$D_i = (T_{1,i}, T_{2,i}, \ldots, T_{m-1,i}), \qquad 1 \le i \le k$$

Then we have

$$\omega = (s+2)k'm - (2s+1)k' - s$$
$$\omega' = \omega_0 = k'm$$

and

$$\frac{\omega}{\omega_0} = s + 2 - \frac{2s+1}{m} - \frac{s}{k'm} \to s + 2 - \frac{2s+1}{m} \qquad \text{as} \quad k' \to \infty \quad \blacksquare$$

5.5 BIN PACKING

In this section† we deal with the very important special case $s = 1$, $<$ is empty, all $\tau_i = 1$, and $m \ge n$. This has become known as the "bin-packing" problem in the literature for the obvious reason that the scheduling problem in this case is equivalent to the problem of "packing" the sequence of "weights" $(R_1(T_1), R_1(T_2), \ldots, R_1(T_n))$ into a minimum number of "bins" (i.e., unit time slots) of unit capacity (i.e., maximum resource usage is 1) so that no bin contains a total weight exceeding one. As in Chapter 1 we note that the preceding is a complementary statement of the problem of minimizing the number of processors required to meet a given deadline ω common to all tasks. Without loss of generality we can assume that the execution times are normalized so that $\omega = 1$. In the latter problem the processors now become a "free" resource, and the processing time "resource" is bounded at $\omega = 1$. In the following it is convenient to take the former point of view, in which the problem is regarded as a special case of the model in the previous section.

† The contents and presentation of this section are based on portions of [JDUGG].

This problem is also equivalent to the one-dimensional stock-cutting problem (a variation of the knapsack problem), and efficient algorithms for obtaining optimal or near-optimal packings (i.e., schedules) have obvious practical applications—for example, in table formatting, file allocation, coil slitting (the formation of varying widths of coils of material formed from a single standard width), cable-length optimization problems, and generally, whenever a number of "pieces" of different "lengths" must be obtained from pieces having a standard length.

We modify the notation slightly for this section (to conform with that in standard use) as follows:

1. The "weight" $R_1(T_i)$ is denoted a_i. We can assume $0 < a_i \le 1$.
2. The sequence of weights is denoted by $L = (a_1, a_2, \ldots, a_n)$.
3. The minimum number of bins into which the elements of L can be packed is denoted by L^*.
4. The ith bin, denoted by B_i, corresponds to the time interval $[i - 1, i)$.

There are four bin-packing algorithms which will constitute our primary concern. In each of the algorithms, a_1 is packed first and a_k is packed before a_{k+1} is packed for all $k \ge 1$.

1. First-fit (or FF). Each a_k is placed into the lowest indexed bin into which it will fit.
2. Best-fit (or BF). Each a_k is placed into a bin for which the resulting unused capacity is minimal.
3. First-fit decreasing (or FFD). The L is arranged into a nonincreasing list and FF is applied to the resulting list.
4. Best-fit decreasing (or BFD). The same as 3, with BF replacing FF.

The corresponding numbers of bins required by these algorithms when used on a list L are denoted by $FF(L)$, $BF(L)$, $FFD(L)$, and $BFD(L)$, respectively.

We begin with a simple example illustrating a type of list for which FF and BF behave poorly.

Example 16 Let n be divisible by 18 and let δ satisfy $0 < \delta < 1/84$. Define a list $L = (a_1, a_2, \ldots, a_n)$ by

$$
a_i = \begin{cases} \left(\dfrac{1}{6}\right) - 2\delta & \text{for} \quad 1 \le i \le \dfrac{n}{3} \\[2mm] \left(\dfrac{1}{3}\right) + \delta & \text{for} \quad \dfrac{n}{3} < i \le \dfrac{2n}{3} \\[2mm] \left(\dfrac{1}{2}\right) + \delta & \text{for} \quad \dfrac{2n}{3} < i \le n \end{cases}
$$

Clearly, $L^* = n/3$, since the elements can be packed perfectly by placing one element of each type in each bin. However, it is easily checked that both the first fit and the best fit algorithm applied to L will result in a packing that consists of $n/18$ bins each containing six elements of size $(1/6) - 2\delta$, $n/6$ bins each containing two elements of size $(1/3) + \delta$, and $n/3$ bins each containing a single element of size $(1/2) + \delta$. The two packings are shown in Fig. 5.38. Thus we have

$$\frac{\text{FF}(L)}{L^*} = \frac{\text{BF}(L)}{L^*} = \frac{n/18 + n/6 + n/3}{n/3} = \frac{5}{3}$$

By slightly modifying the list L given in Example 16, we can force even worse behavior, as shown by the following result.

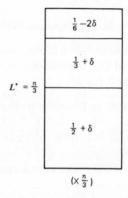

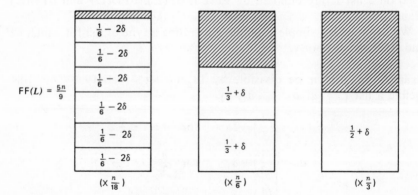

Figure 5.38 The 5/3 example.

Theorem 5.8 For every $k \geq 1$ there exists a list L with $L^* = k$ and

$$FF(L) = BF(L) > \frac{17}{10} L^* - 8$$

Proof As in the previous example, the elements of L belong to three regions, with sizes nearly equal to $\frac{1}{6}$, $\frac{1}{3}$, and $\frac{1}{2}$, respectively. The number of elements belonging to each region is the same. Those of the first region precede those of the second region, which in turn precede those of the third region in L.

Let n be a positive integer divisible by 17 and let δ be chosen so that $0 < \delta \ll 18^{-n/17}$. The first region consists of $n/17$ *blocks* of 10 numbers each. We denote the 10 numbers in the ith block of the first region by $a_{0,i}, a_{1,i}, \ldots, a_{9,i}$. These numbers are defined as follows, where $\delta_i = \delta \cdot 18^{(n/17)-i}$ for $1 \leq i \leq n/17$:

$$a_{0,i} = \left(\frac{1}{6}\right) + 33\delta_i$$

$$a_{1,i} = \left(\frac{1}{6}\right) - 3\delta_i$$

$$a_{2,i} = a_{3,i} = \left(\frac{1}{6}\right) - 7\delta_i$$

$$a_{4,i} = \left(\frac{1}{6}\right) - 13\delta_i$$

$$a_{5,i} = \left(\frac{1}{6}\right) + 9\delta_i$$

$$a_{6,i} = a_{7,i} = a_{8,i} = a_{9,i} = \left(\frac{1}{6}\right) - 2\delta_i$$

Let the first $10n/17$ elements in the list L be $(a_{0,1}, a_{1,1}, \ldots, a_{9,1}, a_{0,2}, a_{1,2}, \ldots, a_{9,2}, \ldots)$. Notice that $a_{0,i} + a_{1,i} + \cdots + a_{4,i} = \left(\frac{5}{6}\right) + 3\delta_i$ and $a_{5,i} + a_{6,i} + \cdots + a_{9,i} = \left(\frac{5}{6}\right) + \delta_i$. Thus for all i, the first five elements of block i will occupy bin $2i - 1$, and the last five elements of block i will occupy bin $2i$ when either the first-fit algorithm or the best-fit algorithm is applied. To see this, we need only observe that $a_{4,i}$, the smallest element in block i, will not fit into any of the preceding bins because the least filled of these, bin $2i - 2$, has contents totaling $\left(\frac{5}{6}\right) + \delta_{i-1} = \left(\frac{5}{6}\right) + 18\delta_i$. Also, the smallest of $a_{5,i}, a_{6,i}, \ldots, a_{9,i}$, which is $\left(\frac{1}{6}\right) - 2\delta_i$, will not fit into bin $2i - 1$, which has contents totaling $\left(\frac{5}{6}\right) + 3\delta_i$. Thus the $n/17$ blocks in the first region must occupy $2n/17$ bins.

We next turn to the second region. Here the elements are all about equal to $\frac{1}{3}$ and they are again divided into $n/17$ blocks of 10 elements each, the elements of the ith block being denoted by $b_{0,i}, b_{1,i}, \ldots, b_{9,i}$. In L, these elements all follow the $a_{j,i}$ and occur in the order $(b_{0,1}, b_{1,1}, \ldots, b_{9,1}, b_{0,2}, b_{1,2}, \ldots, b_{9,2}, \ldots)$. The values of the $b_{j,i}$ are defined as follows:

$$b_{0,i} = \left(\frac{1}{3}\right) + 46\delta_i$$

$$b_{1,i} = \left(\frac{1}{3}\right) - 34\delta_i$$

$$b_{2,i} = b_{3,i} = \left(\frac{1}{3}\right) + 6\delta_i$$

$$b_{4,i} = \left(\frac{1}{3}\right) + 12\delta_i$$

$$b_{5,i} = \left(\frac{1}{3}\right) - 10\delta_i$$

$$b_{6,i} = b_{7,i} = b_{8,i} = b_{9,i} = \left(\frac{1}{3}\right) + \delta_i$$

The elements of block i occupy bins $(2n/17) + 5i - 4$ through $(2n/17) + 5i$. These contain $b_{0,i}$ and $b_{1,i}$, $b_{2,i}$ and $b_{3,i}$, and so on. To see this, we observe that the contents of the five bins occupied by block i sum to, respectively,

$$\left(\frac{2}{3}\right) + 12\delta_i, \qquad \left(\frac{2}{3}\right) + 12\delta_i, \qquad \left(\frac{2}{3}\right) + 2\delta_i,$$

$$\left(\frac{2}{3}\right) + 2\delta_i, \quad \text{and} \quad \left(\frac{2}{3}\right) + 2\delta_i$$

Thus $b_{5,i} = (\frac{1}{3}) - 10\delta_i$ cannot fall into either of the first two bins and $b_{1,i} = (\frac{1}{3}) - 34\delta_i$ cannot fall into any of the bins of previous blocks, since these are all filled to at least level $(\frac{2}{3}) + 2\delta_{i-1} = (\frac{2}{3}) + 36\delta_i$. Thus the $n/17$ blocks in the second region occupy $5n/17$ bins.

The third region consists of $10n/17$ numbers, each equal to $(\frac{1}{2}) + \delta$. They clearly occupy one bin each. This completes the list L. The total number of bins required by applying either the first-fit algorithm or the best-fit algorithm is exactly n.

However, the elements of the list L can be packed into $(10n/17) + 1$ bins as follows. All but two of these bins contain one of the numbers $(\frac{1}{2}) + \delta$. The remaining space in each of these bins is filled with one of the following combinations:

1. $a_{j,i} + b_{j,i}$ for   some i, j with $2 \le j \le 9$, $1 \le i \le n/17$
2. $a_{0,i} + b_{1,i}$ for   some i, $1 \le i \le n/17$
3. $a_{1,i} + b_{0,i+1}$ for   some i, $1 \le i \le n/17$

This leaves $b_{0,1}$, $a_{1,(n/17)}$ and one number $(\frac{1}{2}) + \delta$, which can easily be

packed into the two remaining bins. We have therefore shown that
$L^* \leq 1 + 10n/17$ so that

$$\frac{FF(L)}{L^*} \geq \frac{17n}{10n + 17} > \frac{17}{10} - \frac{2}{L^*}$$

and similarly,

$$\frac{BF(L)}{L^*} > \frac{17}{10} - \frac{2}{L^*}$$

To obtain values of L^* not congruent to 1 modulo 10, we can form the
list L' by adjoining to L, k elements each with size 1, where k is a fixed
integer ≤ 9. The preceding arguments then show

$$FF(L') = FF(L) + k \qquad \text{and} \qquad L'^* = L^* + k$$

so that

$$\frac{FF(L')}{L'^*} \geq \frac{17}{10} - \frac{8}{L'^*}$$

with the same bound also holding for $BF(L')/L'^*$. This proves Theorem
5.8. ∎

We now show that the examples constructed in the preceding proof are
essentially the worst possible, that is, 17/10 is the asymptotic least upper
bound of the ratios $FF(L)/L^*$ and $BF(L)/L^*$ for large L.

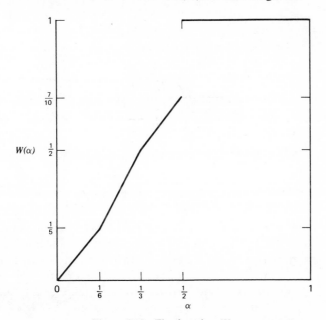

Figure 5.39 The function W.

Theorem 5.9 [U2], [GGU] For every list L, we have

$$\text{FF}(L) \le \frac{17}{10} L^* + 2 \quad \text{and} \quad \text{BF}(L) \le \frac{17}{10} L^* + 2$$

Proof We use only the two following properties of the FF and BF algorithms:

1. No element is placed in an empty bin unless it will not fit into *any* nonempty bin.

2. If there is a unique nonempty bin with lowest level, no element will be placed there unless it will not fit in any lower indexed bin. (The *level* of a bin refers simply to the sum of the weights it contains.)

Define the mapping $W : [0, 1] \to [0, 1]$ as follows (see Fig. 5.39):

$$W(\alpha) = \begin{cases} \dfrac{6}{5}\alpha & \text{for} \quad 0 \le \alpha \le \dfrac{1}{6} \\[2mm] \dfrac{9}{5}\alpha - \dfrac{1}{10} & \text{for} \quad \dfrac{1}{6} < \alpha \le \dfrac{1}{3} \\[2mm] \dfrac{6}{5}\alpha + \dfrac{1}{10} & \text{for} \quad \dfrac{1}{3} < \alpha \le \dfrac{1}{2} \\[2mm] 1 & \text{for} \quad \dfrac{1}{2} < \alpha \le 1 \end{cases}$$

Claim 1 Let some bin be filled with $b_1, b_2, \ldots, b_k$. Then

$$\sum_{i=1}^{k} W(b_i) \le \frac{17}{10}$$

Proof If $b \le \frac{1}{2}$, then $W(b)/b \le \frac{3}{2}$. The extreme ratio is reached only when $b = \frac{1}{3}$ and is less otherwise. Thus the claim is immediate unless one b_i is greater than $\frac{1}{2}$. We can take this one to be b_1, and we must now show that if

$$\sum_{i=2}^{k} b_i < \frac{1}{2}, \quad \text{then} \quad \sum_{i=2}^{k} W(b_i) \le \frac{7}{10}$$

It should be noted that since the slope of $W(b)$ is the same in the regions $[0, \frac{1}{6}]$ and $[\frac{1}{3}, \frac{1}{2}]$, any b_i that is in the second region can be replaced without loss of generality by the two numbers $\frac{1}{3}$ and $b_i - \frac{1}{3}$. We therefore assume that $b_i \le \frac{1}{3}$ for $2 \le i \le k$. Moreover, if b_j and $b_{j'}$ are both $\le \frac{1}{6}$, they can be combined into one, and $\Sigma_i W(b_i)$ will not decrease; in fact it may increase. Thus we can assume that at most one of the b_i's, $i \ge 2$, is in the range $(0, \frac{1}{6}]$ and the rest are in $(\frac{1}{6}, \frac{1}{3}]$.

We have consequently reduced the proof to the consideration of four cases:

1. $k = 2$, $b_2 \leq \frac{1}{3}$
2. $k = 3$, $\frac{1}{6} < b_2 \leq b_3 \leq \frac{1}{3}$
3. $k = 3$, $b_2 \leq \frac{1}{6} < b_3 \leq \frac{1}{3}$
4. $k = 4$, $b_2 \leq \frac{1}{6} < b_3 \leq b_4 \leq \frac{1}{3}$

Case 1 is immediate because $b_2 \leq \frac{1}{2}$ implies $W(b_2) \leq \frac{7}{10}$. In case 2, $W(b_2) + W(b_3) = (\frac{9}{5})(b_2 + b_3) - \frac{1}{5} \leq (\frac{9}{5})(\frac{1}{2}) - \frac{1}{5} = \frac{7}{10}$, since $b_2 + b_3 \leq \frac{1}{2}$. For case 3, $W(b_2) + W(b_3) = (\frac{6}{5})b_2 + (\frac{9}{5})b_3 - \frac{1}{10} \leq \frac{1}{5} + \frac{3}{5} - \frac{1}{10} = \frac{7}{10}$. And finally, in case 4, $W(b_2) + W(b_3) + W(b_4) \leq (\frac{6}{5})b_2 + (\frac{9}{5})(b_3 + b_4) - \frac{1}{5} = (\frac{9}{5})(b_2 + b_3 + b_4) - (\frac{3}{5})b_2 - \frac{1}{5} \leq \frac{9}{10} - \frac{1}{5} = \frac{7}{10}$, since $b_2 + b_3 + b_4 \leq \frac{1}{2}$. $\blacksquare$ *i.e. the bin of smaller index that has greatest amount of empty space*

Let us define the _coarseness of a bin_ to be the largest α such that some bin with smaller index is filled to level $1 - \alpha$. The coarseness of the first bin is 0.

Claim 2 Suppose bins are filled according to either the FF or the BF algorithm, and some bin B has coarseness α. Then every member of B that was placed there _before B_ was more than half full exceeds α.

Proof Until the bin has been filled to a level greater than $\frac{1}{2}$, it must be either empty, or the unique nonempty bin of lowest level (by property 1 of the placement algorithm), so by constraints 1 and 2 any element placed in the bin must not fit in any bin with lower index, hence must exceed α. $\blacksquare$

i.e, no lower indexed bin is more than half full.

Claim 3 Let a bin of coarseness $\alpha < \frac{1}{2}$ be filled with numbers $b_1 \geq b_2 \geq \cdots \geq b_k$ in the completed FF-packing (BF-packing). If $\Sigma_{i=1}^{k} b_i \geq 1 - \alpha$, then $\Sigma_{i=1}^{k} W(b_i) \geq 1$.

Proof If $b_1 > \frac{1}{2}$, the result is immediate, since $W(b_1) = 1$. We therefore assume that $b_1 \leq \frac{1}{2}$. If $k \geq 2$, the second element placed in the bin was placed before the bin was more than half full; thus by claim 2 at least two of the elements exceed α. In particular, we must have $b_1 \geq b_2 > \alpha$. We consider several cases, depending on the range of α.

Case 1 $\alpha \leq \frac{1}{6}$. Then $\Sigma_{i=1}^{k} b_i \geq 1 - \alpha \geq \frac{5}{6}$. Since $W(\beta)/\beta \geq \frac{6}{5}$ in the range $0 \leq \beta \leq \frac{1}{2}$, we immediately have $\Sigma_{i=1}^{k} W(b_i) \geq \frac{6}{5} \cdot \frac{5}{6} = 1$.

Case 2 $\frac{1}{6} \leq \alpha \leq \frac{1}{3}$. We consider subcases, depending on the value of k.

$k = 1$: Here, since $b_1 \leq \frac{1}{2}$, we must have $1 - \alpha \leq \frac{1}{2}$ or $\alpha \geq \frac{1}{2}$, which contradicts our assumption that $\alpha \leq \frac{1}{3}$.

$k = 2$: If both b_1 and b_2 are $\geq \frac{1}{3}$, then $W(b_1) + W(b_2) \geq (\frac{6}{5} \cdot \frac{1}{3} + \frac{1}{10})2 = 1$. If both are $< \frac{1}{3}$, then $b_1 + b_2 < \frac{2}{3} < 1 - \alpha$, which contradicts our hypothesis. If $b_1 \geq \frac{1}{3}$, and $b_2 < \frac{1}{3}$, then since both must be greater than α, $\alpha < b_2 < \frac{1}{3} \leq b_1 \leq$

$\frac{1}{2}$. Hence $W(b_1) + W(b_2) = (\frac{9}{5})b_1 - \frac{1}{10} + (\frac{6}{5})b_2 + \frac{1}{10} = (\frac{6}{5})(b_1 + b_2) + (\frac{3}{5})b_1$. Since $b_1 + b_2 \geq 1 - \alpha$ and $b_1 > \alpha$, we have $W(b_1) + W(b_2) \geq (\frac{6}{5})(1 - \alpha)$ $+ (\frac{3}{5})\alpha = 1 + (\frac{1}{5} - (\frac{3}{5})\alpha) \geq 1$, since $\alpha \leq \frac{1}{3}$.

$k \geq 3$: As in the previous case, if two of the b_i are $\geq \frac{1}{3}$, the result is immediate. If $b_1 \geq \frac{1}{3} > b_2 \geq \alpha$, then

$$W(b_1) + W(b_2) + \sum_{i=3}^{k} W(b_i)$$

$$\geq \frac{6}{5}b_1 + \frac{1}{10} + \frac{9}{5}b_2 - \frac{1}{10} + \frac{6}{5}\sum_{i=3}^{k} b_i$$

$$= \frac{6}{5}\sum_{i=1}^{k} b_i + \left(\frac{3}{5}\right)b_2 \geq \left(\frac{6}{5}\right)(1 - \alpha) + \left(\frac{3}{5}\right)\alpha = 1 + \frac{1}{5} - \left(\frac{3}{5}\right)\alpha \geq 1$$

If $\frac{1}{3} > b_1 \geq b_2 > \alpha$, then

$$W(b_1) + W(b_2) + \sum_{i=3}^{k} W(b_i) \geq \left(\frac{9}{5}\right)(b_1 + b_2) - \frac{1}{5} + \frac{6}{5}\sum_{i=3}^{k} b_i$$

$$\geq \left(\frac{6}{5}\right)(1 - \alpha) + \left(\frac{3}{5}\right)(2\alpha) - \frac{1}{5}$$

$$= 1 + \left(\frac{6}{5}\right)\alpha - \left(\frac{6}{5}\right)\alpha = 1$$

Case 3 $\frac{1}{3} < \alpha < \frac{1}{2}$. If $k = 1$, we have $b_1 \geq 1 - \alpha > \frac{1}{2}$, so $W(b_1) = 1$.
If $k \geq 2$, then $b_1 \geq b_2 > \frac{1}{3}$ and the result is immediate.

Claim 4 If a bin of coarseness $\alpha < \frac{1}{2}$ is filled with $b_1 \geq \cdots \geq b_k$, and $\Sigma_{i=1}^{k} W(b_i) = 1 - \beta$, where $\beta > 0$, then either

1. $k = 1$ and $b_1 \leq \frac{1}{2}$, or
2. $\Sigma_{i=1}^{k} b_i \leq 1 - \alpha - (\frac{5}{9})\beta$

Proof If $k = 1$ and $b_1 > \frac{1}{2}$, it is impossible that $\beta > 0$. Therefore, if condition 1 does not hold, we can assume that $k \geq 2$, hence $b_1 \geq b_2 \geq \alpha$, by the reasoning of the previous claim. Let $\Sigma_{i=1}^{k} b_i = 1 - \alpha - \gamma$. Then we can construct a bin filled with $b_3, b_4, \ldots, b_k$ and two other numbers δ_1 and δ_2, selected so that $\delta_1 + \delta_2 = b_1 + b_2 + \gamma$, $\delta_1 \geq b_1$, $\delta_2 \geq b_2$, and neither δ_1 nor δ_2 exceeds $\frac{1}{2}$. By the proof of claim 3 and because both δ_1 and δ_2 exceed α, we know that

$$\sum_{i=3}^{k} W(b_i) + W(\delta_1) + W(\delta_2) \geq 1$$

But since the slope W in range $[0, \frac{1}{2}]$ does not exceed $\frac{9}{5}$, it follows that $W(\delta_1) + W(\delta_2) \leq W(b_1) + W(b_2) + (\frac{9}{5})\gamma$. Therefore, $\gamma \geq (\frac{5}{9})\delta$, and condition 2 holds. ∎

We are now prepared to complete the proof of Theorem 5.9. Let $L = (a_1, a_2, \ldots, a_n)$ and $\bar{W} = \Sigma_{i=1}^{n} W(a_i)$. By claim 1, $(17/10)L^* \geq \bar{W}$.

Suppose that in the FF (BF) algorithm, bins $B'_1, B'_2, \ldots, B'_k$ are all the bins that receive at least one element and for which $\Sigma_j W(a_j) = 1 - \beta_i$ with $\beta_i > 0$, where j ranges over all elements in bin B'_i. We assume that $1 \le i < j \le k$ implies that B'_i had a smaller index than B'_j in the original indexing of all bins. Let γ_i be the coarseness of B'_i. Since B'_i contains no element exceeding $\frac{1}{2}$, we must have each $\gamma_i < \frac{1}{2}$. By claim 4 and the definition of coarseness,

$$\gamma_i \ge \gamma_{i-1} + \left(\frac{5}{9}\right)\beta_{i-1} \qquad \text{for} \quad 1 < i \le k$$

Thus

$$\sum_{i=1}^{k-1} \beta_i \le \frac{9}{5} \sum_{i=2}^{k} (\gamma_i - \gamma_{i-1}) = \frac{9}{5}(\gamma_k - \gamma_1) \le \frac{9}{5} \cdot \frac{1}{2} < 1$$

Since β_k cannot exceed 1, we have

$$\sum_{i=1}^{k} \beta_i \le 2$$

Applying claim 3, we obtain

$$FF(L) \le \bar{W} + 2 \le (1.7)L^* + 2$$

and

$$BF(L) \le \bar{W} + 2 \le (1.7)L^* + 2$$

completing the proof of the theorem. ∎

If the list $L = (a_1, \ldots, a_n)$ is such that for some $\alpha \le \frac{1}{2}$, all a_i are less than or equal to α, the worst-case behavior of the two placement algorithms is not as extreme. In particular, the following result holds.

Theorem 5.10 [GGU] For any positive $\alpha \le \frac{1}{2}$, let $k = \lfloor \alpha^{-1} \rfloor$. Then, we have:

1. For each $l \ge 1$, there exists a list $L = (a_1, \ldots, a_n)$ with all $a_i \in (0, \alpha]$ and $L^* = l$ such that

$$FF(L) \ge \left(\frac{k+1}{k}\right)L^* - \frac{1}{k}$$

2. For any list $L = (a_1, \ldots, a_n)$ with all $a_i \in (0, \alpha]$,

$$FF(L) \le \left(\frac{k+1}{k}\right)L^* + 2$$

Both 1 and 2 hold with FF replaced by BF.

Proof We first describe how to construct lists L, with no element exceeding α, for which

$$\frac{FF(L)}{L^*} = \frac{BF(L)}{L^*} = \frac{k+1}{k} - \frac{1}{kL^*}$$

Let l be any positive integer. The list L is composed of elements that are all very close to $1/(k+1)$. The elements are of two types, described as follows:

$$b_j = \frac{1}{k+1} - k^{2j+1}\delta, \qquad j = 1, 2, \ldots, l-1$$

$$a_{1j} = a_{2j} = \cdots = a_{kj} = \frac{1}{m+1} + k^{2j}\delta, \qquad j = 1, 2, \ldots, l$$

where $\delta > 0$ is chosen suitably small. The list L has the a-type elements occurring in nonincreasing order and the b-type elements occurring in strictly increasing order, interspersed so that each successive pair b_j and b_{j-1} of b-type elements has precisely k a-type elements occurring in between. The list L is then completely specified by the property that b_{l-1} occurs as the second element. We leave it for the reader to verify that

$$FF(L) = BF(L) = \left\lceil \frac{l(k+1)-1}{k} \right\rceil$$

It is easy to see that the elements of L can be packed optimally by placing $b_j, a_{1j}, a_{2j}, \ldots, a_{kj}$ in a single bin for each $j = 1, \ldots, l-1$ and placing $a_{1l}, a_{2l}, \ldots, a_{kl}$ in one additional bin. This gives $L^* = l$. We then have

$$\frac{FF(L)}{L^*} = \frac{BF(L)}{L^*} \geq \frac{l(k+1)-1}{kl} = \frac{k+1}{k} - \frac{1}{kL^*}$$

The upper bound is also easily proved. Suppose that the list L contains no element exceeding $1/k$, k an integer.

Consider an FF-packing of L. Every bin, except possibly the last bin, contains at least k elements. Disregarding the last bin, suppose two bins B_i and B_j, $i < j$, each contain elements totaling less than $k/(k+1)$. Then since B_j contains k elements, B_j must contain an element with size less than $1/(k+1)$. But this element would have fit in B_i and thus could not have been placed in B_j by FF, a contradiction. Thus all but at most two bins must contain elements totaling at least $k/(k+1)$. Thus, letting $w(L)$ denote the sum of all elements in L, we have

$$L^* \geq w(L) \geq \frac{k}{k+1}(FF(L) - 2)$$

so that

$$FF(L) \leq \frac{(k+1)L^*}{k} + 2$$

A similar but slightly more complicated argument can be used to prove this for BF. This proves the theorem. ∎

It follows at once from Theorem 5.10 that if $\alpha \leq \frac{1}{2}$ and $L = (a_1, \ldots, a_n)$ with all $a_i \in (0, \alpha]$ then for all $\varepsilon > 0$

$$\frac{FF(L)}{L^*} \leq 1 + \lfloor \alpha^{-1} \rfloor^{-1} + \varepsilon$$

provided L^* is sufficiently large. The same bound also holds for BF.

The deepest results currently known concerning bin packing involve the first-fit decreasing (FFD) and best-fit decreasing (BFD) algorithms. To describe these results, we let $R_{FFD}(\alpha)$ denote $\overline{\lim}_{L^* \to \infty} FFD(L)/L^*$ where L ranges over all lists for which all elements a_i of L satisfy $a_i \in (0, \alpha]$. For example, the preceding results imply

$$R_{FF}(\alpha) = \begin{cases} \frac{17}{10} & \text{for} \quad \alpha \in (\frac{1}{2}, 1] \\ 1 + \lfloor \alpha^{-1} \rfloor^{-1} & \text{for} \quad \alpha \in (0, \frac{1}{2}] \end{cases}$$

Theorem 5.11 [J1]

$$R_{FFD}(\alpha) = \begin{cases} \dfrac{11}{9} & \text{for} \quad \alpha \in \left(\dfrac{1}{2}, 1\right] \\[2mm] \dfrac{71}{60} & \text{for} \quad \alpha \in \left(\dfrac{8}{29}, \dfrac{1}{2}\right] \\[2mm] \dfrac{7}{6} & \text{for} \quad \alpha \in \left(\dfrac{1}{4}, \dfrac{8}{29}\right] \\[2mm] \dfrac{23}{20} & \text{for} \quad \alpha \in \left(\dfrac{1}{5}, \dfrac{1}{4}\right] \end{cases}$$

The only known proof of Theorem 5.11, due to D. S. Johnson [J1], [JDUGG], is highly ingenious and rather complicated, exceeding 100 pages in length. Needless to say, space limitations prevent us from including it here. The difficult part of the proof—namely, establishing an upper bound on $R_{FFD}(\alpha)$—is based on essentially the same strategy used in obtaining the upper bounds for FF and BF. That is, a "weighting function" is defined which assigns real numbers or "weights" to the elements of L, depending on their size, in such a way that

1. The total "weight" of all the elements in the list L differs from the total number of bins used in the particular packing under consideration (e.g., FF or FFD) by no more than some absolute constant c.

2. The total weight of any legally packed bin must be less than some fixed constant c'.

For FF we had $c' = 17/10$ and $c = 2$; for FFD one can choose $c' = 11/9$ and $c = 4$.

As in the case of FF and BF, the bounds of Theorem 5.11 for FFD also apply to BFD. However, there is a lack of symmetry between the FFD algorithm and the BFD algorithm, as indicated by the following result (which is also required in the proof that $R_{\text{BFD}}(1) = \frac{11}{9}$).

Theorem 5.12 [GGU], [JDUGG]   For all lists $L = (a_1, \ldots, a_n)$, we have

1. $\text{BFD}(L) \leq \text{FFD}(L)$ if   all $a_i \in [\frac{1}{6}, 1]$
2. $\text{BFD}(L) = \text{FFD}(L)$ if   all $a_i \in [\frac{1}{5}, 1]$

Even the proof of Theorem 5.12 runs about 15 pages and is not given here.

Possibly, the complete form of Theorem 5.11 is given by the following conjecture [J2].

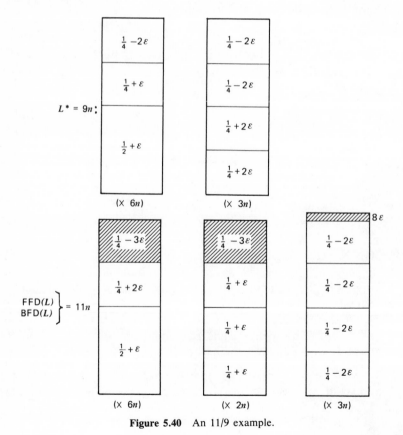

Figure 5.40 An 11/9 example.

Conjecture

$$R_{\text{FFD}}(\alpha) = \begin{cases} \dfrac{11}{9} & \text{for } \alpha \in \left(\dfrac{1}{2}, 1\right] \\[2mm] \dfrac{71}{60} & \text{for } \alpha \in \left(\dfrac{8}{29}, \dfrac{1}{2}\right] \\[2mm] \dfrac{7}{6} & \text{for } \alpha \in \left(\dfrac{1}{4}, \dfrac{8}{29}\right] \\[2mm] 1 + \dfrac{k-2}{k(k-1)} & \text{for } \alpha \leq \dfrac{1}{4}, \quad k = \lfloor \alpha^{-1} \rfloor \end{cases}$$

These values of $R_{\text{FFD}}(\alpha)$ for $\alpha \leq \frac{1}{4}$ are known to be upper bounds by straightforward extensions of the examples given in Figs. 5.42 and 5.43.

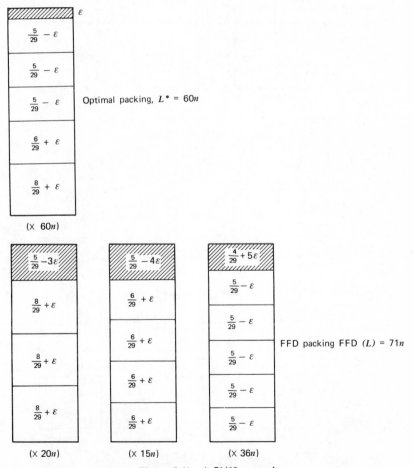

Figure 5.41 A 71/60 example.

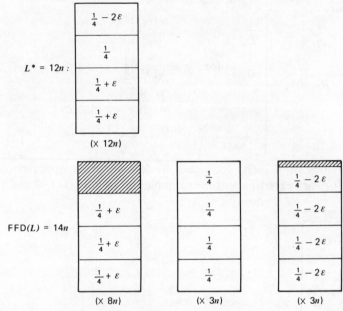

Figure 5.42 A 7/6 example.

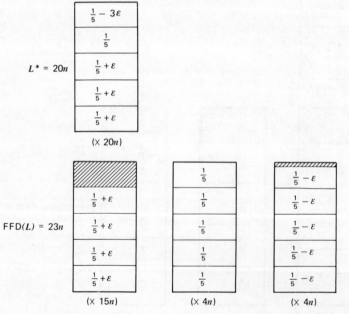

Figure 5.43 A 23/20 example.

In Figs. 5.40 through 5.45 are presented self-explanatory examples showing that the various ranges over which the a_i are allowed to vary in Theorems 5.11 and 5.12 are best possible.

One reason why the proofs of many of the bin-packing results are surprisingly complicated is because of the existence of examples like the following (due to Sylvia Halász [Ha]). This example gives a list L and a *sublist* $L' \subseteq L$ with $FFD(L') > FFD(L)$. Such behavior can be very annoying when one is trying to construct inductive proofs. ■

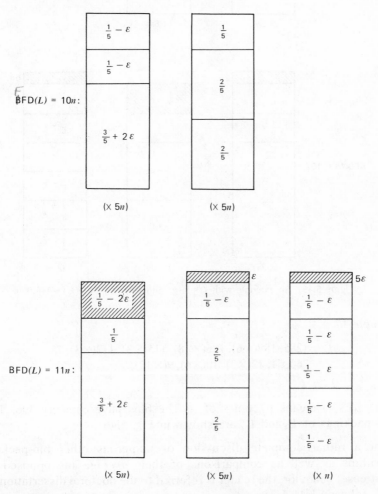

Figure 5.44   An example with L^* large and $BFD(L)/FFD(L) = 10/9$.

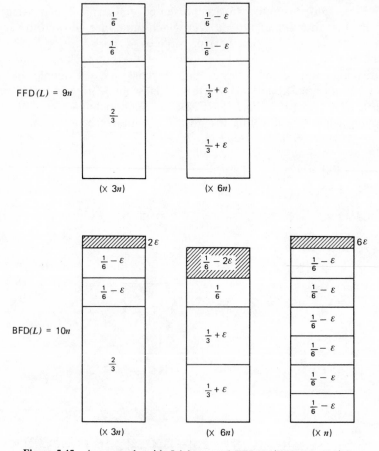

Figure 5.45   An example with L^* large and $FFD(L)/BFD(L) = 11/10$.

Example 17

$$L = (285, 188(\times 6), 126(\times 18), 115(\times 3), 112(\times 3), 75,$$
$$60, 51, 12(\times 3), 10(\times 6), 9(\times 12))$$
$$L' = L - \{75\}$$

where $a(\times b)$ means b copies of a. The bins have capacity 396. The FFD-packings of L and L' are shown in Fig. 5.46.

For a rather complete discussion of numerous other bin-packing algorithms as well as comparisons of their *average* (as opposed to worst-case) behavior, the reader is referred to the doctoral dissertation of D. S. Johnson [J1], [J2].

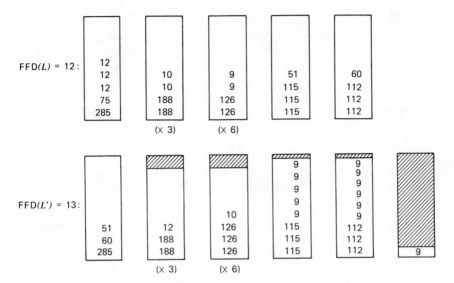

Figure 5.46   Example of $L' \subseteq L$ with FFD$(L') <$ FFD(L).

5.6 BOUNDS FOR SOME OTHER CASES

For the remainder of the chapter, we describe several recent results dealing with bounds on ω/ω_0 for other values of the parameters s, L, $<$, τ, and m.

Without the presence of a processor constraint, the scheduling problem with the parameters $s = 1$, all $\tau_i = 1$, $<$ empty, m, L arbitrary, is just ordinary bin packing for which we have obtained the asymptotic bound on ω/ω_0 of 17/10. When we have just a fixed number m of processors (possibly much smaller than the number n of tasks), this is equivalent to requiring that each bin contain at most m elements. For this situation, the following result of K. L. Krause applies.

Theorem   [Kr]   For $s = 1$, $\tau_i = 1$, $<$ empty, m, L arbitrary, we have

1. $\dfrac{\omega - 2}{\omega_0} < \dfrac{27}{10} - \dfrac{24}{10m}$;

2. There exist examples for which

$$\frac{\omega}{\omega_0} \geq \frac{27}{10} - \frac{37}{10m}$$

Hence the presence of the processor constraint contributes about 1 to the worst-case ratio bound.

If the tasks in L are arranged in the order of decreasing resource requirements, the resulting schedule is just that obtained by applying the FFD algorithm in the corresponding bin-packing problem, again with the additional restriction that no bin contains more than m weights. The finishing time is denoted here by ω_{FFD}.

Theorem [Kr] For $s = 1$, $<$ empty, all $\tau_i = 1$, m arbitrary, we have

$$\frac{\omega_{\text{FFD}} - 1}{\omega_0} \leq 2 - \frac{2}{m} \qquad \text{for} \qquad m \geq 2$$

We next turn to several interesting results concerning the many-resource case (i.e., s is allowed to be arbitrary). Perhaps the most striking is the following.

Theorem 5.13 [GGJY] For $<$ empty, all $\tau_i = 1$, $m \geq n$, s, L arbitrary, we have

$$\omega \leq \left(s + \frac{7}{10}\right)\omega_0 + \frac{5}{2} \tag{31}$$

Furthermore, the coefficient of ω_0 is best possible.

Of course for $s = 1$ this is essentially just Theorem 5.9 (with a slightly weaker constant term). In fact, the inductive proof of Theorem 5.13 relies on Theorem 5.9 to begin the induction.

Comparing this result to that of Theorem 5.6, we see that the restriction that all $\tau_i = 1$ allowed the bound on ω/ω_0 to be strengthened from $s + 1$ to $s + \frac{7}{10}$. It had been previously shown by A. Yao [Y1] that asymptotically ω/ω_0 could not exceed $s + \frac{17}{20}$.

As might be suspected from Theorem 5.5, the restriction that all $\tau_i = 1$ for general $<$ is not sufficient to prevent the ratio ω/ω_0 from blowing up rather badly. The strongest results currently known here are the following.

Theorem 5.14 [GGJY] If all $\tau_i = 1$, $m \geq n$, s, $<$, L arbitrary,

1. $\dfrac{\omega}{\omega_0} \leq \dfrac{1}{2} s\omega_0 + \dfrac{1}{2} s + 1$
2. There exist examples for which

$$\frac{\omega}{\omega_0} \geq \frac{1}{2} s\omega_0 + \frac{1}{2} s + 1 - \frac{2s}{\omega_0}$$

If the schedule is formed by a critical path algorithm then the worst-case bound on ω/ω_0 improves considerably. In particular, the following result can be proved [GGJY].

Theorem 5.15   If all $\tau_i = 1$, $m \geq n$, s, $<$ arbitrary, we have

1. $\dfrac{\omega_{CP}}{\omega_0} \leq \dfrac{17}{10} s + 1$;

2. For any $\varepsilon > 0$, there exist examples for which

$$\frac{\omega_{CP}}{\omega_0} > \frac{17}{10} s + 1 - \varepsilon$$

Recall that in the special case $s = 0$, even with a processor constraint (i.e., allowing $m < n$), T. C. Hu has shown that $\omega_{CP} = \omega_0$ (see Chapter 2).

There are several natural generalizations of the resource model we have been considering for which research work is just beginning. These include allowing processors with different speeds (see Chapter 2), prohibiting certain processors from executing certain tasks, and bin packing with bins of different capacities. Space considerations do not permit us to go into these topics here, however.

CHAPTER SIX

ENUMERATIVE AND ITERATIVE COMPUTATIONAL APPROACHES

W. H. KOHLER
UNIVERSITY OF MASSACHUSETTS

K. STEIGLITZ
PRINCETON UNIVERSITY

6.1 INTRODUCTION

We consider in this chapter the practical computing of solutions to scheduling problems that do not now have polynomial algorithms for finding optimal solutions. As seen in Chapter 4, the general job-shop, and in particular flow-shop, problems fall into this category. Of course, the term "practical" is vague; in some cases we may require a real-time algorithm with only milliseconds to schedule scores of jobs. In other cases several minutes may be available to compute an optimal or suboptimal solution.

We may classify computational methods for producing solutions to scheduling problems (or any combinatorial optimization problems) according to whether they are designed to produce an optimal solution or merely an approximate solution. We call the first, more ambitious, class of methods *exact*, and the second class *approximate*. We also discuss an important third class of algorithms: those which produce approximate solutions whose cost is *guaranteed* to be within some tolerance of optimal. These we call *guaranteed accuracy* methods. When we are faced with problems so large and complex that exact solution appears infeasible, the next best thing is to have a solution of known quality. When the data are uncertain or the cost criterion is to some extent arbitrary, a guaranteed accuracy solution may be every bit as good as the genuine article.

All exact methods for solving the general problems considered in this chapter involve some kind of enumeration—there is no way to avoid the unpleasant explosion in the size of the solution space (at least no way known to us now). The idea is to arrange the enumeration efficiently,

229

using as much information as possible to prune the search tree. We discuss here a general formulation of such backtrack enumeration, all subsumed in the literature under the term "branch-and-bound" algorithms. The presentation here is a generalization of the approach reported in [Ko1, KS1, KS3].

Approximate algorithms include any scheme that might occur to a human being for producing a feasible solution of low cost. Often, valuable insight is gained by studying special cases, and rules optimal for simple situations, such as "smallest-job-first," can be carried over to complex situations. Despite this seeming lack of structure, some general techniques that have emerged in the past decade seem to be effective in a wide variety of problems. One of these is *local neighborhood search*; another is *nonbacktracking branch-and-bound*. We discuss both these approaches, with experimental results for the two-machine, mean finishing-time flow-shop problem.

Finally, we discuss the marriage of exact and approximate methods: the combination of exact and approximate algorithms to get exact solutions faster, or to get answers with guaranteed accuracy. The guaranteed accuracy approach can be viewed as a theorem proving method in a very special system: a feasible schedule is exhibited, together with a proof that its cost is within a certain tolerance of optimal.

In designing an efficient algorithm for a problem too large or difficult for exact solution, one relies heavily on insight and special knowledge of the problem. In the branch-and-bound algorithms, this is reflected in the construction of the lower-bound, dominance, and upper-bound subroutines. There can be no lower bound on the complexity of the branch-and-bound approach—if one knows a perfect lower bound and a perfect heuristic for a starting solution, one is finished before he starts.

In the next section a general framework is introduced for branch-and-bound algorithms; it includes the possibilities of overflowing storage, running out of time, and stopping when a prescribed accuracy has been guaranteed. This is followed by a proof of correctness, and by some recent results on the relative computational requirements as functions of the elimination rules, feasibility function, dominance relation, lower bound, and required accuracy bracket. In the following section we cover approximate algorithms, including heuristic construction procedures and local neighborhood search. Finally, computational results are presented for the two-machine flow-shop problem mentioned earlier. The performance of exact, approximate, and guaranteed accuracy problems is described. The emphasis throughout is on extracting for a given investment in computation power the most useful information—in the form of a feasible solution and lower bounds on optimal solutions.

6.2   BRANCH–AND–BOUND ALGORITHMS FOR PERMUTATION PROBLEMS

6.2.1   Background

Branch-and-bound implicit enumeration algorithms have recently emerged as the principal general method for finding optimal solutions to discrete optimization problems. Application of the branch-and-bound technique has grown rapidly, and a complete list of references would exceed several hundred. Representative examples of this thrust include: flow-shop and job-shop sequencing problems [Ba2, IS, Sc1, Sc2], traveling salesman problems [HK2], general quadratic assignment problems [Gi, PC], and integer programming problems [GM, GN]. Although the branch-and-bound method has been surveyed and generalized by numerous authors [A, Ba1, GN, LW, Mi, Ri, Roy], very little has been proved about the relative computational requirements as a function of the choice of algorithm parameters. One notable exception is the recent work of Fox and Schrage [FS], who compared theoretically the relative number of nodes examined by branch-and-bound integer programming algorithms for three different branching strategies (next-node selection rules).

Branch-and-bound algorithms, although usually more efficient than complete enumeration, have computational requirements that frequently grow as an exponential or high-degree polynomial in the problem size n. In such cases, problems of practical size usually cannot be solved exactly. Recent results in the field of computational complexity strongly suggest (but as yet do not prove) that the computational resources required to find exact solutions to many of these combinatorial problems cannot be bounded by a polynomial in the length of the input data string [BCS1, Ka, U1]. Such problems are said to be *NP-complete* (see Chapter 4).

In many practical situations, an exact solution is not necessary. Any solution whose cost is known to be within a small percentage of the optimal cost would be acceptable. The problem of generating a solution whose cost deviates from the optimal cost by less than a specified percentage has received relatively little attention [Gi, KS3, Ko1]. A related approach is that of generating a solution with some heuristic procedure whose worst case performance can be bounded [DG, GG1, G2] (see Chapter 5). These bounds are fixed. Since they must apply to all cases (including pathological ones), they are frequently quite loose. In the method presented here, the bracket on the maximum deviation is set at any desired value. The bracket can always be achieved in principle, but this may require more than the allotted computational resources. A suboptimal solution produced by a heuristic method can play an important role as an initial upper-bound solution. The branch-and-bound algorithm can either verify that this solution satisfies the desired bracket or generate another solution that does.

In the next two sections we propose a general classification scheme for branch-and-bound algorithms for permutation problems based on a nine-tuple of parameters $(B_p, S, E, F, D, L, U, BR, RB)$, where B_p is the branching or partitioning rule for permutation problems, S is the next-node selection rule, E is the set of node-elimination rules, F is a characteristic function indicating nodes with no feasible completions, D is the node dominance relation, L is the node lower-bound cost function, U is an upper-bound solution cost, BR is the desired tolerance on the accuracy of the solution, and RB is a resource bound including limitations on computation time and space. The general framework for integer programming algorithms recently introduced by Geoffrion and Marsten [GM] is suggestive of this scheme but is less explicit. We demonstrate how the nine-tuple can be used to describe the class of common branch-and-bound algorithms for general permutation problems, including the job-shop problem [ChD, Sc1], whose feasible solution space is a subset of the set of all permutations of n objects. Within this basic framework, we report some theoretical results concerning the relative number of generated nodes and active nodes as functions of the choice of nine-tuple parameters. As we shall see, these results verify some of our intuitive notions and disprove others.

6.2.2 Preliminary Definitions and Notation

1. A *general permutation problem of size n* is a combinatorial optimization problem defined by the triple $(\mathcal{P}, X, f)$ with the following connotation:

    a. The *solution space* $\mathcal{P} \subseteq \mathcal{P}_n \triangleq \{\text{permutations of } n \text{ objects}\} = \{\pi\}$.

    b. The *parameter space* X, each point $x \in X$ represents admissible "data" for the problem.

    c. The *cost function* $f: \mathcal{P} \times X \to R$, where $f(\pi, x)$ is the cost of solution π with parameter value x.

2. A *globally optimal* solution for parameter value x is a solution $\pi^* \in \mathcal{P}$ such that $f(\pi^*, x) \le f(\pi, x)$, for all $\pi \in \mathcal{P}$.

3. Given a set $M = \{i_1, i_2, \ldots, i_j\} \subseteq N \triangleq \{1, 2, \ldots, n\}$, π^M denotes a permutation on the set M.

    a. If $M = N$, π^M is called a *complete permutation* on N.

    b. If $M \subseteq N$, π^M is called a *partial permutation* on N.

    c. If $M = \varphi$, $e \triangleq \pi^\varphi$.

4. Given $\pi_r^M \triangleq (r_1, r_2, \ldots, r_j)$.

    a. $|\pi_r^M| \triangleq$ size of partial permutation $\pi_r^M = |M| = j$.

b. $\bar{M} \triangleq N - M$.

c. If $l \in \bar{M}$, let $\pi_r^M \circ l \triangleq (r_1, r_2, \ldots, r_j, l)$.

d. If π_s^K is a permutation of the set $K \subseteq \bar{M}$ and $\pi_s^K = (s_1, s_2, \ldots, s_k)$, let $\pi_r^M \circ \pi_s^K \triangleq (\cdots ((\pi_r^M \circ s_1) \circ s_2) \cdots \circ s_k)$.

e. $\{\pi_r^M \circ\} \triangleq \{\pi_r^M \circ \pi_s^{\bar{M}} | \pi_s^{\bar{M}}$ is any permutation of $\bar{M}\}$
$\triangleq$ the *completion* of π_r^M
$=$ the set of all *complete* permutations beginning with partial permutation π_r^M

5. Given a set Y of partial permutations on N,
$$\{Y \circ\} \triangleq \{\cup \{\pi_y^K \circ\} | \pi_y^K \in Y\}$$
$\triangleq$ the *completion* of Y

6. Given π_r^M, $M \subseteq N$

a. A *descendant* of π_r^M is any partial permutation $\pi_s^P = \pi_r^M \circ \pi_t^K$ with $K \subseteq \bar{M}$.

b. An *immediate descendant* (*son*) of π_r^M is any descendant $\pi_x^P = \pi_r^M \circ \pi_t^K$ such that K is a singleton set and $K \subseteq \bar{M}$ (i.e., $\pi_x^P = \pi_r^M \circ l$ for some $l \in \bar{M}$).

c. An *ancestor* of π_r^M is any partial permutation π_q^L such that $\pi_r^M = \pi_q^L \circ \pi_t^K$, $K \neq \varphi$.

d. The *immediate ancestor* (*father*) of π_r^M is the ancestor π_q^L such that K is the singleton set; that is, if $\pi_r^M = (r_1, r_2, \ldots, r_j)$, the father of π_r^M is $\pi_q^L = (r_1, r_2, \ldots, r_{j-1})$.

7. A one-to-one into mapping is established between the set of partial solutions of a permutation problem $(\mathscr{P}, x, f)$ and the set of partial permutations on N. Each partial solution is then denoted by its corresponding partial permutation. The terms *partial solution* and *partial permutation* are used synonymously.

6.2.3 Nine-tuple Characterization: $(B_p, S, E, F, D, L, U, BR, RB)$

A class of branch-and-bound algorithms commonly used to solve the general permutation problem $(\mathscr{P}, X, f)$ can be characterized in terms of a nine-tuple $(B_p, S, E, F, D, L, U, BR, RB)$. This is a generalization of the approach used in [KS1]. The nine parameters are defined as follows:

1. *Branching rule* B_p defines the branching process for permutation problems. The object of branching is to partition the set of complete permutations $\mathscr{P}_n$ into disjoint subsets. These subsets are represented by nodes. Each node is labeled by a permutation $\pi_y^{M_y}$ defined on a set M_y for $M_y \subseteq N = \{1, 2, \ldots, n\}$. The node labeled $\pi_y^{M_y}$ represents the set of complete permutations $\{\pi_y^{M_y} \circ\}$. Partial permutation $\pi_y^{M_y}$ is an ancestor of each permutation in the set $\{\pi_y^{M_y} \circ\}$. Branching at node $\pi_b^{M_b} = (b_1, b_2, \ldots, b_k)$ is the process of partitioning set $\{\pi_b^{M_b} \circ\}$ into disjoint

subsets $\{\pi_b{}^{M_b} \circ\} = \bigcup_{l \in \bar{M}_b} \{(\pi_b{}^{M_b} \circ l) \circ\}$. We call $\pi_b{}^{M_b}$ the *branching node*. It follows that $\{(\pi_b{}^{M_b} \circ i) \circ\} \cap \{(\pi_b{}^{M_b} \circ j) \circ\} = \varphi$ for $i, j \in \bar{M}_b$ and $i \neq j$. Nodes $\pi_b{}^{M_b} \circ l$, $l \in \bar{M}_b$ are the sons of branching node $\pi_b{}^{M_b}$. These nodes are said to be *generated at branching step* $\pi_b{}^{M_b}$. (To help simplify this cumbersome notation, π_y is used as a shorthand notation for $\pi_y{}^{M_y}$, with the set M_y understood.)

2. *Selection rule S* is used to choose the next branching node π_b from the set of currently active nodes. Node π_y is *currently active* during the execution of algorithm $(B_p, S, E, F, D, L, U, BR, RB)$ if and only if it has been generated but has not yet been eliminated or branched from. The sons of branching node π_b are generated in lexicographic order. Son $\pi_b \circ l$, $l \in \bar{M}_b$ is added to the set of currently active nodes if (but not only if) (1) it has some feasible completion, that is, $\{(\pi_b \circ l) \circ\} \cap \mathcal{P} \neq \varphi$, (2) it is not eliminated by one of the node elimination rules in E, and (3) it is not lost because the active set exceeds its prespecified maximum size. The algorithm is always initiated by selecting $e = \pi^e$ as the first branching node (e is also assumed to be the first node generated). Termination occurs if the next branching node π_b is a complete solution.

To describe and illustrate some of the common selection rules, let us consider the problem below.

Given: A set of independent tasks $\mathcal{T} = \{T_1, T_2, T_3\}$ with execution times $\tau_1 = 3$, $\tau_2 = 2$, and $\tau_3 = 1$.

Find: A schedule π^* for executing the tasks on a single processor that minimizes the sum of the task finishing times.

In this problem, $\mathcal{P} = \mathcal{P}_3$, $x \in X$ is the vector of execution times, $x = (\tau_1, \tau_2, \tau_3)$, and cost function $f(\pi, x)$ is the sum of the finishing times given schedule $\pi \in \mathcal{P}$ and execution times $x \in X$. For example, when $\pi = (1, 2, 3)$, T_1 finishes at time 3, T_2 at time $3 + 2 = 5$, and T_3 at time $5 + 1 = 6$. Consequently $f(\pi, x) = 14$. Figure 6.1 shows the complete enumeration tree.

a. $S = \text{LLB}$ (*least-lower-bound* rules). Select the currently active node π_a with the least lower-bound cost $L(\pi_a)$. In the case of ties, either select the node that was generated first, LLB_{FIFO} or last, LLB_{LIFO}. In both cases, the order in which the nodes are branched from is controlled by the lower-bound function L. Figure 6.2 shows the order in which the nodes of Fig. 6.1 would be selected for branching under the LLB rules.

b. $S = \text{FIFO}$ (*first-in first-out* rule). Select the currently active node that was generated first. This is a *breadth-first* search strategy that is independent of the lower-bound function L. Figure 6.3 gives the order in which the sample tree would be enumerated under the FIFO rule.

c. $S = \text{LIFO}$ (*last-in first-out* rule). Select the currently active node that was generated last, but skip the active nodes that are complete

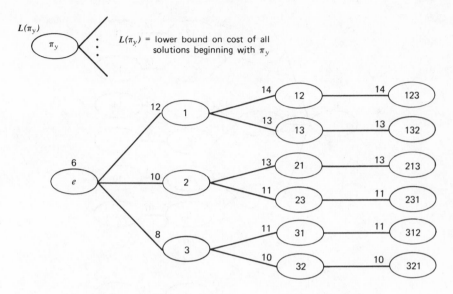

Figure 6.1 Complete enumeration tree for sample problem.

solutions unless there are no incomplete active nodes. This gives a *depth-first* search where the order in which nodes are selected is again independent of the lower-bound function L (see Fig. 6.4).

    d. S = DF/LLB (*depth-first/least-lower-bound* rules). From the set of most recently generated active sons, select the son with the least lower-bound cost, but skip the sets of sons that are complete solutions unless there are no incomplete active nodes. In the case of ties, choose the son that was generated first, DF/LLB$_{FIFO}$, or last, DF/LLB$_{LIFO}$. The order in which our sample tree would be enumerated using the DF/LLB rules (no ties) is illustrated in Fig. 6.5.

    3. *Characteristic function F* is used to eliminate partial permutations known to have no completion in the set of feasible solutions $\mathcal{P}$. In particular, F maps members of the set of partial permutations $\{\pi_y | \{\pi_y \circ\} \subseteq \mathcal{P}_n\}$ into the set $\{0, 1\}$ such that

    a. For every partial permutation π_y, $F(\pi_y) = 1$ if $\{\pi_y \circ\} \cap \mathcal{P} \neq \varphi$.

    b. For every complete permutation π_y^N, $F(\pi_y^N) = 1$ if and only if $\pi_y^N \in \mathcal{P}$.

    Note that our definition does not require $F(\pi_y) = 0$ when $\{\pi_y \circ\} \cap \mathcal{P} = \varphi$ unless π_y is a complete permutation. This recognizes that when π_y is generated, it may not be easy to ascertain that it has no feasible completion. The set of all partial permutations π_y with $F(\pi_y) = 1$ is represented by **P**. This is the set of possible partial solutions.

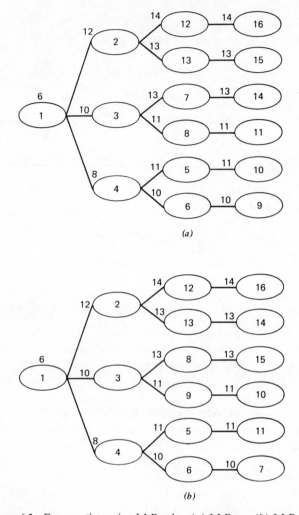

Figure 6.2   Enumeration using LLB rules. (a) LLB$_{\text{FIFO}}$, (b) LLB$_{\text{LIFO}}$.

4. *Dominance relation D* is a binary relation defined on the set of partial solutions of $(\mathcal{P}, x, f)$. Given any partial solution (node) π_y with $\{\pi_y \circ\} \cap \mathcal{P} \neq \varphi$, let $\hat{\pi}_y{}^N$ represent a minimum-cost complete solution beginning with π_y. That is, $\hat{\pi}_y{}^N \in \{\pi_y \circ\} \cap \mathcal{P}$ with $f(\hat{\pi}_y{}^N, x) = \min\{f(\pi_w, x)|\pi_w \in \{\pi_y \circ\} \cap \mathcal{P}\}$. $\mathcal{D}$ is the transitive binary relation defined on the set of partial solutions such that $\pi_y \mathcal{D} \pi_z$ if and only if

    a. $\{\pi_y \circ\} \cap \mathcal{P} \neq \varphi$ and $\{\pi_z \circ\} \cap \mathcal{P} \neq \varphi$.
    b. $f(\hat{\pi}_y{}^N, x) \leq f(\hat{\pi}_z{}^N, x)$.

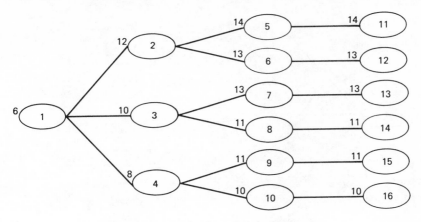

Figure 6.3 Enumeration using the FIFO rule.

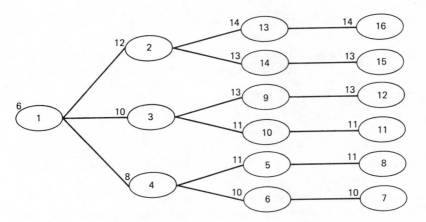

Figure 6.4 Enumeration using the LIFO rule.

The relation D is a subset of $\mathscr{D}$ chosen to have the following properties:

    a. (Transitivity) $\pi_w D \pi_y$ and $\pi_y D \pi_z$ only if $\pi_w D \pi_z$.

    b. (Consistency) $\pi_y D \pi_z$ only if $L(\pi_y) \leq L(\pi_z)$.

    Since $D \subseteq \mathscr{D}$, it follows immediately that $\pi_y D \pi_z$ only if the minimum-cost descendant $\hat{\pi}_y^N$ of node π_y has cost less than or equal to the minimum-cost descendant $\hat{\pi}_z^N$ of node π_z. When $\pi_y D \pi_z$, π_y is said to *dominate* π_z. This is similar to the technique suggested by Szwarc for the flow-shop scheduling problem [Sz]. It is usually assumed that D is defined to contain at least all pairs $\pi_y D \pi_z$ with $L(\pi_y) \leq L(\pi_z)$ and $M_y = N$. When using the branch-and-bound algorithm, pairs of the form (π_y, π_z) are tested for membership in D. Consequently, the choice of relation D

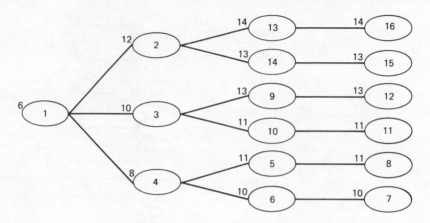

Figure 6.5 Enumeration using the DF/LLB rules.

usually involves a compromise between a powerful relation and one for which membership is easily testable.

5. *Lower-bound function L* assigns to each partial solution $\pi_y \in \mathbf{P}$ a real number $L(\pi_y)$ representing a lower-bound cost for all complete solutions in the set $\{\pi_y \circ\} \cap \mathscr{P}$. The L is required to have the following properties for all $\pi_y, \pi_z \in \mathbf{P}$.

   a. If π_z is a descendant of π_y, then $L(\pi_z) \geq L(\pi_y)$.

   b. For each complete solution π_y^N, $L(\pi_y^N) = f(\pi_y^N, x)$.

When choosing L, usually a compromise must be made between a tight lower-bound function—that is, one that computes a lower bound $L(\pi_y)$ that is very close to the actual minimum-cost descendant $f(\hat{\pi}_y^N, x)$—and a lower-bound function that is easy to compute.

Consider the sample problem given earlier in Fig. 6.1. In this case partial solution $\pi_y^{M_y} = (y_1, y_2, \ldots, y_j)$ represents the solution where task T_{y_1} is executed first, followed by T_{y_2}, and so on. A lower bound on the sum of the finishing times of all tasks starting with partial solution $\pi_y^{M_y}$ was computed as

$$L(\pi_y) = \sum_{y_i \in M_y} \text{finishing time of task } T_{y_i}$$

$$+ \sum_{y_i \in \bar{M}_y} (\text{finishing time of } T_{y_j} + \tau_{y_i})$$

6. *Upper-bound cost U* is the cost $f(\pi_u^N, x)$ of some complete solution π_u^N known at the beginning of the algorithm. If no complete solution is known, U is assumed to be initialized at some cost $U = \infty$ greater than all possible costs. At each stage of the algorithm, the least-cost known

solution is denoted by $\hat{\pi}_u^N$ with cost $\hat{U} = f(\hat{\pi}_u^N, x)$. We have demonstrated [KS3] that an initial upper-bound solution that is close to the optimal cost may substantially reduce the total computation.

7. *Elimination rules E* are a set of rules for using the dominance function D and upper-bound cost U to render inactive (eliminate) newly generated and currently active nodes. Given algorithm $(B_p, S, E, F, D, L, U, BR, RB)$, let π_b be the current branching node, $\pi_b \circ l$ an immediate descendant in the set of feasible partial solutions $\mathbf{P}$, and π_a a member of the currently active set at branching step π_b, $\pi_b \neq \pi_a$. The set E represents some subset of the following three rules:

a. *U/DBAS* (*upper bound tested for dominance of descendants of branching node and members of currently active set*). If $L(\pi_b \circ l) > \hat{U}$, then all members of $\{(\pi_b \circ l) \circ\} \cap \mathscr{P}$ have costs greater than the upper-bound solution $\hat{\pi}_u^N$, where $\hat{U} \triangleq f(\hat{\pi}_u^N, x)$. In this case $\pi_b \circ l$ is eliminated after being generated and before becoming active. If $L(\pi_a) > \hat{U}$, all members of $\{\pi_a \circ\} \cap \mathscr{P}$ have costs greater than the upper-bound solution $\hat{\pi}_u^N$, and π_a is removed (eliminated) from the active set.

b. *AS/DB* (*active node set tested for dominance of descendants of branching node*). Each currently active node is tested for dominance of each descendant of the branching node. If $\pi_a D(\pi_b \circ l)$, then $\pi_b \circ l$ is eliminated after being generated and before becoming active.

c. *DB/AS* (*descendants of branching node tested for dominance of currently active node set*). Each descendant of the current branching node is tested for dominance of each currently active node. If $(\pi_b \circ l)D\pi_a$, then π_a is removed (eliminated) from the set of currently active nodes.

If E contains rules AS/DB and DB/AS, the set of active nodes may depend on the order in which AS/DB and DB/AS are applied. We assume that AS/DB is applied before DB/AS.

8. *Bracket BR* is a real number, $0 \leq BR \leq 1$, representing the desired maximum relative deviation of the optimal cost from an acceptable solution. At each stage of the algorithm, $\hat{U}$ represents the cost of the best-known complete solution and $\hat{L}$ represents the known lower bound on the cost of an optimal solution. When $(\hat{U} - \hat{L})/\hat{U} \leq BR$, we have

$$(1 - BR)\hat{U} \leq \hat{L}$$

Consequently, the cost $f(\pi^*, x)$ of an optimal solution π^* is bounded by

$$(1 - BR)\hat{U} \leq f(\pi^*, x) \leq \hat{U}$$

If BR is chosen to be 0, the current best solution $\hat{\pi}_u^N$ is acceptable only if it is optimal, whereas if BR is chosen to be 0.05, it is acceptable if the optimal cost is no more than 5% below the upper-bound cost $\hat{U}$. Our computational experience indicates that if a bracket of 5 to 10% is acceptable, the required computation may be significantly reduced [KS3].

9. *Resource bound RB* is a vector whose components are upper bounds on the total expendable execution time and the usable storage for active nodes and immediate descendants of the branching node. In particular, $RB = \langle \text{TIMELIMIT}, \text{MAXSZAS}, \text{MAXSZDB} \rangle$, where TIMELIMIT is the prespecified maximum execution time, $\text{MAXSZAS} \geq 1$ is the maximum allowable size for the set of active nodes, and $\text{MAXSZDB} \geq 1$ is the maximum allowable size for the set of descendants of each branching node. If the required computation exceeds TIMELIMIT, the algorithm terminates and outputs the final status of the search. If the storage limits are exceeded, one or more partial solutions, which may have had an optimal solution as a descendant, will be lost because of overflow. A lower bound on the cost of all lost descendants is established by keeping the least lower-bound cost of the nodes that overflow. This is designated $\hat{L}_{\text{OFS}}$. The lower bound on an optimal solution, $\hat{L}$, can be no greater than $\hat{L}_{\text{OFS}}$.

6.2.4 Descriptive Notation and Chart Representation

The following notation describes the detailed operation of algorithm $BB = (B_p, S, E, F, D, L, U, BR, RB)$:

$\quad$ **P** $\quad \triangleq$ set of all feasible partial solutions to $(\mathcal{P}, x, f)$
$\qquad\qquad = \{\pi_y{}^{M_y} \mid M_y \subseteq N \text{ and } F(\pi_y) = 1\}$

$\text{BFS}(\pi_b) \quad \triangleq$ set of previous branching nodes (*branched-from* nodes) at the beginning of branching step π_b

$\text{DB}(\pi_b) \quad \triangleq$ set of feasible immediate descendants generated during branching step π_b and not lost because of overflow
$\qquad\qquad \subseteq \{(\pi_b{}^{M_b} \circ l) \mid l \in \bar{M}\}$

$\text{AS}(\pi_b) \quad \triangleq$ set of currently active nodes at the beginning of branching step π_b

$\text{OFS}(\pi_b) \quad \triangleq$ set of *all* nodes that have overflowed either $\text{AS}(\pi_y)$ or $\text{DB}(\pi_y)$ for some $\pi_y \in \text{BFS}(\pi_b)$
$\qquad\qquad =$ set of all nodes that have overflowed by the start of branching step π_b

$\text{ES}(\pi_b) \quad \triangleq$ set of all feasible nodes eliminated by one of the elimination rules in E during branching step π_b

$\hat{U}(\pi_b) \quad \triangleq$ cost of minimum-cost upper bound solution at the beginning of branching step π_b

$\hat{L}_{\text{AS}}(\pi_b) \quad \triangleq$ lower bound on the cost of all solutions in the completion of the set of active nodes at the beginning of branching step π_b

$\hat{L}_{\text{OFS}}(\pi_b)$ $\triangleq$ lower bound on the cost of all solutions in the completion of the set of overflow nodes at the beginning of branching step π_b

$\triangleq \infty$ if OFS $= \varphi$

$\hat{L}(\pi_b)$ $\triangleq \min(\hat{L}_{\text{AS}}(\pi_b), \hat{L}_{\text{OFS}}(\pi_b))$

= lower bound on the cost of an optimal solution at the beginning of branching step π_b

Using this notation, the elimination rules in E can be expressed as one of two types: (1) for each π_z in the set B, eliminate π_z if $\hat{U}(\pi_b) < L(\pi_z)$, or (2) for each π_z in the set B, eliminate π_z if there exists some π_y in the set A such that $\pi_y D \pi_z$. With $E_i : A \rightarrow B$ representing rule E_i, the complete set of elimination rules is illustrated in Fig. 6.6.

The general branch-and-bound algorithm $BB = (B_p, S, E, F, D, L, U, BR, RB)$ is charted in Fig. 6.7 using the D-chart notation of Bruno and Steiglitz [BSt]. When implementing BB, the set of branched-from nodes BFS and the set of overflow nodes OFS would not be stored. They are included on the chart for descriptive purposes. In this case $\hat{L}_{\text{OFS}}$ is updated every time a node with lower-bound cost less than the current value of $\hat{L}_{\text{OFS}}$ overflows AS or DB. Figure 6.8 contains a detailed D-chart of a straightforward implementation of the elimination rules. Other computationally more efficient implementations can be used, but the simplicity of the given implementation is conceptually useful.

6.2.5 Proof of Correctness

In this section several lemmas are proved to establish that the general branch-and-bound algorithm $(B_p, S, E, F, D, L, U, BR, RB)$ terminates (1)

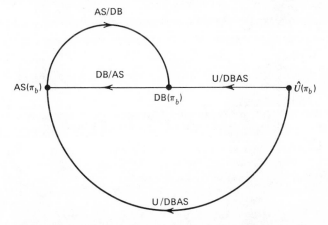

Figure 6.6 Diagram of complete set of elimination rules E.

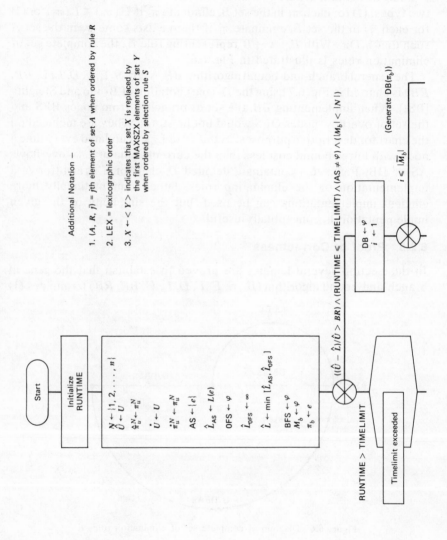

Additional Notation –

1. $(A, R, j) = j$th element of set A when ordered by rule R

2. LEX = lexicographic order

3. $X \leftarrow \langle Y \rangle$ indicates that set X is replaced by the first MAXSZX elements of set Y when ordered by selection rule S

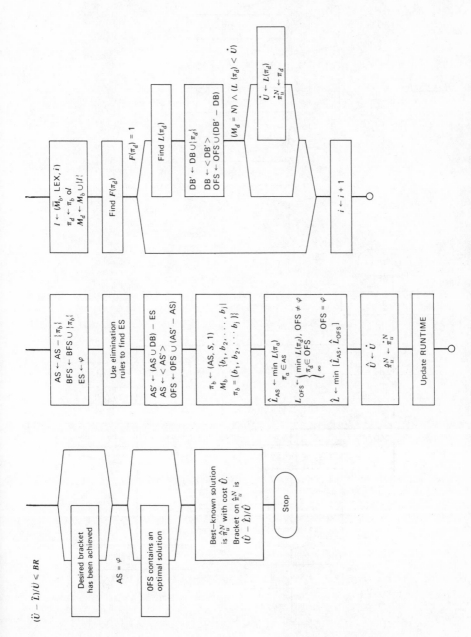

Figure 6.7 Chart representation of branch-and-bound algorithm (B_p, S, E, F, D, L, U, BR, RB).

243

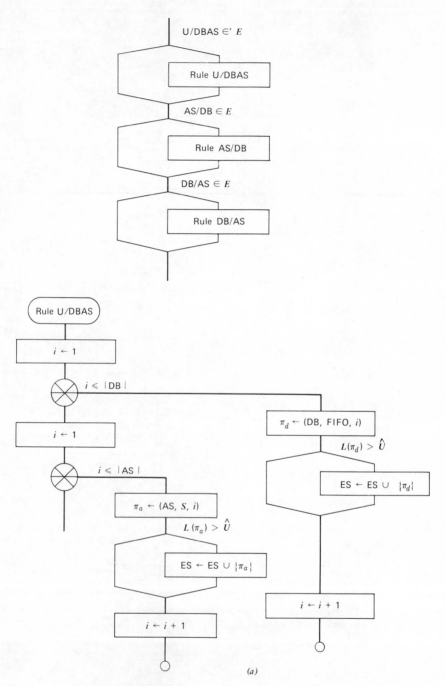

Figure 6.8 Implementation of elimination rules. (a) part A; (b) part B.

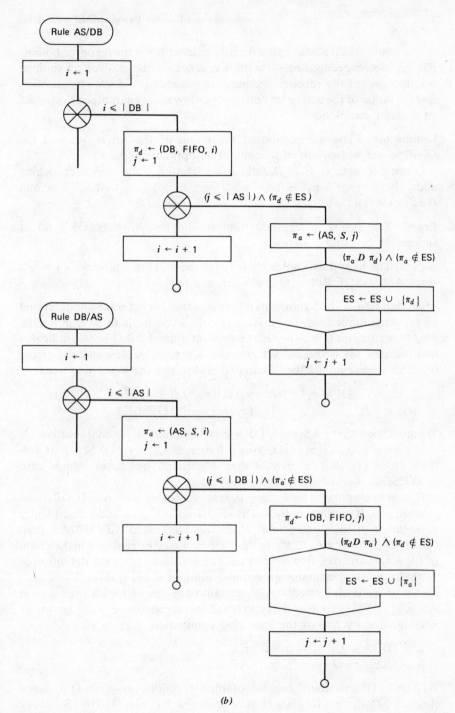

(b)

245

with a solution that achieves the desired bracket BR if the resource bounds RB are not exceeded, or (2) with a bracket on the cost of an optimal solution even if the resource bounds are exceeded. We start by showing that the union of the active set and the overflow set is guaranteed to contain an optimal completion.

Lemma 6.1 (The completion of the union of the active set and the overflow set is guaranteed to contain an optimal solution.)

Given $BB = (B_p, S, E, F, D, L, U, BR, RB)$. If π_b is the current branching node, there exists a $\pi_y^N \in \{[AS(\pi_b) \cup OFS(\pi_b)] \circ\}$ such that $\pi_y^N \in \mathscr{P}$ and $f(\pi_y^N, x) = f(\pi^*, x)$.

Proof The proof is by induction on the set $AS(\pi_b) \cup OFS(\pi_b)$ at successive branching nodes.

Basis The hypothesis holds trivially for the first branching node $e = \pi^\varphi$, since $AS(e) \cup OFS(e) = \{e\} \cup \varphi = \{e\}$, and $\{e \circ\} = \{\pi^\varphi \circ\} = \mathscr{P}_n \supseteq \mathscr{P}$.

Induction step The hypothesis is assumed true for branching node π_b and all previous branching nodes. We show the hypothesis to be true for the next branching node π_c. The chart representation of BB (Fig. 6.7) indicates that the new set is the old set plus the new feasible descendants of the branching node minus the eliminated nodes and the branching node:

$$AS(\pi_c) \cup OFS(\pi_c) = [(AS(\pi_b) \cup \{(\pi_b \circ l) | l \in \bar{M}_b, F(\pi_b \circ l) = 1\}) - (ES(\pi_b) \cup \{\pi_b\})] \cup OFS(\pi_b) \tag{1}$$

We must show that $\{(AS(\pi_c) \cup OFS(\pi_c)) \circ\}$ contains an optimal solution.

Suppose $\pi_y \in AS(\pi_b) \cup OFS(\pi_b)$, but $\pi_y \notin AS(\pi_c) \cup OFS(\pi_c)$. It follows from (1) that π_y was either eliminated by E, in which case $\pi_y \in ES(\pi_b)$, or branched from, $\pi_y = \pi_b$.

If π_y was eliminated by E, then π_y was eliminated with rule U/DBAS or rule DB/AS. If eliminated by U/DBAS, $L(\pi_y) > \hat{U}(\pi_b)$, and consequently no member of $\{\pi_y \circ\}$ is optimal. If π_y was eliminated with DB/AS, then $(\pi_b \circ l) D \pi_y$ for some $l \in \bar{M}_b$. In this case π_y would be replaced in the union of the active and overflow sets by $(\pi_b \circ l)$. It follows from the definition of D that $\{(\pi_b \circ l) \circ\}$ contains an optimal solution if $\{\pi_y \circ\}$ does.

If $\pi_y = \pi_b$, each immediate descendant of π_b, $\pi_b \circ l$ for all $l \in \bar{M}_b$, is in $AS(\pi_c) \cup OFS(\pi_c)$ unless it has no feasible completions, $F((\pi_b \circ l)) = 0$, or is eliminated by one of the following elimination rules in E:

1. U/DBAS. $L((\pi_b \circ l)) > \hat{U}(\pi_b)$.
2. AS/DB. $\pi_a D (\pi_b \circ l)$, $\pi_a \in AS(\pi_b)$.

If $F((\pi_b \circ l)) = 0$, there are no optimal solutions in $\{(\pi_b \circ l) \circ\}$, since $\{(\pi_b \circ l) \circ\} \cap \mathscr{P} = \varphi$. If $(\pi_b \circ l)$ is eliminated by rule U/DBAS, every complete solution in $\{(\pi_b \circ l) \circ\} \cap \mathcal{P}$ has cost greater than $\hat{U}(\pi_b)$, the cost of upper-bound solution $\hat{\pi}_u^N$. Rule AS/DB eliminates descendants $(\pi_b \circ l)$ only if there exists another currently active node $\pi_z \in \mathrm{AS}(\pi_b) \cap \mathrm{AS}(\pi_c)$ such that $\pi_z D (\pi_b \circ l)$. It follows from the definition of D that $\{\pi_z \circ\}$ contains an optimal solution if $\{(\pi_b \circ l) \circ\}$ does.

We conclude that for each $\pi_y \in [\mathrm{AS}(\pi_b) \cup \mathrm{OFS}(\pi_b)] - [\mathrm{AS}(\pi_c) \cup \mathrm{OFS}(\pi_c)]$, either π_y has no optimal completion or there exists some $\pi_z \in \mathrm{AS}(\pi_c) \cup \mathrm{OFS}(\pi_c)$ such that $\pi_z \mathscr{D} \pi_y$, that is, $f(\hat{\pi}_z^N, x) \leq f(\hat{\pi}_y^N, x)$. Consequently, $\{[\mathrm{AS}(\pi_c) \cup \mathrm{OFS}(\pi_c)] \circ\}$ contains an optimal solution if $\{[\mathrm{AS}(\pi_b) \cup \mathrm{OFS}(\pi_b)] \circ\}$ does. ∎

Corollary 6.1 (The completion of the active set contains an optimal solution if the required storage has not exceeded the prespecified bounds.)

Given $BB = (B_p, S, E, F, D, L, U, BR, RB)$. If π_b is the current branching node and no nodes have been lost from AS or DB because of overflow, there exists a $\pi_y^N \in \{\mathrm{AS}(\pi_b) \circ\}$ such that $\pi_y^N \in \mathcal{P}$ and $f(\pi_y^N, x) = f(\pi^*, x)$.

Proof Proof follows directly from Lemma 6.1 because $\mathrm{OFS}(\pi_b) = \varphi$ if no nodes have overflowed AS or DB. Consequently, $\mathrm{AS}(\pi_b) \cup \mathrm{OFS}(\pi_b) = \mathrm{AS}(\pi_b)$ for each branching node π_b. ∎

Lemma 6.2 (When the actual resource requirements do not exceed the prespecified bounds, the algorithm will terminate with a solution that satisfies the desired cost bracket.)

Given $BB = (B_p, S, E, F, D, L, U, BR, RB)$. If $\mathrm{RUNTIME} \leq \mathrm{TIMELIMIT}$, $|\{(\pi_b \circ l) | l \in \bar{M}_b, F(\pi_b \circ l) = 1\}| \leq \mathrm{MAXSZDB}$, and $|[\mathrm{AS}(\pi_b) \cup \mathrm{DB}(\pi_b)] - [\mathrm{ES}(\pi_b) \cup \{\pi_b\}]| \leq \mathrm{MAXSZAS}$, for all $\pi_b \in \mathrm{BFS}(\pi_t)$, where π_t is the branching node at the time of termination, BB terminates with a solution $\hat{\pi}_u^N$ such that

$$(1 - BR)\hat{U}(\pi_t) \leq f(\pi^*, x) \leq \hat{U}(\pi_t) = f(\hat{\pi}_u^N, x)$$

Proof Since the requested storage has not exceeded the available storage, $\mathrm{OFS}(\pi_b) = \varphi$; consequently $\hat{L}_{\mathrm{OFS}}(\pi_t) = \infty$. Therefore $\hat{L}(\pi_t) = \min[\hat{L}_{\mathrm{AS}}(\pi_t), \hat{L}_{\mathrm{OFS}}(\pi_t)] = \hat{L}_{\mathrm{AS}}(\pi_t) = \min\{L(\pi_a) | \pi_a \in \mathrm{AS}(\pi_t)\}$. The function L is defined to have the following properties for all $\pi_y, \pi_z \in \mathbf{P}$:

1. $L(\pi_z) \geq L(\pi_y)$ if π_z is a descendant of π_y.
2. $L(\pi_y^N) = f(\pi_y^N, x)$ for each complete solution π_y^N.

It follows directly that $\hat{L}(\pi_t)$ is a lower bound on the cost of all complete solutions in the set $\{\mathrm{AS}(\pi_t) \circ\}$. Since $\{\mathrm{AS}(\pi_t) \circ\}$ is guaranteed to contain an optimal solution by Corollary 6.1, $\hat{L}(\pi_t)$ is a lower bound on the cost of an optimal solution, that is, $\hat{L}(\pi_t) \leq f(\pi^*, x)$.

Branching will terminate at $\pi_b = \pi_t$ if and only if one of the following is true:

1. $(\hat{U}(\pi_b) - \hat{L}(\pi_b))/\hat{U}(\pi_b) \leq BR$.
2. RUNTIME > TIMELIMIT.
3. $|M_b| = |N|$.

Assume that termination occurs because of condition 1. Then we can write

$$\hat{U}(\pi_t) - \hat{L}(\pi_t) \leq BR \cdot \hat{U}(\pi_t)$$

or

$$(1 - BR)\hat{U}(\pi_t) \leq \hat{L}(\pi_t)$$

We have already shown that $\hat{L}(\pi_t) \leq f(\pi^*, x)$ and we know that $f(\pi^*, x) \leq f(\hat{\pi}_u^N, x) = \hat{U}(\pi_t)$. Consequently

$$(1 - BR)\hat{U}(\pi_t) \leq f(\pi^*, x) \leq \hat{U}(\pi_t) = f(\hat{\pi}_u^N, x)$$

where $\hat{\pi}_u^N$ is the upper-bound solution at the time of termination.

Now assume termination occurs because of condition 2. This contradicts our assumption that the required resources do not exceed the prespecified bounds.

Finally, assume that BB terminates because $|M_b| = |N|$. This occurs when the next branching node is already a complete solution. We show that this can occur only if condition 1 $(\hat{U}(\pi_t) - \hat{L}(\pi_t))/\hat{U}(\pi_t) \leq BR$ is also true. We must consider four cases, one for each class of branching rule: LLB, FIFO, LIFO, and DF/LLB.

When $S = $ LLB branching node π_b is such that $\hat{L}(\pi_b) = \min\{L(\pi_a)|\pi_a \in AS(\pi_b)\}$. Since $|M_b| = |N|$, π_b must be a complete solution with cost $f(\pi_b, x) = L(\pi_b) = \hat{L}(\pi_b)$. Since $AS(\pi_b)$ contains an optimal solution (Corollary 6.1), we conclude that $\pi_t = \pi_b$ must be optimal. This means that $\hat{U}(\pi_t) = f(\pi_t, x)$ and $\hat{U}(\pi_t) - \hat{L}(\pi_t) = f(\pi_t, x) - f(\pi_t, x) = 0$. Consequently $(\hat{U}(\pi_t) - \hat{L}(\pi_t))/\hat{U}(\pi_t) = 0 \leq BR$.

When $S = $ FIFO all active nodes of size k are selected for branching before any active node of size $k + 1$. Consequently if $|M_b| = |N| = |\{1, 2, \ldots, n\}|$, there are no active nodes in $AS(\pi_b)$ of size $n - 1$ or less. Since $AS(\pi_b)$ must contain an optimal completion and all nodes in $AS(\pi_b)$ are complete, $\hat{L}(\pi_b) = \min\{L(\pi_a)|\pi_a \in AS(\pi_b)\} = f(\pi^*, x)$. As in the previous case with $\pi_b = \pi_t$, $(\hat{U}(\pi_t) - \hat{L}(\pi_t))/\hat{U}(\pi_t) = 0 \leq BR$.

When $S = $ LIFO or DF/LLB, all active nodes of size $k < n$ are selected for branching before any active node of size n. Consequently if π_b is such that $|M_b| = |N|$, $AS(\pi_b)$ must consist of complete solutions. As in the previous case, this means that when $\pi_t = \pi_b$, $(\hat{U}(\pi_t) - \hat{L}(\pi_t))/\hat{U}(\pi_t) = 0 \leq BR$. ∎

Lemma 6.3 (The branch-and-bound algorithm will always generate a lower bound on the cost of an optimal solution; and if a complete solution is known, its maximum deviation from the optimal cost is also given.)

Given $BB = (B_p, S, E, F, D, L, U, BR, RB)$. If π_t is the branching node at the time of termination of BB, the cost of an optimal solution π^* is bounded by $\hat{L}(\pi_t) \le f(\pi^*, x) \le \hat{U}(\pi_t)$. If a complete solution is known, $\hat{\pi}_u{}^N$ is the minimum-cost known solution and $\hat{U}(\pi_t) = f(\hat{\pi}_u{}^N, x)$. Also, $(\hat{U}(\pi_t) - \hat{L}(\pi_t))/\hat{U}(\pi_t)$ is a bracket on the difference between the cost of this known solution and an optimal solution.

Proof It follows from the definition of the lower-bound function L that for each feasible partial solution $\pi_y \in \mathbf{P}$, $L(\pi_y) \le L(\pi_y{}^N) = f(\pi_y{}^N, x)$ for all completions $\pi_y{}^N \in \{\pi_y \circ\} \cap \mathscr{P}$. We also know from Lemma 6.1 that $AS(\pi_t) \cup OFS(\pi_t)$ is guaranteed to contain an optimal solution. Consequently, we have

$$\hat{L}(\pi_t) = \min [\hat{L}_{AS}(\pi_t), \hat{L}_{OFS}(\pi_t)]$$
$$= \min \{L(\pi_y) | \pi_y \in AS(\pi_t) \cup OFS(\pi_t)\}$$

Using the previous inequality, we can write

$$\hat{L}(\pi_t) \le \min \{f(\pi_y{}^N, x) | \pi_y{}^N \in \{\pi_y \circ\} \cap \mathscr{P}, \text{ where}$$
$$\pi_y \in AS(\pi_t) \cup OFS(\pi_t)\} = f(\pi^*, x)$$

We have established that $\hat{L}(\pi_t) \le f(\pi^*, x)$.

We now show that $f(\pi^*, x) \le \hat{U}(\pi_t)$ and $\hat{\pi}_u{}^N$ is the minimum-cost known solution with cost $f(\hat{\pi}_u{}^N, x) = \hat{U}(\pi_t)$. For the initial branching node $\pi_b = e$, $\hat{U}(e)$ is assigned the value U, the cost of the best solution $\pi_u{}^N$ known before BB is begun: U is one of the nine-tuple parameters. If $U \ne \infty$, then $\hat{\pi}_u{}^N$ is initialized as the known solution $\pi_u{}^N$; otherwise, $\hat{\pi}_u{}^N$ is undefined until some solution is generated. If improved solutions are generated during the current branching step, the best is stored as $\overset{*}{\pi}_u{}^N$ with cost $f(\overset{*}{\pi}_u{}^N, x) = \overset{*}{U}$ (see Fig. 6.7). Before the next branching step begins, $\hat{\pi}_u{}^N$ and $\hat{U}$ are replaced by the best-known solution $\overset{*}{\pi}_u{}^N$ and its cost $\overset{*}{U}$. Both $\hat{\pi}_u{}^N$ and $\hat{U}$ remain constant throughout the branching step, making the analysis in the next section easier. We conclude that $f(\pi^*, x) \le \hat{U}(\pi_t)$, and if a complete solution is known at the beginning of branching step π_t, it is given by $\hat{\pi}_u{}^N$ with cost $f(\hat{\pi}_u{}^N, x) = \hat{U}(\pi_t)$.

We now can write

$$\hat{L}(\pi_t) \le f(\pi^*, x) \le \hat{U}(\pi_t) = f(\hat{\pi}_u{}^N, x)$$

and therefore

$$\frac{f(\hat{\pi}_u{}^N, x) - f(\pi^*, x)}{f(\hat{\pi}_u{}^N, x)} \le \frac{\hat{U}(\pi_t) - \hat{L}(\pi_t)}{\hat{U}(\pi_t)}$$

where $(\hat{U}(\pi_t) - \hat{L}(\pi_t))/\hat{U}(\pi_t)$ is a bracket on the difference between the cost of the best-known solution and an optimal solution.   ∎

6.2.6 Theoretical Comparison of Computational Requirements

In this section the relative computational requirements of branch-and-bound algorithms are studied as functions of the parameters E, F, D, L, U, and BR for fixed B_p, S, and RB. We assume that the required resources (time and storage) never exceed the resource bounds RB. This is denoted by $RB \triangleq \infty$. In this case Lemma 6.2 guarantees that the algorithm will terminate with a solution that satisfies the desired bracket BR.

The comparisons presented here are valid for any measure of computation that is a monotone nondecreasing function of the size of the sets $BFST \triangleq BFS(\pi_t) \cup \{\pi_t\}$, $AS(\pi_b)$, and $DB(\pi_b)$, for all $\pi_b \in BFST$, where π_t is the branching node at the time of termination. For example, the total number of nodes generated $|\cup DB(\pi_b)|_{\pi_b \in BFS(\pi_t)}$ is a monotone nondecreasing function of the size of $DB(\pi_b)$ for all $\pi_b \in BFST$. This can be used as a rough measure of relative execution time. The maximum size of the active node set $\max_{\pi_b \in BFST} |AS(\pi_b)|$ is a monotone nondecreasing function of $BFST$ and $AS(\pi_b)$, $\pi_b \in BFST$, and can serve as a measure of the maximum storage requirement.

We are interested in determining the choice of parameters E_i, F_i, D_i, L_i, U_i, and BR_i for $BB_1 = (B_p, S_1, E_1, F_1, D_1, L_1, U_1, BR_1, RB_1 = \infty)$ and $BB_2 = (B_p, S_2, E_2, F_2, D_2, L_2, U_2, BR_2, RB_2 = \infty)$ such that the following set of relationships is valid for all $\pi_b \in BFST_1$:

1. $BFS_1(\pi_b) \subseteq BFS_2(\pi_b)$.
2. $AS_1(\pi_b) \subseteq AS_2(\pi_b)$.
3. $DB_1(\pi_b) \subseteq DB_2(\pi_b)$.
4. $\hat{U}_1(\pi_b) \le \hat{U}_2(\pi_b)$.
5. $\hat{L}_1(\pi_b) \ge \hat{L}_2(\pi_b)$.

In addition to these, the following relationships will also be verified for all $\pi_b \in BFST_1$:

6. If $\pi_y \in BFS_2(\pi_b) - BFS_1(\pi_b)$, then $L_1(\pi_y) > \hat{U}_1(\pi_b)$ or $\{\pi_y \circ\} \cap \mathscr{P} = \varphi$.
7. If $\pi_y \in AS_2(\pi_b) - AS_1(\pi_b)$, then $L_1(\pi_y) > \hat{U}_1(\pi_b)$ or $\{\pi_y \circ\} \cap \mathscr{P} = \varphi$.

The complete set of relationships 1 through 7 is denoted by $(*)$.

In comparing parameters, we use the following definitions:

1. $E_2 \subseteq E_1$ if the set of elimination rules E_2 is a subset (not necessarily proper) of the set of rules E_1.

2. $F_1 \leq F_2$ if for every partial permutation (node) π_y such that $\{\pi_y \circ\} \subseteq \mathscr{P}_n$, $F_1(\pi_y) = 1$ only if $F_2(\pi_y) = 1$.

3. $D_2 \subseteq D_1$ if for every pair of partial solutions π_y and π_z, $\pi_y D_2 \pi_z$ only if $\pi_y D_1 \pi_z$.

4. $L_2 \leq L_1$ if for every partial solution π_y with $F_1(\pi_y) = 1$, $L_2(\pi_y) \leq L_1(\pi_y)$.

5. $U_1 \leq U_2$ if the initial upper-bound solution under BB_1 has a cost less than or equal to the initial upper-bound solution under BB_2.

6. $BR_1 \geq BR_2$ if the acceptable solution bracket under BB_1 is greater than or equal to the acceptable solution bracket under BB_2.

We next compare the relative computational requirements of BB_1 and BB_2 when the parameters $E, F, D, L, U,$ and BR are related in the manner just described.

The first theorem shows that the computational requirements will not increase if elimination rule U/DBAS is added to E. A complete proof is given, since it is representative of the techniques used to prove other theorems in this section.

Theorem 6.1 (The computational requirements will not increase (but may decrease) when nodes are eliminated because their lower-bound cost exceeds the upper-bound cost.)

Given $BB_1 = (B_p, S, E_1, F, D, L, U, BR, RB = \infty)$ and $BB_2 = (B_p, S, E_2, F, D, L, U, BR, RB = \infty)$. If $E_1 = E_2 \cup \{U/DBAS\}$, the $(*)$ relationships are true for all $\pi_b \in \mathrm{BFST}_1$.

Proof The proof is by induction on successive branching nodes until BB_1 terminates.

Basis $(*)$ is trivially true for the initial branching node $\pi_b = e = \pi^\varphi$. In particular,

1. $\mathrm{BFS}_1(e) = \mathrm{BFS}_2(e) = \varphi$.
2. $\mathrm{AS}_1(e) = \mathrm{AS}_2(e) = \{e\}$.
3. $DB_1 = DB_2 = \{l \,|\, l \in \bar\varphi = N \text{ and } F(l) = 1\}$.
4. $\hat{U}_1(e) = \hat{U}_2(e) = U$.
5. $\hat{L}_1(e) = \hat{L}_2(e) = L(e)$.
6. $\mathrm{BFS}_2(e) - \mathrm{BFS}_1(e) = \varphi$.
7. $\mathrm{AS}_2(e) - \mathrm{AS}_1(e) = \varphi$.

Induction step To index successive branching nodes, let π_k denote the kth branching node when the complete tree of feasible partial solutions **P** is enumerated using rule S and nodes are *not* eliminated by any elimination rule. When elimination rules are added as in BB_1 or BB_2, π_k will not be branched from if it or one of its ancestors was eliminated from the active set. If π_k is not active it is skipped, all variables remain unchanged, and the next potential branching node π_{k+1} is selected. Since $S_1 = S_2 = S$ and $L_1 = L_2 = L$, the branching sequences under BB_1 and BB_2 correspond to subsequences of the order just given. These subsequences are found by considering only those nodes that are actually branched from. We prove (*) by induction on successive candidate nodes π_k until BB_1 terminates at $\pi_k = \pi_t$. As the inductive hypothesis we assume (*) to be true for $\pi_b = \pi_k$. We show (*) to be true for the next potential branching node π_{k+1}. The induction step is verified by considering each of the following possible cases:

1. $\pi_k \in \mathrm{BFST}_1 \cap \mathrm{BFST}_2$.
2. $\pi_k \in \mathrm{BFST}_1 \cap \overline{\mathrm{BFST}_2}$.
3. $\pi_k \in \overline{\mathrm{BFST}_1} \cap \mathrm{BFST}_2$.
4. $\pi_k \in \overline{\mathrm{BFST}_1} \cap \overline{\mathrm{BFST}_2}$.

Suppose case 1, $\pi_k \in \mathrm{BFST}_1 \cap \mathrm{BFST}_2$. Then π_k is branched from in BB_1 and BB_2. We can then write $\mathrm{BFS}_1(\pi_{k+1}) = \mathrm{BFS}_1(\pi_k) \cup \{\pi_k\} \subseteq \mathrm{BFS}_2(\pi_k) \cup \{\pi_k\} = \mathrm{BFS}_2(\pi_{k+1})$, since $\mathrm{BFS}_1(\pi_k) \subseteq \mathrm{BFS}_2(\pi_k)$ by the inductive hypothesis (*1). We have thus proved (*1) for π_{k+1}.

To show (*2), $\mathrm{AS}_1(\pi_{k+1}) \subseteq \mathrm{AS}_2(\pi_{k+1})$, we note that since the storage requirements never exceed the resource bounds RB, we can write $\mathrm{AS}_i(\pi_{k+1}) = (\mathrm{AS}_i(\pi_k) \cup \mathrm{DB}_i(\pi_k)) - \mathrm{ES}_i(\pi_k)$, for $i = 1, 2$. By the inductive hypothesis (*2) $\mathrm{AS}_1(\pi_k) \subseteq \mathrm{AS}_2(\pi_k)$ and (*3) $\mathrm{DB}_1(\pi_k) \subseteq \mathrm{DB}_2(\pi_k)$. Consequently, $\mathrm{AS}_1(\pi_{k+1}) \subseteq \mathrm{AS}_2(\pi_{k+1})$ if $\mathrm{ES}_1(\pi_k) \supseteq \mathrm{ES}_2(\pi_k) \cap (\mathrm{AS}_1(\pi_k) \cup \mathrm{DB}_1(\pi_k))$. We show that if $\pi_z \in \mathrm{ES}_2(\pi_k) \cap (\mathrm{AS}_1(\pi_k) \cup \mathrm{DB}_1(\pi_k))$, then $\pi_z \in \mathrm{ES}_1(\pi_k)$ as well. This proves (*2) for π_{k+1}. Since $\pi_z \in \mathrm{ES}_2(\pi_k) \cap (\mathrm{AS}_1(\pi_k) \cup \mathrm{DB}_1(\pi_k))$, then π_z must have been eliminated in BB_2 by some rule in set $E_2 \subseteq E$. We now consider each possible case and show that π_z will also be eliminated in BB_1.

If π_z was eliminated in BB_2 by U/DBAS, then $E_1 = E_2$ and $\mathrm{AS}_1(\pi_{k+1}) = \mathrm{AS}_2(\pi_{k+1})$, since $BB_1 = BB_2$. It follows therefore that π_z would be eliminated in BB_1.

If π_z was eliminated in BB_2 by rule AS/DB, then $\pi_y D \pi_z$ for some $\pi_y \in \mathrm{AS}_2(\pi_k)$. Since $\mathrm{AS}_1(\pi_k) \subseteq \mathrm{AS}_2(\pi_k)$ by the inductive hypothesis, we can write $\mathrm{AS}_2(\pi_k) = (\mathrm{AS}_2(\pi_k) - \mathrm{AS}_1(\pi_k)) \cup \mathrm{AS}_1(\pi_k)$. When $\pi_y \in \mathrm{AS}_1(\pi_k)$, then $\pi_y D \pi_z$ and π_z is also eliminated in BB_1 by rule AS/DB. When $\pi_y \in (\mathrm{AS}_2(\pi_k) - \mathrm{AS}_1(\pi_k))$, then $L(\pi_y) = L_1(\pi_y) > \hat{U}(\pi_k)$ by the inductive hypothesis (*7). Since $L(\pi_y) \leq L(\pi_z)$ if $\pi_y D \pi_z$ (consistency requirement on D), we see that $L(\pi_z) \geq L(\pi_y) > \hat{U}(\pi_k)$ and π_z would be eliminated in BB_1 by rule U/DBAS.

If π_z was eliminated in BB_2 by rule DB/AS, then $\pi_d D \pi_z$ for some

$\pi_d \in DB_2(\pi_k)$. But since $DB_1(\pi_k) = DB_2(\pi_k)$ when $F_1 = F_2 = F$, π_z would also be eliminated in BB_1.

We conclude that $\pi_y \in ES_2(\pi_k) \cap (AS_1(\pi_k) \cup DB_1(\pi_k))$ only if $\pi_y \in ES_1(\pi_k)$ as well. Consequently, (∗2) is true for π_{k+1}.

Since we have already proved that $AS_1(\pi_{k+1}) \subseteq AS_2(\pi_{k+1})$, it follows that $\pi_{k+1} \in BFST_1$ only if $\pi_{k+1} \in BFST_2$. If $\pi_{k+1} \in BFST_1$, then $DB_1(\pi_{k+1}) = DB_2(\pi_{k+1})$, since $F_1 = F_2 = F$. If $\pi_{k+1} \notin BFST_1$, then $DB_1(\pi_{k+1}) = \varphi \subseteq DB_2(\pi_{k+1})$. This proves (∗3) for π_{k+1}.

To show (∗4)—$\hat{U}_1(\pi_{k+1}) \leq \hat{U}_2(\pi_{k+1})$—we use the inductive hypothesis $\hat{U}_1(\pi_k) \leq \hat{U}_2(\pi_k)$ and note that the only new solutions generated between steps π_k and π_{k+1} are in the set of immediate descendants of π_k. If $\pi_k \circ l$, $l \in \bar{M}_k$, is a feasible complete solution, then $F(\pi_k \circ l) = 1$ and $\pi_k \circ l \in DB_1(\pi_k) = DB_2(\pi_k)$. Any improved upper-bound solution generated at step π_k would be found in both BB_1 and BB_2 and consequently $\hat{U}_1(\pi_{k+1}) \leq \hat{U}_1(\pi_k)$, $\hat{U}_2(\pi_{k+1}) \leq \hat{U}_2(\pi_k)$, and $\hat{U}_1(\pi_{k+1}) \leq \hat{U}_2(\pi_{k+1})$. Relationship (∗4) has been proved for π_{k+1}.

Since we have already proved (∗3)—$AS_1(\pi_{k+1}) \subseteq AS_2(\pi_{k+1})$—it follows that $\hat{L}_{AS_1}(\pi_{k+1}) \triangleq \min \{L(\pi_a) | \pi_a \in AS_1(\pi_{k+1})\} \geq \min \{L(\pi_a) | \pi_a \in AS_2(\pi_{k+1})\} \triangleq \hat{L}_{AS_2}(\pi_{k+1})$. Since the storage requirements never exceed the resource bounds, $OFS_1(\pi_{k+1}) = OFS_2(\pi_{k+1}) = \varphi$, and therefore $\hat{L}_{OFS_1}(\pi_{k+1}) = \hat{L}_{OFS_2}(\pi_{k+1}) = \infty$. Consequently $\hat{L}_1(\pi_{k+1}) \triangleq \min [\hat{L}_{AS_1}(\pi_{k+1}), \hat{L}_{OFS_1}(\pi_{k+1})] \geq \min [\hat{L}_{AS_2}(\pi_{k+1}), \hat{L}_{OFS_2}(\pi_{k+1})] \triangleq \hat{L}_2(\pi_{k+1})$, and (∗5) is proved for π_{k+1}.

From the inductive hypothesis (∗6) for π_k, if $\pi_y \in BFS_2(\pi_k) - BFS_1(\pi_k)$, then $L_1(\pi_y) > \hat{U}_1(\pi_k)$ or $\{\pi_y \circ\} \cap \mathcal{P} = \varphi$. But since $\pi_k \in BFST_1 \cap BFST_2$, $BFS_2(\pi_{k+1}) - BFS_1(\pi_{k+1}) = BFS_2(\pi_k) - BFS_1(\pi_k)$. Also, $\hat{U}_1(\pi_{k+1}) \leq \hat{U}_1(\pi_k)$. Consequently, if $\pi_y \in BFS_2(\pi_k) - BFS_1(\pi_{k+1})$, then $L_1(\pi_y) > \hat{U}_1(\pi_{k+1})$ or $\{\pi_y \circ\} \cap \mathcal{P} = \varphi$.

Finally we show (∗7), if $\pi_y \in AS_2(\pi_{k+1}) - AS_1(\pi_{k+1})$, then $L_1(\pi_y) > \hat{U}_1(\pi_{k+1})$ or $\{\pi_y \circ\} \cap \mathcal{P} = \varphi$. Since the storage bounds are not exceeded, we can write $AS_2(\pi_{k+1}) - AS_1(\pi_{k+1}) = [(AS_2(\pi_k) \cup DB_2(\pi_k)) - ES_2(\pi_k)] - [(AS_1(\pi_k) \cup DB(\pi_k)) - ES_1(\pi_k)]$. The right-hand side can be rewritten as follows:

$$= [(AS_2 \cup DB_2) \cap \overline{ES_2}] \cap \overline{[(AS_1 \cup DB_1) \cap \overline{ES_1}]}$$
$$= [(AS_2 \cup DB_2) \cap \overline{ES_2}] \cap [\overline{AS_1 \cap DB_1}) \cup ES_1]$$
$$= [(AS_2 \cap \overline{ES_2}) \cup (DB_2 \cap \overline{ES_2})] \cap [(\overline{AS_1 \cap DB_1}) \cup ES_1]$$
$$= (AS_2 \cap \overline{ES_2}) \cap [(\overline{AS_1 \cap DB_1}) \cup ES_1] \cup (DB_2 \cap \overline{ES_2})$$
$$\cap [(\overline{AS_1 \cap DB_1}) \cup ES_1]$$
$$= [(AS_2 \cap \overline{AS_1} \cap \overline{ES_2} \cap \overline{DB_1}) \cup (AS_2 \cap \overline{ES_2} \cap ES_1)]$$
$$\cup [(DB_2 \cap \overline{DB_1} \cap \overline{ES_2} \cap \overline{AS_1}) \cup (DB_2 \cap \overline{ES_2} \cap ES_1)]$$
$$= [(AS_2 - AS_1) \cap (\overline{ES_2 \cap DB_1})] \cup [(AS_2 \cup DB_2) \cap (\overline{ES_2} \cap ES_1)]$$
$$\cup [(DB_2 - DB_1) \cap (\overline{ES_2} \cap AS_1)]$$

When $\pi_y \in AS_2(\pi_{k+1}) - AS_1(\pi_{k+1})$, we show that $L_1(\pi_y) > \hat{U}(\pi_{k+1})$ or $\{\pi_y \circ\} \cap \mathscr{P} = \varphi$ for each of the three special cases given by the final form of the expression just set forth.

First, if $\pi_y \in [(AS_2(\pi_k) - AS_1(\pi_k)) \cap (\overline{ES_2(\pi_k)} \cap \overline{DB_1(\pi_k)})]$, then $\pi_y \in (AS_2(\pi_k) - AS_1(\pi_k))$, and it follows from the inductive hypothesis (*7) that $L(\pi_y) = L_1(\pi_y) \geq \hat{U}_1(\pi_k) \geq \hat{U}_1(\pi_{k+1})$ or $\{\pi_y \circ\} \cap \mathscr{P} = \varphi$.

If $\pi_y \in [(AS_2(\pi_k) \cup DB_2(\pi_k)) \cap (\overline{ES_2(\pi_k)} \cap ES_1(\pi_k))]$, then π_y was eliminated at branching step π_k in BB_1 but not in BB_2. This could happen only if π_y were eliminated by rule U/DBAS $\in E_1$. In this case $L_1(\pi_y) = L(\pi_y) > \hat{U}_1(\pi_k) \geq \hat{U}_1(\pi_{k+1})$ and (*7) is proved for π_{k+1}.

Finally, if $\pi_y \in [(DB_2(\pi_k) - DB_1(\pi_k)) \cap (\overline{ES_2(\pi_k)} \cap \overline{AS_1(\pi_k)})]$, then $\pi_y \in (DB_2(\pi_k) - DB_1(\pi_k))$. But $(DB_2(\pi_k) - DB_1(\pi_k)) = \varphi$, since $F_1 = F_2 = F$ and consequently the last case is impossible. This completes our proof of inductive hypotheses (*1) through (*7) for *case 1*.

Now suppose case 2, $\pi_k \in BFST_1 \cap \overline{BFST_2}$. The node π_k will be branched from in BB_i if and only if $\pi_k \in AS_i(\pi_k)$. By inductive hypothesis (*2) $AS_1(\pi_k) \subseteq AS_2(\pi_k)$, and consequently $\pi_k \in AS_2(\pi_k)$ if $\pi_k \in AS_1(\pi_k)$. It then follows that $\pi_k \in BFST_1$ only if $\pi_k \in BFST_2$. Consequently $BFST_1 \cap \overline{BFST_2} = \varphi$ and case 2 is proved to be impossible.

Next suppose case 3, $\pi_k \in \overline{BFST_1} \cap BFST_2$. Then $\pi_k \in AS_2(\pi_k) - AS_1(\pi_k)$. Again we must prove inductive hypotheses (*1) through (*7) for π_{k+1}. Since $\pi_k \in \overline{BFST_1} \cap BFST_2$, we can write $BFS_1(\pi_{k+1}) = BFS_1(\pi_k)$ and $BFS_2(\pi_{k+1}) = BFS_2(\pi_k) \cup \{\pi_k\}$. It then follows from (*1) that $BFS_1(\pi_{k+1}) = BFS_1(\pi_k) \subseteq BFS_2(\pi_k) \subseteq BFS_2(\pi_k) \cup \{\pi_k\} = BFS_2(\pi_{k+1})$. This proves (*1) for π_{k+1}.

To prove (*2) $AS_1(\pi_{k+1}) \subseteq AS_2(\pi_{k+1})$, we note that $AS_1(\pi_{k+1}) = AS_1(\pi_k)$ because π_k was not branched from in BB_1. But $AS_2(\pi_{k+1}) = (AS_2(\pi_k) \cup DB_2(\pi_k)) - ES_2(\pi_k)$, since $\pi_k \in BFST_2$ and the storage limits are not exceeded. Since $AS_1(\pi_k) \subseteq AS_2(\pi_k)$ by inductive hypothesis (*2), $AS_1(\pi_{k+1}) \subseteq AS_2(\pi_{k+1})$ if $ES_2(\pi_k) \cap AS_1(\pi_k) = \varphi$. Suppose $ES_2(\pi_k) \cap AS_1(\pi_k) \neq \varphi$. Then there exists some $\pi_z \in ES_2(\pi_k) \cap AS_1(\pi_k)$ and π_z must have been eliminated from BB_2 by some rule in E_2. We have three possible cases to consider, one for each of the possible elimination rules in E_2.

If π_z was eliminated by rule U/DBAS, then $E_1 = E_2 \cup \{U/DBAS\} = E_2$ and BB_1 and BB_2 would be identical. Consequently, $\overline{BFST_1} \cap BFST_2 = \varphi$ and this case would be impossible.

If π_z was eliminated by rule AS/DB, then $\pi_y D \pi_z$ for some $\pi_y \in AS_2(\pi_k)$ and $\pi_z \in DB_2(\pi_k)$. Consequently $\pi_z \notin AS_2(\pi_k)$, and it follows from inductive hypothesis (*2) that $\pi_z \notin AS_1(\pi_k)$. The contradiction proves this case to be impossible.

Finally, if π_z was eliminated by rule DB/AS, then $\pi_z \in AS_2(\pi_k) \cap AS_1(\pi_k)$ and $\pi_d D \pi_z$ for some $\pi_d \in DB_2(\pi_k) = \{\pi_k \circ l \mid l \in \bar{M}_k$ and

$F(\pi_k \circ l) = 1\}$. By the monotone nondecreasing property of lower bound L, $L(\pi_d) \geq L(\pi_k)$, and by the consistency requirement on D, $L(\pi_d) \leq L(\pi_z)$. But since $\pi_k \in AS_2(\pi_k) - AS_1(\pi_k)$, we know by inductive hypothesis (∗7) that $L_2(\pi_k) = L(\pi_k) > \hat{U}_1(\pi_k)$ or $\{\pi_k \circ\} \cap \mathcal{P} = \varphi$. The second possibility can be immediately eliminated, since this would mean that $\{\pi_d \circ\} \cap \mathcal{P} \subseteq \{\pi_k \circ\} \cap \mathcal{P} = \varphi$ and consequently $\pi_d \, \cancel{D} \, \pi_z$ because this violates the definition of D. In the first possibility we see that $L(\pi_z) \geq L(\pi_d) \geq L(\pi_k) > \hat{U}_1(\pi_k)$. It follows that $\pi_z \notin AS_1(\pi_k)$ because it would have been eliminated in BB_1 by rule U/DBAS or rule DB/AS. Again this leads to a contradiction and this case is impossible. This concludes our proof of (∗2) for π_{k+1}.

The proof of (∗3) for π_{k+1} is the same as our earlier proof for *case 1*.

The proof of (∗4) $\hat{U}_1(\pi_{k+1}) \leq \hat{U}_2(\pi_{k+1})$ follows because $\hat{U}_1(\pi_{k+1}) = \hat{U}_1(\pi_k)$ and any new solutions $\pi_d \in DB(\pi_k)$ generated during branching step π_k in BB_2 must have cost $L(\pi_d) \geq L(\pi_k)$. By inductive hypothesis (∗7), $L(\pi_k) = L_1(\pi_k) > \hat{U}_1(\pi_k)$ or $\{\pi_k \circ\} \cap \mathcal{P} = \varphi$. Consequently $\hat{U}_1(\pi_{k+1}) = \hat{U}_1(\pi_k) \leq \hat{U}_2(\pi_{k+1})$, and (∗4) is proved for π_{k+1}.

Statement (∗5) $\hat{L}_1(\pi_{k+1}) \geq \hat{L}_2(\pi_{k+1})$ follows directly from (∗2), $AS_1(\pi_{k+1}) \subseteq AS_2(\pi_{k+1})$ as proved in *case 1*.

By inductive hypothesis (∗7) we know that since $\pi_k \in AS_2(\pi_k) - AS_1(\pi_k)$, then $L(\pi_k) = L_1(\pi_k) > \hat{U}_1(\pi_k)$ or $\{\pi_k \circ\} \cap \mathcal{P} = \varphi$. Also by the inductive hypothesis on (∗6) we know that if $\pi_y \in BFS_2(\pi_k) - BFS_1(\pi_k)$, then $L_1(\pi_y) > \hat{U}_1(\pi_k)$ or $\{\pi_y \circ\} \cap \mathcal{P} = \varphi$. Since $BFS_2(\pi_{k+1}) - BFS_1(\pi_{k+1}) = (BFS_2(\pi_k) \cup \{\pi_k\}) - BFS_1(\pi_k)$ and $\hat{U}_1(\pi_k) = \hat{U}_1(\pi_{k+1})$ when $\pi_k \in BFST_1$, we conclude that if $\pi_y \in BFS_2(\pi_{k+1}) - BFS_1(\pi_{k+1})$, then $L_1(\pi_y) > \hat{U}_1(\pi_{k+1})$ or $\{\pi_y \circ\} \cap \mathcal{P} = \varphi$. This proves (∗6) for π_{k+1}.

We are left to prove (∗7) if $\pi_y \in AS_2(\pi_{k+1}) - AS_1(\pi_{k+1})$, then $L_1(\pi_y) > \hat{U}_1(\pi_{k+1})$ or $\{\pi_y \circ\} \cap \mathcal{P} = \varphi$. Since $\pi_k \notin BFST_1$, $DB_1(\pi_k) = ES_1(\pi_k) = \varphi$ and consequently $AS_1(\pi_{k+1}) = AS_1(\pi_k)$. For $AS_2(\pi_{k+1})$ we have $AS_2(\pi_{k+1}) = (AS_2(\pi_k) \cup DB_2(\pi_k)) - ES_2(\pi_k)$, since the storage bounds are not exceeded. Consequently,

$$
\begin{aligned}
AS_2(\pi_{k+1}) - AS_1(\pi_{k+1}) &= [(AS_2(\pi_k) \cup DB_2(\pi_k)) - ES_2(\pi_k)] - AS_1(\pi_k) \\
&= [(AS_2 \cup DB_2) \cap \overline{ES_2}] \cap \overline{AS_1} \\
&= [(AS_2 \cap \overline{AS_1}) \cup (DB_2 \cap \overline{AS_1})] \cap \overline{ES_2} \\
&= [(AS_2(\pi_k) - AS_1(\pi_k)) \cup DB_2(\pi_k)] \cap \overline{ES_2}(\pi_k).
\end{aligned}
$$

If $\pi_y \in AS_2(\pi_{k+1}) - AS_1(\pi_{k+1})$, then either $\pi_y \in AS_2(\pi_k) - AS_1(\pi_k)$ or $\pi_y \in DB_2(\pi_k)$. In the first case inductive hypothesis (∗7) for π_k tells us that $L_1(\pi_y) > \hat{U}_1(\pi_k) = \hat{U}_1(\pi_{k+1})$ or $\{\pi_y \circ\} \cap \mathcal{P} = \varphi$. In the second case $\pi_y \in DB_2(\pi_k)$, where $\pi_k \in AS_2(\pi_k) - AS_1(\pi_k)$. Since π_y is a descendent of π_k, we conclude that $L(\pi_y) = L_1(\pi_y) \geq L_1(\pi_k) > \hat{U}_1(\pi_k)$ or $\{\pi_y \circ\} \cap \mathcal{P} = \varphi$.

Finally, *suppose case 4*, $\pi_k \in \overline{BFST_1} \cap \overline{BFST_2}$. In this case π_k is not branched from in BB_1 or BB_2, and all parameters remained unchanged at branching step π_{k+1}. The inductive step holds trivially. ∎

The next theorem confirms that the elimination of partial solutions with no feasible completions will not increase the computational requirements.

Theorem 6.2 (The computational requirements will not increase when a stronger characteristic function is used to eliminate infeasible partial solutions.)

Given $BB_1 = (B_p, S, E, F_1, D, L, U, BR, RB)$ and $BB_2 = (B_p, S, E, F_2, D, L, U, BR, RB)$. If $F_1 \leq F_2$ the $(*)$ relationships are true for all $\pi_b \in BFST_1$.

Proof A formal proof of this theorem would be similar to that of the previous theorem. We note that if $F_1(\pi_y) = 0$, by definition of F_1, $\{\pi_y \circ\} \cap \mathscr{P} = \varphi$, and from the definition of dominance relation D, π_y cannot be used to dominate any other partial solutions. If π_y is generated in BB_2 with $F_2(\pi_y) = 1$, then π_y has no feasible completion and it cannot eliminate any other partial solutions. The $(*)$ relationships follow for all $\pi_b \in BFST_1$, since all partial solutions π_y in BB_2 with $F_1(\pi_y) = 0$ are eliminated in BB_1 without changing any other parameters. ∎

Although the previous theorems confirm our intuitive feeling about the usefulness of elimination rule U/DBAS and a stronger characteristic function, examples that contradict our intuition about the universal value of a stronger dominance relation can be constructed. Knowing this, we conclude that the computational requirements of $(B_p, S, E, F, D, L, U, BR, RB)$ are not necessarily monotone nonincreasing functions of the dominance relation D. We present a counterexample for one choice of parameters, but it is easy to find counterexamples for other choices as well.

Theorem 6.3 (The computational requirements may increase when a stronger dominance relation is used.)

Given $BB_1 = (B_p, S, E, F, D_1, L, U, BR, RB)$ and $BB_2 = (B_p, S, E, F, D_2, L, U, BR, RB)$. If $D_2 \subseteq D_1$, the $(*)$ relationships are not necessarily true for all $\pi_b \in BFST_1$.

Proof An example demonstrates that the $(*)$ relationships are not necessarily true for all $\pi_b \in BFST_1$. The complete search tree of the example is given in Fig. 6.9. Solution space $\mathscr{P} = \mathscr{P}_4$ and consequently $F(\pi_y) = 1$ for all π_y. The lower-bound cost associated with each node π_y, $L(\pi_y)$, is written to the upper left of the corresponding node in the tree. For ease of notation, $\pi_a \triangleq (a_1, a_2, \ldots, a_j)$ is denoted by $a_1 a_2 \cdots a_j$, and membership in the dominance relation D_i, $\pi_y D_i \pi_z$, is denoted by the pair (π_y, π_z). Now let $BB_1 = (B_p, LLB, \{DB/AS\}, 1, D_1, L, \infty, 0, \infty)$ and $BB_2 = (B_p, LLB, \{DB/AS\}, 1, D_2, L, \infty, 0, \infty)$, where $D_2 = \{(24, 4), (23, 3)\} \cup \{(\pi_y, \pi_z) | L(\pi_y) \leq L(\pi_z),$ and $M_y = \{1, 2, 3, 4\}\}$ and $D_1 = D_2 \cup \{(12, 2)\}$. The $U = \infty$ indicates that no solution is known at the start of the algorithm. Since $BR = 0$, termination will occur when $\hat{L}(\pi_b) = \hat{U}(\pi_b)$.

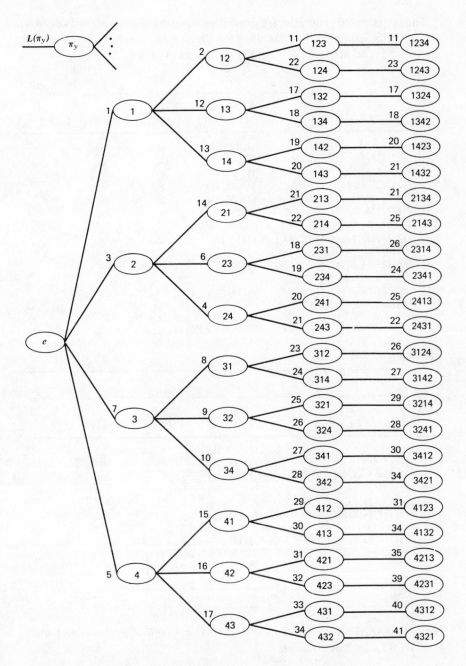

Figure 6.9 Complete search tree for Theorem 6.3.

The steps of BB_1 and BB_2 are described in terms of the ordered sets AS, DB, and ES, where (A, R, j) signifies the jth element of set A when ordered by rule R. The steps of BB_1 and BB_2 are as follows:

BB_1

π_b	$(AS_1(\pi_b), LLB, j)$	$(DB_1(\pi_b),$ LEX, $k)$	$(ES_1(\pi_b),$ FIFO, $l)$	$\hat{L}_1(\pi_b)$	$\hat{U}_1(\pi_b)$
e	(e)	$(1, 2, 3, 4)$	φ	0	∞
1	$(1, 2, 4, 3)$	$(12, 13, 14)$	(2)	1	∞
12	$(12, 4, 3, 13, 14)$	$(123, 124)$	φ	2	∞
4	$(4, 3, 123, 13, 14, 124)$	$(41, 42, 43)$	φ	5	∞
3	$(3, 123, 13, 14, 41, 42, 43, 124)$	$(31, 32, 34)$	φ	7	∞
31	$(31, 32, 34, 123, 13, 14, 41, 42,$ $43, 124)$	$(312, 314)$	φ	8	∞
32	$(32, 34, 123, 13, 14, 41, 42, 43,$ $124, 312, 314)$	$(321, 324)$	φ	9	∞
34	$(34, 123, 13, 14, 41, 42, 43, 124,$ $312, 314, 321, 324)$	$(341, 342)$	φ	10	∞
123	$(123, 13, 14, 41, 42, 43, 124,$ $312, 314, 321, 324, 341, 342)$	(1234)	$(13, 14, 41, 42,$ $43, 124, 312,$ $314, 321, 324,$ $341, 342)$	11	∞
1234 $\pi^* = 1234$	(1234)			11	11

BB_2

π_b	$(AS_2(\pi_b), LLB, j)$	$(DB_2(\pi_b),$ LEX, $k)$	$(ES_1(\pi_b),$ FIFO, $l)$	$\hat{L}_1(\pi_b)$	$\hat{U}_1(\pi_b)$
e	(e)	$(1, 2, 3, 4)$	φ	0	∞
1	$(1, 2, 3, 4)$	$(12, 13, 14)$	φ	1	∞
12	$(12, 2, 4, 3, 13, 14)$	$(123, 124)$	φ	2	∞
2	$(2, 4, 3, 123, 13, 14, 124)$	$(21, 23, 24)$	$(3, 4)$	3	∞
24	$(24, 23, 123, 13, 14, 21, 124)$	$(241, 243)$	φ	4	∞
23	$(23, 123, 13, 14, 21, 241,$ $243, 124)$	$(231, 234)$	φ	6	∞
123	$(123, 13, 14, 21, 231, 234,$ $241, 243, 124)$	(1234)	$(13, 14, 21, 231,$ $234, 241,$ $243, 124)$	11	∞
1234 $\pi^* = 1234$	(1234)			11	11

We note that $BFST_1 \not\subseteq BFST_2$ and the $(*)$ relationships are not valid for all $\pi_b \in BFST_1$. In this example

$$\left| \bigcup_{\pi_b \in BFST_1} DB_1(\pi_b) \right| = 22 > \left| \bigcup_{\pi_b \in BFST_2} DB_2(\pi_b) \right| = 17$$

and

$$\max_{\pi_b \in \text{BFST}_1} |AS_1(\pi_b)| = |AS_1(123)| = 13 > \max_{\pi_b \in \text{BFST}_2} |AS_2(\pi_b)| = |AS_2(123)| = 9 \quad \blacksquare$$

The next three theorems show how the computational requirements change when the lower-bound function and the initial upper-bound solution are improved.

Theorem 6.4 (When using the FIFO or LIFO selection rules, the computational requirements will not increase if a tighter lower-bound function or a better initial upper-bound solution is used.)

Given $BB_1 = (B_p, S, E, F, D, L_1, U_1, BR, RB = \infty)$ and $BB_2 = (B_p, S, E, F, D, L_2, U_2, BR, RB = \infty)$. If $S = $ FIFO or LIFO, $L_1 \geq L_2$, and $U_1 \leq U_2$, the (*) relationships are true for all $\pi_b \in \text{BFST}_1$.

Proof A formal inductive proof of this theorem would be similar to that of Theorem 6.1. We note that since $S = $ FIFO or LIFO, the order of branching is the same for BB_1 and BB_2 because it is independent of the lower-bound function. The theorem is proved by considering two distinct cases: (1) U/DBAS $\notin E$, and (2) U/DBAS $\in E$. In the first case, $\text{BFS}_1(\pi_b) = \text{BFS}_2(\pi_b)$ and $AS_1(\pi_b) = AS_2(\pi_b)$ for all $\pi_b \in \text{BFST}_1$. In both cases the (*) relationships can be shown to be true for all $\pi_b \in \text{BFST}_1$. The BB_1 will terminate before the BB_2 if at the last branching node π_t in BB_1, $(\hat{U}_1(\pi_t) - \hat{L}_1(\pi_t))/\hat{U}_1(\pi_t) \leq BR < (\hat{U}_2(\pi_t) - \hat{L}_2(\pi_t))/\hat{U}_2(\pi_t)$. $\blacksquare$

The next theorem shows that when $S = $ LLB or DF/LLB, it is in fact possible for the computational requirements to increase if an improved lower-bound function is used. This behavior is possible, but the computational requirements would be expected to decrease in most cases.

Theorem 6.5 (When $S = $ LLB or DF/LLB, the computational requirements may increase if a tighter lower-bound function is used.)

Given $BB_1 = (B_p, S, E, F, D, L_1, U, BR, RB)$ and $BB_2 = (B_p, S, E, F, D, L_2, U, BR, RB)$. If $S = $ LLB or DF/LLB and $L_1 \geq L_2$, the (*) relationships are not necessarily true for all $\pi_b \in \text{BFST}_1$.

Proof An example shows that the (*) relationships are not necessarily true for all $\pi_b \in \text{BFST}_1$. Lower-bound functions L_1 and L_2 are defined by the partial search trees of Fig. 6.10. We examine the case when $S = $ DF/LLB, but the same problem can be used as a counterexample when $S = $ LLB.

Let $BB_1 = (B_p, \text{DF/LLB}_{\text{LIFO}}, \varphi, 1, \varphi, L_1, \infty, 0, \infty)$ and $BB_2 = (B_p, \text{DF/LLB}_{\text{LIFO}}, \varphi, 1, \varphi, L_2, \infty, 0, \infty)$. Since $BR = 0$ and $RB = \infty$, termination will occur when the upper-bound solution has been proven optimal, that is, when $\hat{L}_i(\pi_b) = \hat{U}_i(\pi_b)$. Algorithms BB_1 and BB_2 execute the following steps:

BB_1

π_b	$(AS_1(\pi_b), DF/LLB_{LIFO}, j)$	$(DB_1(\pi_b),$ LEX, $k)$	$(ES_1(\pi_b),$ FIFO, $l)$	$\hat{L}_1(\pi_b)$	$\hat{U}_1(\pi_b)$
e	(e)	$(1,2,3,4)$	φ	0	∞
1	$(1,2,3,4)$	$(12,13,14)$	φ	1	∞
14	$(14,13,12,2,3,4)$	$(142,143)$	φ	2	∞
143	$(143,142,13,12,2,3,4)$	(1432)	φ	2	∞
142	$(1432,142,13,12,2,3,4)$	(1423)	φ	2	3
13	$(1423,1432,13,12,2,3,4)$	$(132,134)$	φ	2	3
134	$(134,132,1423,1432,12,2,3,4)$	(1342)	φ	2	3
132	$(1342,132,1423,1432,12,2,3,4)$	(1324)	φ	2	3
12	$(1324,1342,1423,1432,12,2,3,4)$	$(123,124)$	φ	2	3
124	$(124,123,1324,1342,1423,1432,2,3,4)$	(1243)	φ	2	3
123	$(1243,123,1324,1342,1423,1432,2,3,4)$	(1234)	φ	2	3
1234	$(1234,1243,1324,1342,1423,1432,2,3,4)$		φ	2	2
	$\pi^* = 1234$				

BB_2

π_b	$(AS_2(\pi_b), LLB_{LIFO}, j)$	$(DB_2(\pi_b),$ LEX, $k)$	$(ES_1(\pi_b),$ FIFO, $l)$	$\hat{L}_2(\pi_b)$	$\hat{U}_2(\pi_b)$
e	(e)	$(1, 2, 3, 4)$	φ	0	∞
1	$(1,2,3,4)$	$(12,13,14)$	φ	1	∞
12	$(12,14,13,2,3,4)$	$(123,124)$	φ	2	∞
123	$(123,14,13,124,2,3,4)$	(1234)	φ	2	∞
1234	$(1234,14,13,124,2,3,4)$			2	2
	$\pi^* = 1234$				

We see that $BFST_1 \nsubseteq BFST_2$ and the (*) relationships are not valid for all $\pi_b \in BFST_1$. In particular, we note that

$$\left| \bigcup_{\pi_b \in BFST_1} DB_1(\pi_b) \right| = 19 > \left| \bigcup_{\pi_b \in BFST_2} DB_2(\pi_b) \right| = 10$$

and

$$\max_{\pi_b \in BFST_1} |AS_1(\pi_b)| = |AS_1(124)| = 9 > \max_{\pi_b \in BFST_2} |AS_2(\pi_b)| = |AS_2(123)| = 7 \quad \blacksquare$$

Theorem 6.6 (When $S = $ LLB or DF/LLB, the computational requirements will not increase if a better initial upper-bound solution is used.)

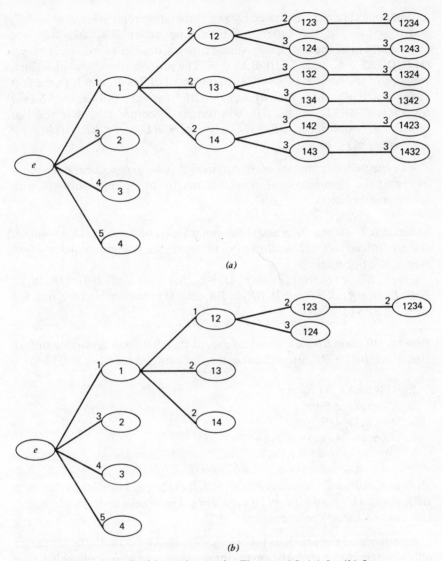

Figure 6.10   Partial search trees for Theorem 6.5: (a) L_1, (b) L_2.

Given $BB_1 = (B_p, S, E, F, D, L, U_1, BR, RB = \infty)$ and $BB_2 = (B_p, S, E, F, D, L, U_2, BR, RB = \infty)$. If $S = \text{LLB}$ or DF/LLB and $U_1 \leq U_2$, the (*) relationships are true for all $\pi_b \in \text{BFST}_1$.

Proof   Let π_k be the kth branching node when the complete tree of feasible partial solutions is enumerated using rule S and lower-bound

L, and nodes are not eliminated by any elimination rule. Since $S = S_1 = S_2$ and $L = L_1 = L_2$, the orders of branching under BB_1 and BB_2 are subsequences of the previously stated order. Consider two distinct cases: (1) U/DBAS $\notin E$, and (2) U/DBAS $\in E$. The proof of the (*) relationships for each of the two cases is similar to the proof of Theorem 6.1. In the first case we actually show that $BFS_1(\pi_b) = BFS_2(\pi_b)$ and $AS_1(\pi_b) = AS_2(\pi_b)$ for all $\pi_b \in BFST_1$. Again BB_1 will terminate before BB_2 if at the last branching node π_t in BB_1, $(\hat{U}_1(\pi_t) - \hat{L}_1(\pi_t))/\hat{U}_1(\pi_t) \le BR < (\hat{U}_2(\pi_t) - \hat{L}_2(\pi_t))/\hat{U}_2(\pi_t)$. ∎

As expected, our final theorem confirms that we may reduce, but cannot increase, the computational requirements by accepting solutions with larger cost brackets.

Theorem 6.7   (If the difference between the cost of an acceptable solution and an optimal solution is allowed to increase, the computational requirements will not increase.)

Given $BB_1 = (B_p, S, E, F, D, L, U, BR_1, RB = \infty)$ and $BB_2 = (B_p, S, E, F, D, L, U, BR_2, RB = \infty)$. If $BR_1 \ge BR_2$, the (*) relationships are true for all $\pi_b \in BFST_1$.

Proof BB_1 and BB_2 are identical except that BB_1 may terminate before BB_2, since $BR_1 \ge BR_2$. In particular, it is obvious that for all $\pi_b \in BFST_1$

1. $BFS_1(\pi_b) = BFS_2(\pi_b)$.
2. $AS_1(\pi_b) = AS_2(\pi_b)$.
3. $DB_1(\pi_b) = DB_2(\pi_b)$.
4. $\hat{U}_1(\pi_b) = \hat{U}_2(\pi_b) = \hat{U}(\pi_b)$.
5. $\hat{L}_1(\pi_b) = \hat{L}_2(\pi_b) = \hat{L}(\pi_b)$.

Moreover, BB_1 will terminate before BB_2 if at the last branching node π_t in BB_1, $BR_1 \ge (\hat{U}(\pi_t) - \hat{L}(\pi_t))/\hat{U}(\pi_t) > BR_2$. These relationships are a special case of the (*) relationships. ∎

All but one of the previous theorems were concerned with the change of only a single parameter. However, these results are also applicable to the more general case where we would like to know if the computational requirements of $BB_1 = (B_p, S_1, E_1, F_1, D_1, L_1, U_1, BR_1, RB_1)$ are less than or equal to the computational requirements of $BB_2 = (B_p, S_2, E_2, F_2, D_2, L_2, U_2, BR_2, RB_2)$. For example, if $S_1 = S_2 = S$, $E_1 = E_2 \cup \{$U/DBAS$\}$, $F_1 \le F_2$, $D_1 = D_2 = D$, $L_1 = L_2 = L$, $U_1 \le U_2$, $BR_1 \ge BR_2$, and $RB_1 = RB_2 = \infty$, the computational requirements of BB_1 will not exceed those of BB_2. This can be proven as follows:

$$BB_1 = (B_p, S, E_1, F_1, D, L, U_1, BR_1, \infty)$$
$$\leq (B_p, S, E_2, F_1, D, L, U_1, BR_1, \infty) \qquad \text{(Theorem 6.1)}$$
$$\leq (B_p, S, E_2, F_2, D, L, U_1, BR_1, \infty) \qquad \text{(Theorem 6.2)}$$
$$\leq (B_p, S, E_2, F_2, D, L, U_2, BR_1, \infty) \qquad \text{(Theorem 6.6)}$$
$$\leq (B_p, S, E_2, F_2, D, L, U_2, BR_2, \infty) \qquad \text{(Theorem 6.7)}$$
$$= BB_2$$

6.2.7 Comments on the Branch-and-Bound Approach

We have used the nine-tuple $(B_p, S, E, F, D, L, U, BR, RB)$ to characterize a class of exact and approximate branch-and-bound algorithms for general permutation problems. The relative computational requirements of different algorithms in this class were then compared theoretically as functions of the choice of parameters E, F, D, L, U, and BR for fixed B_p, S, and $RB = \infty$. Figure 6.11 summarizes the results. Theorem 6.1 shows that we cannot lose by eliminating the currently active and newly generated nodes that exceed an upper-bound solution cost. Theorem 6.2 shows that the computational requirements will not increase when nodes with no feasible completion are eliminated. Although the computational requirements may increase when a stronger dominance relation is used (Theorem 6.3), these are usually pathological cases. Even when the (*) relationships are true, we have no guarantee that the measured running time will not increase. For example, a stronger dominance relation may take more time to compute. Theorems 6.4 and 6.5 reveal that the (*) relationships are guaranteed to hold when a tighter lower-bound function is used along with the FIFO and LIFO selection rules, but not necessarily with the LLB or DF/LLB rules. In practice, a tighter lower-bound function usually reduces the total computation, but once again any additional computation required to generate the tighter bound must be offset before overall savings are possible. As expected, Theorems 6.4, 6.6, and 6.7 demonstrate that a better initial upper-bound solution and a broader bracket cannot increase the computa-

Parameter		(*) Relationships	
1. $E_1 = E_2 \cup U/DBAS$		True	(Theorem 6.1)
2. $F_1 \leq F_2$		True	(Theorem 6.2)
3. $D_1 \supseteq D_2$		False	(Theorem 6.3)
4. $L_1 \geq L_2$	a. S = FIFO or LIFO	True	(Theorem 6.4)
	b. S = LLB or DF/LLB	False	(Theorem 6.5)
5. $U_1 \leq U_2$		True	(Theorems 6.4 and 6.6)
6. $BR_1 \geq BR_2$		True	(Theorem 6.7)

Figure 6.11 Relative computational requirements as a function of parameters E, F, D, L, U, and BR for fixed B_p, S, and $RB = \infty$.

tion. Computational experience with flow-shop problems shows that the computation can be significantly reduced by using a good initial upper-bound solution and a small nonzero bracket [KS3], as we learn in Section 6.4.

The branch-and-bound formulation described in this section is intimately related to dynamic programming, but we postpone a discussion of this relationship until Section 6.5. We next survey approximate algorithms and then present some computational results for a specific flow-shop problem.

6.3 APPROXIMATE ALGORITHMS

6.3.1 Limited Backtrack Branch-and-Bound

When using the branch-and-bound method, one may intentionally curtail the storage used (by the choice of MAXSZAS or MAXSZDB), ensuring that the final result is not necessarily exact. An extreme example of this occurs when we refuse to backtrack at all; we simply branch from the node with the least lower bound at successively deeper levels until we reach a complete solution after n assignments [As]. This corresponds to MAXSZAS = MAXSZDB = 1. We call this procedure "nonbacktrack" branch-and-bound, and it entails evaluating the lower bound at $O(n^2)$ nodes.

Since we limit a priori the sizes of the node sets, we simply discard any overflow information. We do, however, keep track of the lowest lower bound associated with a discarded node; this enables us to exhibit a lower bound on the solution when we are finished. This lower bound, together with the upper bound represented by the best complete solution, is used to guarantee the accuracy of our solution.

Another limitation may be the computation time. If we have a complete solution when we exceed the time estimate, this, together with the least lower bound of a member of the active set, provides a tolerance on the accuracy of our solution.

6.3.2 Heuristic Constructions

We cannot make many generalizations about heuristic constructions. Given a problem, a human being may think of a way to generate a solution with low cost, with very little (or no) theoretical justification. For example, in the traveling salesman problem, one may use the rule of visiting from the ith city the nearest unvisited city. This so-called nearest-neighbor method is not particularly good, but it illustrates the arbitrary nature of such constructions.

Another example is provided by the heuristic algorithms discussed in

Chapter 5. Here one can sometimes bound the performance for the worst case, but further computation does not in general improve the bound or produce an optimal solution.

We again emphasize, however, that heuristic construction procedures, arbitrary and elusive as they may be, can be used to advantage in conjunction with branch-and-bound algorithms to provide initial solutions and upper bounds [Hi, S].

6.3.3 Local Neighborhood Search

An entirely different approach to obtaining approximate solutions to combinatorial problems has been applied successfully to a wide variety of problems over the past 15 years and has only recently emerged as a general technique. We call this technique *local neighborhood search* (LNS), although others have called it *natural selection* [DFFN], *heuristic prog-ramming* [Kro, KrS], *local search* [SWKr], and *neighborhood search* [Sa, WSB], to name the most common. Given a permutation problem of size n $(\mathcal{P}, X, f)$ (recall Section 6.2.2), we can describe the technique as follows [CE, Kro, Li, LK, RS, Ro, Sa, SWKr, WSB]:

1. For each $\pi \in \mathcal{P}$, there is defined a subset of $\mathcal{P}$ called the *neighbor-hood* $N(\pi)$ of π. When such a neighborhood $N(\pi)$ has been defined for every $\pi \in \mathcal{P}$, we say a neighborhood N has been defined for the problem.

2. An algorithm I is given which simply chooses an initial solution $\pi_1 \in \mathcal{P}$. Often algorithm I is randomized to produce different solutions on successive applications.

3. A policy Q is given for searching $N(\pi)$ and choosing for successive i some $\pi_{i+1} \in N(\pi_i)$ such that

$$f(\pi_{i+1}, x) < f(\pi_i, x)$$

if such an improved solution point exists in $N(\pi_i)$. When for some k

$$f(\pi_k, x) \le f(\pi, x) \qquad \text{for all } \pi \in N(\pi_k)$$

π_k is said to be *locally optimal* with respect to the neighborhood N.

The idea of such algorithms is to search in some neighborhood of a given solution, adopting improvements as they are found, and continuing the process until no further local improvement is possible. This is possibly repeated from different starting solutions, and the best solution is retained. This class of algorithms is denoted by LNS(I, Q, N), where:

1. I is the method for choosing initial solutions.
2. Q is the policy for searching the neighborhood and accepting improvements.
3. N is the neighborhood searched for improvements.

As an example of a very successful application of this technique, we describe Shen Lin's [Li] approach to the traveling salesman problem, which can in fact be considered a scheduling problem. After Lin, a tour is called λ-opt if it is impossible to obtain a tour with smaller cost by replacing any λ of its links by any other set of λ links. At any tour π, we need to search a neighborhood of size $O(n^\lambda)$, where n is the number of cities. Lin generated λ-opt tours by choosing random initial tours and adopting the first improvement found in searching each neighborhood. He found that 3-opt tours are very much better than 2-opt tours in the sense that (1) every 3-opt tour is also 2-opt, (2) the average length of 3-opt tours is considerably less than the average tour length of 2-opt tours, and (3) the probability of a 3-opt tour being optimal is significantly higher than that of a 2-opt tour. He also found that 4-opt tours were not worth generating, in that they required much more time to produce, whereas their probability of being optimal was not noticeably better. This tradeoff between neighborhood size and quality of solution is a recurrent theme in applications of the LNS method. Lin argues that one should choose between two algorithms A_1 and A_2 not only on the basis of which one produces optimal tours more frequently, but also on the basis of the algorithms' relative computation times. Thus A_1 may be preferred to A_2 because A_2 may require disproportionately more time, even though A_2 produces optimal tours more frequently. If we have time for k_i experiments with algorithm A_i, and if A_i produces an optimal tour with probability p_i, we should choose the algorithm for which the probability of success

$$p_i^* = 1 - (1 - p_i)^{k_i}$$

is maximized.

One can argue further that the best neighborhood to choose may vary with the size of the problem n, according to the following plausibility argument. Suppose, for example, that we have a family of neighborhoods of size $s = s(n, \lambda)$ and that the probability of optimality is $p = p(n, \lambda)$. We wish to minimize with respect to λ the probability of failure

$$1 - p^* = (1 - p)^{t/cs} \cong e^{-tp/cs}$$

where we have a total of t seconds of computation time, we require cs seconds to find a locally optimal solution, and p is small at the solution of the equation. (Note that we have assumed that the total computation time is proportional to the size of the neighborhood; this seems to be true for 3-opt in the traveling salesman problem, but is not true in general. The truth of the assumption depends critically on how many steps must be taken from starting point to local optimum.) Thus the λ that maximizes the ultimate probability of success is approximately that which maximizes the ratio p/s, and this depends in general on n. Lin found empirically that $p \cong 2^{-n/10}$ for 3-opt. Taking a wild guess for the purposes of discussion, let us assume that $p(n, \lambda) = e^{-an/\lambda}$. Then if $s = n^\lambda$, the optimum λ is $(an/\ln n)^{1/2}$. Similar comments apply if we are concerned with the closeness of the final cost to optimal instead of the probability of optimality.

For a given problem, the design of LNS(I, Q, N) requires a careful choice of the nature of N as well as its size, and of I and Q as well. Reference [KS2] suggests an approach in which N is "learned" experimentally by an evolutionary process. Krone discusses the problem of defining neighborhood "structure" and describes in detail two case studies in which LNS was applied to scheduling problems; we refer the reader to his thesis [Kro] for details. As a final comment on neighborhoods, [Sa, WSB, SWKr] take up the question of when neighborhoods lead to globally optimal solutions, indicating that such an exact neighborhood for the traveling salesman problem must have size $O(n!)$.

The method of choosing initial solutions I can be either random, constructive (such as might be obtained from limited backtrack branch-and-bound or a heuristic construction), or a combination of the two, obtained by randomizing a constructive procedure. The usual reason for randomizing a constructive procedure is to obtain a variety of starting solutions which, while different from one another, all have exceptionally low cost. The question of whether the local optima produced from biased starts are preferable to those produced from purely random starts is an important one, and the answer depends on the problem. In the traveling salesman problem, it seems that purely random starting tours work best, although in one method it is desirable to start with "good" tours [SW]. In other problems it is essential to start with good solutions, since the neighborhoods that are practical are too small to produce good solutions from totally random ones [SWK1, Gra, GS]. In an application to the package placement problem [HKu], Hanan and Kurtzberg remark that the question in that case is unresolved. Intuitively, the weaker the neighborhood in a given problem, the more one can gain by biasing the starting solutions.

We conclude the general discussion of LNS with consideration of the choice of Q, the policy for searching the neighborhood and accepting improvements. It seems to be generally true that it is not worth the extra effort to search the entire neighborhood for the best improvement, the so-called steepest descent strategy. Rather, the usual procedure is to adopt the first improvement encountered, which means that it is usually necessary to search completely only the final neighborhood. The last search is called the "check-out period" by Lin. There are two main orderings for searching the neighborhood: first, the neighborhood may be ordered randomly for each search; and second, the neighborhood may be lexicographically ordered by indexing in a fixed way. In the latter case, one can either restart the lexicography or continue it circularly from the point at which the previous neighborhood search ended. These are called variations A and B, respectively, by Krone [Kro]. The possible advantage to variation B is that it avoids the likely retracing of unsuccessful transformations, which are likely to remain unsuccessful after an improvement.

In summary, the design of a good LNS algorithm for a given problem is partly art, partly science; ingenuity and insight into the problem at hand are usually rewarded richly. In the next section we take up the application of the computational methods discussed up to this point to a particular flow-shop problem.

6.4 COMPUTATIONAL RESULTS FOR A FLOW–SHOP PROBLEM

6.4.1 Background

We now give some computational results when the previous exact and approximate algorithms are applied to the classical n-job two-machine flow-shop problem where mean flow time is to be minimized.* In this sequencing problem, each job J_j, $1 \leq j \leq n$, is assumed to consist of at most two distinct tasks, where each task can be performed on only one of two distinct machines, P_1 or P_2. The processing time required by job J_j on machine P_i is denoted by τ_{ij}. In keeping with the flow-shop assumption that the operations of each job are processed by the machines in the same order, we assume that each job completes its processing on machine P_1 before it begins processing on machine P_2. Permutation schedules result when each machine processes the jobs in the same order (permutation), with no unnecessary idle time between operations. When the mean of the job finishing times is used as the measure of schedule performance, it is well known that the class of permutation schedules is guaranteed to contain an optimal solution [CMM]. Although the mean finishing-time criterion has not received as much attention as the schedule-length (makespan or maximum finishing-time) criterion [As, CMM, DH, E1, Gu, Me], Ignall and Schrage [IS] presented computational results for an exact branch-and-bound approach and Krone and Steiglitz [KrS] applied LNS techniques to the general m-machine case. The exact and approximate algorithms presented here for the two-machine problem demonstrate the computational effectiveness of coupling LNS and branch-and-bound to generate solutions with a guaranteed accuracy.

* As indicated in Table 1.2, this problem is known to be NP-complete.

6.4.2 Application of Exact Branch-and-Bound

In our application of exact branch-and-bound algorithms to our flow-shop problem, we are concerned with the following choices of parameters:

1. $S = \text{LLB}_{\text{FIFO}}$ (*least lower bound*). Select the currently active node with the least lower-bound cost. In the case of ties, select the node that was generated first.

2. $E = \{\text{U/DBAS, U/DB, AS/DB}\}$

   b. U/DBAS (*upper-bound tested for dominance of descendants of the branching node and members of the active set*). Eliminate those descendants of the active set whose lower-bound costs exceed the current upper bound U.

   b. U/DB (*upper-bound tested for dominance of descendants of the branching node*). Eliminate those descendants of the branching node whose lower-bound costs exceed the current upper bound U.

   c. AS/DB (*active node set tested for dominance of descendants of the branching node*). Eliminate those descendants of the branching node that are dominated by a member of the active set.

3. $F(\pi_y) = 1$ for every π_y, hence $\mathscr{P} = \mathscr{P}_n$.

4. $D = D_{\text{IS}}$ (*Ignall and Schrage* [IS]). Let π_y and π_z be two nodes that represent partial schedules involving the same subset of jobs M_y, where $|M_y| = r$, let $F_{ij}(\pi)$ be the finishing time of job J_j on machine P_i under the partial schedule π, and let x_k denote the kth job of schedule π_x.

   Then

$$(\pi_y, \pi_z) \in D_{\text{IS}} \text{ (i.e., } \pi_y \text{ dominates } \pi_z) \text{ if and only if}$$

$$F_{2y_r}(\pi_y) \leq F_{2z_r}(\pi_z) \quad \text{and} \quad \sum_{i \in M_y} F_{2i}(\pi_y) \leq \sum_{i \in M_y} F_{2i}(\pi_z)$$

5. $L = L_{\text{IS}}$ (*Ignall and Schrage* [IS]). This is the lower-bound function of [IS]. We use the quantities

$\tau_{1i} = $ execution time of job J_i on machine 1

$\tau_{2i} = $ execution time of job J_i on machine 2

$F_{2i} = F_{2i}(\pi_t) = $ finishing time of job J_i on machine 2, under schedule π_t

Given a partial solution π_y defined on the set of jobs M_y, where $|M_y| = r$, the sum of the finishing times for any schedule $\pi_t \in \{\pi_y \circ\}$ is

$$S = \sum_{i \in M_y} F_{2i} + \sum_{i \in \bar{M}_y} F_{2i} \tag{2}$$

where the F_{2i} in the second sum are computed under schedule π_t. The second sum can be lower bounded as follows: if each job could start on machine P_2 immediately after being finished on machine P_1, then

$$\sum_{i \in \bar{M}_y} F_{2i} = S_1 = \sum_{k=r+1}^{n} [F_{1t_r} + (n - k + 1)\tau_{1t_k} + \tau_{2t_k}]$$

where schedule π_t has the jobs in the order t_k. If, on the other hand, each job on machine P_2 must wait only for the preceding job on machine P_2 to finish, we have

$$\sum_{i \in \bar{M}_Y} F_{2i}(\pi_t) = S_2 = \sum_{k=r+1}^{n} [\max(F_{2t_r}(\pi_t), F_{1t_r}(\pi_t) + \min_{i \in \bar{M}_y} \tau_{1i}) + (n - k + 1)\tau_{2t_k}]$$

If either of the two preceding conditions is not met, the second sum in (2) can only increase; thus we have

$$S \geq \sum_{i \in M_y} F_{2i} + \max(S_1, S_2)$$

Furthermore, S_1 is minimized by choosing π_t so that the jobs τ_{1i_k}, $i_k \in \bar{M}_y$, are in ascending order, with the result $S_1 = \hat{S}_1$. Also, S_2 is minimized by choosing π_t so that the jobs τ_{2i_k}, $i_k \in \bar{M}_y$ are in ascending order, with the result $S_2 = \hat{S}_2$. Therefore

$$S \geq \sum_{i \in M_y} F_{2i} + \max(\hat{S}_1, \hat{S}_2)$$

Note that since the ordering of τ_{1i_k} and τ_{2i_k} need be done only once for the problem, the lower bound can be computed at π_y in time $0(n)$.

6. Let U denote the upper bound given at the start of the algorithm. This is distinguished from $\hat{U}(\pi_b)$, the upper bound known during execution of the algorithm when π_b is the current branching node. Then we have two possibilities:

    a. $U = \infty$, when no initial solution is given.

    b. $U < \infty$, when some initial solution is given.

7. Wishing the exact solution, we set $BR = 0$.

8. $RB = $ (TIMELIMIT, MAXSZAS, MAXSZDB). The bound on computation time TIMELIMIT was set at various values for different runs and is indicated with the numerical results. MAXSZDB was taken to be n (ensuring that DB never overflows), except in the nonbacktrack cases where MAXSZDB = 1. Finally, MAXSZAS = 999; and further computation is terminated if the size of AS exceeds MAXSZAS.

We employ the two following exact branch-and-bound algorithms:

$BB_1 = (B_p, \text{LLB}_{\text{FIFO}}, \{AS/DB, U/DB\}, F = 1, D_{IS}, L_{IS}, U_1, BR = 0, RB)$

$BB_2 = (B_p, \text{LLB}_{\text{FIFO}}, \{\text{AS/DB}\}, F = 1, D_{\text{IS}}, L_{\text{IS}}, U_2 = \infty, BR = 0, RB)$

where U_1 is an upper bound generated by methods described in Section 6.3 and in more detail in the next section.

6.4.3 Application of Nonbacktrack Branch-and-Bound

A tree search with no backtracking can be used to generate a complete solution, whose cost then is an upper bound for all costs. Such an algorithm results from choosing the following parameters:

$$S = \text{LLB}_{\text{FIFO}}, \quad E = \varphi, \quad F = 1, \quad D = \varphi, \quad L = L_{\text{IS}}, \quad U = \infty,$$

$$RB = (\text{TIMELIMIT}, \text{MAXSZAS}, \text{MAXSZDB}) = (\infty, 1, 1)$$

In this case the least lower-bound descendant at each branching node becomes the next branching node. This algorithm is denoted by BBLB(1); it is similar to one described in [As].

6.4.4 Application of Local Neighborhood Search

We are concerned here with the following choices:

1. *a.* $I = \text{UPRS}$ (*u*niform *p*seudo*r*andom *s*tart), in which starting solutions are generated using random permutations.
    b. $I = \text{BBLB}(1)$, in which the single result of algorithm BBLB(1) is used as the start.
2. $Q = \text{RFI}$ (*r*andom *f*irst *i*mprovement), in which the neighborhood is enumerated randomly and the first improvement encountered is accepted.
3. *a.* $N = \text{BSI}$ (*b*ackward *s*ingle *i*nsertion) is the set of permutations (solutions) generated by inserting the job currently in position i after the job currently in position j, $i < j$. For example, $i = 2$, $j = 4$ transforms solution *abcde* into solution *acdbe*.
    b. $N = \text{FSI}$ (*f*orward *s*ingle *i*nsertion) is the set of permutations generated by inserting the job currently in position i before the job currently in position j, $i > j$. For example, $i = 4$, $j = 2$ transforms solution *abcde* into solution *adbce*.
    c. $N = \text{API2}$ (*a*djacent *p*air interchange 2) is the set of permutations generated by first interchanging the jobs in positions i and $i + 1$, and then, if a second number $j \neq i$ is specified, interchanging the jobs then in positions j and $j + 1$. For example, $i = 2$, $j = 4$, transforms *abcde* into *acbed*. Also, $i = 2$, $j = 3$ transforms *abcde* into *acdbe*.
    d. $N = \text{BSI} \cup \text{API2}$.

All these neighborhoods are of size $O(n^2)$.

6.4.5 Problem Data

Twenty-five standard sets of random data, five sets for each of the problem sizes $n = 5, 10, 15, 20$, and 50, were used to test exact and approximate algorithms. The processing times τ_{ij} were selected as independent integer samples from the uniform distribution Prob $\{\tau_{ij} = r\} = 1/10$. Rather than computing the mean finishing time, which may not be integer valued, the sum of the finishing times was adopted as an equivalent measure of schedule cost.

6.4.6 Performance of Approximate Techniques

Local neighborhood search and nonbacktrack branch-and-bound were used to generate suboptimal solutions to the 25 test problems. In the first set of experiments, the LNS algorithm was used with parameters $I = $ PRS; $Q = $ RFI; and the neighborhoods $N = $ BSI, FSI, API2, and BSI $\cup$ API2.

Table 6.1 shows the best solution produced by each neighborhood and indicates the number of times it was produced and the number of starting solutions used (i.e., "Number" = number of times best solution found/number of starting solutions used). The starred solutions have been proved optimal by an exact technique, and the underlined solutions are the best-known suboptimal solutions for those data sets. Problems of size $n = 5$ have not been included because they are relatively simple problems and all neighborhoods frequently produced the optimal solution for each data set. A comparison of the solution quality based on this small number of data sets shows that the difference between neighborhoods is insignificant. No one neighborhood was uniformly better than any other on all data sets. In particular, it is interesting to note that BSI $\cup$ API2 is not uniformly better than BSI or API2.

Branch-and-bound without backtracking, BBLB(1), was also employed to generate suboptimal solutions. The solutions generated by this nonbacktracking heuristic were generally not as good as the local neighborhood search solutions, but they required less than half the computation time. The next step was to use these solutions as improved nonrandom starting solutions for local neighborhood search: LNS(BBLB(1), RFI, N) was tested with two neighborhood sets $N = $ BSI and FSI. For small problems $(n \leq 15)$, we found that the solutions generated with these improved starting solutions were about the same as with the random starting solutions, but the improved start usually generated better solutions for the larger problems $(n = 20, 50)$. Also, the BSI generating set produced uniformly better solutions than FSI for the 50-job problems but about the same quality for the smaller problems. The solutions are tabulated in Table 6.1, along with the optimal or best-known solution for each data set.

TABLE 6.1 BEST SOLUTIONS GENERATED BY APPROXIMATE TECHNIQUES

| | | | LNS(PRS, RFI, N) | | | | | | | | | LNS(BBLB(1), RFI, N) | | | |
| | | | N = BSI | | N = FSI | | N = API2 | | N = BSI∪API2 | | BBLB(1) | N = BSI | | N = FSI | |
n	Data set	Best-known solution	Best solution	Number	Best solution	Number	Best solution	Number	Best solution	Number	Solution	Best solution	Number	Best solution	Number
10	1	298*	299	2/10	298*	3/10	304	2/10	299	1/10	305	298*	6/10	298*	5/10
	2	326*	326*	3/10	326*	7/10	326*	5/10	326*	5/10	335	326*	9/10	326*	10/10
	3	375*	375*	4/10	375*	6/10	375*	3/10	375*	3/10	375*	375*	1/1	375*	1/1
	4	340*	340*	1/10	340*	5/10	340*	1/10	340*	5/10	340*	340*	1/1	340*	1/1
	5	291*	291*	1/10	291*	8/10	291*	4/10	291*	3/10	294	291*	1/10	291*	10/10
15	1	598	605	2/10	599	1/10	602	3/10	598	1/10	667	603	3/10	600	5/10
	2	608*	608*	6/10	608*	8/10	608*	9/10	608*	8/10	609	608*	10/10	608*	10/10
	3	573	576	1/10	573	1/10	574	1/10	577	1/10	600	578	1/10	578	6/10
	4	713*	713*	8/10	713*	7/10	713*	7/10	713*	8/10	713*	713*	1/1	713*	1/1
	5	634*	639	1/10	636	1/10	642	1/10	637	1/10	638	638	1/1	638	1/1
20	1	954	971	1/10	956	1/10	958	1/10	955	1/10	956	956	1/1	954	10/10
	2	1161	1166	1/10	1173	1/10	1177	1/10	1170	2/10	1310	1161	1/10	1170	1/10
	3	957	958	2/10	958	1/10	962	1/10	957	1/10	991	957	1/10	958	4/10
	4	1015	1020	1/10	1018	1/10	1019	1/10	1016	1/10	1041	1015	1/10	1019	5/10
	5	881*	885	1/10	886	1/10	884	1/10	890	2/10	886	885	10/10	885	10/10
50	1	6295	6334	1/5	6327	1/5					7127	6295	1/5	6324	1/5
	2	5046	5151	1/5	5079	1/5					5807	5046	1/5	5068	1/5
	3	6300	6392	1/5	6455	1/5					6990	6300	1/5	6409	1/5
	4	6362	6519	1/5	6460	1/5					6389	6362	1/5	6382	1/5
	5	5726	5927	1/5	5949	1/3					6017	5726	1/5	5805	1/5

* Optimal solution.

273

When $n \geq 15$, the average time required to generate a solution using LNS(UPRS, RFI, BSI) was greater than the sum of the times required by BBLB(1) and LNS(BBLB(1), RFI, BSI). This suggests that a good heuristic for large mean finishing-time flow-shop problems is to generate an improved starting solution using nonbacktrack branch-and-bound and then to try to improve the solution with local neighborhood search.

The average number of neighbors that are tested (selected and cost compared to base solution cost) before finding a local optimum can be used as a relative measure of execution time requirements for local search. This also measures the number of cost-function evaluations performed. For n-job m-machine flow-shop problems, each cost evaluation requires time that grows linearly with the product nm, since the finishing times of each of n jobs on m machines must be computed by recursively building the permutation schedule until all n jobs have been assigned a starting time on each of m machines. Experimental results for the 5 problem sets indicate that the number of neighbors tested using LNS(UPRS, RFI, N) and LNS(BBLB(1), RFI, N) for N = BSI, FSI, API2, and BSI $\cup$ API2, grows as $n^{2.3}$ to $n^{2.5}$, and the execution time as $n^{3.3}$ to $n^{3.7}$. Thus the number of neighbors tested seems to grow slightly faster than the neighborhood size $O(n^2)$. Nonbacktrack branch-and-bound always generates $n(n-1)/2 + 1$ nodes, each requiring a lower-bound function evaluation; consequently the execution time increases approximately as n^3.

6.4.7 Performance of Exact and Guaranteed Algorithms

The branch-and-bound approach used by Ignall and Schrage [IS] for the two-machine mean finishing-time problem is equivalent to BB_2 described earlier, except that they use LLB_{LIFO}, breaking ties in the selection rule with a last-in-first-out policy, instead of our first-in-first-out policy. This change was found to have a negligible effect on the experimental results to be described. From the analysis in Section 6.2.6 we know that the computational requirements of this algorithm may be reduced, and cannot be increased, by adding upper-bound elimination rule U/DBAS to E. In addition, it was shown that the computational requirements are a monotone nonincreasing function of the initial upper-bound cost U. Indeed, the next set of computational results demonstrates that the average computational requirements for the same finishing-time flow-shop problem can be significantly reduced by adding a slightly weaker version of rule U/DBAS to E and using a good suboptimal solution as the initial upper bound U.

In our computational experiments, we assumed that the upper-bound cost at each branching node would be used only to eliminate the descendants of that branching node, not the currently active set. This new rule is denoted by U/DB. Rule U/DB is weaker than U/DBAS because an active node π_a not eliminated by the upper bound when generated—that is, when $L(\pi_a) \not> U(A(\pi_a))$, where $A(\pi_a)$ denotes the father of π_a—may have $L(\pi_a) > U(\pi_b)$ at some later branching node π_b if an improved solution was found. If we neglect to recheck for possible dominance of the active set when the upper bound is improved, we may leave some unnecessary nodes on the active list, and these nodes may be branched from. However, in our experiments, the initial upper bound U was often an optimal solution; consequently U/DB and U/DBAS would eliminate the same nodes. Furthermore, since we used the LLB selection rule exclusively, the set of branched-from nodes cannot include nodes with lower bound greater than the optimum cost (Lemma 6, [KS1]). Therefore, using U/DB rather than U/DBAS did not change the branched-from set. Now consider

$$BB_2 = (B_p, \text{LLB}_{\text{FIFO}}, 1, \{\text{AS/DB}\}, D_{\text{IS}}, L_{\text{IS}}, \infty, BR, RB)$$
$$BB_1 = (B_p, \text{LLB}_{\text{FIFO}}, 1, \{\text{AS/DB}, \text{U/DB}\}, D_{\text{IS}}, L_{\text{IS}}, U_1, \text{BR}, \text{RB})$$

where U_1 = best solution generated by LNS(BBLB(1), RFI, BSI), and $BR = 0$. The computational requirements of BB_2 and BB_1 are displayed in Table 6.2. The column S denotes the condition under which the algorithm terminated for each data set: $R1 \triangleq \hat{L} = \hat{U}$, upper-bound solution proved optimal; $ET \triangleq$ execution time equals or exceeds TIMELIMIT; $EN \triangleq$ number of currently active nodes equals MAXSZAS. When termination occurs under ET or EN, the cost of the least lower-bound active node is listed as the final lower-bound cost. When termination occurs under $R1$, the final lower-bound bound cost is the cost of an optimal solution π^*.

Both BB_1 and BB_2 terminated with optimal solutions ($R1$) for all problems of size $n = 10$, but examination of Table 6.2 reveals that the computational requirements of BB_1 are significantly less than those of BB_2. The maximum-number-of-active-nodes statistic can be interpreted as the minimum storage needed to execute the algorithm. An average storage requirement for problems of a given size n was found by averaging this statistic. When $n = 10$, the average storage requirement for BB_1 was only 15% of the average storage requirement of BB_2; and the average execution time used by BB_1 was only 13% of that used by BB_2. When the time required to generate the initial upper-bound solution is included, the time required by LNS(BBLB(1), RFI, BSI) for 10 starts per data set, there is still an average savings of 76%. The improvement in execution time and storage occurs because all descendants π_d with lower-bound costs $L(\pi_d)$ greater than upper-bound cost U are immediately eliminated by rule U/DB. These descendants never become active, and it is unnecessary to test whether they are dominated by existing active nodes under rule AS/DB.

TABLE 6.2 COMPUTATIONAL REQUIREMENTS OF EXACT AND GUARANTEED ACCURACY TECHNIQUES

$BB_3: BR = .05(n = 10, 15, 20),\ 10(n = 50)$

			BB_2				BB_1							BB_3						
				Maximum						Maximum							Maximum			
			Final	number of	Total		Initial		Final	number of	Total			Initial		Final	number of	Total		
	Data		lower	active	nodes	RUNTIME*	upper		lower	active	nodes	RUNTIME*	$\frac{\hat{U}-L}{\hat{U}}$	upper		lower	active	nodes	RUNTIME*	$\frac{\hat{U}-L}{\hat{U}}$
n	set	S	bound	nodes	generated	(seconds)	bound	S	bound	nodes	generated	(seconds)		bound	S	bound	nodes	generated	(seconds)	
10	1	R1	298	381	724	2.787	298	ET	298	50	622	.319	.0	298	AB	285	33	75	.046	.045
	2	R1	326	132	178	.256	326	R1	326	12	109	.048	.0	326	AB	320	4	11	.013	.018
	3	R1	375	61	83	.060	375	R1	375	4	64	.030	.0	375	AB	367	1	11	.010	.021
	4	R1	340	54	69	.045	340	R1	340	2	43	.022	.0	340	AB	339	1	11	.011	.003
	5	R1	291	456	1579	8.079	291	R1	291	95	1366	1.026	.0	291	AB	282	6	11	.011	.031
15	1	EN	580	999	1819	17.062	603	ET	589	942	5726	30.072	.023	603	AB	573	242	553	1.221	.050
	2	R1	608	237	291	.743	608	R1	608	11	168	.089	.0	608	AB	606	2	16	.016	.033
	3	EN	563	999	1716	16.829	578	EN	567	999	4263	29.856	.019	578	AB	550	21	30	.026	.048
	4	R1	713	428	738	3.073	713	R1	713	29	497	.264		713	AB	709	4	16	.016	.006
	5	EN	629	999	2242	22.271	638	R1	634	167	4605	3.872	.0	638	AB	607	49	153	.128	.049
20	1	EN	923	999	2494	26.631	956	ET	943	893	16524	40.026	.014	956	AB	909	87	299	.320	.049
	2	EN	1122	999	1495	15.764	1161	EN	1122	999	1738	15.842	.035	1161	AB	1111	17	21	.024	.043
	3	EN	940	999	1887	22.160	957	EN	944	999	6656	32.531	.014	957	AB	935	10	21	.023	.023
	4	EN	976	999	1650	16.802	1015	EN	980	999	3244	23.156	.036	1015	AB	968	8	21	.022	.046
	5	EN	876	999	2462	27.367	885	R1	881	124	5415	4.436	.0	885	AB	858	4	21	.022	.031
50	1	EN	5842	999	1130	10.882	6295	EN	5842	999	1130	10.635	.065	6295	AB	5835	50	51	.114	.073
	2	EN	4716	999	1050	9.507	5046	EN	4716	999	1050	9.260	.065	5046	AB	4716	50	51	.117	.065
	3	EN	5795	999	1070	10.516	6300	EN	5795	999	1070	10.017	.080	6300	AB	5788	50	51	.117	.081
	4	EN	5945	999	1046	10.304	6362	EN	5946	999	1079	9.920	.050	6362	AB	5925	43	51	.106	.069
	5	EN	5050	999	1136	10.390	5726	EN	5050	999	1136	9.855	.118	5726	EN	5050	999	1136	10.330	.118

* On the IBM 360/91, FORTRAN H compiler.

When the problem size is greater than 10, the storage and execution time limits are frequently exceeded. However, since the computational requirements of BB_1 are less than or equal to the requirements of BB_2, BB_1 generally gets closer to an optimal solution before termination. In some cases (problems 15-5 and 20-5), BB_1 reached an optimal solution but BB_2 exceeded the computational limits. When both algorithms are terminated for exceeding storage or execution time limits, the final lower bound achieved by BB_1 is at least as great and frequently greater than the bound achieved by BB_2. Because we are using the LLB branching rule, the active node with the least lower-bound cost is always the current branching node. This lower-bound cost, denoted by $\hat{L}$, together with the final upper bound $\hat{U}$ can be used to bracket the cost of an optimal solution. Table 6.2 indicates brackets $(\hat{U} - \hat{L})/\hat{U}$ of 0 to 2.3% for problems of size $n = 15$, 0 to 3.6% for problems of size $n = 20$, and 5.0 to 11.8% for problems of size $n = 50$.

These experiments show that a good suboptimal solution should be obtained before attempting to generate an optimal solution with branch-and-bound. The use of elimination rule U/DB together with a good initial upper-bound solution significantly reduces the necessary computation; and if the branch-and-bound algorithm exceeds the allowed storage or execution time limits, the known upper-bound solution and the least lower-bound active node nevertheless give a close bracket on the cost of an optimal solution.

6.4.8   Bracketing with Suboptimal Solutions

When an optimal solution is not necessary, even more dramatic computational savings are possible. In this section we use the branch-and-bound algorithm to verify that a suboptimal solution exceeds the optimal cost by no more than a prespecified amount. This technique for achieving a prespecified bracket has been suggested by other authors and is discussed in [GN, Hi, S, Gi]. We again use BB_1, but now given prespecified bracket BR, $0 \leq BR < 1$. The case when $BR = 0$ was discussed in the previous section. Table 6.2 shows the computational requirements of BB_1 when $BR = 0.05$ for $n = 10$, 15, and 20, and $BR = 0.10$ for $n = 50$; $S = AB$ signifies that BB_1 achieved the prespecified bracket. In most cases the bracket was achieved at the first branching step (the total number of nodes generated is then $n + 1$) and the required execution time was insignificant compared with the optimum-producing branch-and-bound requirements. This is a result of the optimality of the initial upper-bound solutions and the very close bound generated by the lower-bound function L. When the bracket was tightened to $BR = 0.01$, the average computational requirements were not significantly different from the optimal case, since both methods usually exceeded the allowed computational limits. However, on data sets where this was not the case, savings were achieved.

6.4.9 Conclusions from Computational Results

The computational results for the algorithms described for our flow-shop problem indicate the following conclusions:

1. The computational requirements of optimum-producing branch-and-bound algorithms can be decreased by using a good initial upper-bound solution together with an upper-bound dominance rule such as U/DB or U/DBAS.

2. When an exact solution to a problem is desired, the total computation (the computation required to obtain an initial upper-bound solution, plus the computation required by the optimum-producing algorithm) may be significantly reduced by first computing a good suboptimal solution.

3. Optimum-producing branch-and-bound algorithms may be computationally competitive with approximate algorithms for problems as large as $n = 20$.

4. When a suboptimal solution guaranteed to satisfy a prespecified bracket is sufficient, the branch-and-bound technique can be used to verify the quality of a suboptimal solution or to generate another suboptimal solution satisfying the desired bracket. Brackets of 5 to 10% frequently result in dramatic computational savings over the optimum-producing (0%) requirements.

5. Branch-and-bound without backtracking used as a startup, together with local neighborhood search, provides an effective heuristic for this problem.

6.5 RELATIONSHIP BETWEEN BRANCH–AND–BOUND AND DYNAMIC PROGRAMMING

6.5.1 Background

Dynamic programming was first applied to a variety of sequencing problems by Held and Karp [HK1]. Later, Lawler and Moore [LM] found improved algorithms for several special cases. More recently, Sahni [Sah] and Horowitz and Sahni [HS] have demonstrated similar dynamic programming algorithms for problems of scheduling independent tasks under various processor and cost assumptions. We do not attempt to review this work in detail, but a sample problem demonstrates how the dynamic programming approach is related to branch-and-bound.

6.5.2   Sample Problem

We consider a problem of processing n independent tasks on a single processor. The execution time of task T_i is a nonnegative integer τ_i. In addition, a deferral cost or *loss* $w_i(t)$, where $w_i(t)$ is a monotone nondecreasing function of t, is incurred if T_i is completed at time t. The objective is to find a schedule that minimizes the total loss over all n tasks. An optimal schedule can be represented by a permutation π where $\pi(j) = k$ if task T_k is the jth task to be processed. Held and Karp [HK1] derived a recurrence relation that solves the general problem in $O(n2^n)$ steps. Kohler [Ko1] later used the same approach to demonstrate an equivalent $O(n2^n)$ branch-and-bound algorithm.

6.5.3   Dynamic Programming Approach to a Special Case

Lawler and Moore [LM] were the first to recognize that when

$$w_i(t) = \begin{cases} l_i & t > d_i \\ 0 & t \leq d_i \end{cases}$$

(i.e. when a fixed loss l_i is incurred if T_i does not meet some due date d_i), the problem can be solved by finding an optimal partition of the tasks into two sets. We call this the *fixed-loss due-date scheduling* (FLDS) problem. The tasks in the first set J are all processed by their due dates, and $\bar{J}$ is the remaining set of tardy tasks for which a loss is incurred. The sets J and $\bar{J}$ can be found by ordering all tasks by their due dates, earliest due date first, and applying the following dynamic programming argument [LM].

Let $f(j, t)$ be the minimum total loss for the first j tasks, subject to the constraint that task j is completed no later than t. Establish the following boundary conditions

$$f(0, t) = 0 \qquad t \geq 0$$
$$f(j, t) = +\infty \qquad j = 1, 2, \ldots, n; \qquad t < 0$$

and then solve the recurrence equation

$$f(j, t) = \min \begin{cases} f(j, t-1) \\ w_i(t) + f(j-1, t-\tau_j), \qquad j = 1, 2, \ldots, n; \qquad t \geq 0 \\ l_i + f(j-1, t) \end{cases}$$

Since all tasks are completed by $\omega = \sum_{i=1}^{n} \tau_i$, this equation need only be computed for $0 \leq t \leq \omega$. The tasks that are given zero processing time by the solution of the equation are in the set $\bar{J}$ of tardy tasks, whereas the remainder, those in J, are processed on time in order of nondecreasing due dates. The tasks in $\bar{J}$ are processed in any order following those in J. Since our recurrence equation must be solved for n values of j for each t between 0 and ω, it can be solved in $O(n\omega)$ steps.

6.5.4 Binary Tree Representation of Solution Space

A variation of this dynamic programming method can be more easily understood and related to branch-and-bound. As before, assume that the tasks are indexed in order of nondecreasing due dates (i.e., $d_1 \le d_2 \le \cdots \le d_n$). Then all feasible solutions (partitions) can be encoded as sequences of literals $\alpha_1\alpha_2 \cdots \alpha_n$, where $\alpha_i = i$ or $\bar{i}$. If $\alpha_i = i$, then $T_i \in J$ and task T_i is executed in order and finishes by its due date d_i; but if $\alpha_i = \bar{i}$, then $T_i \in \bar{J}$ and task T_i is tardy. The leaves of a complete binary tree of height n can be used to represent all possible sequences. For example, if $n = 4$ we have the tree of Fig. 6.12, where the root is designated e and the remaining nodes by sequences of the form $\alpha_1\alpha_2 \cdots \alpha_r$. Leaf $\bar{1}2\bar{3}4$ represents the partition $J = \{T_2, T_4\}, \bar{J} = \{T_1, T_3\}$.

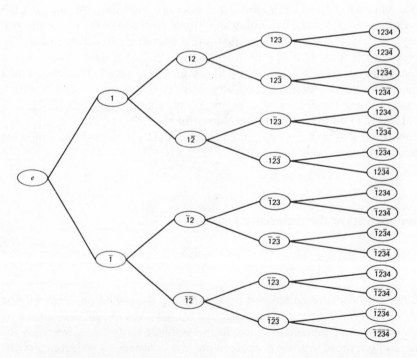

Figure 6.12   Binary tree representation of all possible solutions to a four-task FLDS problem.

Consider the four-task FLDS problem specified by:

$$
\begin{array}{lll}
d_1 = 2 & l_1 = 3 & \tau_1 = 2 \\
d_2 = 4 & l_2 = 2 & \tau_2 = 3 \\
d_3 = 5 & l_3 = 1 & \tau_3 = 2 \\
d_4 = 6 & l_4 = 2 & \tau_4 = 3
\end{array}
$$

Parameters d_i, l_i, and τ_i are, respectively, the due date, loss, and processing time for task T_i. With each node (partial partition) $\alpha_1 \alpha_2 \cdots \alpha_r$ of the binary tree, we associate a two-tuple $(\bar{l}, \bar{\tau})$, where $\bar{l}$ is the total loss incurred by tasks already in $\bar{J}$ and $\bar{\tau}$ is the total processing time of tasks already in J; that is,

$$
\bar{l} = \sum_{\alpha_i = \bar{i}} l_i \qquad \text{and} \qquad \bar{\tau} = \sum_{\alpha_i = i} \tau_i
$$

These two-tuples are assigned as labels on the nodes. Figure 6.13 is a pruned version of Fig. 6.12, in which infeasible partial solutions and their descendants have been crossed out. For example, node 12 and its descendants are not feasible because task T_2 cannot be completed by its due date if task T_1 precedes it. (It is easy to check for feasibility. Just verify that each task assigned to J meets its due date.) We assume that all tasks assigned to $\bar{J}$ are tardy. In some cases this can only be achieved by inserting unnecessary idle time between the tasks in J and those in $\bar{J}$. For example, node $\overline{1234}$ represents a solution in which all tasks are tardy. An optimal schedule requires no idle time between tasks; consequently, schedules with idle time are not of interest.

6.5.5   A Dynamic Programming Algorithm

We now find an optimal solution by a dynamic programming algorithm similar to those used by Sahni [Sah] and Horowitz and Sahni [HS]. The algorithm proceeds by computing a sequence of sets $S^{(0)}, S^{(1)}, \ldots, S^{(n)}$. Each $S^{(i)}$ is a lexicographically ordered set of two-tuples $(\bar{l}, \bar{\tau})$, where components $\bar{l}$ and $\bar{\tau}$ correspond to the total loss and total processing time, respectively, of a node of depth i in the associated binary tree.

FLDS Dynamic Programming Algorithm

Input: d_i, l_i, τ_i, $1 \le i \le n$ such that $d_1 \le d_2 \le \cdots \le d_n$
Output: a minimum loss schedule $\alpha_1 \alpha_2 \cdots \alpha_n$
Method:
   Step 1   [Initialize] $S^{(0)} \longleftarrow \{(0, 0)\}$

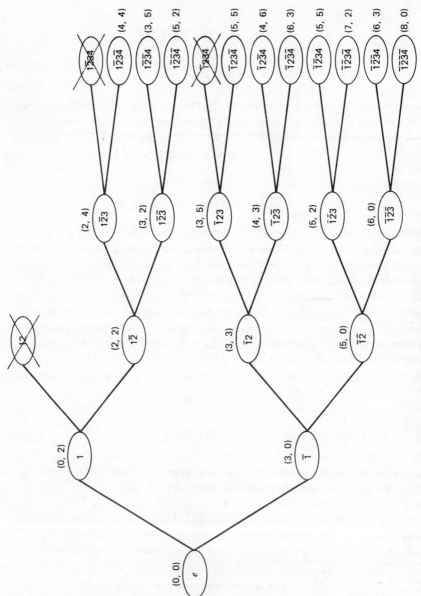

Figure 6.13 Tree representing feasible solutions to sample problem.

Step 2   [Generate $S^{(1)}, S^{(2)}, \ldots, S^{(n)}$]
    for $i = 1, 2, \ldots, n$ **do**
    begin $V \leftarrow \varphi; \ \bar{V} \leftarrow \varphi$
        for each tuple $(\bar{l}, \bar{\tau})$ in $S^{(i-1)}$ **do**
        begin
           if $\bar{\tau} + \tau_i \le d_i$ **then** $V \leftarrow V \cup \{(\bar{l}, \bar{\tau} + \tau_i)\}$
           $\bar{V} \leftarrow \bar{V} \cup \{(\bar{l} + l_i, \bar{\tau})\}$
        end

          merge V and $\bar{V}$ to obtain $S^{(i)}$
          If during the merge we encounter $(\bar{l}_\alpha, \bar{\tau}_\alpha)$ and
          $(\bar{l}_\beta, \bar{\tau}_\beta) \in V \cup \bar{V}$ such that $\bar{l}_\alpha \le \bar{l}_\beta$ and $\bar{\tau}_\alpha \le \bar{\tau}_\beta$,
          eliminate $(\bar{l}_\beta, \bar{\tau}_\beta)$
    end

Step 3   [Optimal solution] The tuple in $S^{(n)}$ with the smallest $\bar{l}$ is the
        label of an optimal solution $\alpha_1 \alpha_2 \cdots \alpha_n$.

This algorithm searches the tree of partial solutions in a straightforward
breadth-first manner. The method used to merge and eliminate tuples in
step 2 distinguishes it from other common enumeration techniques. Note
that if nodes $\alpha_1 \alpha_2 \cdots \alpha_r$ and $\beta_1 \beta_2 \cdots \beta_r$ have associated tuples $(\bar{l}_\alpha, \bar{\tau}_\alpha)$ and
$(\bar{l}_\beta, \bar{\tau}_\beta)$ with $\bar{l}_\alpha \le \bar{l}_\beta$ and $\bar{\tau}_\alpha \le \bar{\tau}_\beta$, the best complete solution starting with
$\alpha_1 \alpha_2 \cdots \alpha_r$ is at least as good as the best complete solution starting with
$\beta_1 \beta_2 \cdots \beta_r$. Consequently, partial solution $\beta_1 \beta_2 \cdots \beta_r$ can be eliminated,
since it is dominated by $\alpha_1 \alpha_2 \cdots \alpha_r$. Also, for each node $\alpha_1 \alpha_2 \cdots \alpha_{i-1}$ with
an associated tuple $(\bar{l}, \bar{\tau})$ in $S^{(i-1)}$, if $\bar{\tau} + \tau_i > d_i$, then $\alpha_1 \alpha_2 \cdots \alpha_{i-1} i$ is not
feasible and is not included in $S^{(i)}$. The elimination rule and the feasibility
test ensure that none of the $S^{(i)}$ contains more than $M = \min [\Sigma_{i=1}^{n} l_i, \Sigma_{i=1}^{n} \tau_i,$
$d_n] + 1$ tuples. Since the number of nodes at depth i in a binary tree is at
most 2^i, 2^n is another bound on the size of $S^{(i)}$.

An inductive argument can be used to show that the elements of sets V
and $\bar{V}$ and the merged set $S^{(i)}$ are generated in lexicographic order. Since
neither V nor $\bar{V}$ contains more tuples than $S^{(i-1)}$, whose size is bounded by
$\min [M, 2^n]$, V and $\bar{V}$ can be generated and merged (step 2) to obtain $S^{(i)}$ in
$O(\min [M, 2^n])$ steps. This is repeated n times before an optimal solution is
found. Therefore, the total number of steps is $O(\min [nM, n2^n])$. Note that
the worst-case requirements are bounded by nM and $n2^n$. The $n2^n$ bound is
independent of the problem data, whereas the nM bound depends on the
parameter values l_i, τ_i, and d_i. If l_i, τ_i, and d_i are drawn from known bounded
distributions with bounds $\bar{L}$, $\bar{T}$, and $n\bar{D}$, respectively, $M \le$
$\min [n\bar{L}, n\bar{T}, n\bar{D}]$. In this special case the number of steps to compute an
optimal solution is $O(n^2)$.

Table 6.3 shows the steps of the FLDS dynamic programming algorithm
when used to solve the sample four-task problem. Note that V, $\bar{V}$ and $S^{(i)}$

TABLE 6.3 STEPS OF FLDS DYNAMIC PROGRAMMING ALGORITHM

i	V	$\bar{V}$	Eliminated tuples	$S^{(i)}$
0	—	—	—	$((0,0))$
1	$((0,2))$	$((3,0))$	—	$((0,2),(3,0))$
2	$((3,3))$	$((2,2),(5,0))$	$((3,3))$	$((2,2),(5,0))$
3	$((2,4),(5,2))$	$((3,2),(6,0))$	$((5,2))$	$((2,4),(3,2),(6,0))$
4	$((3,5),(6,3))$	$((4,4),(5,2),(8,0))$	$((6,3))$	$((3,5),(4,4),(5,2),(8,0))$

Optimal solution: $(\bar{l}, \bar{\tau}) = (3,5) \Rightarrow 1\bar{2}\bar{3}4$

are lexicographically ordered. The final solution can be found by associating each tuple with its corresponding node in the binary tree of Fig. 6.13.

6.5.6 Equivalent Branch-and-Bound Algorithm

An equivalent branch-and-bound algorithm for the FLDS problem can be characterized by the nine-tuple $BB_{\text{FLDS}} = (B_b, \text{FIFO}, \{\text{AS/DB, DB/AS}\}, F_{\text{FLDS}}, D_{\text{FLDS}}, L_{\text{FLDS}}, \infty, 0, \infty)$. The parameters are defined as follows:

1. B_b is the branching rule for binary partition problems. Let π_α^r denote a node of the form $\alpha_1 \alpha_2 \cdots \alpha_r$, where $\alpha_i = i$ or $\bar{i}$. Then $\{\pi_\alpha^r \circ\}$ represents the leaves of the complete subtree with π_α^r as root. This is the set of complete solutions with partial solution π_α^r as a common ancestor. Branching rule B_b partitions the set $\{\pi_\alpha^r \circ\}$ into two disjoint subsets $\{(\pi_\alpha^r \circ (r+1)) \circ\}$ and $\{(\pi_\alpha^r \circ \overline{(r+1)}) \circ\}$. This branching rule leads to an obvious modification of the general branch-and-bound algorithm for permutation problems given in Fig. 6.7. Each node π_α^r now has two descendants $(\pi_\alpha^r \circ (r+1))$ and $(\pi_\alpha^r \circ \overline{(r+1)})$.

2. $S = \text{FIFO}$. The FIFO selection rule will cause the binary tree to be searched in a breadth-first manner.

3. $E = \{\text{AS/DB, DB/AS}\}$. When used in conjunction with the dominance relation D_{FLDS}, this set of rules will ensure that all dominated nodes are eliminated.

4. Characteristic function F_{FLDS} eliminates all partial solutions that are not feasible. In particular, given $\pi_\alpha^r = \alpha_1 \alpha_2 \cdots \alpha_r$, then

$$F_{\text{FLDS}}(\pi_\alpha^r) \triangleq \begin{cases} 1 & \text{if for each } i \text{ with } \alpha_i = i, \text{ task } T_i \text{ finishes} \\ & \text{by its due-date } d_i \\ 0 & \text{otherwise} \end{cases}$$

5. Given any two nodes $\pi_\alpha^j = \alpha_1 \alpha_2 \cdots \alpha_j$ and $\pi_\beta^k = \beta_1 \beta_2 \cdots \beta_k$ with corresponding two-tuples $(\bar{l}_\alpha, \bar{\tau}_\alpha)$ and $(\bar{l}_\beta, \bar{\tau}_\beta)$. Dominance relation D_{FLDS} is

defined such that $(\pi_\alpha{}^j, \pi_\beta{}^k) \in D_{\text{FLDS}}$ if and only if $j = k$, $\bar{l}_\alpha \leq \bar{l}_\beta$, and $\bar{\tau}_\alpha \leq \bar{\tau}_\beta$. This is equivalent to the condition used to eliminate tuples in the dynamic programming algorithm.

6. The lower-bound cost $L_{\text{FLDS}}(\pi_\alpha)$ associated with each node π_α is defined as the cost of the partial solution $\pi_\alpha = \alpha_1 \alpha_2 \cdots \alpha_r$, that is, $L_{\text{FLDS}}(\pi_\alpha) \triangleq \Sigma_{\alpha_i = \bar{i}} \, l_i = \bar{l}_\alpha$

7. $U = \infty$, since we assume no solution is known beforehand.

8. $BR = 0$, since an optimal solution is desired.

9. $RB = \infty$. For comparison with the FLDS dynamic programming algorithm, we assume that the storage and execution time resources are as large as necessary.

Algorithm BB_{FLDS} executes the steps outlined in Table 6.4. By refering to Fig. 6.13, these steps can be compared with the steps of the dynamic programming algorithm as given in Table 6.3. This comparison reveals that the same nodes are generated and eliminated, except for the last step, in which BB_{FLDS} terminates as soon as node $1\bar{2}\bar{3}4$ is generated and verified as optimal. The only significant difference is that the dynamic programming algorithm generates all the required nodes at each level of the tree before merging and eliminating, whereas the branch-and-bound algorithm checks each new node as it is generated. Since the batch method used in the dynamic programming algorithm requires fewer total comparisons to check for dominance, it is more efficient. The general branch-and-bound algorithm can also be modified to achieve this efficiency.

TABLE 6.4 STEPS OF BB_{FLDS} ALGORITHM

π_b	$AS(\pi_b)$	$DB(\pi_b)$	$ES(\pi_b)$	$\hat{L}(\pi_b)$	$\hat{U}(\pi_b)$
e	(e)	$(1,\bar{1})$	φ	0	∞
1	$(1,\bar{1})$	$(1\bar{2})$	φ	0	∞
$\bar{1}$	$(\bar{1},1\bar{2})$	$(\bar{1}2,1\bar{2})$	$(\bar{1}2)$	2	∞
$1\bar{2}$	$(1\bar{2},1\bar{2})$	$(1\bar{2}3,1\bar{2}\bar{3})$	φ	2	∞
$\bar{1}\bar{2}$	$(\bar{1}\bar{2},1\bar{2}3,1\bar{2}\bar{3})$	$(\bar{1}2\bar{3},1\bar{2}\bar{3})$	$(\bar{1}2\bar{3})$	2	∞
$1\bar{2}3$	$(1\bar{2}3,1\bar{2}\bar{3},\bar{1}2\bar{3})$	$(1\bar{2}3\bar{4})$	φ	2	∞
$1\bar{2}\bar{3}$	$(1\bar{2}\bar{3},\bar{1}2\bar{3},1\bar{2}3\bar{4})$	$(1\bar{2}3\bar{4},1\bar{2}\bar{3}4)$	φ	3	4
$\overline{123}$	$(\bar{1}2\bar{3},1\bar{2}3\bar{4},$ $1\bar{2}\bar{3}4,1\bar{2}\bar{3}\bar{4})$	—	—	3	3

$$\frac{\hat{U} - \hat{L}}{\hat{U}} = 0 \Rightarrow \hat{\pi} \Rightarrow 1\bar{2}\bar{3}4 \text{ is an optimal solution.}$$

6.5.7 COMMENTS

The relationship between branch-and-bound and dynamic programming has been demonstrated by means of a sample problem. In general, given a sequencing problem and a dynamic programming algorithm to solve it, an equivalent branch-and-bound algorithm can also be found. This relationship should not be surprising. In both cases, the underlying search space can be modeled as a finite directed tree of partial solutions, and the objective is to locate and isolate an optimal solution while explicitly enumerating only a small portion of the complete tree. The application of branch-and-bound and dynamic programming techniques to other scheduling problems can be found in the work of Horowitz and Sahni [HS], Kohler [Ko2], Rinnoy Kan et al. [RLL], and Sahni [Sah].

6.6 FINAL REMARKS

We have examined in some detail computational techniques for obtaining practical solutions to scheduling problems that resist analytical solution. These scheduling problems fall into the general category of "large" combinatorial optimization problems, many of which are NP-complete and seem to be chronically difficult. The emphasis in this chapter has been on obtaining with a given amount of computational resources the most useful sort of information when we actually want to schedule tasks—in the form of optimal schedules (when possible), or in the form of schedules guaranteed to be within a given tolerance of optimal.

This work draws on the efforts of many workers, and some are represented in the references. The direction of this research seems to be toward a "numerical analysis" for combinatorial problems—some theory and methodology which will enable us to work with numerical problems and to produce predictably good results with a predetermined amount of effort. To pursue an analogy with continuous variable problems, one cannot hope to produce numerically the "exact" solution of a nonlinear optimization problem, or even a linear programming problem. One can expect, however, to obtain solutions within useful tolerances of exact by controlling the effects of finite word length arithmetic. In the same way, might it not be overly ambitious to ask for the "optimal" solution to a large NP-complete problem?

Results along the lines just mentioned have recently been reported [Sah, SG, GJ3]. In particular [Sah], the fact that the computation time for the fixed-loss due-date scheduling problem discussed in Section 6.5 is bounded by $O(nM)$ leads to the conclusion that for this problem (and some related problems) solutions within a bracket $BR = \varepsilon$ can be obtained in time $O(n^3/\epsilon)$. On the other hand, [SG] shows that there are approximate versions of NP-complete problems (more precisely P-complete in the notation of [SG]), which are also NP-complete, and [GJ3] shows that an approximate version of the graph-coloring problem is in some sense as hard as the graph-coloring problem itself. Thus as Sahni and Gonzales [SG] point out, some "hard" combinatorial problems are "harder" than others.

These remarks suggest several areas for future investigation. First, it seems worthwhile to explore further the complexity of "approximate" combinatorial problems—problems that require the production of good rather than optimal solutions. Related to this area is the general question of sensitivity of solution to data parameters in such problems. Finally, it appears that the development of algorithms for solving such problems has just begun. More work is needed to develop automatic methods for constructing lower bounds, finding good neighborhoods for local neighborhood search, and improving the branch-and-bound approach in general.

REFERENCES

[A]   Agin, N., "Optimum Seeking with Branch and Bound," *Management Science*, **13**, 4 (1966), B:176–B:185.

[AGU]   Aho, A. V., M. R. Garey, and J. D. Ullman, "The Transitive Reduction of a Directed Graph," *SIAM Journal on Computing*, **1** (1972), 131–137.

[AHU]   Aho, A. V., J. E. Hopcroft and J. D. Ullman, *The Design and Analysis of Computer Algorithms*, Addison-Wesley, Reading, Mass., 1974.

[As]   Ashour, S., "An Experimental Investigation and Comparative Evaluation of Flow-Shop Scheduling Techniques," *Operations Research*, **18**, 3 (1970), 541–549.

[B1]   Baer, J. L., "A Survey of Some Theoretical Aspects of Multiprocessing," *Computing Surveys*, **5**, 1 (1973).

[B2]   Baer, J. L., "Optimal Scheduling on Two Processors of Different Speeds," *Computer Architectures and Networks*, E. Gelenbe and R. Mahl (Eds.), North Holland Publishing Company, 1974, pp. 27–45.

[Ba1]   Balas, E., "A Note on the Branch-and-Bound Principle," *Operations Research*, **16**, 2 (1968), 442–444. Errata, **16**, 4 (1968), 886.

[Ba2]   Balas, E., "Machine Sequencing via Disjunctive Graphs: An Implicit Enumeration Algorithm," *Operations Research*, **17**, 6 (1969), 941–957.

[Bak]   Baker, K., *Introduction to Sequencing and Scheduling*, John Wiley & Sons, 1974.

[BCJ]   Bruno, J., E. G. Coffman, Jr., and D. B. Johnson, "On Batch Scheduling of Jobs with Stochastic Service Times and Cost Structures on a Single Server," Technical Report No. 154, Computer Science Department, Pennsylvania State University, August 1974 (to appear, *Journal of Computer and System Sciences*).

[BCS1]   Bruno, J., E. G. Coffman, Jr., and R. Sethi, "Scheduling Independent Tasks to Reduce Mean Finishing Time," *Communications of the ACM*, **17**, 7 (1974), 382–387.

[BCS2]   Bruno, J., E. G. Coffman, Jr., and R. Sethi, "Algorithms for Minimizing Mean Flow Time," *Proceedings, IFIPS Congress*, North Holland Publishing Company, August 1974, pp. 504–510.

[BH]   Bruno, J. and M. Hofri, "On Scheduling Chains of Jobs on One Processor with Limited Preemptions," Technical Report No. 153, Computer Science Department, Pennsylvania State University, March 1974 (to appear, *SIAM Journal on Computing*).

[BLR]   Brucker, P., J. K. Lenstra, and A. H. G. Rinooy Kan, "Complexity of Machine Scheduling Problems," *Technical Report* BW 43/75, Mathematisch Centrum, Amsterdam, 1975 (to appear, *Operations Research*).

[Bo]   Bowden, E. K., "Priority Assignment in a Network of Computers," *IEEE Transactions on Computers*, **C-18** (1969), 1021–1026.

[Br]   Brucker, P., "On Hu's 'Cutting the Longest Queue' Algorithm," Technical Report No. 14, Series B, University of Regensburg, West Germany, July 1973.

[BrH]   Brinch-Hansen, P., *Operating Systems Principles*, Prentice-Hall, Englewood Cliffs, N.J., 1973.

[BSe]   Bruno, J. and R. Sethi, "On the Complexity of Mean Flow-Time Scheduling," Technical Report, Computer Science Department, Pennsylvania State University, 1975.

[BSt]   Bruno, J. and K. Steiglitz, "The Expression of Algorithms by Charts," *Journal of the ACM*, **19**, 3 (1972), 517–525.

[C]   Chvatál, V. (personal communication).

[CC]   Cody, R. and E. G. Coffman, Jr., "Record Allocation for Minimizing Expected Retrieval Costs on Drum-Like Storage Devices," *Proceedings, 8th Annual Princeton Conference on Information Sciences and Systems*, March 1973 (to appear, *Journal of the ACM*).

[CD]   Coffman, E. G., Jr. and P. J. Denning, *Operating Systems Theory*, Prentice-Hall, Englewood Cliffs, N.J., 1973.

[CE]   Christofides, N., and S. Eilon, "Algorithms for Large-Scale Travelling Salesman Problems," *Operational Research Quarterly*, **23**, 4 (1972), 511–518.

[CG]   Coffman, E. G., Jr. and R. L. Graham, "Optimal Scheduling for Two Processor Systems," *Acta Informatica*, **1**, 3 (1972), 200–213.

[ChD]   Charlton, J. M. and C. C. Death, "A Method of Solution for General Machine-Scheduling Problems," *Operations Research*, **18**, 4 (1970), 689–707.

[CL]   Coffman, E. G., Jr. and J. Labetoulle, "Deterministic Scheduling to Minimize Mean Number in System," Technical Report, Institut de Recherche d'Informatique et d'Automatique, Rocquencourt, France, 1975.

[CLi]   Chen, N. F. and C. L. Liu, Technical Report, Computer Science Dept., University of Illinois, 1975.

[CMM]   Conway, R. W., W. L. Maxwell, and L. W. Miller, *Theory of Scheduling*, Addison-Wesley, Reading, Mass., 1967.

[Co]   Coffman, E. G., Jr., "A Survey of Mathematical Results in Flow-Time Scheduling for Computer Systems," *Proceedings, GI 73*, Hamburg, Springer-Verlag, 1973, pp. 25–46.

[Coo]   Cook, S. A., "The Complexity of Theorem Proving Procedures," *Proceedings, 3rd ACM Symposium on Theory of Computing*, 1971, 151–158.

[CR]   Cook, S. A. and R. A. Rechkow, "Time-Bounded Random Access Machines," *Journal of Computer and System Sciences*, **7**, 4 (1973), 354–375.

[CS]   Coffman, E. G., Jr. and R. Sethi, "Algorithms Minimizing Mean-Flow-Time Schedule-Length Properties," Technical Report, Computer Science Department, Pennsylvania State University, 1973 (to appear, *Acta Informatica*).

[CW]   Chandra, A. K. and C. K. Wong, "Worst-Case Analysis of a Placement Algorithm Related to Storage Allocation," *SIAM Journal on Computing* (to appear).

[D]   Dannenbring, D. G., "An Evaluation of Flow-Shop Heuristics," Technical Report, University of North Carolina, 1974.

[DFFN]   Dunham, B., D. Fridshal, R. Fridshal, and J. H. North, "Design by Natural Selection," IBM Research Report No. RC-476, June 1961.

[DG]   Denning, P. J. and G. S. Graham, "A Note on Subexpression Ordering in the Execution of Arithmetic Expressions," *Communications of the ACM*, **16**, 11 (1973), 700–702. Erratum: *Communications of the ACM*, **17**, 8 (1974), 455.

[DH]   Day, J. E. and M. P. Hottenstein, "Review of Sequencing Research," *Naval Research and Logistics Quarterly*, **17**, 1 (1970), 11–40.

[E]   Edmonds, J., "Paths, Trees, and Flowers," *Canadian Journal of Mathematics*, **17** (1965), 449–467.

[EEI]   Eastman, W. L., S. Even, and I. M. Isaacs, "Bounds for the Optimal Scheduling of *n* Jobs on *m* Processors," *Management Science*, **11** (1964), 268–278.

[EK]   Edmonds, J. and R. Karp, "Theoretical Improvements in Algorithmic Efficiency for Network Flow Problems," *Journal of the ACM*, **19**, 2 (1972), 248–264.

[El]   Elmaghraby, S. E., "The Machine Sequencing Problem—Review and Extensions," *Naval Research and Logistics Quarterly*, **15**, 2 (1968), 205–232.

[FF]   Ford, L. R. and D. R. Fulkerson, *Flows in Networks*, Princeton University Press, Princeton, N.J., 1962.

[FKN]   Fujii, M., T. Kasami, and K. Ninomiya, "Optimal Sequencing of Two Equivalent Processors," *SIAM Journal on Applied Mathematics*, **17**, 3 (1969), 784–789. Erratum, **20**, 1 (1971), 141.

[FS]   Fox, B. L. and L. E. Schrage, "The Value of Various Strategies in Branch-and-Bound" (unpublished report), June 1972.

[G1]   Graham, R. L., "Bounds for Certain Multiprocessing Anomalies," *Bell System Technical Journal*, **45** (1966), 1563–1581.

[G2]   Graham, R. L., "Bounds on Multiprocessing Timing Anomalies," *SIAM Journal on Applied Mathematics*, **17**, 2 (1969), 416–429.

[G3]   Graham, R. L., "Bounds on Multiprocessing Anomalies and Related Packing Algorithms," *Proceedings, AFIPS Conference*, **40** (1972), 205–217.

[Ga]   Garey, M. R., "Optimal Task Sequencing with Precedence Constraints," *Discrete Mathematics*, **4** (1973), 37–56.

[GG1]   Garey, M. R. and R. L. Graham, "Bounds on Scheduling with Limited Resources," *Operating Systems Review*, **7**, 4 (1973), 104–111.

[GG2]   Garey, M. R. and R. L. Graham, "Bounds for Multiprocessing Scheduling with Resource Constraints," *SIAM Journal on Computing*, **4** (1975), 187–200.

[GGJY]   Garey, M. R., R. L. Graham, D. S. Johnson, and A. C. Yao, "Multiprocessor Scheduling as Generalized Bin-Packing," (to appear, *Journal of Combinatorial Theory (A)*).

[GGU]   Garey, M. R., R. L. Graham, and J. D. Ullman, "Worst-Case Analysis of Memory Allocation Algorithms," *Proceedings, 4th Annual ACM Symposium on the Theory of Computing*, 1972, pp. 143–150.

[Gi]   Gilmore, P. C., "Optimal and Suboptimal Algorithms for the Quadratic Assignment Problem," *SIAM Journal on Applied Mathematics*, **10**, 2 (1962), 305–313.

[GJ1]   Garey, M. R. and D. S. Johnson, "Complexity Results for Multiprocessor Scheduling Under Resource Constraints," *Proceedings, 8th Annual Princeton Conference on Information Sciences and Systems*, 1974.

[GJ2]   Garey, M. R. and D. S. Johnson, "Deadline Scheduling of Equal Execution Time Tasks on Two Processors," Technical Report, Bell Laboratories, Murray Hill, N.J., 1975.

[GJ3]   Garey, M. R. and D. S. Johnson, "The Complexity of Near-Optimal Graph Coloring," Technical Report, Bell Laboratories, Murray Hill, N.J., 1975 (to appear, *Journal of the A.C.M.*).

[GJS]   Garey, M. R., D. S. Johnson, and R. Sethi, "The Complexity of Flowshop and

Jobshop Scheduling," Technical Report No. 168, Computer Science Dept., The Pennsylvania State University, 1975.

[GM]   Geoffrion, A. M. and R. E. Marsten, "Integer Programming Algorithms: A Framework and State of the Art Survey," *Management Science*, **18**, 9 (1972), 465–491.

[GMM]   Gapp, W., P. S. Mankelar, and L. G. Mitten, "Sequencing Operations to Minimize In-Process Inventory Costs," *Management Science*, **11** (1965), 476–484.

[GN]   Garfinkel, R. S. and G. L. Nemhauser, "A Survey of Integer Programming Emphasizing Computation and Relations among Models," *Mathematical Programming*, T. C. Hu and S. M. Robinson (Eds.), Academic Press, New York, 1973, pp. 77–156.

[Gr]   Graham, G. S. (personal communication).

[Gra]   Gratzer, F. J., *Computer Solution of Large Multicommodity Flow Problems*, Ph.D. thesis, Electrical Engineering Department, Princeton University, 1970.

[GS]   Gratzer, F. J. and K. Steiglitz, "A Heuristic Approach to Large Multicommodity Flow Problems," *Proceedings of the Symposium on Computer-Communications Networks and Teletraffic*, Microwave Research Institute Symposia Series, Vol. XXII, Brooklyn Polytechnic Press, New York, 1972, pp. 311–324.

[Gu]   Gupta, J. N. D., "Economic Aspects of Production Scheduling Systems," *Journal Operations Research Society of Japan*, **13**, 4 (1971), 169–193.

[H]   Hu, T. C., "Parallel Sequencing and Assembly Line Problems," *Operations Research*, **9**, 6 (1961), 841–848.

[Ha]   Halasz, S. (personal communication).

[Hi]   Hillier, F. S., "A Bound-and-Scan Algorithm for Pure Integer Linear Programming with General Variables," *Operations Research*, **17** (1969), 638–679.

[HK1]   Held, M. and R. Karp, "A Dynamic Programming Approach to Sequencing Problems," *SIAM Journal on Applied Mathematics*, **10**, 1 (1962), 196–210.

[HK2]   Held, M. and R. Karp, "The Traveling-Salesman Problem and Minimum Spanning Trees: Part II," *Mathematical Programming*, **1**, 1 (1971), 6–25.

[HKu]   Hanan, M. and J. M. Kurtzberg, "Placement Techniques," Ch. 5, *Design Automation of Digital Systems*, M. A. Breuer (Ed.), Prentice-Hall, Englewood Cliffs, N.J., 1972.

[Ho1]   Horn, W. A., "Single-Machine Job Sequencing with Treelike Precedence Ordering and Linear Delay Penalties," *SIAM Journal on Applied Mathematics*, **23** (1972), 189–202.

[Ho2]   Horn, W. A., "Minimizing Average Flow Time with Parallel Machines," *Operations Research*, **21** (1973), 846–847.

[HS]   Horowitz, E. and S. Sahni, "Exact and Approximate Algorithms for Scheduling Non-Identical Processors," Technical Report, Computer Science Program, University of Southern California, 1974 (to appear, *Journal of the A.C.M.*).

[HSe]   Horvath, E. C. and R. Sethi, "Preemptive Schedules for Independent Tasks," Technical Report No. 162, Computer Science Department, The Pennsylvania State University, 1975.

[HU]   Hopcroft, J. E. and J. D. Ullman, "Set Merging Algorithms," *SIAM Journal on Computing*, **2**, 4 (1973), 294–303.

[IS]   Ignall, E. and L. Schrage, "Application of the Branch and Bound Technique to Some Flow-Shop Scheduling Problems," *Operations Research,* **13**, 3 (1965), 400–412.

[J1]   Johnson, D. S., *Near-Optimal Bin-Packing Algorithms,* Ph.D. thesis, Electrical Engineering Department, Massachusetts Institute of Technology, 1974.

[J2]   Johnson, D. S., "Fast Algorithms for Bin Packing," *Journal of Computer and System Sciences,* **8** (1974), 272–314.

[J3]   Johnson, D. S., "Fast Allocation Algorithms," *Proceedings, 13th Annual IEEE Symposium on Switching and Automata Theory,* 1972, 144–154.

[Ja1]   Jackson, J. R., "An Extension of Johnson's Results on Job-Lot Scheduling," *Naval Research and Logistics Quarterly,* **3**, 3 (1956).

[Ja2]   Jackson, J. R., "Scheduling a Production Line to Minimize Maximum Tardiness," Research Report No. 43, Management Sciences Research Project, University of California at Los Angeles, January 1955.

[JDUGG]   Johnson, D. S., A. Demers, J. D. Ullman, M. R. Garey, and R. L. Graham, "Worst-Case Performance Bounds for Simple One-Dimensional Packing Algorithms," *SIAM Journal on Computing,* **3** (1974), 299–326.

[Jo]   Johnson, S. M., "Optimal Two-and-Three-Stage Production Schedules, *Naval Research and Logistics Quarterly,* **1**, 1 (1954).

[K1]   Kaufman, M. T., "Anomalies in Scheduling Unit-Time Tasks," Stanford Electronics Laboratory Technical Report No. 34, 1972.

[K2]   Kaufman, M. T., "An Almost-Optimal Algorithm for the Assembly Line Scheduling Problem," *IEEE Transactions on Computers,* **TC-74** (1974), 1169–1174.

[Ka]   Karp, R. M., "Reducibility Among Combinatorial Problems," *Complexity of Computer Computation,* R. E. Miller and J. W. Thatcher (Eds.), Plenum Press, New York, 1972, pp. 85–104.

[Kn]   Knuth, D. E., *The Art of Computer Programming:* Vol. 1, *Fundamental Algorithms,* Addison-Wesley, Reading, Mass., 1968.

[Ko1]   Kohler, W. H., *Exact and Approximate Algorithms for Permutation Problems,* Ph.D. thesis, Electrical Engineering Department, Princeton University, 1972.

[Ko2]   Kohler, W. H., "A Preliminary Evaluation of the Critical Path Method for Scheduling Tasks on Multiprocessor Systems," Technical Report NSF GK 37400-74-2, Department of Electrical and Computer Engineering, University of Massachusetts, 1974.

[Kol]   Kolesar, P. J., "A Branch and Bound Algorithm for the Knapsack Problem," *Management Science,* **13**, 9 (1967), 723–735.

[Kr]   Krause, K. L., *Analysis of Computer Scheduling with Memory Constraints,* Ph.D. thesis, Computer Science Department, Purdue University, 1973.

[Kro]   Krone, M. J., *Heuristic Programming Applied to Scheduling Problems,* Ph.D. thesis, Electrical Engineering Department, Princeton University, 1970.

[KrS]   Krone, M. and K. Steiglitz, "Heuristic Programming Solution of a Flowshop Scheduling Problem," *Operations Research,* **22**, 3(1974), 629–638.

[KS1]   Kohler, W. H. and K. Steiglitz, "Characterization and Theoretical Comparison of Branch-and-Bound Algorithms for Permutation Problems," *Journal of the ACM,* **21**, 1 (1974), 140–156.

[KS2]   Kohler, W. H. and K. Steiglitz, "Evolutionary Learning of Neighborhoods for Heuristic Programs and Application to a Sequencing Problem," *Proceedings, 9th Allerton Conference on Circuit and System Theory*, October 1971, 377–389.

[KS3]   Kohler, W. H. and K. Steiglitz, "Exact, Approximate, and Guaranteed Accuracy Algorithms for the Flow-Shop Problem $n/2/F/\bar{F}$," *Journal of the ACM*, **22**, 1(1975), 106–114.

[L]   Labetoulle, J., "Some Theorems on Real Time Scheduling," *Computer Architecture and Networks*, E. Gelenbe and R. Mahl (Eds.), North Holland Publishing Company, 1974, pp. 285–298.

[La1]   Lawler, E. L., "On Scheduling Problems with Deferral Costs," *Management Science*, **11** (1964), 280–288.

[La2]   Lawler, E. L., "Optimal Sequencing of a Single Machine Subject to Precedence Constraints," *Management Science*, **19** (1973), 544–546.

[Li]   Lin, S., "Computer Solutions to the Traveling Salesman Problem," *Bell System Technical Journal*, **44**, 10 (1965), 2245–2269.

[LiL1]   Liu, J. W. S. and C. L. Liu, "Performance Analysis of Heterogeneous Multiprocessor Computing Systems," *Computer Architecture and Networks*, E. Gelenbe and R. Mahl (Eds.), North Holland Publishing Company, 1974.

[LiL2]   Liu, J. W. S. and C. L. Liu, "Bounds on Scheduling Algorithms for Heterogeneous Computer Systems," *Proceedings, IFIPS 74 Congress*, North Holland Publishing Company, August 1974.

[LL]   Liu, C. L. and J. W. Layland, "Scheduling Algorithms for Multiprogramming in a Hard Real-Time Environment," *Journal of the ACM*, **20**, 1 (1973), 46–61.

[LK]   Lin, S., and B. W. Kernighan, "An Effective Heuristic for the Traveling-Salesman Problem," *Operations Research*, **21**, 2 (1973), 498–516.

[LM]   Lawler, E. L. and J. M. Moore, "A Functional Equation and its Application to Resource Allocation and Sequencing Problems," *Management Science*, **16**, 1 (1969), 77–84.

[LS]   Lam, S. and R. Sethi, "Worst-case Analysis of Two Scheduling Algorithms," Technical Report, Computer Science Department, Pennsylvania State University, 1975.

[LW]   Lawler, E. L. and D. E. Wood, "Branch-and-Bound Methods: A Survey," *Operations Research*, **14**, 4 (1966), 699–719.

[M]   Misra, J., "Constructive Proofs of Two Scheduling Algorithms," Technical Report, IBM, Gaithersburg, Md., April 1974.

[Mc]   McNaughton, R., "Scheduling with Deadlines and Loss Functions," *Management Science*, **12**, 7 (1959).

[MC1]   Muntz, R. R. and E. G. Coffman, Jr., "Preemptive Scheduling of Real Time Tasks on Multiprocessor Systems," *Journal of the ACM*, **17**, 2 (1970), 324–338.

[MC2]   Muntz, R. R. and E. G. Coffman, Jr., "Optimal Preemptive Scheduling on Two-Processor Systems," *IEEE Transactions on Computers*, **C-18**, 11 (1969), 1014–1020.

[Me]   Mellor, P., "A Review of Job Shop Scheduling," *Operational Research Quarterly*, **17**, 2 (1966), 161–171.

[Mi]   Mitten, L. G., "Branch-and-Bound Methods: General Formulation and Properties," *Operations Research*, **18**, 1 (1970), 24–34.

[Mo]   Moore, J. M., "An *n* Job, One Machine Sequencing Algorithm for Minimizing the Number of Late Jobs," *Management Science*, **15** (1968), 102–109.

[Mu]   Munkres, J., "Algorithms for the Assignment and Transportation Problems," *SIAM Journal on Applied Mathematics*, **5** (1957), 32–38.

[Mur]   Muraoka, Y., *Parallelism, Exposure and Exploitation in Programs*, Ph.D. thesis, Computer Science Department, University of Illinois, 1971.

[N]   Nollemeier, H., "*E* in Branch-and-Bound-Verfahren-Generator," *Computing*, **8** (1971), 99–106.

[PC]   Pierce, J. F. and W. B. Crowston, "Tree-Search Algorithms for Quadratic Assignment Problems," *Naval Research and Logistics Quarterly*, **18**, 1 (1971), 1–36.

[R]   Rothkopf, M. H., "Scheduling Independent Tasks on Parallel Processors," *Management Science*, **12**, 5 (1966).

[Ri]   Rinnooy Kan, A. H. G., "On Mitten's Axioms for Branch-and-Bound," Working Paper W/74/45/03, Graduate School of Management, Interfaculteit Bedr'jfskunde, Delft, The Netherlands, April 1974.

[RLL]   Rinnooy Kan, A. H. G., B. J. Lageweg, and J. K. Lenstra, "Minimizing Total Costs in One-Machine Scheduling," Technical Report No. BW33/74, Mathematisch Centrum, Amsterdam, 1974.

[Ro]   Roth, R. H., "An Approach to Solving Linear Discrete Optimization Problems," *Journal of the ACM*, **17**, 2 (1970), 303–313.

[Roy]   Roy, B., "Procedure d'Exploration par Séparation et Evaluation," *Revue Française d'Informatique et de Recherche Operationelle*, **6** (1969), 61–90.

[RS]   Reiter, S. and G. Sherman, "Discrete Optimizing," *SIAM Journal on Applied Mathematics*, **13**, 3 (1965), 864–889.

[S]   Salkin, H. M., "On the Merit of the Generalized Origin and Restarts in Implicit Enumeration," *Operations Research*, **18**, (1970), 549–554.

[Sa]   Savage, S. L., *The Solution of Discrete Linear Optimization Problems by Neighborhood Search Techniques*, Ph.D. thesis, Computer Science Department, Yale University, March 1973.

[Sah]   Sahni, S., "Algorithms for Scheduling Independent Tasks," Department of Computer Science, University of Minnesota, 1974 (to appear, *Journal of the A.C.M.*).

[Sc1]   Schrage, L., "Solving Resource-Constrained Network Problems by Implicit Enumeration—Nonpreemptive Case," *Operations Research*, **18**, 2 (1970), 263–278.

[Sc2]   Schrage, L., "Solving Resource-Constrained Network Problems by Implicit Enumeration—Preemptive Case," *Operations Research*, **20**, 3 (1972), 668–677.

[Se]   Sethi, R., "Scheduling Graphs on Two Processors" (to appear, *SIAM Journal on Computing*).

[Se2]   Sethi, R., "Complexity of Flow-Shop Scheduling," Technical Report No. 161, Computer Science Department, Pennsylvania State University, December 1974.

[Sev]   Sevcik, K. C., "Scheduling for Minimum Total Cost Using Service Time Distributions," *Journal of the ACM*, **21** (1974), 66–75.

[SG]   Sahni, S. and T. Gonzalez, "P-Complete Problems and Approximate Solutions,"

Technical Report 74-5, Computer, Information, and Control Sciences Department, University of Minnesota, March 1974.

[Si1]   Sidney, J. B., "One Machine Sequencing with Precedence Relations and Deferral Costs—Part I," Working Paper No. 124, "Part II," Working Paper No. 125, Faculty of Commerce and Business Administration, University of British Columbia, 1972.

[Si2]   Sidney, J. B., "An Extension of Moore's Due-Date Algorithm," *Symposium on the Theory of Scheduling and Its Applications*, S. M. Elmagrabhy (Ed.), Springer-Verlag, 1973, 393–398.

[Sm]   Smith, W. E., "Various Optimizers for Single-Stage Production," *Naval Research and Logistics Quarterly*, 3, 1 (1956).

[SS]   Schindler, S. and W. Simonsmeier, "The Class of All Optimal Schedules for Two Processor Systems," *Proceedings, 7th Annual Princeton Conference on Information Sciences and Systems*, 1973.

[SW]   Steiglitz, K. and P. Weiner, "Some Improved Algorithms for Computer Solution to the Traveling Salesman Problem," *Proceedings, 6th Allerton Conference on Circuit and System Theory*, October 1968, 814–821.

[SWKl]   Steiglitz, K., P. Weiner, and D. J. Kleitman, "The Design of Minimum Cost Survivable Networks," *IEEE Transactions on Circuit Theory*, CT-16, 4 (1969), 455–460,

[SWKr]   Savage, S. L., P. Weiner, and M. J. Krone, "Convergent Local Search," Research Report No. 14, Computer Science Department, Yale University, March 1973.

[Sz]   Szarc, W., "Optimal Elimination Methods in the mn Flow-Shop Scheduling Problem," *Operations Research*, 21, 6 (1973), 1250–1259.

[T]   Tarjan, R. E., "Efficiency of a Good but not Linear Set Union Algorithm," Memorandum ERL-M434, Department of Electrical Engineering and Computer Science, University of California, Berkeley, March 1974.

[U1]   Ullman, J. D., "Polynomial Complete Scheduling Problems," *Operating Systems Review*, 7, 4 (1973), 96–101.

[U2]   Ullman, J. D., "The Performance of a Memory Allocation Algorithm," Technical Report No. 100, Electrical Engineering Department, Princeton University, 1971.

[WSB]   Weiner, P., S. L. Savage, and A. Bagchi, "Neighborhood Search Algorithms for Finding Optimal Traveling Salesman Tours Must Be Inefficient," Research Report No. 13, Computer Science Department, Yale University, March 1973.

[Y1]   Yao, A. C., "Scheduling Unit-Time Tasks With Limited Resources," *Proceedings Sagamore Computer Conference*, 1974.

[Y2]   Yao, A. C., "On Scheduling With Limited Resources" Computer Science Dept., University of Illinois, unpublished manuscript (to appear).

INDEX